SPHERE LIBRARY

HISTORY OF LITERATURE IN THE ENGLISH LANGUAGE

Volumes marked with an asterisk are already published.
The remainder are in preparation.

HISTORY OF LITERATURE
IN THE ENGLISH LANGUAGE

Vol. 4 Dryden to Johnson

Dryden to Johnson

EDITED BY ROGER LONSDALE

PR
85
S7
v.4

SPHERE BOOKS LIMITED
30/32 Gray's Inn Road, London, WC1X 8JL

First published in Great Britain in 1971 by Sphere Books
© Sphere Books 1971
A library edition of this volume is available from
The Cresset Press,
2 Clement's Inn,
Strand, London W.C.2

Set in Linotype Pilgrim

Printed in Great Britain by
Hazell Watson & Viney Ltd.
Aylesbury, Bucks

CONTENTS

INTRODUCTION

The aim of the contributors to this volume has not been to provide a handbook of information about the period it covers or to summarize received opinion about its literature. They have tried to avoid, on the one hand, burdening the literature with a dead weight of 'background' material or, on the other, of reading it in an historical void. The volume deals with the major figures and the main developments within the significant genres in this period, providing such information about their context as will illuminate and enrich their meaning. The twelve contributors have been encouraged to combine information with individuality of response to the literature itself. The essays will reveal differences of emphasis and approach which can in themselves be instructive. Different kinds of information—biographical, historical or literary—will seem more or less appropriate to particular authors and will also be dictated by the interests of the critic himself. The variety and vitality of judgement and informed reading which results will, it is hoped, prove a welcome alternative to a dogged or doctrinaire single-handed coverage of all aspects of the period.

Recent literary history has contrived to break down confidence in the old periodisation of English literature. Useful landmarks like the Restoration of Charles II in 1660 and the publication of the *Lyrical Ballads* in 1798 have tended to become submerged by the complexity of the factors which influence literary history: the lives of individual writers, philosophical and scientific developments, economic and political history, as well as the processes of purely literary influences and fashions, and the interplay of individual genius with public taste. The Restoration of 1660 remains a useful signpost in this flux, as long as faith in its historical significance is balanced by the knowledge that the less dramatic Revolution of 1688 was to have more profound significance for English society. As far as literary history is concerned, we can see that Waller and Denham, for example, who seemed to following generations the

9

forefathers of the new refinement of English poetry, were writing well before 1660 and that John Milton published his greatest poetry after that date.

Restoration literature and the plays of John Dryden have been dealt with in earlier volumes of this *History*. But the early essays in the present volume will repeatedly reveal the relationships of early eighteenth-century literature with the Restoration period. Dryden's poetry and criticism, central to what has come to be called Augustan literature, has in fact been discussed here by Howard Erskine-Hill. He emphasizes Dryden's optimistic identification in 1660 of the new age with Rome under Augustus, a comparison which, seriously or ironically, was to be repeated and explored for almost a century. A new refinement was felt to be a cause for self-congratulation, as Dryden claimed in 1672 when writing of the previous age (Epilogue to *The Second Part of the Conquest of Granada*):

> Wit's now arriv'd to a more high degree;
> Our native Language more refin'd and free.
> Our Ladies and our men now speak more wit
> In conversation, than those Poets writ.

Erskine-Hill's essay emphasizes the importance to an understanding of Dryden—supremely the poet of public life—of the Restoration and of events leading to the Revolution of 1688. If this approach through the involvement of Dryden's poetry with contemporary events is crucial, Erskine-Hill is also concerned to stress the interplay between the historical context and the changing personal tone of the poetry itself. Dryden's energy and exuberance are characteristic of his century; but his use of the heroic couplet and his exploitation of the mock-heroic form towards the end of his career, which involved a recognition of the disparity between Augustan literary ideals and what Erskine-Hill calls 'unideal reality', relate him, with many other factors, to the literature which followed his death in 1700.

Characteristically, Swift thought the application of the word 'Augustan' to the later seventeenth century 'absurd'. The controversy between the Ancients and the Moderns with which he was involved early in his career is in some ways crucial to an understanding of the conflict in this period between optimism about scientific and philosophical progress and the pessimism of the conservatives who believed in the traditional allegiance to classical achievements as a model and an ideal. Kathleen Williams illuminates the biographical, religious and historical context of Swift's satires, which explains the hostility of Swift and many of his most gifted contemporaries to literary, scientific and political developments in the age. Pope, Swift's younger friend, shared a similar gloom about the effect on literary and intellectual ideals and on standards of public morality of the new social and economic order which followed the Revolution of 1688. Most of the outstanding creative writers between 1660 and 1740 were involved in political activity of one sort or another. If the political attitudes of Swift, Pope and their circle do not explain their literary art, knowledge of them can help to elucidate and focus their achievements. One concern of the editor's essay on Pope is to stress the way in which he responded to developments in his society and to show how this is a factor giving coherence to his poetry as a whole.

By 1737, when Pope sarcastically addressed George II in his imitation of Horace, 'To Augustus', the epithet 'Augustan', once expressive of so much optimism and idealism, was being used for ironic and derogatory purposes. Swift and Pope can, of course, seem to dominate their age in a misleading way. Dr. Johnson wrote of their letters in his *Life of Pope* that 'whoever should form his opinion of their age from their representation, would suppose them to have lived amidst ignorance and barbarity, unable to find among their contemporaries either virtue or intelligence, and persecuted by those that could not understand them.' Among their contemporaries, Addison and Steele in fact show how literature adapted itself to the growing reading public (implicitly deplored by Swift and Pope) and how the new ideals of elegance and delicacy apparent in many cultural aspects of the age could combine with middle-class moral standards. F. W. Bateson's lively discussion of Addison and Steele and, in particular, of their distinctive contribution to the periodical essay, approaches *The Tatler* and *The Spectator* through both the social context and the personalities of the two essayists.

Bateson's remarks on Addison's incipient 'romanticism' point to the new developments of the first decades of the eighteenth century. Charles Peake, writing on the poetry of Pope's contemporaries, stresses the new interests of this period. Acknowledging its desire for stability and conformity, he shows how change and experiment still occurred within familiar poetic forms. It was hardly a great period for English drama, even if the London theatres flourished throughout the century. Yet the drama reflects changing tastes in an illuminating way and it did produce its comic masterpieces. Ian Donaldson discusses the variety and uncertainty of theatrical taste in the eighteenth century and shows how surviving Restoration conventions were modified by the theatre's response to social changes. He approaches comedy through contemporary attitudes to laughter as social behaviour and traces the emergence of sentimental comedy well before the period sometimes referred to as 'The Age of Sensibility'.

Like most significant literature up to 1740, the drama was involved in various ways with politics. One result was Walpole's Stage Licensing Act in 1737 which, as Donaldson suggests, was incidentally to encourage the emergence of fiction as a serious literary form. Defoe's novels (offered as authentic narratives) had appeared two decades earlier and Mark Kinkead-Weekes examines the blend of bourgeois morality with vivid realism in Defoe and the next major English novelist, Samuel Richardson. They share, as Kinkead-Weekes stresses, a conscious detachment from the polite Augustan culture which can seem dominant in this period. Writing for a quite different audience from Pope and Swift, they were both concerned to examine man and his environment with a new detailed attentiveness. While clarifying aspects of their fiction which may be obscure to the modern reader, Kinkead-Weekes refuses to treat their novels as simply reactions to social situations : his concern is ultimately with the 'unique informing vision' of each novelist.

One reaction of the traditional, aristocratic culture to the new fiction and its values was expressed in Fielding's novels. C. J. Rawson approaches Fielding through the plays which he wrote early in his career and through his relationship—one of fascinated repugnance—with Richardson's *Pamela*. Fielding's irony and conservatism are modified by a growing emphasis on 'benevolence', the faith in the basic goodness of human nature which was by now pervading English thought and literature. Rawson goes on to show how even the tough and lively surface of Smollett's fiction could soften under the influence of the new cult of sensibility. Sensibility and sentiment are inevitably matters also discussed in Ian Jack's essay on Sterne, although he also stresses Sterne's relationhip to (if largely by reaction against) the earlier novelists and brings out the element of 'learned fooling' in his fiction.

Many aspects of 'The Age of Sensibility' can be traced back to the high 'Augustan' period of the early eighteenth century. At the same time, what has been identified as 'Augustan Humanism' can be shown to survive to the end of the century in the writings of Johnson, Goldsmith, Gibbon, Reynolds and Burke. But the 1740s, the decade in which Pope and Swift died, in which the novel came to sudden maturity, and in which a new generation of poets began to pursue fresh aims and follow different models, surely contains the transition to a new period, whose main interests are outlined in Arthur Johnston's essay on poetry and criticism to the death of Samuel Johnson. He shows how the attention of both poets and critics turned away from the Roman culture which had provided the dominant orientation of earlier English literature since the Restoration, towards the inspiration of Greek poetry, of the Bible, of earlier English literature, of primitive and medieval poetry and of superstition. If in this period of experiment and changing ideals Samuel Johnson has still seemed the representative figure of the age, it should be remembered that in many ways he was the spokesman for older allegiances and that he often viewed contemporary literary tendencies with distaste. His stature in the popular literary tradition is to be explained not merely by his own critical and creative achievements, but by his role as the hero of Boswell's inimitable biography. Aware of the limitations of Boswell's superb but in some ways idiosyncratic portrayal of Johnson, John Hardy places a corrective emphasis on the facts of Johnson's life, while presenting a detailed picture of all of his literary activities, including some often neglected works. In this way his account of Johnson also throws light on the life of a professional man of letters in the eighteenth century.

The detachment of literature from its 'background' has been deliberately avoided in this volume: the social or intellectual context of a major writer has been discussed as it appeared to illuminate his own work. William Frost's essay on religious and philosophical themes is not offered as a guidebook to intellectual trends in the period. Frost places many of the major authors discussed earlier in the volume, as well as such philosophers and historians as Shaftesbury, Hume and Gibbon, in a fresh perspective which emphasizes certain unifying preoccupations of the period, in particular the way in which religious experience was treated in its literature. His essay ends by commenting on two major achievements of the later eighteenth century, which help to define the period at which the volume ends. Gibbon's *Decline and Fall of the Roman Empire* (1776–88), recently described as 'a veritable paradigm of the world-view of English neo-classicism', brings to an end a period absorbed, inspired and eventually depressed by the glory that was Rome. Gibbon's account of the collapse of that civilization retrospectively illuminates the aspirations and misgivings of many of his predecessors in the century.

Boswell's *Life of Johnson*, as John Hardy suggests, fascinates partly because of the contrast between the two men whose relationship contributes so much to the biography. The confrontation of Boswell's unsteady, self-indulgent, 'romantic' personality with Johnson's troubled commonsense expresses a crucial tension of the century as a whole. If Boswell's acute interest in the idiosyncrasies and heroic stature of Johnson as an individual looks ahead to the interests of the following century, this biography, constructed from the conversation and letters of Johnson and his friends and from the storehouse of Boswell's own remarkable journal, reminds us that the later eighteenth century was a period when informal and sociable literary modes flourished. It is regrettable that limitation of space has not allowed more to be said in the following pages about the brilliant letters, journals and memoirs which characterize the period, although the names of many of their writers will be mentioned, including Lady Mary Wortley Montagu, Lord Chesterfield, Lord Hervey, Horace Walpole, Thomas Gray, John Wesley, James Boswell, Fanny Burney, Mrs. Thrale, William Cowper and many others.

For William Frost, Boswell's pages provide an image of 'a society supremely confident about its central values, in some perplexity about their exact application or their detailed exposition, but at peace with itself and embarked on an enterprise of harmonious clarification.' These words eloquently express much that is most memorable about the literature discussed in this volume. Yet by the time Boswell's *Life of Johnson* appeared in 1791, what seemed, for better or worse, a new era had begun, not merely for France but, as many thought, for humanity as a whole. By 1793, in the second edition of the *Life*, Boswell already felt called on to oppose Johnson's 'strong, clear, and animated enforcement of religion, morality, loyalty, and subordination to the new 'Philosophy' which, 'with a malignant industry has been employed against the peace, good order, and happiness of society.' The 'Peace of the Augustans', if it had ever existed, was surely at an end.

R.L.

ANNALS

1660–1791

1660 Parliament recalls Charles II; the Restoration; the Royal Society established; the theatres reopen.

Daniel Defoe b.

Dryden, *Astræa Redux*.

1662 Pascal d.

Butler, *Hudibras*, Part I (II, 1663; III, 1677); Fuller, *Worthies of England*.

1664 Matthew Prior b. Sir John Vanbrugh b.

1665 The Great Plague.

La Rochefoucauld, *Maximes*; Marvell, *The Character of Holland*.

1666 Fire of London.

Boileau, *Satires*; Molière, *Le Misanthrope*.

1667 Cowley d.

Jonathan Swift b. John Arbuthnot b.

Dryden, *Annus Mirabilis*; Milton, *Paradise Lost*; Molière, *Tartuffe*; Racine, *Andromaque*.

1668 Dryden poet-laureate.

Denham, *Poems*; Dryden, *An Essay of Dramatic Poesy*; La Fontaine, Fables I.

1669 Denham d.

1670 William Congreve b.

Pascal, *Pensées*.

1671 Milton, *Paradise Regained* and *Samson Agonistes*.

1672 Joseph Addison b. Richard Steele b.

Buckingham (and others), *The Rehearsal*.

1673 Molière d.

Milton, *Poems* (enlarging the 1645 volume).

1674 Herrick d. Milton d. Traherne d.

Boileau, *Le Lutrin*, *L'Art Poétique*.

1675 Wycherley, *The Country Wife*.

1676 Dryden, *Aureng-Zebe*; Etherege, *The Man of Mode*.

1667 Racine, *Phèdre*; Wycherley, *The Plain Dealer*.

1678 The Popish Plot.

Marvell d.

Henry St. John, Lord Bolingbroke b.

Bunyan, *The Pilgrim's Progress I*; Dryden, *All for Love*.

1680	Butler d. Rochester d.
	Rochester, *Poems*.
1681	Dryden, *Absalom and Achitophel I*; Marvell (d. 1678), *Poems*; Oldham, *Satyrs upon the Jesuits*.
1682	Browne d.
	Dryden, *Mac Flecknoe*, *Religio Laici*, *The Medall*.
1683	Oldham d.
1685	Charles II d. Accession of James II.
	John Gay b.
1687	Waller d.
	Dryden, *The Hind and the Panther*; Newton, *Principia*.
1688	The Revolution.
	Bunyan d.
	Alexander Pope b.
1689	Accession of William III and Mary II.
	Samuel Richardson b.
1690	Locke, *Essay Concerning Human Understanding*.
1691	Etherege d.
1693	Dryden, *Satires of Juvenal and Persius*.
1694	Mary II d. William III reigns alone.
	Voltaire b.
	Congreve, *The Double Dealer*.
1695	Vaughan d.
1697	William Hogarth b.
	Defoe, *Essay upon Projects*; Dryden, *The Works of Virgil Translated*; Vanbrugh, *The Relapse*.
1698	Collier, *Short View of the Immorality and Profaneness of the Stage*.
1699	Garth, *The Dispensary*.
1700	Dryden d.
	James Thomson b. John Dyer b.
	Congreve, *The Way of the World*; Dryden, *Fables*.
1701	Steele, *The Christian Hero*; Swift, *Contests in Athens and Rome*.
1702	Accession of Queen Anne.
	Defoe, *Shortest Way With the Dissenters*; *The Daily Courant* (first daily newspaper).
1703	John Wesley b.
1704	John Locke d.
	Defoe, *The Review* (to 1713); Swift, *A Tale of a Tub*, *The Battle of the Books*; Newton's *Optics* translated.
1706	Union with Scotland.
	Defoe, *Apparition of Mrs. Veal*; Watts, *Horae Lyricae*.
1707	Farquhar d.
	Henry Fielding b.
	Prior, *Poems*.
1708	Philips, *Cyder*.
1709	First Copyright Act.

Samuel Johnson b.

A. Philips, *Pastorals*; Pope, *Pastorals*; Rowe's edition of Shakespeare (concluded 1710); Steele, *The Tatler* (to 1711).

1711 David Hume b.

Addison, *The Spectator* (to 1712); Pope, *Essay on Criticism*; Shaftesbury, *Characteristicks of Men and Manners*; Swift, *Miscellanies*.

1712 Rousseau b.

Arbuthnot, *History of John Bull*; Pope, *Rape of the Lock* (in two Cantos); Swift, *Proposal for Correcting the English Language*.

1713 Treaty of Utrecht. The Scriblerus Club.

Laurence Sterne b.

Addison, *Cato*; Pope, *Windsor-Forest*; Steele, *The Guardian*; Countess of Winchilsea, *Miscellany Poems*.

1714 Accession of George I.

William Shenstone b.

Gay, *The Shepherd's Week*; Mandeville, *The Fable of the Bees*; Pope, *The Rape of the Lock* (5 cantos).

1715 First Jacobite Rebellion. Rowe poet-laureate.

Pope, *The Iliad* vol. I (completed 1720), *The Temple of Fame*; Spenser, *Works* (edited by J. Hughes).

1716 Wycherley d.

Thomas Gray b.

Gay, *Trivia*.

1717 Horace Walpole b. David Garrick b.

Gay, Pope and Arbuthnot, *Three Hours After Marriage*; Pope, *Works* (vol. II, 1735).

1718 Rowe d. Parnell d. Laurence Eusden poet-laureate.

Prior, *Poems*.

1719 Addison d. Garth d.

Defoe, *Robinson Crusoe*.

1720 South Sea Bubble.

Defoe, *Memoirs of a Cavalier*, *Captain Singleton*.

1721 William Collins b. Mark Akenside b. Tobias Smollett b.

1722 Christopher Smart b. Joseph Warton b.

Defoe, *Journal of the Plague Year*, *Moll Flanders*, *Colonel Jacque*; Parnell, *Poems* (edited by Pope).

1723 Adam Smith b. Sir Joshua Reynolds b.

1724 Defoe, *Roxana*; Swift, *The Drapier's Letters*.

1725 Hutcheson, *Original of our Ideas of Beauty and Virtue*; Pope's edition of Shakespeare, *Odyssey* I–III (completed 1726; with Broome and Fenton); Young, *The Universal Passion*.

1726 Vanbrugh d.

Bolingbroke, *The Craftsman* (to 1736); Swift, *Gulliver's Travels*; Theobald, *Shakespeare Restored*; Thomson, *Winter*.

1727 Accession of George II.
Newton d.
Dyer, *Grongar Hill*; Gay, *Fables* I (II 1737); Newton, *Principia* (1st English translation); Pope, Swift, Arbuthnot, *Miscellanies* (to 1732); Thomson, *Summer*.

1728 Thomas Warton jnr. b.
Gay, *The Beggar's Opera*; Law, *A Serious Call to a Devout and Holy Life*; Pope, *Dunciad* (in 3 Books); Thomson, *Spring*.

1729 Steele d. Congreve d.
Edmund Burke b. Thomas Percy b.
Gay, *Polly, an Opera*; Swift, *A Modest Proposal*.

1730 Colley Cibber poet-laureate.
Oliver Goldsmith b. (?)
Thomson, *The Seasons* (collected edition); Fielding, *Tom Thumb* (and other comedies)

1731 Defoe d.
William Cowper b. Charles Churchill b.
Lillo, *The London Merchant*; Pope, *Epistle to Burlington*; *The Gentleman's Magazine* started.

1732 Gay d.
Pope, *Epistle to Bathurst*.

1733 Pope, *Essay on Man* I–III (IV 1734), *Epistle to Cobham*, *Imitation of Horace, Sat.II.i*; Swift, *The Life and Genuine Character of Dr. Swift*; Voltaire, *Letters Concerning the English Nation*.

1734 Pope, *Horace, Sat.II.ii*.

1735 Arbuthnot d.
Johnson, *A Voyage to Abyssinia*; Pope, *Epistle to a Lady*, *Epistle to Arbuthnot*, *Satires of Donne*.

1737 Edward Gibbon b.
Green, *The Spleen*; Pope, *Horace, Epistles* I.i., II.i. and ii, *Letters* (authorized edition); Shenstone, *Poems*.

1738 Johnson, *London*; Pope, *One Thousand Seven Hundred and Thirty-Eight* (later *Epilogue to the Satires*); Swift, *A Collection of Genteel Conversation*.

1739 Hume, *A Treatise of Human Nature*; Johnson, *Marmor Norfolciense, Complete Vindication of the Licensers of the Stage*; Swift, *Verses on the Death of Dr. Swift*.

1740 James Boswell b.
Cibber, *An Apology for his Life*; Richardson, *Pamela* vols. I–II (III–IV 1742).

1741 Arbuthnot, Pope, Swift and others, *Memoirs of Scriblerus*; Fielding, *Shamela*; Hume, *Essays Moral and Political*.

1742 Collins, *Persian Eclogues*; Fielding, *Joseph Andrews*; Pope, *The New Dunciad* (Book IV); Young, *The Complaint, or Night Thoughts* I–IV (V 1743, VI–VII 1744, VIII–IX 1745).

1743 Blair, *The Grave*; Collins, *Verses on Hanmer's Shakespeare*; Fielding, *Miscellanies* (incl. *Jonathan Wild*); Pope, *The Dunciad* (Books I–IV).

1744 Pope d.
Akenside, *The Pleasures of Imagination*; Johnson, *Life of Savage*; J. Warton, *The Enthusiast*.

1745 Second Jacobite Rebellion.
Swift d.
Akenside, *Odes*; Johnson, *Observations on Macbeth*; Swift, *Directions to Servants*.

1746 Collins, *Odes*; J. Warton, *Odes*.

1747 Gray, *Ode on Eton College*; Johnson, *Drury Lane Prologue, Plan of a Dictionary*; T. Warton, *The Pleasures of Melancholy*.

1748 Thomson d.
Dodsley, *Collection of Poems* I–III (IV 1755, V–VI 1758); Hume, *Philosophical Essays*; Richardson, *Clarissa Harlowe*; Smollett, *Roderick Random*; Thomson, *The Castle of Indolence*.

1749 Collins, *Ode on the Death of Thomson*; Fielding, *Tom Jones*; Hartley, *Observations on Man*; Johnson, *The Vanity of Human Wishes, Irene: a tragedy*.

1750 Johnson, *The Rambler* (to 1752).

1751 Bolingbroke d.
Richard Brinsley Sheridan b.
Gray, *Elegy*; Smollett, *Peregrine Pickle*; *L'Encyclopédie* (to 1780).

1752 Thomas Chatterton b. Frances Burney b.
Smart, *Poems*; Fielding, *Amelia*.

1753 Richardson, *Sir Charles Grandison* I–IV (V–VII 1754); Smollett, *Ferdinand Count Fathom; The Adventurer* (to 1754).

1754 Fielding d.
George Crabbe b.
T. Warton, *Observations on the Fairie Queene*.

1755 Fielding, *A Voyage to Lisbon*; Johnson, *Dictionary*; Smollett, translation of *Don Quixote*.

1756 William Godwin b.
Burke, *Origin of our Ideas of the Sublime and Beautiful*; J. Warton, *Essay on the Genius and Writing of Pope* I (II 1782).

1757 Cibber d. William Whitehead poet-laureate.
William Blake b.
Gray, *Odes*; Home, *Douglas*; Smollett, *History of England* (concl. 1758); Hume, *Four Dissertations*.

1758 Dyer d.
Gibbon, *Essai sur l'étude de la littérature*; Johnson, *The Idler* (to 1760).

1759   British Museum opens.
Collins d.
Robert Burns b.
Goldsmith, *Present State of Polite Learning*; Johnson, *Rasselas*;
Smith, *The Theory of Moral Sentiments*; Young, *Conjectures
on Original Composition*; Voltaire, *Candide*.

1760   Accession of George III.
William Beckford b.
Goldsmith, *Chinese Letters* (to 1761; as *Citizen of the World*
1762); Macpherson, *Fragments of Ancient Poetry*; Sterne,
Tristram Shandy I–II (III–VI 1761–2, VII–VIII 1765, IX 1767),
Sermons (concl. 1769).

1761   Richardson d.
Churchill, *The Rosciad*; Hurd, *Letters on Chivalry and
Romance*; Kames, *The Elements of Criticism*; Macpherson,
Fingal; Smollett, *Sir Lancelot Greaves*.

1763   Meeting of Johnson and Boswell.
Churchill, *Poems* I (II 1765); Smart, *A Song to David*.

1764   Churchill d.
Ann Radcliffe b.
Goldsmith, *The Traveller*; Evans, *Specimens of the Ancient
Welsh Bards*; Reid, *An Enquiry into the Human Mind*;
Shenstone, *Works* I–II (III 1769).

1765   Young d.
Collins, *Poetical Works*; Goldsmith, *Essays*; Johnson's edition
of Shakespeare; Percy, *Reliques of Ancient English Poetry*;
Walpole, *The Castle of Otranto*.

1766   Brooke, *The Fool of Quality*; Goldsmith, *The Vicar of Wakefield*; Smollett, *Travels*.

1767   Herder, *Fragmente*.

1768   Sterne d.
Boswell, *An Account of Corsica*; Goldsmith, *The Good
Natur'd Man*; Gray, *Poems*; Sterne, *A Sentimental Journey*.

1769   Shakespeare Jubilee at Stratford.
Chatterton, *Elinoure and Juga*; Reynolds, *Discourses* (to
1790); Smollett, *The Adventures of an Atom*; Sterne, *A Political Romance*.

1770   Akenside d. Chatterton d.
William Wordsworth b. James Hogg b.
Beattie, *An Essay on Truth*; Goldsmith, *The Deserted Village*;
Johnson, *The False Alarm*; Percy, *Northern Antiquities*.

1771   Gray d. Smollett d. Smart d.
Walter Scott b.
Beattie, *The Minstrel* I (II 1774); Johnson, *Thoughts on Falk-
land's Islands*; Mackenzie, *The Man of Feeling*; Smollett,
Humphry Clinker; Klopstock, *Oden*.

1772   Samuel Taylor Coleridge b.
      Graves, *The Spiritual Quixote*.

1773   Chesterfield d.
      Fergusson, *Poems* I (II 1779); Goldsmith, *She Stoops to Conquer*; Herder and Goethe, *Von deutscher Art und Kunst*.

1774   Goldsmith d.
      Chesterfield (d. 1773), *Letters to his Son*; Goldsmith, *Retaliation*; Johnson, *The Patriot*; Richardson, *A Philosophical Analysis of some of Shakespeare's Characters*; T. Warton, *A History of English Poetry* I (II 1778, III 1781).

1775   War of American Independence.
      Jane Austen b. Charles Lamb b. W. S. Landor b. M. G. Lewis b.
      Johnson, *Journey to the Western Islands*; Mason, *Memoirs of Mr. Gray*; Sheridan, *The Rivals*; Sterne, *Letters from Yorick to Eliza*; Tyrwhitt's edition of Chaucer's *Canterbury Tales*.

1776   Hume d.
      Burney, *History of Music* I (II 1782, III–IV 1789); Gibbon, *Decline and Fall of the Roman Empire* I (II–III 1781, IV–VI 1788); Smith, *The Wealth of Nations*.

1777   Chatterton, *Poems, supposed to have been written by Thomas Rowley*.

1778   Voltaire d. Rousseau d.
      William Hazlitt b.
      Burney, *Evelina*; Chatterton, *Miscellanies*.

1779   Garrick d.
      Cowper and Newton, *Olney Hymns*; Johnson, *Prefaces, Biographical and Critical, to the Works of the English Poets* (concl. 1781; as *Lives of the Poets*, 1781).

1781   Sheridan, *The Critic*; Schiller, *Die Raüber*; Kant, *Kritik der reinen Vernunft*.

1782   Burney, *Cecilia*; Cowper, *Poems*; Laclos, *Les Liaisons Dangereuses*.

1783   Blake, *Poetical Sketches*; Crabbe, *The Village*; Sheridan, *The School for Scandal*.

1784   Johnson d.
1785   T. Warton poet-laureate.
      Thomas de Quincey b. Thomas Love Peacock b.
      Boswell, *A Tour to the Hebrides*; Cowper, *Poems* II; Reeve, *The Progress of Romance*.

1786   Beckford, *Vathek*; Burns, *Poems Chiefly in the Scottish Dialect*; Piozzi, *Anecdotes of Johnson*.

1787   Hawkins, *Life of Johnson*.
1788   George Gordon Byron b.
      Collins (d. 1759), *Ode on the Popular Superstitions of the Highlands*.

1789   French Revolution.
      Blake, *Songs of Innocence, The Book of Thiel*; Bowles, *Sonnets*.

1790 T. Warton d. Henry James Pye poet-laureate.
      Blake, *The Marriage of Heaven and Hell*; Burke, *Reflections on the French Revolution*; Malone's edition of Shakespeare; Goethe, *Faust, ein Fragment*.
1791 Boswell, *The Life of Johnson*.

I

JOHN DRYDEN:

THE POET AND CRITIC

Howard Erskine-Hill, Jesus College, Cambridge

I

Poets, critics and historians have rightly praised Dryden's splendid vigour and variety of expression; for a century after his death conventional tribute was paid to his art of versification, but such qualities can never be absolute values. If Dryden deserves the place usually accorded to him as a great poet, it is not because his versification is efficiently regular and readable, but because it is expressively varied in accordance with subject, purpose and mood. It is because the variety of his expression is a mark not only of matchless craftsmanship but of his capacity for a many-sided response to the ideas, issues and events of life. It is because his vigour is more than the 'articulate energy' of his style but the proper manifestation of a staunch and penetrating human understanding. These gifts and skills marry to form works of art almost ostentatious in their life, shape and point. It cannot be too much stressed that in Dryden's work we have not merely a repository of literary skills but the voice of a richly accomplished artist speaking to us of the active, peopled seventeenth-century world in which he was involved and which he judged.

Of a poet whom one calls great one demands an individual poetic character. Milton would not be a great poet if he closely resembled Spenser or Chaucer. Dryden has two strong characterising qualities. The first is that, more clearly than any other English poet including Pope, Dryden is a poet of public life. And here we must guard against the common modern assumption that personal concerns are always richer and more satisfying than public ones. Much of the value of Dryden for the modern reader is precisely that for this poet the concept of the public was endowed with an authentic excitement, dignity and splendour wholly lacking in our time. Moreover in several of his later works Dryden becomes skilful in the effective introduction of a personal tone into a predominantly public poem. The second characterising quality of Dryden is his extraordinary capacity to blend the comic with the heroic, the elaborate with the plain, the mundane with the magnificent, in a variety of ways, so that his best work is unusual in its simultaneous satisfaction of different propensities in the reader. Indeed his richest poems seem to spring from a tension between opposing tendencies in Dryden himself.[1]

Dryden was born on 9 August 1631 at Aldwinkle, Northamptonshire, of a family of landed gentry tending to parliamentarian and Puritan sympathies. He was educated at Westminster School and Trinity College, Cambridge, and probably held some small office in the service of the Lord Protector in the last years of the Interregnum. The tension in his poetry to which I have referred has not yet appeared in his first notable poem, the *Heroique Stanza's . . . to the Glorious Memory of . . . Oliver Late Lord Protector* (1659) where the nature of his subject leads him to demonstrate his heightened sense of public grandeur, his concern with the heroic and its due praise, in simple and direct fashion. It represents, in fact, a temporary victory over the weakness for excessive elaboration shown in other of his earlier poems. Conceits and parallels abound, but are kept in the control of strong and exalted statement:

30

That old unquestion'd Pirate of the Land
Proud *Rome*, with dread, the fate of *Dunkirk* h[e]ar'd;
And trembling wish't behind more *Alpes* to stand,
Although an *Alexander* were her guard.

31

By his command we boldly crost the Line
And bravely fought where *Southern Starrs* arise,
We trac'd the farre-fetched Gold unto the mine
And that which brib'd our fathers made our prize.

32

Such was our Prince . . . .

(117–25)[2]

The truth of T. S. Eliot's claim that Dryden is a "descendant of Marlowe" may be seen here; we can feel the excitement of human aspiration and discovery, but Dryden's more developed

24

wit and emphatic form give the lines their own kind of strength, and ironic life.[3] The rest of the poem is not of this standard.

It is not surprising that for so public a poet as Dryden the two most momentous events of his life were the Restoration of King Charles II in 1660, and the departure into exile of his brother, James II, in 1688. Dryden not only celebrated the Restoration in his next public poem, *Astræa Redux* (1660), but the theme of restoration moves through his major poetry, and is, for example, powerfully and significantly recalled at the end of his most famous poem, *Absalom and Achitophel*. Nor is it surprising or disturbing that Dryden should now praise Charles who had so lately praised Cromwell; Johnson well said that if Dryden changed, he changed with the nation, and Sir Walter Scott noted rightly the restraint of the *Heroique Stanza's* in praising neither Cromwell's rise to power, nor, as might have seemed natural at the time, his son and successor.[4] To all who lived through that remarkable event, the Restoration cannot but have powerfully appealed to the imagination : its peacefulness, its rejoicing, the strong sense of providence, and of a harmony re-established with the best of the nation's past, well attested by Evelyn in a great passage of his *Diary* (29 May 1660). As a poet Dryden responded in two main ways to meet the challenge of the event. He put aside the alternately rhyming stanza of the lines to Cromwell, which he thought appropriate to deeds of heroic enterprise, and adopted the more plain order of the heroic couplet. Then probably from Waller's *Panegryric to my Lord Protector* (1655) (and possibly also from Marvell's 'Horatian Ode', still unpublished but conceivably circulated in manuscript in the 1650s), he took the deeply suggestive parallel between the establishment of a British ruler after civil war, and the consolidation of power by Octavius Caesar, to become the Emperor Augustus of Virgil and Horace.[5] Dryden improves upon Waller in that he recognizes that the intrinsic importance of the parallel is too great to provide a merely local allusion; it must become the dominant myth of the poem. Thus his poem is entitled *Astræa Redux* : the return of the goddess of Justice (after the Age of Iron), and by its epigraph from the Fourth Eclogue of Virgil, as well as by allusions in the text, the poem associates this with the return of a Golden Age on the establishment of strong and just civil order in Rome by Caesar Augustus. But Virgil's Fourth Eclogue is less obviously a poem of compliment than a religious prophecy; its appropriateness as a prophecy of Christ was a living conception in the seventeenth century if no longer believed in literally. Dryden did not hesitate to associate his Christian religion with the momentous Roman compliment to Charles, and made him David returned from exile as well as Augustus ending the civil wars. Thus Dryden helped to inaugurate formally the myth and ideal of Augustanism as applied to Britain, with its hope for strong and harmonious rule, a flourishing of the arts of peace, and the favour of providence on both.[6] The gravity of the historical and religious allusion accords well with the plain dignity of the heroic couplets. The poem does not strive for the excitement of the *Heroique Stanza's* but, as perhaps Dryden felt, for the welcoming of tried virtue and proven right with a more sober splendour. This he achieves at the beginning and end of his poem, the first with its ominous strength :

> Now with a general Peace the World was blest,
> While Ours, a World divided from the rest,
> A dreadful Quiet felt, and worser farre
> Then Armes, a sullen Intervall of Warre . . .

leading through a series of modulated reflections, to full revelation of Charles in the pattern of providence in the last :

> Oh Happy Age! Oh times like those alone
> By Fate reserv'd for Great *Augustus* Throne!
> When the joint growth of Armes and Arts foreshew
> The World a Monarch, and that Monarch *You*.

$$(1-4, 320-3)$$

It is in the centre that the poem fails. It lacks form and forward drive. Marvell's much greater 'Horatian Ode' shows that an occasional poem may need a story-line to give it shape, and Marvell also places at the very centre of his poem the dramatic scene which was the point of historical transition : the execution of Charles I, which in its brilliant theatrical metaphor looks back to the Elizabethans, while in the Horatian parallel with Octavius and Cleopatra it anticipates the dominant Augustan myth of the coming century. *Astræa Redux*, on the other hand, is more important for its ideas than its execution.

By 1666 Dryden, already thirty-five, was working on the longest and most ambitious of his early poems. Taking the title of a series of seditious anti-Royalist pamphlets, *Annus Mirabilis*, he sought to provide the Court with a powerful and welcome piece of poetic propaganda—and a very great deal more than that. 1666, by virtue of the coincidence of its numbers, was expected by some to be a year of portents and prodigies. The

26

puritan astrologer William Lilly had forecast there would in this year be neither king nor royal claimant. These expectations established, providence unluckily supplied the period 1665–66 with the Great Plague and the Great Fire, which were inevitably taken by those disaffected with the royal government as judgments upon the nation for restoring the monarchy. Dryden's purpose, in turning the title back upon the disaffected, was to stress that Charles's victories in the First Dutch War hardly suggested a providence unfavourable to the Restoration, and that the Fire was to be interpreted less a punishment for the Restoration than the Interregnum; above all a test of London's renewed loyalty to its sovereign.[7] The poem thus treats of a successful naval war waged for commercial advantage, followed by a disaster bravely endured; Dryden judged it to be "Historical, *not* Epick, *though both the Actions and Actors are as much Heroick, as any Poem can contain.*"[8] He found no conflict between high literary ambition and writing for a political occasion, blending the two so well that it was over two hundred years before scholarship recovered the immediate purpose of the work. In a sense, *Annus Mirabilis* combines the two types of heroism dealt with respectively in *Heroique Stanza's* and *Astræa Redux*: active, aggressive enterprise, and the equal heroism of a wise, enduring fortitude. Each is seen as an essential mark of national glory under a wise and strong King secure in the affection of his people. Few other English poems have celebrated national glory with such enthusiasm.

Reverting, for this poem of action, to quatrains "*because I have ever judg'd them more noble, and of greater dignity, both for the sound and number, then any other Verse in use amongst us,*"[9] making constant allusion to Virgil's *Aeneid*, straining every poetic nerve to elevate his subject to the pitch of the heroic, while yet maintaining an undercurrent of satirical wit, Dryden produced an extraordinary poem. Its main fault is obvious and should be mentioned at once. In his repeated efforts to raise and embellish his subject-matter, Dryden in effect fails to do justice to its intrinsic human interest which would have come through in plainer style, but now often fails to penetrate the screen of baroque similitudes which he interposes. He can leave no literal statement as it is, but must always follow with a comparison: "*So hear the skaly Herd . . .*", "*So glad Egyptians see . . .*", "*Thus with their Amazons . . .*", "*Thus Israel safe . .*", "*Such port the Elephant bears . . .*" and so forth.[10] While these comparisons are rarely without their ingenious relevance, much of the poem is spoiled by over-elaboration.

Dryden made an error of critical judgment and, failing to learn from the Virgil he so often echoed, took the artistic challenge of his subject to be panegyrical when in fact it was narrative.[11] And as in *Astræa Redux*, we are perhaps most troubled by the poem's weakness at its centre. This having been said, the poem remains an astonishing manifestation of energy and brilliance. Nowhere more so than in its opening, in the description of the Great Fire, and at the end, the contemporary reader must have been aware of a powerful new talent on the literary scene.

I

    In thriving Arts long time had *Holland* grown,
        Crouching at home, and cruel when abroad :
    Scarce leaving us the means to claim our own.
        Our King they courted, and our Merchants aw'd.

2

    Trade, which liked bloud should circularly flow,   5
        Stop'd in their Channels, found its freedom lost
    Thither the wealth of all the world did go,
        And seem'd but shipwrack'd on so base a Coast.

3

    For them alone the Heav'ns had kindly heat,
        In Eastern Quarries ripening precious Dew :   10
    For them the *Idumæan* Balm did sweat,
        And in hot *Ceilon* Spicy Forrests grew.

4

    The Sun but seem'd the Lab'rer of their Year;
        Each wexing Moon suppli'd her watry store,
    To swell those Tides, which from the Line did bear   15
        Their brim-full Vessels to the *Belg'an* shore.

5

    Thus mighty in her Ships, stood *Carthage* long,
        And swept the riches of the world from far;
    Yet stoop'd to *Rome*, less wealthy, but more strong :
        And this may prove our second Punick War.   20
                         (1–20)

Dryden has, in this opening of his poem, imperiously yoked a number of different qualities together into one powerful team. There is first and fundamentally the achievement of strong, measured and emphatic statement, fitted variously to its content by modulation of rhythm and syntax (note the flagging force of l.6 created by the cæsura; the pointed antithesis of l.19; the unchecked sweep forward of l.7). There is the Marlovian revelling in exotic richness, whose possession is cunningly made to seem like impiety in the Dutch and a glorious challenge to the English. There is the superbly open and unashamed satirical attitude to Holland ('Crouching at home, and cruel when abroad') which is yet kept a minor *motif* in the total harmony—the well deployed pun in 'so base a Coast,' prepared for and enriched by 'Crouching' in l.2, is in no way smart or obtrusive. Admiration for exotic wealth and satirical scorn for the base Dutch pull the poetry in opposite directions and create a fine tension, but one finally controlled by the masterful syntax and resounding rhyme, which drives towards the grand introduction of the Roman analogy in the fifth stanza. Dryden here measures Britain up to a triumphant Roman Republic with an almost breathless historical excitement, the more effectively conveyed by language which is strong and plain. This passage illustrates what is best in the first two thirds of the poem. It can already be seen that if this is heroic verse, it is so in a growingly complex way, which can accommodate an outwardly genial if mordant satiric element.

The description of the Great Fire, however, gains a further strength. In the earlier part of the poem, despite promising moments, the Roman analogy is never properly extended. In the later part Dryden fully develops an impressive and relevant analogy between the Fire, and forces of rebellion and disorder in the kingdom. The Fire is personified and compared to 'some dire Usurper Heav'n provides,/To scourge his Country with a lawless sway,' the allusion to Cromwell being sharpened by what would appear to be an echo, in stanza 215, of Marvell's lines on Cromwell in the *Horatian Ode*:

> Then burning through the air he went
> And palaces and temples rent . . .
>
> (21–2)

to which Dryden would in that case be replying. The Fire/Rebellion is built up into a terrifying image:

217

> In this deep quiet, from what source unknown,
>   Those seeds of fire their fatal birth disclose:
> And first, few scatt'ring sparks about were blown,
>   Big with the flames that to our ruine rose.

29

Then, in some close-pent room it crept along,
    And, smouldring as it went, in silence fed :
Till th'infant monster, with devouring strong,
    Walk'd boldly upright with exalted head.

Now, like some rich or mighty Murderer,
    Too great for prison, which he breaks with gold :
Who fresher for new mischiefs does appear,
    And dares the world to tax him with the old :

So scapes th'insulting fire his narrow Jail . . . .

(865–77)

With perfect naturalness the analogy is continued; the Fire is
compared to factions, armies and the Hydra-headed anarchic
mob. It becomes a complete image of rebellion without ceasing
to be a fire. And against this image, King Charles is displayed
in his proper role of monarch opposing the destruction of his
people by action and prayer. The language of the prayer is grave
and plain, in effective and probably designed contrast to the
exuberant, sometimes humorous elaboration of the narrative
of the naval war. Providence now looks with favour upon
Britain and its monarch. The Fire is checked, King and citizens
are grown close in loyalty through suffering and endeavour,
and a new and grander city ('More great then humane, now,
and more *August*') rises from flames apparently destructive but
in the event purgatorial. The Rebellion and Restoration have
been re-enacted, their meaning re-affirmed, the favour of providence asserted. Through his art Dryden has harmonised and
interpreted an historical sequence which might have borne a
very different reading; in the treatment of the Fire especially
the poem would not have succeeded as propaganda had it failed
as art. In the last stanzas, with an easy transition, Dryden
turns back to his original theme of eastern wealth and the war.
Despite serious faults, remarkable powers of imagination are
displayed in *Annus Mirabilis*; to dismiss or ignore it is to de-
prive ourselves of one of the great pleasures of Dryden's work.

For twelve years after the publication of *Annus Mirabilis*
Dryden wrote chiefly for the stage. It was the period of his
rhyming heroic tragedies, but the theatre also drew from his
pen comedy, opera, songs, prologues and epilogues (in themselves a notable and enjoyable part of his poetic achievement,
which should not be ignored) and the *Essay of Dramatic Poesy*
(1668). New directions developed in his thought and practice,
so that he by no means came to his next major poem from
the position adopted in his last. The first development concerned his disappointed desire to celebrate his native country
and the Stuart dynasty in a national epic, the subject of which
was to be 'great, the *Story* English, and neither too far distant
from the present Age, nor too near approaching it.' The King
and the Duke of York were to be 'the Heroes of the Poem.'[12]
But, as Dryden was later to confess, 'being encourag'd only
with fair Words, by King *Charles* II, my little Sallary ill paid,
and no prospect of a future Subsistance, I was then dis-
courag'd . . .'[13] The significant background to this is of course
the publication of Milton's *Paradise Lost* (to which Dryden early
gave generous and unfashionable praise) in 1667; and his own
appointment as Poet Laureate and Historiographer Royal in
1668 and 1670 respectively. The second development is more
unexpected. It can be divined in Dryden's very intelligent trans-
position of *Paradise Lost* into a rhyming opera, *The State of
Innocence*, in 1677. This fascinating work, whose design, atmosphere and language are naturally Milton's in the main, shows
sudden, unmistakable touches of the mature Dryden. Lines
such as : 'From Heav'n to rise States-General of Hell,' 'And all
dissolved in *Hallelujahs* lie', evince a powerful, alert irony; all
the strength of the mundane rises into the language, but nowhere more so than in the line rightly singled out for praise by
T. S. Eliot: '. . . all the sad variety of Hell.'[14] This worldly
and disenchanted phrase, quite unlike Milton, comes from
Dryden the man of the Restoration world. Another way to see
the same development is to consider the change in Dryden's
drama from *The Conquest of Granada* through *Aureng-Zebe*
(1676) to *All for Love* (1670–77). The ranting heroics of the first
are modified in the second by the figure of the Old Emperor, a
startling blend of high passion and dry world-weary comedy,
and by the treatment of the truly heroic and virtuous Aureng-

zebe himself, whose famous speech in Act IV strikes a new note for the author of *Annus Mirabilis* :

> When I consider Life, 'tis all a Cheat :
> Yet, fool'd with hope, Men favour the Deceit.
> Trust on, and think to Morrow will repay :
> To Morrow's falser than the former Day . . .
> I'm tir'd of waiting for this Chymick Gold,
> Which Fools us Young, and Beggars us when Old.[15]

This forceful, worldly tone, whose language is so expressively plain and low, is far from the heroic. Coming from Aureng-Zebe, as his reaction to an appalling series of undeserved disappointments, it is dramatic and strikes no more of an attitude than its place in the play warrants.[16] And this leads on to the rich, but flexible and unobtrusive blank verse of *All for Love* in 1677. Still retaining his epic ideal, Dryden had come to see the need to dismount from the elaborately caparisoned high horse of *Annus Mirabilis*. The world impinged upon him in various ways, and he must respond in varying modes.

It was perhaps for this reason that Dryden adopted the mock-heroic mode, practised by his contemporaries Rochester ('The Disabled Debauchee') and Boileau (*Le Lutrin*), in *Mac Flecknoe*, written probably in 1678 (published 1682). The mode, which applies an heroic manner to low subjects for a comic and critical purpose, fulfilled opposite trends in Dryden, and brought them into creative equilibrium. Indeed *Mac Flecknoe*, seems to have been written to please himself, and is one of the few examples of personal lampoon in his work. It is an uproarious attack upon the worthy and interesting dramatist Thomas Shadwell. What provoked it is still obscure, but it must have been something more than the critical dispute which had continued for ten years between the two dramatists.[17] Dryden seized upon the death of Richard Flecknoe, a figure generally considered 'the bottom of all Poetry,' and through parodying the epic and Augustan theme of the aged ruler determining and blessing his successor, made Shadwell the Son of Flecknoe, and hapless target of a poem whose plan of attack varies widely and unfairly from the large-spirited Augustan irony of :

> Besides his goodly Fabrick fills the eye,
> And seems design'd for thoughtless Majesty :

32

to the unashamed Billingsgate of :

> Echoes from *Pissing-Alley*, *Sh[adwell]* call ....
>
> (25–6, 47)

This contrast expresses the progress of the work, from the sonorous Virgilian opening :

> All humane things are subject to decay,
> And, when Fate summons, Monarchs must obey :
> This *Fleckno* found, who, like *Augustus*, young
> Was call'd to Empire, and had govern'd long ....
>
> (1–4)

to the booby-trap of its farcical conclusion, when the interminably declaiming Flecknoe is precipitated in mid-flow through a trap-door, leaving Shadwell to succeed him as ruler over the 'Realms of *Non-sense*.' Much in *Mac Flecknoe* would become more luminous had we a detailed knowledge of its immediate background. Yet enough can be seen to appreciate that it is a short poem of quality and importance, using considerable literary accomplishment to create satire of superb patronage, of jovial, almost forgiving contempt, readier to turn to the broadly comic than the sharply destructive. In this respect it anticipates Dryden's characters of Doeg (Settle) and Og (Shadwell) in Tate's *Second Part of Absalom and Achitophel* (1682) : not mock-heroic indeed, but among the most richly and exuberantly comic poetry Dryden ever wrote. *Mac Flecknoe* is also notable, with Rochester's 'Upon Nothing', in laying the poetic foundation for Pope's later and greater *Dunciad*, and for the widely embracing Augustan concept of Dullness. It shows a new and ingenious variation on the Augustan ideal, as expressed in *Astræa Redux*, bringing its high literary meaning into encounter, for the first time, with un-ideal reality. Finally, not to get the work out of proportion, we must remember that *Mac Flecknoe* is a very good joke.[18]

We now come to a poem which, far more than *Mac Flecknoe*, gave Dryden the chance to write in heroic style, yet at the same time recognize the unheroic aspects of his subject. With such human perception and subtlety did Dryden now blend the two that *Mac Flecknoe* looks mechanical by comparison. This poem was *Absalom and Achitophel* (1681). It is a work which grew out of a particular crisis in English history, and it is first necessary to consider the events which led Dryden to write it.

Despite the high hopes of 1660, the reign of Charles II had

been far from harmonious in its first twenty years. The religious and political conflicts of the Civil War were neither resolved nor dispelled, merely driven underground, while the nation struggled to re-unite. As time went on, the chief issues seemed to re-emerge, and turn upon the question of the royal succession. Queen Catherine proved barren; the King had no legitimate child. The heir-apparent was the Duke of York, but he had become a Roman Catholic. The Protestant Succession was thus in danger, and with it the basis of Tudor and Stuart monarchy since Elizabeth. But the available remedies were severe and dangerous, especially to friends of the royal prerogative : either to enact by Parliament severe limitations upon the Duke on his attaining the throne, even to the extent of a Protestant regency; or to exclude the Duke from succession by act of Parliament, in favour, perhaps, of the King's illegitimate but Protestant son, the Duke of Monmouth. The first course Charles was prepared to envisage, despite a love of his son and dislike of his brother. The second was that sought by the Earl of Shaftesbury, the King's brilliant and ambitious dismissed Chancellor. It must be noted that his solution, if adopted, would have finally made kings and servants of Parliament. To this situation, already complex and explosive, was added, in 1678, the notorious Popish Plot, whose full origins still defy the historian. Clearly Titus Oates, the remarkable political confidence-man who *appears* to have been its author, realized the rich profits there might be at such a time in discovering a Roman Catholic design on the life of the King. Charles never believed in the plot, but was obliged from political realism to make concessions to the mounting public hysteria, vigorously exploited by Shaftesbury for his political ends. Hostile pressures upon the King were exerted, however, chiefly through Parliament. Charles could dissolve and defy Parliament only in so far as he could dispense with it as a source of money. Thus the availability of a large secret subsidy from King Louis XIV offered him one way out of his difficulties. The other way, more honourable and harder to achieve, was to bring Parliament round to an acceptable formula of Limitation. Like a wise politician Charles tried for both. Despite a notable victory for Limitation in the Lords, the Commons remained obstinate for Exclusion. Charles dissolved Parliament, summoned a new one at Oxford for March 1681; meanwhile clinched his deal with Louis XIV. He then tried once again for Limitation, but to no avail. In a dramatic encounter in the Lords, Shaftesbury handed Charles a proposal to make Monmouth his heir, offering to undertake all parliamentary legalisation. 'Let there be no delusion,' the King replied,

> I will not yield, nor will I be bullied. Men usually become more timid as they become older; it is the opposite with me, and for what may remain of my life I am determined that nothing will tarnish my reputation. I have law and reason and all right-thinking men on my side; I have the Church . . . and nothing will ever separate us.[19]

Parliament was then again dissolved, and by a well-judged and successful political act Charles won moderate opinion of the kingdom to his side in a *Declaration To All His Loving Subjects*. Shaftesbury was committed to the Tower in June; his trial was to follow in November. Without doubt the Laureate was now required to produce a work which would strengthen the royal case in the eyes of all but the most obdurately disaffected. Probably Charles appealed to Dryden personally, and suggested that his *Declaration* be included.

The assignment was delicate yet challenging. Dryden himself increased his difficulty by again resolving that a work of art would do more good to the royal cause in which he believed than a mere party piece. The *desiderata* were many and complex. The poem was to be directed against Shaftesbury, but if Dryden were to give an heroic sense of the monarch having surmounted a great national crisis, Shaftesbury must be presented as neither contemptible, ridiculous, nor perhaps entirely evil. He must be an infinitely dangerous but impressive adversary. Monmouth, on the other hand, retained his father's love. His part in the crisis must be softened; he must seem to have been *betrayed* into a disloyalty none could deny. Charles must seem strong and heroic at the moment of his triumph, but the monarch himself had tacitly admitted earlier weakness in his remarks to Shaftesbury; his candour and good sense left Dryden free to be delicately critical of his past conduct. In contrast to all this, the nation had just emerged from the hysterical excesses of the Plot; here scorn and contempt were appropriate, and ranging from the King to (say) Titus Oates there were other well known figures, such as Villiers, Duke of Buckingham, and Slingsby Bethel, each of whom demanded treatment at different points on the scale from the heroic to the satiric. Finally, it was necessary that Dryden, whose subject was once again historical, and part of a sequence of events not necessarily concluded, should shape his material into a coherent unified pattern. In every respect Dryden successfully met the challenge.

Despite the difficulties it imposed, he was also helped by history. He was an eager and shrewd student of the human scene; the characters of *Absalom and Achitophel* are so much more vivid than those of his drama because they are taken from life, nor can it be said that he grossly distorted any contemporary figure to serve his political end. His treatment of Charles, Shaftesbury, Monmouth, and their various supporters, seems to have been remarkably close to historical truth—though we must remember that he was probably ignorant of Charles's French subsidy.

Dryden's first step was to cast over the contemporary figures and events a transparent biblical disguise. The whole sequence was recast as Absalom and Ahithophel conspiracy against King David, as recounted in II *Samuel*, 15–17. This device offered a number of advantages. First the practical one : Dryden could write about recognizable figures without using their real names. Secondly the biblical trappings had the effect of slightly distancing the subject and presenting it anew : a way of saying that the poem was an autonomous work of art. Thirdly and most important, the biblical parallel with one stroke put a compelling moral and religious interpretation upon the events which were Dryden's subject, appealing not only to the authority of a familiar episode of Hebrew history, but also to the already widely used identification of Charles as a new David, and of Shaftesbury as a new Ahithophel, the biblical type of the rebellious political conspirator and a type of Lucifer's conspiracy and rebellion against God. It is sometimes said that by his biblical parallel Dryden 'universalized' what would otherwise have been no more than an ephemeral political broadside. This is to misunderstand the poem. The life of the work lies above all else in its particularity, in our sense that its characters are individuals caught up in a particular crisis at a particular time. Dryden indeed saw fundamental principles at stake in the situation, and brought a broad range of religious, political and social wisdom to bear upon it, including the story of David and Ahithophel. But who can say that his characters or his principles are truly 'universal', and why should it be necessary when we can see humanity in the particular?

Let us now approach the poem more closely, looking first at its range, then at its structure. Fundamental is Dryden's treatment of the Plot and the people; in his very style and terms he *disposes* of that national folly, but without failing to take it seriously :

From hence began that Plot, the Nation's Curse,
Bad in it self, but represented worse.
Rais'd in extremes, and in extremes decry'd;
With Oaths affirm'd, with dying Vows deny'd.
Not weigh'd, or winnow'd by the Multitude;
But swallow'd in the Mass, unchew'd and Crude.
Some Truth there was, but dash'd and brew'd with Lyes;
To please the Fools, and puzzle all the Wise.

(108–115)

The bold, confident, antithetical style, in itself an expression of
health and order, triumphs over the murky and confused depths
of the Plot. Dryden has drawn his distinctions, weighed up and
dismissed the Plot, but yet acknowledges how 'several Factions
from this first Ferment/Work up to Foam, and threat the
Government.' This image of unstable popular emotion, something which partakes of the formless destructive fury of the sea,
yet also, in more homely terms, of the seething liquid periodic-
ally boiling over in the pot, underlies the whole poem; such
actions which are attempted, such order which is restored,
exploit or contend with this unstable element. The same in-
stability is recognized when Dryden speaks particularly of the
English political public of the mid-seventeenth century :

God's pamper'd people whom, debauch'd with ease,
No King could govern, nor God could please;
(Gods they had tri'd of every shape and size
That God-smiths could produce, or Priests devise :) ...
They who when *Saul* was dead, without a blow,
[*Saul* : Oliver Cromwell]
Made foolish *Ishbosheth* the Crown forgo;
[*Ishbosheth* : Richard Cromwell]
Who banisht *David* did from *Hebron* bring,
[*Hebron* : here, the Low Countries]
And, with a Generall Shout, proclaim'd him King ...
Now, wondred why, so long, they had obey'd
An Idoll Monarch which their hands had made :
Thought they might ruine him they could create;
Or melt him to that Golden Calf, a State.

(47–50, 57–60, 63–6)

With all the usual strengths of Dryden's poetry granted, this
passage shows a new brilliance. It lies in the outrageous apparent impiety of the third and fourth lines, the audacious pun
on 'Idoll', the sudden breathtaking translation from 'Golden Calf'

to 'State': the whole affirming, paradoxically, the deeply traditional view that God made man not man God, that God appointed kings for their subjects to obey, or chaos would come again. Energetic, ordered, concise, the passage is one in which every word, balance, and allusion seems to break into fresh insight. But now, rising out of the restless discontent of the people, certain individual figures are depicted: Corah (Titus Oates):

> Sunk were his Eyes, his Voyce was harsh and loud,
> Sure signs he neither Cholerick was, nor Proud ...
> His Memory, miraculously great,
> Could Plots, exceeding mans belief, repeat;
>
> (646–7, 650–1)

(note the vividly particular descriptive detail, the exuberant irony of 'miraculously', the incredulous inflexion of the speaking voice in the last line); Shimei (Slingsby Bethel) who 'Did wisely from Expensive Sins refrain' (note the moral shock and humour in the placing of the adjective); Zimri (the Duke of Buckingham) of whose portrait Dryden later said: ' 'Tis not bloody, but 'tis ridiculous enough': who

> ... in the course of one revolving Moon,
> Was Chymist, Fidler, States-Man, and Buffoon:
> Then all for Women, Painting, Rhiming, Drinking:
> Besides ten thousand freaks that dy'd in thinking.
>
> (549–52)

In this portrait we cannot find trenchant low diction as much as in the portraits and passages above; the style has been modified with the rank and character of the subject. It is also growing more inward; we are not shown what Zimri looked like, as we are Corah; instead with almost hallucinatory vividness we are given a poetic image of his various, ever-shifting mind. Even more inward is the powerful portrayal of Achitophel himself, Sagacious, Bold, and Turbulent of wit':

> Pleas'd with the Danger, when the Waves went high
> He sought the Storms ...
>
> (153, 160–1)

Starting with Dryden's poetry about the people, we have, with the portrait of Achitophel, mounted from the satiric to the heroic. While fully facing the danger to civil harmony of Achitophel's restless dynamism, Dryden depicts him largely without low and contemptuous language, and often in terms of open admiration. He is a great soul who dares more than ordin-

38

ary men dare, though he dares for evil. There remains, perhaps most brilliant of all, the portrait of David before the crisis, in a kind of Hebrew Golden Age of sexual freedom:

> When Nature prompted, and no law deny'd
> Promiscuous use of Concubine and Bride;
> Then, *Israel's* Monarch, after Heaven's own heart,
> His vigorous warmth did, variously, impart
> To Wives and Slaves: And, wide as his Command,
> Scatter'd his Maker's Image through the Land
>
> (5–10)

Through the biblical parallel Dryden found the perfect way of recognizing, while seeming to admire, Charles's faults; it is a most delicate and witty piece of equivocation, such as that witty monarch and all who loved him would appreciate. But there is more than this. The progeny of a king is inevitably a political issue; David's genial warmth, and love of his eldest illegitimate son, bespeaks an easy and affectionate humanity, not the sterner qualities required to rule successfully over a 'Headstrong, Moody, Murmuring' people. Dryden has struck a balance. We apprehend political weakness, yet before the onset of political trouble give our sympathy to David as a man, so appropriate a warmth and largeness of conception is there in Dryden's portrayal.

The poem has so far been discussed only as a collection of brilliantly varied characters. Much of the new strength, colour and interest in it is due to its characters, which show Dryden responding more richly and humanly to his world than he had before. Yet there is more to *Absalom and Achitophel* than this; the poem is an architectural masterpiece. The whole is organized into a series of significant balances and contrasts. The genial, mild David of the beginning of the poem is contrasted with the next portrait, that of the fiery and impatient Achitophel; the two confront one another across Dryden's description of the English people (the 'Headstrong, Moody, Murmuring race') which the first seeks to rule, the second to exploit. This exemplifies also a contrast between dominant individuals in the foreground, the restless people in the background, which runs through the whole poem. Again, in the second half of the poem, the 'Hydra . . . of sprouting heads' of the rebel followers is contrasted with the 'short File' of loyalists, though an actual symmetry is achieved by the fact that Dryden gives three long portraits from the first, one long and five of the briefest from the second, thus adroitly honouring more while stressing the weakness of David's support. These lists, in their turn, face one another across the account of Absalom's seduction of the people, with his brilliantly delusive and dishonest speech; it is as though they take up their stations as the public strife begins. Absalom's speech to the people is in itself a public development from that earlier and more crucial speech of seduction : Achitophel's to Absalom. The second recalls the first; the seduced proves an apt pupil of the seducer; conflict in the state develops out of the conflict in the individual. The connection between the two seduction speeches makes the poem more than a series of formal and static contrasts, and gives it forward impetus. But what above all gives the poem movement and suspense, the feel of history in the making, is Achitophel's seduction of Absalom itself. On the success of this the fable of the whole poem turns, and it is notable that Dryden has now sufficiently learned the importance of the middle of a poem to give the temptation scene a near-central position. Absalom is placed in the formal position for a tragic conflict, torn, as the illegitimate son of a king, between 'mounting Spirits' and a 'mean Descent', and Achitophel while seeming to appeal to the first, appeals in fact to the second. The archetypal Temptation and Fall, which Dryden recalls at the crucial moment, is always in the background.[20] Tempted upward, he does not rise but falls. Achitophel's speech is indeed in the great tradition of Renaissance rhetoric of temptation : Lucifer to Eve; Comus to the Lady; Volpone to Celia; the song to Guyon from the Bower of Bliss in *Faerie Queene* II. In keeping with this tradition, it displays a richness of poetic imagery further from the satiric levels of the poem even than the portrait of Achitophel or the later noble panegyric to Barzillai (Ormonde) :

> The Young-mens Vision, and the Old mens Dream!
> Thee, *Saviour*, Thee. . . .

(239–40)

but it must be read in its entirety. This is the only part of the poem that does not match or contrast with another part; it rises like a dome from the formal symmetries of the rest of the work, and this is a mark of its importance. A final important aspect of the design remains to be mentioned : the relation between the beginning and the end. It was Johnson who said of the end, where David puts down the opposition with a speech, that the rebellion vanishes absurdly into air like the enchanted castle when 'the destined knight' blows his horn.[21] He is wrong for a number of reasons. Scott noted the historical justification: that Charles's speech (actually the *Declaration*) constituted a carefully timed political act which *had* disarmed the opposition.[22] And what Dryden does in the poem, in the most marked of his formal contrasts which is also in a sense a development, is to show us the monarch as a man at the beginning, the monarch *as* monarch at the end. In re-asserting the rightful political hierarchy, David acts for God who gives His consent. The Restoration, hitherto imperfect, now for the first time becomes genuine; the Virgilian Golden Age is re-invoked, and the hoped-for splendours of a new Augustan Era begin. On the ideal level this is true, and the poem is as finely rounded off as it was begun. Yet for me it is a merit of the poem that its conclusion begs just half a question. Will the 'Moody, Murmuring' people stay 'willing' long? With Heaven's consent perhaps so, but we are reminded that the Augustan edifice of order stood on a precarious foundation. This insight is fundamental to the character of the poem; unlike Shakespeare's great tragedies of state it dramatizes not the working out but the containment of conflict. It is to this end that its abounding vigour of statement, its audacious satiric life, its glowing rhetorical richness and its splendidly formal architecture all move.

III

Dryden's next two considerable poems, *The Medall: A Satyre Against Sedition*, and *Religio Laici or a Layman's Faith*, appeared in 1682. The first, a further attack on Shaftesbury prompted by the King, is a good round piece of indignant invective. It lacks variation of tone, but is not long, and the poem shows enough verve to carry it through without monotony. *Religio Laici* is altogether more remarkable, and shows a new aspect of Dryden's varied talent. The occasion of the poem was the publication in 1682 of Henry Dickinson's translation of Simon's *Histoire Critique du Vieux Testament* (1678); exercised by the difficulties this work put in the way of all who saw the Bible as the sole and sufficient basis of religious faith, Dryden wrote a grave and candid examination of Christian belief, feeling his way in humble and pragmatic fashion between the extremes of Roman Catholicism and Deism. Quite apart from its subject, the poem is utterly unlike his chief earlier works, and has no splendour of style or form. It is plain, fit, and sound to the heart. Yet it has considerable variation of tone and effect. Its moving and beautiful opening, based on a passage from Donne's *Biathanatos*, is celebrated:

41

> Dim, as the borrow'd beams of Moon and Stars
> To *lonely, weary, wandring* Travellers,
> Is *Reason* to the *Soul* ....
>
> (1–3)

From all Dryden's work this is the best instance to refute Wordsworth's obtuse claim that there is not a single image from Nature in Dryden.[23] How different (and how appropriate to its theme) is the dry, infinitely worldly tone of the following :

> In *Pleasure* some their glutton Souls would steep;
> But found their Line too short, the Well too deep;
> And leaky Vessels which no *Bliss* cou'd keep.
> Thus, *anxious Thoughts* in *endless Circles* roul,
> Without a *Centre* where to fix the *Soul* :
> In this wilde Maze their vain Endeavours end.
>
> (33–38)

The latter part of this passage shows something of a debt to Rochester's atheistic 'Satyre against Mankind'. But it is notable that while Rochester denounces the perplexities and pretensions of the various kinds of believer with scorn, Dryden writes from the position of involvement. Hence such effective details as the emotive choice of adjectives in l.2 : '. . . *lonely, weary, wandring* . . .'; hence the humble and serious way in which Dryden answers the arguments with which he disagrees, showing here the catholic and impartial appreciation of different points of view which is the prime virtue of his criticism; hence the modest and unassuming manner in which he plots a personal and reasonable Christian path through the 'wilde Maze.'[24] It is one of the finest religious poems in the language and reads as a work of absolute integrity.

Charles II died on the 6 February 1685, and within five weeks Dryden had performed his laureately duty with his *Threnodia Augustalis*. It is surprising that Dryden of all people should fail to carry out this public duty with a convincing emotion, but Johnson rightly said that it shows 'a desire of splendor without wealth.'[25] It is hollowly elaborate and sometimes unctuous, though there are one or two fine moments. But Dryden's heart was now in poetry of religious argument; he had, with much power and feeling, just been producing translations out of Lucretius, and his next major performance was to be the long poem of controversy and Catholic apologetics, *The Hind and the Panther* (1687). It is his longest and most involved original poem. On the personal level it gives an account of Dryden's conversion to the Roman Catholic faith, early in the reign of the

Catholic James II. On the level of church controversy it attempts to thrash out the salient differences between the Anglican (the Panther) and Catholic (the Hind) communions. On the political level it gives, in considerable detail, the relative positions of the two churches to the monarchy and to the nonconformist churches, in the reign of James II.[26] It is a monument to the tensions, hopes and fears of those remarkable three years; indeed any attempt to see in *The Hind and the Panther* the traditional ascent of an ageing poet from profane to sacred matter overlooks the irreducibly political nature of the third part of the poem.[27] Dryden deploys the allegorical beast-fable, which is the method of the poem, with tact and sense. His characterizations are vivid, and are revealed as the more pointed when one considers earlier seventeenth-century examples of the mode.[28] The poem is well arranged, with the lively introduction to the different 'beasts' in the first part, the main body of controversy between Hind and Panther in the second, and the two (highly political) inset fables, of the Swallows by the Panther, of the Doves by the Hind, in the third part. Nevertheless in the long stretches of close argument between the two beasts we are little aware of this larger pattern, and the poem perhaps demands a more intense concern with the intrinsic importance of its subject than the modern reader can grant. Yet once again the poetic quality is high; the basic explanatory mode, 'As fittest for Discourse, and nearest Prose,' is vigorous and clear, and frequently rises into great vividness of asperity or beauty. It repays in poetic pleasure the extra effort it asks.

In 1688 the tensions which the Laureate had recognized in *Absalom and Achitophel* and *The Hind and the Panther* broke out into invasion and rebellion. James Stuart, portrayed in Dryden's work as resolute and strong, lost control of the favourable political situation he had inherited from his brother. William of Orange landed and James, after prolonged indecision, deserted by all on whom he most relied, departed into exile. For Dryden, so long concerned with the fortune, strengths and failings of the royal brothers, the Glorious Revolution must have seemed like the sad end of an age. Incapacitated now from office by his religion, he chose rather to write for his bread than expose himself a second time to the charge of being a religious turncoat. He stuck to his religious and political convictions, saw Thomas Shadwell (the foolish Mac Flecknoe, he once so vividly satirized) succeed him as Laureate, and lived for the remaining twelve years of his life an unprovocative but firm Papist and Jacobite. It is equally to this, as to the poet's interest and talent,

43

that we owe his large literary undertakings during these years: the translations of Juvenal and Persius with the important 'Discourse Concerning Satire' (1693), the *Eclogues, Georgics* and *Aeneid* of Virgil (1697), and the versions chiefly of Boccaccio and Chaucer published as *Fables Ancient and Modern* in 1700, the last year of his life. That each of these groups achieves the quality of original poetry has always been recognized. But his translation of the *Aeneid* was the most ambitious, arduous, and is the most interesting of them all. With a characteristic candour that grew in dignity with age, Dryden said of his effort:

> What *Virgil* wrote in the vigour of his Age, in Plenty and at Ease, I have undertaken to *Translate* in my Declining Years: struggling with Wants, oppress'd with Sickness, curb'd in my Genius, lyable to be misconstrued in all I write . . . what I have done, Imperfect as it is . . . will be judg'd in after Ages . . . to be no dishonour to my Native Country. . . .
> ('Postscript to the Reader', 1–4, 14–16)

Dryden admits his version to be imperfect. It must naturally be judged in the first place by the *Aeneid* itself, and it is clear by this standard that the seventeenth-century poem is not only inferior in general, but fails to respond to some of the highest and most important qualities of the original.[29] Against this we must remember the improbability of *any* translation matching up to a great original, and that the *Aeneid* is one of the greatest poems of literature. By the lower but not low standard which recognizes the importance of Dryden's achievement in *Annus Mirabilis, Absalom and Achitophel* and *Religio Laici*, the Dryden *Aeneid* is a highly impressive individual poem, by no means to be neglected because it is also a translation.

The poem is characteristically of its age and of Dryden's pen, and in no way more so than politically. To announce and carry through any but a narrowly academic translation of the *Aeneid*, at this time, was a quasi-political act. The 'Dedication of the Aeneis' shows Dryden, predictably, putting stress on the political and court-poet aspects of Virgil's work. The epic told of the founding of the Roman state and looked ahead to the empire of Augustus. The production of an English *Aeneid* implied a comparison between contemporary England and Augustan Rome. Thus Dryden's publisher, Tonson, besought him to dedicate the poem to William III (which was staunchly refused) and angered the old Jacobite by the illustrations, 'For in every figure of Eneas, he has causd him to be drawn like K. William, with a hookd Nose.' [30] Virgil is woven into the fabric of English history at this time; the dead Charles and the exiled James were inextricably involved with the Augustan Myth for Dryden. Thus, far from working for a parallel between Aeneas and William, he was at pains to make his English *Aeneid* express what for him was the truth; those punished in the underworld include men 'who Brothers' better Claim disown,/Expel their Parents, and usurp the Throne.' Dryden changed the sense of his text (Ruaeus's edition of 1675) to make this pointed reference to William and Mary. Later in the same passage he refers to 'Hosts of *Deserters*' who broke faith for gold; again the reference is to 1688.[31] But Dryden's Stuart loyalty is not confined to a scattering of Jacobite allusions. It is also more subtly and pervasively present. When, in Book VII, Latinus holds out for a certain time against pressure from his subjects to declare war on the Trojans, Dryden slightly points the passage, and we become aware that he is re-working a fundamental situation common to the Virgilian episode and Charles II's predicament in the Exclusion Crisis and Plot :

> With Fates averse, the Rout in Arms resort,
> *To Force their Monarch, and insult the Court.*
> But like a Rock unmov'd . . .
> So stood the Pious Prince unmov'd : and long
> *Sustain'd the madness of the noisie Throng.*

> (vii. 807–9, 813–14)

—yet in the end it is vain for him to fight the storm. Dryden's *Aeneid* arose from a conviction of the relevance of Virgil to the present, and of the present to Virgil. How close in tone (it has been noted) is the character of Drances, in Book XI, to *Absalom and Achitophel* :

> Factious and rich, bold at the Council Board,
> But cautious in the Field, he shun'd the Sword;
> A close Caballer, and Tongue-valiant Lord.

> (xi. 512–14)

Throughout Dryden displays impressive understanding of the dignity, difficulty, at times the tragedy, of political situations, conveying this compellingly in the poetry. From a wealth of examples, Diomede's rejection of Latinus' request for help against Aeneas, is especially fine; and the more plain and stirring speech of Numanus against the Trojans.[32]

Looking at the Dryden *Aeneid* from a more strictly aesthetic point of view, it is clear that throughout it seeks to heighten and elaborate the original, imparting to it an added physical turbulence, and substituting for the high dignity and pathos of Virgil a very human kind of bravura. Sometimes this quality is hollow and external, the clanking armour round the feeble warrior as Swift depicted Dryden in the *Battle of the Books*, but usually it weds with the content to form a baroque poem of the age which produced St. Paul's Cathedral, but not, for example, the Parthenon, or the Roman temple of Fortuna Virilis. Consider the identical last line of Book X (the death of Mezentius) and Book XII (the death of Turnus and conclusion of the poem): 'And the disdainful Soul came rushing thro' the Wound.' At neither point does the Ruaeus Virgil quite sustain the line, which combines ideas from both. Even then, 'disdainful' is stronger than Virgil's '*indignata*' and, in keeping, 'came rushing' more fiery than '[*animam*] *diffundi*', or '*fugit*'. That Dryden uses the same line twice, combining *both* Virgil's lines, shows that he wished to link the death of Turnus with the death of Mezentius; Aeneas had now overcome *both* his formidable foes and the poem was the more formally rounded off with a spirited flourish. Yet each of the new words is perfectly appropriate to the persons concerned. This is characteristic. Consider finally, not one of the abundance of splendid passages, but a representative middle one. As Troy burns, Aeneas appeals to his followers to make a hopeless last stand :

> Brave Souls, said I, but Brave, alas! in vain :
> Come, finish what our Cruel Fates ordain.
> You see the desp'rate state of our Affairs;
> And Heav'ns protecting Pow'rs are deaf to Pray'rs.   470
> The passive Gods behold the *Greeks* defile
> Their Temples, and abandon to the Spoil
> Their own Abodes : we, feeble few, conspire
> To save a sinking Town, involv'd in Fire.
> Then let us fall, but fall amidst our Foes,   475
> Despair of Life, the Means of Living shows . . .
> So rush'd we forth at once, resolv'd to die,
> Resolv'd in Death the last Extreams to try.
> We leave the narrow Lanes behind, and dare ⎫   485
> Th' unequal Combat in the publick Square : ⎬
> Night was our Friend, our Leader was Despair. ⎭
> What Tongue can tell the Slaughter of that Night?
> What Eyes can weep the Sorrows and Affright!
> An ancient and imperial City falls,   490
> The Streets are fill'd with frequent Funerals . . . .
>   (ii. 467–76, 483–91)

There are faults here. 'Frequent Funerals' where Virgil referred to the many corpses of the slain is perhaps insensitively Latinate. Line 475 seems ineloquently compressed, line 489 mechanical. But how good the rest is! How authentically contemporary 'the desp'rate state of our Affairs' and the 'publick Square'; how well he has imagined the difference between fighting in the open square and narrow lanes; how well his *enjambement* and cæsura in lines 471–4 express the desperate contrast between retreating gods and defiant men; how well the triplet expands from the physical facts to the spiritual! Why should we not enjoy whole-heartedly the not altogether Virgilian grandeur of the first and penultimate lines? The Dryden *Aeneid*, in truth, gives us too much finely characteristic poetry for appreciation to be easy. Daunted by its length, we neglect its range and richness, or hurry imperceptively through.

IV

The later short poems of Dryden are among the most effective and brilliant of his work. The dignified and moving elegy 'To the Memory of Mr. Oldham' (1684) should first be mentioned. It is poetry at the opposite extreme from the complexity of the Metaphysicals: poetry of statement, strong, elevated and plain:

> Farewel, too little and too lately known,
> Whom I began to think and call my own;
> For sure our Souls were near ally'd .... (1–3)

In such a poem modulation of tone is all-important. The heroic air of the opening changes to one of restrained irony and unpatronizing reproof in the middle:

> What could advancing Age have added more?
> It might (what Nature never gives the young)
> Have taught the numbers of thy native Tongue.
> (12–14)

This skilfully brings the heroic tribute to the young poet into contact with human reality, strengthening the feeling in the return to the heroic at the end. Wedded to this pattern of elevated but not impersonal statement are its two dominant Virgilian allusions: the comparison between the old and young satirists and Nisus and Euryalus, the two young competitors and heroes of *Aeneid* V. Nisus, with whom Dryden here compares himself, fell in the track, but in so doing made possible the victory of his friend. They later die for the cause of Aeneas in a valiant, voluntary exploit. This allusion is taken up at the end by the tribute to Oldham as the '*Marcellus* of our Tongue'— from the prophecy of Anchises to Aeneas in *Aeneid* VI. Though widely distant in time, Nisus, Euryalus and Marcellus all showed brilliant promise of contribution to the Augustan state, but were tragically cut off in youth. It is this promise which Dryden now equates with his and his young friend's poetic activity, but, in telling use of the pagan background to convey loss, the 'generous fruits' of poetic achievement are, at the conclusion, encompassed with darkness. So Marvell, in 'To His Coy Mistress', kept out of the poem his belief in a Christian immortality, to heighten the sense of life.

A poem somewhat similar in preoccupation, though not in form, is the epistle 'To My Dear Friend Mr. Congreve' (1694). It differs in form from 'To Mr. Oldham' since Dryden has pitched the tone at a lower, easier, more conversational level, appropriate to an epistle to a friend. But this poem too is concerned with the Augustan ideal. This is the 'promis'd hour' of the first line; as A. W. Hoffman has well said, 'the solemn suggestions have been made smilingly', through the use of the colloquial opening 'Well then' and the slight shock in the phrase 'The present Age of *Wit*.' [33] Thus Dryden congratulates Congreve on his achievement in drama, sees it as combining the strengths of the ages before and after the Civil War, and implicitly criticizes his own plays. A comparison of the literature of the two periods follows, resolving their achievements respectively into 'Strength' and 'Grace', and working out an architectural metaphor. Congreve is praised as 'You, the best Vitruvius' (the great Roman Augustan architect) for resolving the two into a harmony. An analogy between kingly succession and poetic succession is next deployed, whereby Dryden alludes to the deposition of James, and his own deposition from the laureateship.[34] If Shadwell and Rymer (Tom the first and second) have succeeded him in literary office, Congreve is the true heir, as James is the true king; Augustanism in England depends on the nation's recognition of each. The epistle has proceeded, by analogy, from the theme of writing to the theme of rule (both essential parts of the Augustan ideal); it concludes in more personal vein with lines whose richness resides in their blend of plain, candid admission and stately, public rhetoric :

> Already I am worn with Cares and Age;
> And just abandoning th'Ungrateful Stage. .
> But You, whom ev'ry Muse and Grace adorn,

Whom I foresee to better Fortune born,
Be kind to my Remains; and oh defend,
Against Your Judgement, Your departed Friend!
(66-7, 70-3)

These two poems succeed chiefly through a noble plainness; in two other of his later short poems, the Ode 'To the Memory of Mrs. Anne Killigrew' (1685) and *Alexander's Feast* (1697), Dryden exerted his talent to achieve effects of the most elaborate splendour. The first of these, the most brilliant of Dryden's panegyrical poems, celebrates rather than mourns the untimely death of a young poetess and painter, the daughter of the almoner to the Duke of York and of a family conspicuously loyal to the throne. She in no way deserved the heavenly harmony of praise Dryden devoted to her, but realistic description was not his purpose. He could, when he chose, be a mordantly exact observer of his human environment, but as James Kinsley observes, in an essay which goes to the heart of Dryden's work, 'the lamentable reality could be countered only by a persistent exemplification of the ideal.' [35] In this poem Dryden affirms the true nature and role of the artist: its affinity with the harmony of a Christian heaven, its marriage to moral purity in a degraded world, its reverence for the remains of classical antiquity whose living spirit it receives, its spirited and loyal depiction of the true monarch and consort in their sacred office, and its final return to a celestial music which, as in the later *Song for St. Cecilia's Day* (1687), will triumph at the world's end. Anne Killigrew's activities are happily contrived to exemplify this progression, and it is thus with an appropriate splendour that Dryden enacts the part he praises:

Whether, adopted to some Neighbouring Star,
Thou rol'st above us, in thy wand'ring Race,
  Or, in Procession fixt and regular,
  Mov'd with the Heavens Majestick Pace;
  Or, call'd to more Superior Bliss,
Thou tread'st, with Seraphims, the vast Abyss:
What ever happy Region is thy place,
Cease thy Celestial Song a little space;
(Thou wilt have Time enough for Hymns Divine,
  Since Heav'ns Eternal Year is thine.)
Hear then a Mortal Muse thy Praise rehearse,
  In no ignoble Verse . . .
(6-17)

Though he deals with things heavenly, his splendour is of a human kind. There is no sense of the otherworldly; we are in the world of Baroque painting, or Purcell's music, where genuine reverence and aspiration issue in an unashamed delight in spirited movement, variety and elaboration of effect.

But Dryden achieved poetic splendour in different ways. His splendour in honour of the sacred, in the 'Anne Killigrew' Ode, is quite different from *Alexander's Feast*, where he again blends the comic and the heroic, but in a new way. In *Mac Flecknoe* and *Absalom and Achitophel* Dryden achieved this by the varying juxtaposition of high and low; in *Alexander's Feast* it has evolved to a point where the triumphant Alexander *is* also comic; the genuine victor is, in a rather terrible way, the plaything of Timotheus the musician. Like the *St. Cecilia* Ode, *Alexander's Feast* was written for musical setting (on this occasion by Jeremiah Clarke) and performance in a festival of music. It is a libretto as well as a poem, and the marked division between recitative and chorus, with the frequent opportunity for repetition which the poem *gives* the singer, without sacrifice of logical or poetic effect, show that Dryden bore well in mind the nature of his task.[36] But even without music the poem is a compelling myth, for in celebrating the power of music Dryden offers a new and enigmatic image of the relation between artist and ruler. In *Annus Mirabilis* and *Absalom and Achitophel* Dryden had taken sequences of events and moulded them into the harmony of moral, political and artistic interpretations; here the harmony which purports to celebrate what *has* happened begins to initiate events, and the roles are reversed. The great conqueror in his splendour, 'Aloft in awful State,' 'Assumes the God' in response to sublime flattery, carouses like a soldier, fights all his battles again in drunken euphoria, laments the fall of his foe and the chances of the world, puts conquest and honour behind him for love, and the power of art over the victor issues terribly in the final 'Zeal to destroy' as the 'blooming *Eastern* Bride' lights her lover to his prey and fires another Troy. Timotheus runs the gamut of attitudes to conquest and each time Alexander responds; each time the poetry affirms his vitality and splendour it reduces him morally. While its incantatory repetition—'Happy, happy, happy Pair! /None but the Brave/None but the Brave . . .'—irresistibly builds up the atmosphere of heady celebration, the poem exposes the vulgar triumph of amoral conquest in most devastating fashion, and the hint of the fallen Darius 'Great and Good' (which makes Alexander maudlin) joins with the allusion to the fall of

Troy at the end to suggest that martial victory is one thing, heroism in the cause of the right quite another. Alexander is no Aeneas. To recall what Dryden made of his almost contemporary *Aeneid* translation is to realize the political *animus* behind the Ode. It is not an exact political allegory, but in 1697 William III had just triumphed over Louis XIV who supported the fallen cause of James II; and James had, like Darius, been 'Deserted at his utmost Need,/By those his former Bounty fed.' [37] The poem makes a general political allusion which is a part, but a part only, of its meaning; its full greatness lies in the way Dryden, like Timotheus, relentlessly brings out the moral truth behind the worldly triumph he purports to celebrate. The Ode is the peculiar creation of a man who responded with a natural ardour to the idea of public triumph, but who also put the world behind him for a principle. Once again the artistic richness arises from a tension of opposites.

Dryden's considerable lyrical gift can be seen from *Alexander's Feast*; it is a thread of poetry which runs throughout his work, from the Cavalier delicacy of the First Song from *An Evening's Love* (1671); through the rustic vigour of the harvest song ('We ha' cheated the Parson, we'll cheat him agen . . .'), and the classical grace of Venus's song, from *King Arthur*, both splendidly set by Purcell; through the dying fall of the Song from *Cleomenes* (1692), so dramatic in its context; the declamatory lyricism of the two Odes to Music; to the marvellously courageous bravura of the 'Secular Masque' from *The Pilgrim*, in which Dryden in the last year of his life reviewed the outgoing century and welcomed the new. The three phases of the seventeenth century, the reigns of James I and Charles I, the Civil War, and the Restoration, are summed up with the utmost simplicity by Momus as the reigns of hunting, war and love, and then the whole century, in the vicissitudes of which the old poet had been so deeply involved as artist and man, is with devastating simplicity dismissed.

> *All, all, of a piece throughout;*
> *Thy Chase had a Beast in view;*
> *Thy Wars brought nothing about;*
> *Thy Lovers were all untrue.*
> *'Tis well an Old Age is out,*
> *And time to begin a New.*

> (92–7)

Realistic worldly penetration is balanced against the buoyant tone and gallant dance of words in which Dryden dismisses with the century the world of his own life. There is gallantry and bravura in the way so much is left unsaid, and only the pattern triumphs, the impeccable work of art which is the 'Secular Masque' itself.

It remains to complete this portrait of Dryden by recognition of his stature as a critic. His reputation as 'the father of English criticism' (Johnson's words) deserves to rest chiefly on five works: *An Essay of Dramatic Poesy* (1668), the *Heads of an Answer to Rymer* (1677), *The Grounds of Criticism in Tragedy* (1679), *A Discourse Concerning Satire* (1693) and the *Preface to the Fables* (1700) with its perceptive praise of Chaucer. Of these, the first is a dialogue, the second a series of MS. notes unpublished in his lifetime, the rest prefaces to his works, the characteristically personal and flexible form in which most of his criticism is couched. But while these five works are in their different ways classics, the wealth of fine insight and precept scattered through his other prefaces—especially those concerning the art of translation—should never be forgotten.

The world of learning from which Dryden's criticism grew is in many ways remote from modern concern. To take the most accessible instance, the redemption of Shakespeare and contemporary dramatists from the strictures of neo-classical criticism, exemplified particularly by Rymer's *Tragedies of the Last Age* (1678), is taken for granted today. Yet through the viewpoint of Neander in the *Essay*, and in *The Heads of an Answer* and *The Grounds of Criticism*, Dryden effectively disengaged the appreciation of Shakespeare from an insensitively rigid dramatic doctrine. More fundamental still is Dryden's importance in establishing descriptive criticism in English, going beyond the practice of Sidney's *Apology* and Jonson's *Discoveries* in giving precept and example, but offering also sustained examination of individual works. The discussion of Jonson's *Epicoene*, in the *Essay*, was a milestone in English letters. In some other respects the *Essay* is less than satisfactory, and has perhaps been overrated. Undoubtedly it presents some of the most important critical issues of the time concerning drama (Ancient versus Modern literary achievement; English Elizabethan drama versus French neo-classical drama; rhyming plays as against blank verse—all essentially connected issues as Dryden narrows his focus onto the immediate present); undoubtedly Dryden

appears consistently to be urging one central concept: that the dramatist imitates human nature in order to delight and thereby to instruct (which was the traditional view), but that excellence of drama is to be measured by the liveliness of the representation and the keen delight experienced by the audience; [38]

and undoubtedly the dialogue is closely associated, by setting and style, with contemporary Restoration London, in its aristocratic and lettered aspect. But, in this the earliest of Dryden's main critical works, we lack the sense of the dialogue being a mode in which truth is naturally established by exchange, in which viewpoints needing to be countered *are* always countered, and in which all major issues raised come to satisfying resolution.[39]

Yet it is precisely this virtue, lacking in the *Essay*, which makes the general attitude and quality of mind with which Dryden goes about the critical task impressive in the later criticism. This we have already seen in *Religio Laici*. It is a sensitivity to conflicting arguments, a catholic ability to see the value in several sides of a question, a real and modest care (in one who talks so often and unaffectedly about himself) in coming to his final decision. This is his great virtue, and what we should learn from him. In the line of English critics, he has indeed a less subtle and original intelligence than Coleridge, but deserves to rank above Johnson, Arnold and the earlier Eliot in at least one very important respect: that his criticism, though like theirs it has a personal dimension, indulges so rarely in dogmatic summary judgements.

These qualities are strongly displayed in the *Discourse Concerning Satire* which in my view is the greatest of his critical writings. Here the comparative discussion of Horace, Persius and Juvenal, the three chief Roman satirists, of potent influence upon English poetry of the Augustan Age, is a splendid example of his catholic literary appreciation and personal humility. It may be argued that the *Discourse* is rambling and erratic, that the first third is not about satire at all but epic. To a formalist the charge is true. But the *Discourse* is also a personal document. It is given personal, organic unity by the fact that Dryden had always intended to be an epic poet, had never abandoned the heroic strain, and yet ended up in great measure a satirist. He had just translated Persius and Juvenal; he was just about to translate the *Aeneid*. The impulse to the heroic and the impulse to the satiric, which give the creative tension of his best poems, are in balance, too, in the *Discourse*; here too the opposites are synthesized in his final, long-deferred preference of the 'Tragical Satyre' of Juvenal to the urbane familiarity of Horace.[40] And

53

the whole work is couched in a prose so fluent, copious and expressive, easy without the affected easiness of Addison, dignified without the formalized stateliness of Johnson, so full and yet so pointed, that to read it is an education and a delight.

Dryden was in every sense a professional writer. He wrote by virtue of his office, he wrote for occasions and he wrote for money. Often he wrote hastily and confessed the fault. He soon developed the technique to save him from writing ill, and if his prolific output is uneven, it varies between brilliant and competent, not brilliant and bad. The world laid its hand upon him, yet from this comes his strength : 'When I consider life, 'tis all a cheat . . . ,' 'In *Pleasure* some their glutton Souls would steep/ Yet find their Line too short, the Well too deep . . .'—the human force of that plain language is a great part of what he has to offer. Yet in the midst of worldly pressure and worldly disappointment, he also sustained his sense of the splendour of his poetic vocation; his poetry rose still from the strong and plain to the heroic, magnificent and ideal :

> Henceforth a Series of new time began,
> The mighty Years in long Procession ran :
> Once more the godlike *David* was restor'd . . .

and mastered like a monarch the whole range between. Indeed the reader who can be indifferent to Dryden is in some measure deaf to poetry and blind to life.

1. E. M. W. Tillyard writes of the 'addition of the burlesque to the serious' being 'potentially Dryden's original contribution to the course of the English epic', *The English Epic and Its Background*, London, 1954, p. 473, but the truth is more complex.

2. Unless otherwise stated, all quotations from Dryden are taken from James Kinsley, ed., *The Poems of John Dryden*, 4 vols., Oxford, 1958. To the notes in this, the standard English edition of Dryden, I am everywhere in debt.

3. T. S. Eliot, 'John Dryden,' in *Homage to John Dryden*, London, 1924, p. 13.

4. Samuel Johnson, 'The Life of Dryden,' *The Lives of the English Poets*, ed. George Birkbeck Hill, Oxford, 1905, i. 334; *The Works of John Dryden*, ed. Walter Scott, London, 1808, ix. 3–4.

5. The reference of Marvell's title seems to be to Ode xxxvii of the First Book of Horace, especially the last three stanzas : *The Poems of Edmund Waller*, ed. G. Thorn Drury, London, 1893, ii. 17 (ll. 169–72).

6. See George Sherburn, 'The Restoration and the Eighteenth Century,' *A Literary History of England*, ed. A. C. Baugh, London, 1948, p. 699; and Howard Erskine-Hill, 'Augustans on Augustanism,' *Renaissance and Modern Studies*, xi (1967), 55–8.

7. See E. N. Hooker, 'The Purpose of Dryden's *Annus Mirabilis*,' *Huntington Library Quarterly*, x (1946), 49–67, reprinted in *Essential Articles for the Study of John Dryden*, ed. H. T. Swedenberg, London, 1966, pp. 281–99.

8. Kinsley, ed. cit., i. 44 (ll. 27–28).

9. Ibid., i. 44 (ll. 36–38).

10. Ll. 59, 183, 195, 367, 235; ibid., i. 52–68 (my italics except for the proper names).

11. My view of the poem's faults agrees largely with Mark Van Doren, *John Dryden*, 1920; Cambridge, 1931, pp. 36–38; and Alan Roper, *Dryden's Poetic Kingdoms*, London, 1965, pp. 74–78. A more favourable view is maintained by E. N. Hooker and H. T. Swedenberg, eds., *The Works of John Dryden*, i. (London, 1956), pp. 260–67.

12. Dedication to *Aureng-Zebe* (1676); George Saintsbury, ed., *John Dryden [Plays]*, London, 1904, i. 340–41 (1949 edition).

13. 'Discourse Concerning Satire' (1693); Kinsley, ed. cit. ii. 617 (ll. 636–8).

14. *The Comedies, Tragedies and Operas Written by John Dryden, Esq.*, London, 1701, i. 596, 594; T. S. Eliot, op. cit., p. 20.

15. *Aureng-Zebe*, IV. i; Saintsbury, ed. cit., p. 398.

16. See the criticism of the Pelican *Guide to English Literature*, ed. Boris Ford, London, 1957, iv. 101 (1962 edition).

17. Kinsley, ed. cit., iv. 1914–15.

18. A good full account of *Mac Flecknoe* is chap. III of Ian Jack, *Augustan Satire*, Oxford, 1952, pp. 41–52.

19. David Ogg, *England in the Reign of Charles II*, Oxford, 1934, ii. 618–19.

20. *Absalom and Achitophel*, ll. 373–4; note also l. 30 and 'To the Reader', ll. 40–42; Kinsley, i. 266, 217, 216.

21. Samuel Johnson, 'The Life of Dryden,' *Lives of the English Poets*, ed. cit., i. 437.

22. Walter Scott, 'The Life of John Dryden,' ed. cit., i. 248–9; and see the defence of the conclusion of *Absalom and Achitophel* in Bernard Schilling, *Dryden and the Conservative Myth*, London, 1961, pp. 289–90, 305–6.

23. *The Early Letters of William and Dorothy Wordsworth*, ed. E. de Selincourt, Oxford, 1935, p. 541 (Wordsworth to Scott, 7 Nov. 1805).

24. Recent criticism has put less stress on the 'scepticism' of *Religio Laici*, and seen the poem as 'securely within the tradition of Anglican Christian humanism' (see E. J. Chiasson, 'Dryden's Apparent Scepticism in *Religio Laici*,' *Harvard Theological Review* (1961), reprinted in H. T. Swedenberg, ed. cit., pp. 245–60, especially 256).

25. 'The Life of Dryden,' *Lives of the English Poets*, ed. cit., i. 439.

26. For an evidently autobiographical passage, see Part i, ll. 62–99; Kinsley, ii. 471–2.

27. See F. T. Prince, 'Dryden Redivivus,' *Review of English Literature*, i (1960), 78.

28. See James Kinsley, 'Dryden's Bestiary,' *Review of English Studies*, N.S. iv (1953), 331–36.

29. See L. Proudfoot, *Dryden's Aeneid and its Seventeenth Century Predecessors*, Manchester, 1960, pp. 208–19. Also useful is William Frost, *Dryden and the Art of Translation*, New Haven, 1955, pp. 81–92.

30. *The Letters of John Dryden*, ed. C. E. Ward, Durham, North Carolina, 1942, p. 93 (Dryden to his sons, 3 Sept. 1697).

31. *Virgil's Aeneis*, vi. 824–5, 832; Kinsley, ed. cit., iii. 1222. See J. M. Bottkol, 'Dryden's Latin Scholarship,' *Modern Philology*, xl (1943), 241–55, reprinted in H. T. Swedenberg, ed. cit., esp. pp. 401–3. Dryden sometimes achieves such references by departing from Ruaeus to follow earlier translations, which take on fresh topicality in the post-1688 situation.

32. *Virgil's Aeneis*, xi. 386–452; ix. 810–50; ed. cit., iii. 1365–6, 1312–13.

33. Ll. 1–2; Kinsley, ed. cit., ii. 852. A. W. Hoffman, *John Dryden's Imagery*, Gainesville, 1962, p. 133.

34. Ll. 45–46; Kinsley, ed. cit., ii. 853. As Alan Roper observes, in *Dryden's Poetic Kingdoms*, pp. 168–76, the succession of the deposed Edward II by his lineal heir, Edward III, was cited against the deposition of James II. The two Edwards are seen in hopeful analogy with James and his young son.

35. James Kinsley, 'Dryden and the Art of Praise,' *English Studies*,

xxxiv (1953), 57–64, reprinted in H. T. Swedenberg, ed. cit., esp. p. 547.

36. See, on the Odes to Music: Ernest Brenecke, 'Dryden's Odes and Draghi's Music,' *Publications of the Modern Language Association*, xlix (1934), 1–34, reprinted in H. T. Swedenberg, ed. cit., pp. 425–65; and John Hollander, *The Untuning of the Sky: Ideas of Music in English Poetry, 1500–1700*, Princeton, 1961, pp. 401–22.

37. Alan Roper, op. cit., pp. 8–9, considers and rejects the possibility of this topical reference in *Alexander's Feast*. His rejection is only plausible if we are assuming that the Ode would have to be political allegory in the manner of *Absalom and Achitophel*. But clearly it is a different kind of poem; the *general* allusion to William's present triumph and James's earlier defeat is, it seems to me, compelling.

38. Dryden, *Of Dramatick Poesie*, ed. James T. Boulton, Oxford, 1964, p. 17.

39. See the interesting discussion of the *Essay* by George Watson in his edition of Dryden's *Of Dramatic Poesy and Other Critical Essays*, 2 vols., London, 1962, I, ix–xii.

40. A. W. Verrall came close to making these points, in his *Lectures on Dryden*, ed. M. de G. Verrall, Cambridge, 1914, pp. 61–2.

BIBLIOGRAPHY

I *Editions:*

The Poems of John Dryden, ed. James Kinsley, 4 vols., Oxford, 1958. The standard scholarly edition, comprising poems, verse translations, and prose originally published with any part of the poetry.

The Poems and Fables of John Dryden, ed. James Kinsley, Oxford, 1962 (Oxford Standard Authors). The text of the four-volume edition, omitting translations and notes.

The Poetical Works of Dryden, ed. George R. Noyes, Cambridge, Mass., 1909, 1937, 1950. A complete one-volume edition, including the translations and with useful notes.

The Works of John Dryden, ed. Sir Walter Scott, rev. George Saintsbury, 18 vols., Edinburgh, 1882–93. Still valuable.

The Works of John Dryden, ed. E. N. Hooker and H. T. Swedenberg, vol. i (London, 1956) : *Poems 1649–1680.* The American scholarly edition still in progress.

Letters, ed. C. E. Ward, Durham, North Carolina, 1942.

Of Dramatic Poesy and Other Critical Essays, ed. G. Watson, 2 vols., London, 1962. Contains all the strictly critical writings, together with notes, summaries of topics and a general introduction.

Bibliography

Macdonald, Hugh, *John Dryden: A Bibliography*, Oxford, 1939.

II *Historical Background:*

Ogg, David, *England in the Reign of Charles II*, 2 vols., Oxford, 1934.
—— *England in the Reigns of James II and William III*, Oxford, 1955.

III *Biographical Studies:*

Johnson, Samuel, 'The Life of Dryden' (1779) in *The Lives of the English Poets*, ed. G. B. Hill, Oxford, 1905, Vol. i.

Osborn, James M., *John Dryden: Some Biographical Facts and Problems*, New York, 1940; rev., Gainesville, Florida, 1965. A meticulous survey of biographical studies of Dryden from Thomas Birch to C. E. Ward, with several 'collateral investigations' added.

Saintsbury, George, *The Life of Dryden*, London, 1881. Like Johnson and Scott, Saintsbury is critical as well as biographical.

Scott, Walter, 'The Life of John Dryden,' in his edition of *The Works*, London, 1808, Vol. i. Incorrect in certain points of fact, but more balanced than Johnson and perhaps still the best biography for an understanding of Dryden and his times.

Ward, C. E., *The Life of John Dryden*, Chapel Hill, N.C. and London, 1961. The standard modern biography.

IV *Critical Studies:*

Bredvold, L. I., *The Intellectual Milieu of John Dryden*, Ann Arbor, 1934. An interesting exploration of Dryden's poetry from the point of view of the history of ideas, although this account of Dryden's philosophical scepticism has been challenged by Harth (see below).

Courthope, W. J., *A History of English Poetry*, London, 1903, vol. iii. ch. xvi.

Dryden: A Collection of Critical Essays, ed. B. N. Schilling, Englewood Cliffs, N.J., 1963.

Eliot, T. S., 'John Dryden,' in *Homage to John Dryden*, London, 1924. A fighting defence of Dryden, in a review of Van Doren's book.
—— *John Dryden: Poet, Dramatist and Critic*, London, 1932.

Essential Articles for the Study of John Dryden, ed. H. W. Swedenberg, London, 1966. Contains, among other important essays, James Kinsley's 'Dryden and the Art of Praise.'

Frost, William, *Dryden and the Art of Translation*, New Haven, 1955 (Yale Studies in English, vol. 128).

Hoffman, A. W., *John Dryden's Imagery*, Gainesville, Florida, 1962. One of the most stimulating of modern critical books about Dryden.

Harth, Phillip, *Contexts of Dryden's Thought*, Chicago, 1968.

Hollander, John, *The Untuning of the Sky: Ideas of Music in English Poetry. 1500–1700*, Princeton, 1961. Contains a valuable section on Dryden's Odes to Music.

Jack, Ian, *Augustan Satire*, Oxford, 1952. Contains useful chapters on *Mac Flecknoe* and *Absalom and Achitophel*.

Lees, F. N., 'John Dryden,' *The Pelican Guide to English Literature*, ed. Boris Ford, vol. iv, London, 1957.

Miner, Earl, *Dryden's Poetry*, Bloomington, Indiana, 1967.

Nicoll, Allardyce, *Dryden and his Poetry*, London, 1923.

Proudfoot, L., *Dryden's Aeneid and its Seventeenth Century Predecessors*, Manchester, 1960. Contains a forthright and stimulating assessment of Dryden's *Aeneid*.

Roper, Alan, *Dryden's Poetic Kingdoms*, London, 1965. A valuable explication of the poems discussed.

Schilling, B. N., *Dryden and the Conservative Myth*, London, 1961. A study of *Absalom and Achitophel*, with a cogent defence of the poem's conclusion.

Sharrock, Roger, *Selected Poems of John Dryden*, London, 1963. Contains a short but stimulating introduction to his work.

Sherburn, George, 'The Restoration and the Eighteenth Century,' in *A Literary History of England*, ed. A. C. Baugh, London, 1948.

Van Doren, Mark, *John Dryden*, New York, 1920; Cambridge, 1931. A confusingly arranged book but with some good critical insights.

Verrall, A. W., *Lectures on Dryden*, Cambridge, 1914. Still one of the best critical works on Dryden.

2

JONATHAN SWIFT

Kathleen Williams, University of California, Riverside

I

Jonathan Swift was born in Ireland of English parents, in 1667, and died there in 1745. Though so much of his life was spent in Ireland and though in his later years he became deeply involved in Irish affairs, he thought of himself as an Englishman. Both in England and in Ireland, Swift led an active public life, some knowledge of which is important to the understanding of his satire. His life will accordingly be briefly dealt with before his works are considered. His grandfather, Thomas Swift, had a small estate in Herefordshire and was vicar of Goodrich during the Civil War, in which he gallantly put his fortune at the disposal of the King. The devotion of the vicar of Goodrich to the royalist cause meant that his sons had their fortunes to seek. Several of them went to Ireland including the fifth son, Jonathan, who like his elder brother Godwin took to the legal profession. He died very young, leaving a wife, a daughter, and a posthumous son Jonathan, who became 'the Dean'. Swift was born, therefore, into a fatherless family dependent upon others for its survival. His uncles helped, and Swift received a good education, attending Kilkenny Grammar School and Trinity College, Dublin, where he did passably well, very well in Greek and Latin, but was too impatient with the traditional logic of the schools, still an important part of University education at that time, to distinguish himself. He was then employed as secretary by Sir William Temple, former statesman, man of letters, now living a life of elegant retirement at Sheen and soon at his house Moor Park in Surrey. Sir William's family had apparently long known the family of the Swifts.

In Sir William's house Swift spent ten years from about 1689, though not unbrokenly; he left Temple on two occasions. It seems to have been here, rather than at Trinity College, that Swift made himself into a really well-read and, in some areas, learned man. He read, in Temple's well-stocked library, for several hours every day over a long period and he learned too from Temple himself, a man who had been courtier and diplomat in stirring times and who now lived away from the world and with his books and his garden and his domestic circle; such a man would naturally influence the young Swift. It was at Moor Park too that Swift contracted Ménière's disease,[1] which made him deaf and ill and from which he was to suffer recurrently all his life. And it was at Moor Park that he met the little Esther Johnson who was to become the 'Stella' of the poems and the *Journal*. Esther was the fatherless daughter of Temple's housekeeper, and when Swift arrived she was a child of eight years old. Swift taught her to write, and supervised her reading. His relations both with Esther Johnson and with Hester, or Esther, Vanhomrigh, whom he called Vanessa, seem to have been in large part that of teacher to pupil; in a good phrase of Mr. Nigel Dennis's, Swift's form of love was 'an impassioned education'. Stella remained his closest friend until she died; and his *Journal* and poems to her and his prayers for her in sickness are among the most tender and moving of all his writings.

In 1695 Swift was ordained and presented to the Prebend of Kilroot in the Diocese of Down and Connor in Ireland, a district where the members of Swift's own Church were outnumbered by the Dissenters for whom, in *A Tale of a Tub*, he was soon to display such dislike.

In 1696, however, Temple asked him to return to Moor Park, and, without giving up his Kilroot living, he did so. He was employed largely in preparing for the press Temple's various works, and Temple had an excellent clear prose style which must have helped Swift to achieve his own fine prose. But in 1699 Temple died, and Swift returned to Ireland as domestic chaplain to the newly appointed Lord Justice, the Earl of Berkeley, as a result of which he received a cathedral stall in St. Patrick's Cathedral, Dublin, and the living of Laracor, which included three united parishes and was flourishing compared to Kilroot. In 1701 Berkeley was recalled and Swift returned with him to England. In the same year appeared his first published political tract, *A Discourse of the Contests and Dissensions between the Nobles and the Commons in Athens and Rome*. This is a polished and clever application of conditions in the ancient world to certain contests and dissensions which were at present proceeding in England. Swift was at this stage not entirely ignorant of the practical conduct of great affairs. He must have heard much of such matters from Sir William Temple, he had met King William III, and Temple had sent him on errands to William's court. The *Discourse* displays a Swift very adroit in the drawing of parallels between the ancient and the contemporary political worlds, and a Swift whose political convictions were already taking the shape which they were to retain all his life. Swift was an advocate of mixed government, which he sometimes also calls the 'balance of power', the notion that sovereignty resides not in the King alone, nor in Parliament alone, but in three places, the King, the Lords, and the Commons. This was an idea associated with the Whigs, and Swift was at this time a Whig. Later Swift was to throw in his lot with the Tories, but he always maintained that he kept his old Whig principles and that what changed was not Swift but the Whig party.

Swift became Doctor of Divinity at Trinity College in 1702, and in 1703 he paid another long visit to England, where he took evident delight in the political and social activities of London. On this occasion he took with him the manuscript of *A Tale of a Tub*, which was published in 1704 along with *The Battle of the Books* and *A Discourse on the Mechanical Operation of the Spirit*. The *Tale* is dedicated to the Whig Lord Somers, and though Swift never formally acknowledged that he was the author (it was his almost unvarying practice to publish anonymously) it made his name as a wit and also was possibly responsible for the fact that he never received a bishopric, or for that matter any kind of preferment in England. The *Tale* is in large part a satirical allegory of the history of the church, and Swift's vigorous attacks on Dissent and Catholicism left him open to the charge of ridiculing all religion; this was at least a charge which his political enemies, of whom he soon made many, were only too ready to exploit. The *Tale*, though it was not published until 1704, was probably written in the 1690s, a period when he had been reading very hard both in secular and, doubtless, in theological works, the latter in preparation for his ordination.

At this period Swift had persuaded Esther Johnson, who was still living as a member of the household of Sir William Temple's sister, to remove to Ireland, where she could be near Swift and where, also, her modest income could be stretched further. Esther took with her as companion an older woman (Esther was at this time only about twenty years of age), Rebecca Dingley, another dependent of the Temple family. Esther lived in Ireland until her death, always near Swift but never in the same house with him, and never seeing him without at least one other person present. After her death stories grew up of her secret marriage to Swift, but for this there is no real evidence. Swift stayed in Ireland, fulfilling his duties as vicar of Laracor, until his departure for England in November 1707, when he was commissioned by his superiors in the Church of Ireland to solicit for remission of the First Fruits.[2] Swift made representations to the Whig Lord Treasurer, the Earl of Godolphin, but with no result. But at the same time he was establishing himself in the brilliant London of the wits and men of letters, a world of literature which was not separable from that of politics : in this period great writers—Dryden, Addison, Steele, Pope, Swift himself—regarded public affairs as part of their province, and men like Addison and Prior held government office. Swift himself never held office, but he was soon to become the honoured friend and aide of the two men who replaced the Whig ministry of Somers and Godolphin with a moderate Tory government, Robert Harley, later Lord Oxford, and Henry St. John, later Lord Bolingbroke, himself a man of letters. Swift was already known to the world of letters and politics in London as the author of the brilliant *Tale of a Tub* and the accomplished *Discourse of the Contests and Dissensions*. He now produced, in 1708, *A Letter from a Member of the House of Commons in Ireland, concerning the Sacramental Test*, and early in 1709 *A Project for the Advancement of Religion and the Reformation of Manners*. Neither of these is among his best works, but both added to his reputation when they came to be known as his, and both indicate a movement in Swift's mind away from the Whigs. The reason for this movement is the reason why Swift eventually gave his considerable literary services to Harley's Tory party : he saw the Whigs as deliberately undermining the established Church in England and Ireland, and deliberately building up the power of Dissent.

The Whig government was courting the support of Dissenters by considering the repeal of the Sacramental Test which effectively banned Dissenters (and also Catholics) from public office unless they were prepared, as some of them were, to conform occasionally—that is, to attend Anglican communion once a year to qualify themselves for such office. Swift's *Letter . . . concerning the Sacramental Test* shows his opposition to the repeal, as, more indirectly, does the *Project for the Advancement of Religion* of the same year, which suggests in effect that the Queen should appoint to positions of state only good churchmen (a category which as Swift saw it excluded the Whig statesmen who were hoping to bring about a repeal of the Test). Shortly before these overtly serious works Swift had brought out as well that hilarious hoax, the *Bickerstaff Papers*, in which he ridicules the astrologer and almanac-maker John Partridge by writing his own set of predictions, including one of Partridge's imminent death. Thus by 1709 Swift had established the main lines of his career : serious political principles arising out of a stern morality and an affection for the church which, for him, came nearest to embodying that morality; a power of, and delight in, sheer comedy; and enormous skill in adopting a persona through which to express himself. These characterize his two greatest long works, *A Tale of a Tub* and *Gulliver's Travels*. It was during this visit to England, also, that Swift made the acquaintance of the Vanhomrigh family, whose elder daughter, another Esther, or Hester, became his friend and pupil, the Vanessa of *Cadenus and Vanessa*, one of his best-known poems, and like Stella a centre for much sensational surmise after her death and Swift's. Hester Vanhomrigh, like Stella, died before Swift, and died in Ireland, where she had gone to live more cheaply and presumably also to be nearer Swift.

In the summer of 1709 Swift returned to Ireland, to be sent once again to England in 1710 by his Archbishop, who wished him to try again for the remission of the First Fruits. He again got no promise from Godolphin about the First Fruits, but at this juncture Godolphin fell from power and Harley was appointed Chancellor of the Exchequer and formed a new government. And Harley needed a propagandist; he agreed to approach the Queen in the matter of the First Fruits (though the Church of Ireland never gave Swift credit for his part in the eventual success of this approach) and soon had charmed Swift into writing for the Tories. Swift took over the Tory periodical *The Examiner*, and wrote for it, with considerable success, for some time. He wrote also other political tracts in which he attacked the Whigs and supported the new government, notably *The Conduct of the Allies* (late in 1711) which aimed to persuade public opinion to the Tory point of view that it was high time to bring to an end the long war of the Spanish Succession, in which the English and their allies strove to break the enormous power of Louis XIV of France. The Commander-in-chief of the combined forces, the great Duke of Marlborough, had won some spectacular victories, and Harley and St. John believed that it was time that some benefit, commercial and territorial, should accrue to Britain.

In *The Conduct of the Allies* Swift, building a number of both open and implied accusations upon a basis of fact conveyed to him by the government, brilliantly succeeds in suggesting that Britain is being gulled both by the allies and by her own general, Marlborough; the allies are not pulling their weight in a war entered upon chiefly for their advantage, while Marlborough has a vested interest in keeping the land war going, since he gets from it not only perquisites but even bribes. The pride of the British in such great victories, over all the might of France, as Blenheim and Ramillies, is with great skill turned into resentment and suspicion : Marlborough, the Dutch, the Austrians have solid gains from the war, only Britain has to be content with glory, a glory which is attained at the cost of immeasurable waste.

> It will, no doubt, be a mighty Comfort to our Grandchildren, when they see a few Rags hanging up in *Westminster-Hall*, which cost an hundred Millions, whereof they are paying the Arrears . . .[3]

What are military trophies, robbed of their symbolic value? Nothing but 'a few rags', for which Britain has squandered money and men. We see here, in a political tract written to exploit a particular occasion, certain characteristics visible in Swift's major satires too. We see skill in playing upon natural human reactions such as the fear of being exploited, being made a fool of; the capacity to link particular occasions with large issues like that of the wastefulness of war; and the power of the great satirist to shock the reader into feeling he is suddenly seeing a truth which his own habitual reactions, or perhaps the deliberate deceit of someone else, has hidden from him until now. The tattered standards whose tears and stains testify all the more to their glory become suddenly the rags of beggars; the empty glory of Blenheim and of the palace built for Marlborough to commemorate it will be the ruin of Britain for generations.

In this year (1711) also was published *The Sentiments of a Church-of-England Man, with Respect to Religion and Government*, which was actually written some years before and which shows, in its emphasis on a strong state church, how close Swift had always been to a moderate Toryism, even when he was hoping to gain the First Fruits through the action of a Whig government. Also in 1711 was published another work (again probably written earlier, in 1708) in which Swift shows his concern for a strong church, *An Argument against Abolishing Christianity*, the occasion for which was the agitation for abolition of the Test Act, the act by which those who refused to attend the Anglican service were debarred from public office. This, though comparatively short, is one of the most important of Swift's satires because one of the most brilliant, and will be given more extended discussion along with the major works later in this essay.

Swift now had a brief period of political power and influence. Oxford and Bolingbroke were both his friends, and he exerted his influence to hold together these two very different men, so that the Tory government could survive. With the poets Pope, Gay and Parnell, the Queen's literary-minded physician Dr. John Arbuthnot, and Lord Oxford, he set up the Scriblerus Club, the purpose of which was to ridicule false learning through the invented figure of the misguided pedant Martin Scriblerus. Various works of wit resulted from the foundation of this society, and parts of *Gulliver's Travels* may have had their origin here. But for all his activity and influence Swift did not secure for himself what he hoped for, a bishopric or a deanery in England, where his dearest friends were. Eventually he was presented to the Deanery of St. Patrick's Cathedral in Dublin, where he was to spend the rest of his life. Though he later became passionately involved in Irish politics, he always regarded his life in Ireland as an exile from England which he thought of as his home and in which he had hoped to live. In 1713, he went to Dublin to be installed as Dean, but was soon persuaded by his friends to return to England to try to reconcile Oxford and Bolingbroke, whose personal antipathy and spite were threatening the very existence of the Tory ministry. Swift tried to reconcile them and to persuade the dilatory Oxford to get a grip upon the party, but it was to no avail. Oxford was dimissed, whereupon Swift, to his credit, offered to accompany him in his retirement and disgrace in Herefordshire. But at this juncture (August 1714) the Queen died; the Whigs came in at once with the Hanoverian successor, and Swift was compelled to leave at once for Ireland to take the oaths to the new King. He was to see little more of England.

In Ireland, Swift was quiet for some time, acutely regretting the loss of his hopes, his friends, and his busy life at the heart of affairs in London. But there was much to do in Ireland, settling the affairs of his new office (Swift was a very conscientious clergyman and a very conscientious and strong Dean) in the face of much opposition from Whiggish superiors. As a prominent member of the discredited Tory party he was for some time disliked and distrusted in Dublin, but gradually he began to take an interest in the plight of Ireland, where native

Irish and Anglo-Irish alike suffered at the hands of the English government which treated Ireland as a colony to be exploited for the benefit of the motherland. In about 1720 Swift probably began to write *Gulliver's Travels*, which was to be, with the possible exception of *A Tale of a Tub*, his greatest work. In 1724 came the occasion which made him the idol of Ireland as the patriot Dean, and which produced Swift's second period of political power. The English government, under the Whig first minister, Robert Walpole, was attempting to force upon the Parliament and people of Ireland a supply of small copper coins, which the Irish feared would devalue their coinage. The patent for coining and distributing what came to be known as 'Wood's halfpence' had been granted to an English entrepreneur, William Wood, and the grant was thought to have involved bribery to one of the King's mistresses. In Swift's view, and that of other Irish and Anglo-Irish leaders, the welfare of the people and the dignity of the Parliament of Ireland were being treated as less important than the squalid financial transactions of a few people in England, and he wrote and published a series of letters, under the pseudonym of 'M.B., Drapier'—a simple, honest Dublin Draper enraged at a political action which he believes will ruin his business and which disregards the rights of the nation. With brilliant strategy Swift graduates his attack on the English government, first appealing to the self-interest of each person and then, having roused their anger, turning it upon the essential issue: that Ireland is no colony but a sovereign kingdom of free men, freely owing allegiance to a monarch who also happens to be King of England. For once Swift was able to achieve something he could never do, for all his efforts, before or after the Drapier incident: he united the Irish people behind one line of action, opposition to the English government by refusing to accept Wood's halfpence. In face of this solid determination, the government capitulated, the grant was withdrawn and for the rest of his life Swift, the Drapier, was reverenced by his grateful countrymen. Even more than at the time of *The Conduct of the Allies*, Swift could feel that he had produced effective practical results. It is important to remember that it was during these years of vigorous, successful, exciting action that *Gulliver's Travels* was finished; it was no more the work of a withdrawn disappointed misanthrope than was the hilarious *Tale of a Tub*.

In 1726 Swift visited England to see his friends and also to arrange the publication of *Gulliver's Travels*, and in 1727 he made the journey again, for the last time. In 1729 was published the greatest of all his shorter satires, *A Modest Proposal*. Through most of his years as Dean, Swift had been writing political tracts in an attempt to unite the Irish workers, tradesmen, landlords, and the rest for the good of the country as a whole. The *Modest Proposal* is Swift's proposal to end all proposals, written when he was coming to despair of persuading the different sections of Irish society to combine for their own good instead of following their individual and short-term interest; the practical success of *The Drapier's Letters* was only temporary.

During the later part of his life Swift continued to write, and some of his most effective poems were produced in these years. But as he grew older, more frequently ill with his chronic disease, more alone, with Esther Johnson and other close friends dead, he took refuge increasingly in what he called 'la bagatelle', the writing of punning poems to his remaining friends and similar ways of passing the time. For the last few years of his life he was overtaken by illness and senility, and in 1742, at the age of 75, he was declared of unsound mind. In October 1745 he died.

II

Swift's writings have been in the past much misunderstood because they were read in the light of a false conception of his character. Swift was a doughty political fighter in an age of fierce political passions, and his enemies of the opposite party branded him, quite falsely, as an irreligious priest, a political turncoat, and a misanthrope. Doubtless in his years of lonely senility and illness, Swift became embittered and parsimonious, but through most of his life his friends delighted in his wit, charm, humour, generosity of spirit and humanity. So good a man as Bishop Berkeley thought him one of the best natured and agreeable men in the world, and similar tributes are paid him by friends and acquaintances. Many of his works, from the early *Bickerstaff Papers* or the poem 'Mrs. Frances Harris's Petition' (1709), capturing the tremulous garrulity of a waiting-woman who has lost her purse with all her savings in it, to the delightful mockery of *Polite Conversation* [4] (completed in the 1730's, though begun much earlier), are sheer fun and humour. Swift and his friends would have supposed that he was not misanthropic but realistic and practical; he had no very high opinion of 'man' and made no claims to feel benevolent towards abstractions like 'Mankind' or 'the English', and indeed as a clergyman of the old school he thought of man as fallen. But he dearly loved certain individuals, as he says himself in one of his letters :

> I have ever hated all Nations professions and Communityes and all my love is towards individualls for instance I hate the tribe of Lawyers, but I love Councellor such a one, Judge such a one for so with Physicians (I will not Speak of my own Trade) Soldiers, English, Scotch, French; and the rest but principally I hate and detest that animal called man, although I hartily love John, Peter, Thomas and so forth.[5]

We must not prejudge his greatest book, *Gulliver's Travels*, as the work of a misanthrope; it is a clearsighted view of the bad—and sometimes the good—sides of humanity, as seen by a man both serious and gay, a man of great experience of people in public and private life, writing at the height of his powers.

But *Gulliver's Travels* is the culminating achievement of Swift's writing life; before we come to that there are earlier, and in their kind no lesser, works to consider. And in placing these works in their chronological context we must remember that Swift was born during the Restoration, a period which, for all its faults, had the courage to face facts, however unpalatable: facts about the nature of man and the nature of government, facts about our limited power to manage ourselves or the world about us. The men of the Restoration were striving to make sense of a world shattered by the worst of all conflicts, civil and religious war, a world in which high and noble ideals, on either side, had withered into squalid failures; in which the philosopher Thomas Hobbes (to be followed by his disciple Bernard Mandeville) and the Duc de la Rochefoucauld, a favourite of Swift's, had turned an unillusioned gaze on the motivations of man. Swift would have disagreed with the practical, political and economic conclusions which Hobbes and Mandeville drew from their observations, but his own observations were similar. The fine *Verses on the Death of Dr. Swift, D.S.P.D.* (1739) opens with the lines :

> As *Rochefoucault* his Maxims drew
> From Nature, I believe 'em true;
> They argue no corrupted Mind
> In him; the Fault is in Mankind.

In the eighteenth century, which came more and more to see man as naturally good and society as perfectible, there were inevitably many who were horrified at Swift's view of mankind as being full of faults of head and of heart, his passions astride of his weak reason and driving it wherever they wished to go. Yet this was an ancient view of man, a traditional Christian one only made more stark by the vividly real figures who exemplify in Swift's work what he took to be the truth about man. Man in the gross, he thought with the Christian fathers, was a lump of pride; again man, he thought with La Rochefoucauld and Hobbes, was governed by self-love. In a late poem, 'The Day of Judgement' Swift makes Jove say at the Last Day:

> Offending Race of Human Kind,
> By Nature, Reason, Learning, blind;
> You who thro' Frailty step'd aside,
> And you who never fell—*thro' Pride* . . .
>
> (11–14)

Yet in this situation there was much that could be done, and there were many individuals who did it. Self-love, worked upon by such reason as we have, could lead to love of our fellows and love of God. Swift seems never to have doubted that reason, common decency, and an attention to the moral precepts of Christianity, could produce a worth-while man. But he was clearly very sure that a man could not make himself into anything worth-while unless he faced and recognized the facts of his fallen nature; if we do not face them, we cannot improve upon them. '*Nosce teipsum*,' 'Know thyself': Swift's message is essentially that of generations of classical and Christian thinkers, from the Greeks to the Renaissance. He is one of the last of the Christian humanists, almost out of date already in his own day. Small wonder that a period which was turning its back on this centuries-old tradition should have come more and more to misunderstand him. It was his younger cousin, Deane Swift, who first pointed out that his clerical kinsman was saying, in *Gulliver's Travels*, something essentially similar to the words of the Old Testament prophets. Swift is a satirist, our greatest satirist in prose, and the brilliance with which he takes up, time after time, precisely the right rhetorical stance to get the most out of his material, is perhaps the most important thing to look for if we are to read him aright. But we must remember too that he was a moralist, who claimed that his works in verse and prose were:

> As with a moral view design'd
> To cure the Vices of Mankind.[6]

70

There is one aspect of Swift's work which has not appeared in this brief account of his life, but which is worthy of attention; that is his poetry. Swift wrote verses all his life, and a handful of them are among his best work: *Cadenus and Vanessa*, *Baucis and Philemon*, 'Description of a City Shower,' the second 'Stella's Birth-Day,' the beautifully poised *Verses on the Death of Dr. Swift*, with its half-laughing, half-sad but wholly tolerant vision of the quick forgetfulness of the world when he is dead:

> Poor Pope will grieve a Month; and Gay
> A Week; and Arbuthnot a Day.[7]

The course of Swift's poetry is itself in little a picture of the course of his development. As a young man at Sir William Temple's he wrote a few odes, in the complex stanza and high Pindaric style of the earlier seventeenth century, but he soon came to realize that for him this noble and idealistic kind of writing was wholly false. His poem in heroic couplets, 'Occasioned by Sir William Temple's Late Illness and Recovery' (written in 1693) closes thus:

> There thy enchantment broke, and from this hour
> I here renounce thy visionary pow'r.

He went on writing poetry, but from now on it was poetry which stayed close to the facts of the late seventeenth and early eighteenth centuries.

Swift seems to have had, along with his contemporaries of the Restoration, a strong feeling of the confusion and difficulties of life. Scientists and philosophers were stressing, at this time, the deceptiveness of our senses, and experiments with microscopes and telescopes were bringing this vividly home. With instruments, people were seeing things never seen before; strange experiments were going on. How could one know, even now, that one was seeing things as they were? Our reason is dependent on our senses for its material, and the senses clearly do not provide that material with complete accuracy. It behooves us to walk warily, using our senses and our reason as well as we can, but always remembering their unreliability, just as we must remember the terrible strength of our passions, which also reason must deal with as best it can. This is the atmosphere which thickens in Swift's early poems. When the 'delusion' ended, he proceeded to write (mostly in the octosyllabic couplets used for poetry which does not make any

71

very great claim for itself) some of the best social verse in the language, keeping wonderfully close to the movement of vernacular speech and close, too, to the world of muddled facts that we live in. Out of the facts, a moral observation usually emerges. In the *Verses* on his death, it is an observation upon our self-love, our will to live, our inability to grieve for long because life must, somehow, continue. When news of Dr. Swift's illness goes round, people

> . . . hug themselves and reason thus;
> 'It is not yet so bad with us.'[8]

In the so-called 'obscene' poems (dating from 1730–31), 'The Lady's Dressing-Room,' 'Strephon and Chloe,' 'Cassinus and Peter,' 'A Beautiful Young Nymph Going to Bed,' the unpleasantness of the material is there to point out the inadequacy of a romantic attitude towards the facts of our lives, or the absurdity of taking the surface of a thing—an apparently beautiful but painted woman, for instance—as the reality. Good human relationships are built on knowledge, not on romantic avoidance of the facts, often unpleasing, of our existence as human beings. The same deliberate choice to stay close to the things of this world and make from them what order and shape he could, the same refusal to indulge in any form of wishful thinking is visible in the great prose works. *A Tale of a Tub* and *The Mechanical Operation of the Spirit* examine the reality of lofty religious and literary claims; *The Battle of the Books* examines the claims of modern literary men, philosophers, and scholars to be equal to the great names of the highly civilised classical past, and finds them wanting.

A Tale of a Tub is a very learned work, but it is not necessary to recognize all his allusions in order to understand Swift's meaning. The *Tale* consists of a fairly clear allegorical narrative and a number of digressions, all written as if by a contemporary hack writer, who will write anything so long as it will bring him in something to live on. It is important to remember that Swift's satires are almost always written 'as if by' someone who is not Swift himself. This is a deliberate step. A good satirist must be a good rhetorician;[9] he must concern himself with the difficult task of persuading the reader to accept what may often be rather unacceptable material, upsetting the reader's cherished assumptions and habits. To adopt a persona—that of a third-rate hack writer, that of a Draper or 'Drapier,' that of a dabbler in economics, that of a ship's surgeon like Gulliver— means that one is adopting a particular point of view from which to write, and that point of view can be chosen to present one's material from the best angle, which in the case of satire will be the most devastating angle. Swift's personae are varied in their degree of intelligence or good will, but they all share a certain simplicity, invaluable for casting a new light on familiar and accepted things, which is what the satirist wishes to do. The Drapier's simplicity enables him to show what Wood's halfpence will mean in practice to the common man who knows little of economics; Gulliver's smugger simplicity means that he reveals the evils of his country without realizing he is doing it, with devastating satiric effect.

Of course these personae do not have the consistency and solidity of a character in, or a narrator of, a novel. Swift's concern is to satirize, to use the persona to cast a particular new light on things, not to create a consistent character. Indeed if a satiric persona were too solid, the satirist's purpose would be defeated, because too fully drawn a persona would have to be given very firm characteristics and views and this would limit the satirist's scope. If the persona remains in outline merely, his position can be adjusted this way and that according to the satirist's aim at any given point. Thus the Drapier, in his first letter, is a simple honest tradesman, indignant at the dishonest dealings of William Wood, whom he sees as merely a tradesman like himself though on a larger scale. But in succeeding letters he knows more about difficult legal matters than he at first seemed to do, because Swift wishes to bring out the legal issues implicit in the confrontation of the Parliaments of Ireland and England. Similarly Gulliver is at one point a generous, kindly man, and at another a petty and pompous one; at one point he is a great lover of the human race, at another he abhors it. Each modification of Gulliver's character enables Swift to present to us a different facet of the absurdity, stupidity, or wickedness of humanity.

The 'author' used by Swift in *A Tale of a Tub* is less consistent even than Gulliver or the Drapier. He has no name, and critics usually refer to him as 'the supposed author' or 'the hack,' and it would hardly be accurate to call him a character, so many aspects does he have, and such shifting and inconsistent attitudes. In him simplicity becomes foolishness, complacent self-conceit, and an absurd assumption that everything that concerns *him* or occurs to *his* mind must be highly relevant and important, and worth putting in his book. His chief concern is to write a book of a certain length, which will bring him a certain amount of money. He is quite frank about this; for example he says in 'The Conclusion :'

> I am now trying an Experiment very frequent among Modern Authors; which is, to *write upon Nothing*; When the Subject is utterly exhausted, to let the Pen still move on.[10]

The 'supposed author' is a modern author, whose work embodies the faults of mind and heart which Swift thinks typical of those writers who have abandoned ancient (i.e. classical) standards of objectivity, relevance and importance of content, and good taste. Such faults of mind and heart are visible in the author's style, with its repeated 'I' and 'me' and 'we,' its unstructured, wandering sentences, its air of impetuous mindless haste. The passage concerning the importance to a modern author of indexes, compendiums, and similar aids to an appearance of knowledge, is a good example of how Swift embodies wrong ways of thinking in a muddled breathless style; both the thinking and the way of expressing the thinking convey to us a man whose only concern is to get a long book written with the minimum of effort. It begins :

> By these Methods, in a few Weeks, there starts up many a Writer, capable of managing the profoundest, and most universal Subjects. For, what tho' his *Head* be empty, provided his *Common-place-Book* be full; And if you will bate him but the Circumstances of *Method*, and *Style*, and *Grammar*, and *Invention*; allow him but the common Priviledges of transcribing from others, and digressing from himself, as often as he shall see Occasion : He will desire no more Ingredients towards fitting up a Treatise . . .[11]

The very structure—if it can be called that—of *A Tale of a Tub* embodies those qualities of self-conceit, opportunism, and impertinence which for Swift go to make up his deliberately exaggerated type of the 'modern' author, for the narrative part of the *Tale* takes up less space than the digressions which alternate with chapters of the story. The digressions are frankly ways of enlarging the book; one is called 'A Digression in the Modern Kind' and another 'In Praise of Digressions.' At least, this is what they are for the supposed author. In Swift's satiric scheme, however, they are ways of displaying modern absurdity in their lack of intelligence and order. The supposed author is made by Swift to write irrelevant nonsense; self-congratulatory passages on the brilliance of modern wit, snatches of garbled philosophy, personal opinion or reminiscence. But all this contributes to a satiric order and plan which the true author, Swift, deliberately brings about. All the absurdities and inconsistencies are related to one another as part of a satiric whole because they all illustrate the opportunism of the third-rate, muddle-headed modern writer, his inability to think hard or to feel strongly, his absolute certainty that he, simply in virtue of being modern and up-to-date, the most recent of writers, is bound to be superior to the great writers of the past.

Though the supposed author takes no pains to make them so, the religious allegory and the digressions are in a way connected. The allegory is the story of Peter, Martin, and Jack, three brothers who represent the Catholic Church, the Church of England, and the Dissenters. The three brothers each receive from their dying father a coat cut from a single piece of cloth —Christianity in its primitive purity. They have also a will which instructs them to wear their coats always, and never to alter them in any way. But the brothers after a while wish to appear as men of the world, and to add embroidery, lace, and the rest to their plain coats. In order to do this without disobeying the will Peter, who becomes the leading brother, and who is more book-learned than the others, undertakes to find mention in the will of shoulder-knots, gold lace, and whatever else they wish to wear.

'Tis true, said he, there is nothing here in this Will, totidem verbis, making mention of Shoulder-knots, but I dare conjecture, we may find them inclusive, or totidem syllabis.[12]

When these methods only partially succeed, Peter picks out the word 'shoulder' letter by letter; he has recourse also to allegorical interpretation. Thus the churches became ever more worldly, and ever further from the plain commandments of the will, which is of course the Testament. All this clearly refers to the ingenious interpretations of the Bible, and to the use of tradition, by which the church moved over the centuries further from its primitive purity, and from the plain reality of what Christians were told to do. It involves a process of mental irresponsibility in which reason becomes not a guide but a tool to be used in the service of the passions to gain whatever is desired; reality is confused with fantasy for one's own ends, until one is not known from the other and the plain coats are scarcely visible under their load of fantastic decoration.[13]

Swift thought that this process of mind is exemplified in any philosophy that reduces the complication and difficulty of experience to a number of merely verbal processes, word-spinning being substituted for reality. It is parodied in the *Tale* in the Aeolist theology and in the clothes philosophy of Section II. This is a passage typical of Swift in its satiric inclusiveness and complication. The brothers find they have, in order to live in the world, to decorate their coats because it is the fashion to believe in the philosophy of clothes, according to which the whole universe is a suit of clothes. If this is true of the universe, the macrocosm, it is true also of man, the microcosm; working from the double (that is, literal and metaphorical) meaning of the word 'invests,' the clothes philosophers reach the conclusion 'that the Soul was the outward, and the Body the inward cloathing,' reinforcing this by a mishandling of biblical text and philosophical axiom. This process parodies medieval scholastic reasoning, which survived in the universities of Swift's day and which he, like others, thought of as mere word-spinning. It also satirises materialism; both are unreal ways of thought, leading man into a fantasy world where reason and morality are weakened.

Finally Martin and Jack realize how far they have moved from their father's commands. They are so horrified that they set to work at once to pull off the decorations of centuries, but Martin (the Anglican Church) realises that some of the decorations have been so firmly sewn in that they have become in effect part of the fabric of the coat. He prudently stops his pulling and tearing when he sees that some accretions to the coat of primitive Christianity have become so much a part of it that to pull them away would be to rend the fabric of the coat itself. But Jack, the dissenting church, goes on tearing until his decent coat is in rags, and, we are told, his rags look from a distance very like the fringes and lace which Peter has kept on his coat. It is Martin, therefore, the moderate reformer, who is nearest to what primitive Christianity would be. All of the churches have failed to obey the will; all are at fault compared to that ultimate standard. But it is typical of Swift that, while he is strongly aware of an ideal standard, he does not suppose that, because mortal men can not reach that standard, all effort is vain. The ideal may well be unattainable, yet there is a good that *can* be attained, by honesty and decency and care like Martin's. But to attain it we must, like Martin, know our limitations.

The proliferating madness of the allegory and the digressions culminates in the eighth and ninth sections, the ninth being a digression on Madness. Section eight is part of the religious allegory, being an account of a religious sect, the Aeolists, founded by Jack. The Aeolists are Swift's embodiment of the errors of Dissent, and their practices and their theology provide perhaps the most vivid of all the *Tale's* examples of that wrong, self-concentrated thinking which moves steadily away from the real into a fantasy world. The Aeolists are vivid to us because they are evoked in all their gross physicality. We see the red-faced, breathy Aeolist preacher and his open-mouthed audience, and we are made to experience them in this physical manner because Swift's point is that the Aeolists in their way, like Peter with his doctrine of transubstantiation, confuse the material and the spiritual. The Aeolists think themselves directly inspired, that is 'breathed into' by God; but in fact what they think of as the breath of the spirit is only wind rising, to confuse their brains, from the lower parts of their bodies. Their theology codifies this confusion of material and spiritual; they take biblical metaphors literally and build a theology upon them. The point that Swift makes against the Aeolists in *A Tale of a Tub*, that their reason (readily confused in man) is overthrown by their physical being, which they mistake for the spirit or, in Puritan phrase, the 'Inner light', is made again in *The Mechanical Operation of the Spirit*, published with the *Tale*. Swift's mouthpiece in this short work is a virtuoso scientist, one of those gentlemen of Swift's time who formed societies (the most famous and influential being, of course, the Royal Society) for the investigation of natural phenomena.

The third work printed with *A Tale of a Tub, The Battle of the Books*, is also aimed at self-deceiving pride. This is a gay, amusing work which was written for a particular occasion but which—as is usual in Swift's satires—engages issues central to his thinking. The particular occasion was that Sir William Temple had become involved in what is known as the 'Quarrel of the Ancients and the Moderns.' In the seventeenth and eighteenth centuries the authority of the classical ancients as models in philosophy, science, and literature was being challenged, especially in England and in France, by those who wished to loose modern man from the shackles of the past and free him to develop new ways of thinking and writing. Temple, himself an excellent example of the classically oriented civilization produced by the tendency of education since the Renaissance, was of course on the side of the ancients and of a civilization founded on them, and Swift writes in support of him. *The Battle of the Books*, in which ancient and modern authors take part in a mock-heroic engagement, is set by Swift in the Library of St. James's, of which the great scholar Bentley was keeper, and the *Battle* is directed primarily against what Swift sees, with some justification, as the ill-mannered, arrogant and boorish egoism of Bentley and others who claim that the moderns have surpassed the ancients in various spheres. Bentley was a great scholar, but as an example of civilized behaviour he was certainly inferior to Temple; and to Swift this mattered more than precise scholarship.

The battle is a hilarious and very neatly allegorical affair: for example a few ancients lead an orderly army against the disorganized rabble of the moderns; Dryden, a modern who had translated Virgil, appears in armour too big for him as a man who has taken on too much. But the real issues of the quarrel of the ancients and the moderns, as they seemed to Swift, are brought out in the encounter between the Spider (emblematic of the moderns) and the Bee (emblematic of the ancients and those whose values are formed by them) in a corner of the library where the battle is taking place. The Spider is an exaggerated version of the uncouth Bentley; he lives in his fragile, dusty cobweb which seems to him a great, strong fortress (fortification, and the mathematics it is based on, was one skill in which the moderns claimed to have surpassed the ancients) but which is wrecked by the mere accidental touch of the highly civilized bee, whose elegant and beautifully phrased talk sums up the ancient values just as the Spider's does the modern. Coarse ejaculations and arrogant personal claims sum up the achievements of the moderns. The Spider's chief claim is that he is self-sufficient; he spins his magnificent web out of himself, and his own resources, and is indebted to nothing and no one outside himself: he is an original in our sense of the word, and we would perhaps be inclined to applaud his claim. But to traditional humanists like Swift, this was precisely what was wrong with modern writers and thinkers, that they spin everything out of themselves, and take nothing from the world outside them or from the tried and trusted values of Christian classical tradition. The Spider's web, spun out of his own bowels, fragile, dusty, useful only for catching flies, is Swift's emblem of the ephemerality and worthlessness of whatever is produced without reference to anything but one's own opinions. The Bee, on the other hand, does not spin out of himself but collects his materials from outside himself, works upon them, and produces those useful and attractive things, honey and wax, sweetness and light.

The Renaissance scholar Scaliger, who is on the side of the

ancients, sums up much of Swift's objection to the quarrelsome moderns in his words to Bentley:

> *Thy* Learning *makes thee more* Barbarous, *thy Study of* Humanity, *more* Inhuman; *Thy* Convers *amongst Poets more* groveling, miry, *and* dull.[14]

Knowledge of literature, especially ancient literature, had made Scaliger civilized and humane; this was the use of learning, to a humanist like Swift. But the self-assertive modern remains uncivilized despite all contact with the great civilizations of the past, and inhumane despite his exposure to humane learning. One may say that Swift, like Temple before him, has chosen an unfortunate example, since Bentley was a formidable scholar. Yet the objects of Swift's attack are valid; and they are closely connected with the things attacked in *A Tale of a Tub*. The supposed author of the *Tale* is another arrogant, self-sufficient Spider, spinning away to no purpose, 'producing nothing at last, but Fly-bane and a Cobweb.'[15] *The Battle of the Books* is a work of great charm and some profundity, but it is atypical of Swift in at least one respect: it makes little use of a persona, a 'supposed author'. The satiric effect is made by the allegorical battle, by the actions and talk of the emblematic insects, and by the comments of characters in the fiction, like Scaliger and Aesop.

We may now consider two works which, though brief, are very typical of Swift in their complexity and richness and in the extraordinary economy of their satiric method, involving in each case a persona or mouthpiece from which the utmost effect is gained. The first of these is the *Argument Against Abolishing Christianity*, published in 1711. The *Argument* refers to a particular occasion, but it brings before us the important issues which lie behind that occasion. The particular occasion of the *Argument* was that, as has been mentioned earlier, the Whigs were agitating for the ending of the Test Act. To Swift, this meant that the Presbyterians and other Dissenters would be put well on the way to getting power as they had already done once in the seventeenth century, and that would be the end of the Church of England as by law established, and to Swift the beginning of the end of Christianity. In the *Argument*, he makes his persona discuss that opposition to the continuance of the Christian religion which he finds to be almost universal. Swift means to attack the Whigs who wish to oppose the Test Act and so are, in his view, uninterested in the survival of Christianity, but more importantly he is attacking all those whose practice suggests that, though nominally Christians, they are actually indifferent to the religion which for motives of convenience or expediency they profess to espouse. These people betray their religion into the hands of those who, like the Deists and freethinkers, are actively opposed to it.

Swift chooses with some skill the point of view from which to direct his strategy. The persona here is a 'nominal' Christian: that is, on the level of Swift's opposition to the repeal of the Test Act, he could be an occasional conformer, a Dissenter who takes once a year the statutory Anglican communion which qualifies him for public office; while on the more important level he is any man, Dissenter or mere indifferent, who pays respectable lip-service to the established church while really paying no attention to its instructions. As one might expect from such a timeserver, he is timid, and puts forward very apologetically his revolutionary opinion that 'in the present Posture of our Affairs at home or abroad, I do not yet see the absolute Necessity of extirpating the Christian Religion from among us.' [16] The difference between this nominal Christian and others is that he is naïve enough to put into words what others merely act by, and he is careful to explain that of course he is not arguing for *real* Christianity, but for the nominal kind, Christianity in name only. Swift is using his naïve persona to put before his readers the real state of affairs that they have not recognized because of the dulling effect of habit. They call themselves Christians, but they have never really thought what being a Christian involves. From the country's actions and its literary productions, the persona casually assumes that everyone must realize that real Christianity has been dead for centuries, and his very casualness adds to the shock which makes a reader suddenly aware. This casualness is frequently used by Swift with brilliant effect.

The way in which Swift's persona develops his theme of the social and even economic convenience of keeping up nominal Christianity enlarges on Bernard Mandeville's recognition that 'Religion is one thing and Trade is another'; religion is going on Sundays to church, which is a very convenient place for meeting your business associates, for 'Appointments and Rendezvouzes of Gallantry',[17] and so forth. In the course of the *Argument* many groups of people, for example free-thinkers, Deists [18] and the men of fashion and pleasure, and all those who have lost all such 'prejudices', as the persona calls them, as 'foolish Notions of Justice, Piety, Love of our Country',[19] are satirised, but Swift's main target is the man who is a Christian only because it is useful and respectable to be so.

The second of Swift's two greatest short satires is *A Modest Proposal for preventing the Children of Poor People in Ireland from being a Burden to their Parents or Country; and for making them beneficial to the Publick* (1729). Two phrases in this lengthy title suggest the kind of work this is. Well-meaning 'modest proposals' for improving conditions in the wretched country of Ireland were often written, and their purpose was economic; thus the children here are considered purely as economic entities. A way is suggested of preventing them from being a financial burden to their parents and even of making them 'beneficial to the Publick'. The work is in fact a parody, the grimmest parody Swift ever wrote, of the proposal of a writer who subscribes to the dominant economic theory of the time, the mercantilist theory. According to one of the adages of mercantilism, the riches of a nation consisted in its people. Swift refers to this elsewhere and seems to agree with it, though one may certainly conclude from *A Modest Proposal* that he would have interpreted the maxim to mean 'The riches of a nation consist in a healthy, numerous, industrious and morally sound people', not merely 'the riches of a nation consist of a numerous population all contributing so much a head to the national wealth'. Among other things *A Modest Proposal* aims to reveal the horrors which merely economic thinking can bring. The English government, which forbids Ireland any trade which can compete with England; the Anglo-Irish and Irish absentee landlords who rack-rent their tenants, turn their arable land into pasture and thus throw labourers out of work, and spend all their money not in Ireland where it is made but in England; the tradesmen of Ireland who take advantage of shortages to put up their prices; all these are thinking in terms of immediate financial gain. And immoral economic thinking is in the long term inefficient economic thinking: as Swift says elsewhere, it kills the goose that lays the golden eggs. Under all these stresses, the 'riches', the people, are given no opportunity to be 'beneficial to the Publick'. (The hopeless plight of Ireland in the 1720s can be seen in a straight-forward account by Swift in 1727, *A Short View of the State of Ireland*.[20]) The poorer people, barely keeping alive, are being reduced by the pressure of poverty to a state of hopeless degradation in which ordinary moral decency is too much of a luxury; they treat their pregnant sheep and cows with more consideration than they do their pregnant wives because a child will be only one more financial drag on

81

them, one more mouth to feed, whereas a lamb or calf will feed *them*. So the modest proposer, bearing in mind that the riches of a nation consist in its people, tries to find a way in which this can be made true of the country of Ireland, and the only way that seems open, given the impossibility of any normal lucrative trade, is that the children of the poor should be slaughtered and sold for meat at a year old, before they reach the age when they become 'a Burden to their Parents'. Thus the people will be very literally the riches of their country, being actually sold.[21] Again Swift is trying, as the satirist typically does, to prevent his readers from being any longer blinded to reality by any of the mechanisms we use for our comfort.

The persona of this work is chosen brilliantly to bring out all the issues involved in the State of Ireland. He is well-meaning; he is aware, as others are not, of the cruel miseries which the people are suffering through the fault of others. That, for all his good intentions, he can only think of a scheme like this is in itself an eloquent comment on the state of Ireland. He puts forward a purely economic plan because there is no hope of persuading people to accept the moral plans which alone can succeed. Throughout the *Proposal* the persona uses a vocabulary which equates the children and their mothers with cattle: 'dams', 'breeders', 'carcasses', 'the fore or hind quarter'. Given the conversion of arable land to pasture which left so many farm workers destitute, it is a reasonable satiric conclusion that beasts are being preferred to men, and that the only recourse left for men is to compete with the beasts, producing young for slaughter. The imagery implies, moreover, that the poor are being driven by hardship and hopelessness to a state of degeneracy in which they are scarcely distinguishable from beasts; if men are treated like beasts, they will come to act like beasts. All Swift's pity and anger are expressed in this brilliant satire, with all the more effect for being contained within the persona's desperate last attempt to find a solution to his country's miseries.

III

Our discussion of Swift's two greatest pamphlets, the *Argument* and the *Modest Proposal*, has taken us on an unchronological course. It is time now to move back a few years to the work on which Swift's enduring fame as our greatest prose satirist has been chiefly based, *Gulliver's Travels*. In the *Travels*, we can enjoy Swift's mature thinking about the nature of man (always his central subject, though it is expressed often in terms of politics or economics, literature or religion) embodied in a fiction which gives full scope to the various rhetorical skills of satire which he had so long been practising. As in the *Argument* and the *Modest Proposal*, Swift uses a well-known and popular form, here that of travel literature, parodied and adapted to his own satiric and moral purposes. As in these two pamphlets and the *Tale*, he uses a persona who is himself the object of satire, thus providing himself with a complexity of method able to express the inclusiveness of his satiric aims. *Gulliver's Travels* is essentially a book about human nature, its capacities and its limitations, expressed in the first three voyages in terms of various aspects of human activity and in the last voyage seen openly as Gulliver, representative of man, meets the representatives of two other species in relation to which human nature can be precisely placed.

The *Travels* were published with an elaborate apparatus to suggest that they were the genuine productions of the ship's doctor and later captain, Lemuel Gulliver. There are maps and a notice from the publisher explaining how he came by Gulliver's papers, and in 1727 Swift added a letter from Captain Gulliver to his cousin Sympson, who had prevailed on him to publish. The book begins with a detailed account by Gulliver of his background and life, and in each voyage we are given details of the latitude and longitude, and of the accidents that caused Gulliver to be cast ashore alone on undiscovered territory. All this has the same literary value as the similar detail in a novel by Defoe or Scott; it carries us willingly and comfortably into a solid-seeming fictional world which we are prepared to enjoy. But in Swift's case the solidity is established to be deliberately disturbed as we find ourselves moving into strange places, where men can be six inches high or as tall as steeples, and where a pleasant story becomes steadily more disturbing to our conventional notions. The first voyage of the *Travels* is the most charming—doubtless by design—and has always been the most popular. Gulliver, who changes according to his surroundings (this gives him his flexibility as a satiric persona as well as his interest as a character reacting to the strange things he encounters), is here at his kindliest, being as he is a giant among a people so small they can creep along his legs like tiny animals. The Lilliputians, for their part, have charm too; the charm of the miniature and more particularly of the little, weak creature who yet has indomitable courage, inventiveness, and curiosity in the face of overwhelming and unfamiliar danger. These qualities are shown at once in their intelligent and resourceful binding of Gulliver and in the means they take to feed and clothe him.

Only gradually do we begin to see the other side of Lilliputian behaviour, for example that they are willing to make all the use they can of Gulliver while keeping him a prisoner, and slowly the pettiness of these little men is revealed to us. They are brave—they have to be—and they are well organized; they work competently and quickly as a team. But like a body of ants or bees, they put the survival of their tiny state above everything else. They are very much what man is said to be, a 'political animal', and it is this aspect of human life chiefly that they reveal to us. Their physical smallness is a symbol of the moral smallness of man, and this is an aspect of man that can well be seen in politics, in the banding together of men to surpass their personal weakness in the strength of the state. The emptiness of public grandeur is made clearer to us in a man six inches high than it can be in a man of six feet. The Lilliputian emperor, for example, is 'taller by almost the Breadth of my Nail, than any of his Court; which alone is enough to strike an Awe into the Beholders' [22] and is officially styled 'the most Mighty Emperor of *Lilliput*, Delight and Terror of the Universe, whose Dominons extend five Thousand Blustrugs' ('about twelve Miles in Circumference', Gulliver tells us in parentheses) 'to the Extremities of the Globe'.[23] The qualities required for great office in the state are more clearly seen when they are diminished in the Lilliputian allegory to a physical process of balancing on a rope, yet these things are of passionate importance to Lilliputian courtiers, and even Gulliver, kindly and humble though he is, becomes sufficiently infected by Lilliputian values to pride himself on his rank of Nardac. Lilliputian petty pride of rank and power is made clearer to us when Gulliver loses favour after putting out a palace fire by urinating on it,[24] and again when Gulliver becomes an embarrassment to the empire because of his huge consumption of food. At the council, Gulliver's particular enemies wish to put him to death, despite his great services to Lilliput in putting out of action the fleet of Blefuscu, but by great lenity the sentence is changed to blinding, though the council is swayed even here chiefly by self-interest. Blind, Gulliver can be gradually starved, so that his carcass, at his death, will be smaller and less likely to produce infection in the country. The ruthlessness of the tiny people is underlined by Gulliver's goodness : forewarned by his one friend, he will not crush the little empire out of gratitude to the past kindness of the Emperor, and escapes to Blefuscu instead.

The Lilliputians, clearly, regard the state as an entirely non-moral entity. Where political action is in question, morality has nothing to do with the matter. This is further emphasized by the account Gulliver gives in the sixth chapter of the former, and better, constitution of Lilliput; in the old days, the moral good of the country had been very much the concern of government, and there is no doubt from Swift's political writings (including *A Modest Proposal*) that he believed that even a modern commercial state should do what little it could to encourage morality in its members. Lilliput is, indeed, itself a miniature example of such a commercial state; there is much stress on money and goods, and on the 'perpetual Intercourse of buying and selling, and dealing upon Credit'.[25]

Lilliput, then, shows the pettiness in man, his pride in trifling honours, in money, his political ruthlessness; but its full effect is not made until we look back upon it from the second voyage, to Brobdingnag. Gulliver himself makes in his comments several links between the two voyages, and they are linked by the device on which both of them are based, that of relative size. The device is of course an excellent satiric one. Satire depends for much of its effect on looking at familiar things from a different point of view, so that the reader sees them from a new and unaccustomed angle: it is as if he is seeing them afresh, for the first time. Big men and small men provide an excellent pair of new angles from which to look at men of normal size. But the device of relative size performs a further function too: it suggests the partial dependence of human nature on such mere physical accidents as those of size. Not only do the Lilliputians differ from the Brobdingnagians, but Gulliver himself is a different man according as he is a giant in a land of pygmies or a pygmy in a land of giants. But there is a third, related, function of the big and little men too, as we have seen; as in the Lilliputians Swift worked out precisely the symbolic consequences of smallness, so in the Brobdingnagians does he work out the symbolic consequences of largeness. The Brobdingnagians are man seen large, and one result of this is that we see more clearly our physical grossness; human skin or hair, or the act of eating, greatly magnified, reveal to us how little, physically, we have to pride ourselves upon. Again the now relatively tiny Gulliver is subjected to various degrading physical adventures. But physical size can also symbolize moral largeness. As the best of the Lilliputians were petty, so the best of the giants are generous, warm, and humane. The physical pressure of gigantic men and women is everywhere in this book, for Swift is moving steadily towards the central point of the fourth voyage, that man is a physical as well as a mental and spiritual being, and that all his efforts towards good will go for nothing unless he remembers this. The grossly physical Aeolists of the *Tale*, belching and groaning and believing that such things are manifestations of spirit not of body, point in the same direction. Since Swift's subject is, so often, man's readiness to forget the limitations placed on his reason by his wayward physical passions, physicality is likely to be a marked feature of his most serious satire, whether in prose or in the 'obscene' poems. So in Brobdingnag we see the lasciviousness of the maids of honour, the wretchedness of the beggars with their sores and their lice. But we see also the human warmth and largeness of compassion in the best of the giants, the King, the Queen, and Gulliver's 'nurse' and protectress, the affectionate little girl Glumdalclitch.

Brobdingnag is no perfect state. It has beggars and it has men who exploit others, as Gulliver's first master, increasingly driven by the prospect of unaccustomed gain, exploits him. It is an ordinary human state, which has had political troubles much like those of seventeenth-century England. Such an ordinary state depends, in Swift's view, on the decency of those individuals who make it up, and this in turn will depend in part on the actions and example of those in power. The Brobdingnag visited by Gulliver is fortunate in its monarch, who unlike the Emperor of Lilliput refuses to separate government and morality: his horrified refusal to accept Gulliver's offer of the secret of gunpowder is an example of this. He is a good King, loved by his people, and his intelligence is directed to doing his best for their moral and physical well-being. He believes 'that whoever could make two Ears of Corn, or two Blades of Grass to grow upon a Spot of Ground where only one grew before; would deserve better of Mankind, and do more essential Service to his Country, than the whole Race of Politicians put together.'[26] The highest point of the second voyage is in the sixth chapter. Here Gulliver, by the King's request, gives him an account of public affairs in England, naturally putting them forward in their best light. This in effect means that he speaks of the Houses of Parliament and other institutions as they were ideally supposed to be, not as observation showed them to be in actuality. But the wise King knows what Gulliver will not admit, that human beings are always prone to distort, through bribery and self-interest, what may seem in the abstract an excellent scheme. After questioning Gulliver, he points this out to him. And he concludes his speech with a metaphor which sums up the insect and animal imagery which has worked through the first and second voyages:

> by what I have gathered from your own Relation, and the Answers I have with much Pains wringed and extorted from you; I cannot but conclude the Bulk of your Natives, to be the most pernicious Race of little odious Vermin that Nature ever suffered to crawl upon the Surface of the Earth.[27]

Earlier, in Chapter III, he has used the same image, while gently stroking Gulliver, and has drawn from the device of relative size precisely the moral which Gulliver—who in this book acts with the self-importance of a Lilliputian—is unable to draw: 'how contemptible a Thing was human Grandeur, which could be mimicked by such diminutive Insects as I'.[28]

Near the end of the *Travels*, where Gulliver gives a summing-up of his adventures, there is a hint—a very indirect hint, as is proper to satire—that the Brobdingnagians may be Swift's presentation of the kind of goodness—the kind of moral and emotional largeness—that humanity can attain. Gulliver says, after speaking of the Houyhnhnms of the fourth voyage, 'I shall say nothing of those remote Nations where *Yahoos* preside; amongst which the least corrupted are the *Brobdingnagians*, whose wise Maxims in Morality and Government, it would be our Happiness to observe.'[29] Gulliver has come to equate human beings with Yahoos, and while we are not necessarily expected to agree with him (for Gulliver is not Swift, but simply part of the satiric fiction, as a character in a play is part of the dramatic fiction) we may well be expected to perceive that all men are by definition fallen and corrupt, and that the Brobdingnagians, working on the materials common to all men, have made a better job of it than most; they are the least corrupted of those nations of human beings whom Gulliver has encountered in Europe and on his travels.

The third book of *Gulliver's Travels*, as scholars have shown by reference to Swift's letters, was the last book to be written. It is not closely linked to the first two, interrelated, books, and it is less shapely and satisfying than they. In it Gulliver visits several countries instead of one, and the satiric effect is much less concentrated and coherent. The most important visit made by Gulliver, and that treated at the greatest length, is the visit to the flying island of Laputa and to the fixed land of Balnibarbi beneath, governed by Laputa (which is chiefly occupied by the King and his court). The flying island has political reference to the relation of the English King to his subjects, but more importantly it is a satire on abstract thinking. The men there are normal in size, but distorted in physical appearance, and it is they who are satirized; Gulliver, who as representative of European man carries a large share of the satire elsewhere, is scarcely touched in Laputa. The Laputans have one eye turned in upon their own mental calculations and one turned up to the sky, for their principal interests are the abstract sciences of mathematics, music, and astronomy. Not one eye is turned outward upon the actual world; their distorted human shape is emblematic of the Laputans' loss of their normal human quality in their absorption in abstract matters far from the daily concerns of men. These people live in a world of fantasy, like the characters of *A Tale of a Tub*; they turn in upon themselves as does the Spider in *The Battle of the Books*. An excessive concentration on one's own intellectual abstractions is, in the context of Swift's satire, as effectual a way as excessive self-conceit or reliance on individual inspiration to arrive in a 'mad' world.

Gulliver makes a trip to Balnibarbi, which he finds to be (in sharp contrast to the fruitful Brobdingnag) virtually uncultivated; scarcely an ear of corn or blade of grass is to be seen, and houses are ruinous. The reason for this is that certain inhabitants of Balnibarbi, after a visit to Laputa, had set up an Academy of Projectors in Lagado, the capital. They form many wild schemes in agriculture, architecture, and so on, which the people carry out; but these schemes inevitably miscarry. Gulliver is taken to see the Academy at Lagado, a satiric version of the Royal Society and like it set up under royal patronage. The projectors carry out many strange experiments, which Swift invented by somewhat exaggerating or fitting together some of the odder experiments undertaken in the early days of experimental science. These are of various kinds, but they all share the quality of uselessness and irrelevance to practical or moral concerns. The much admired 'Universal Artist', for example, spends his time in pointlessly converting things into their opposites, turning the useful into the useless and the vital into the dead: sheep are bred without wool, horses' hooves are petrified into stone. Laputa and Lagado produce an atmosphere as chaotic as that of *A Tale of a Tub*. Man's creative and controlling mind gives way to the mere chance of the machine which will in time produce 'Books in Philosophy, Poetry, Politicks, Law, Mathematics and Theology.'[30]

In all this Swift is satirizing not so much the new science as such but the new science as an example of the misuse of the mind. In Swift's humanist tradition, the proper use of the mind is moral and practical. The mental processes of the men of Laputa and Lagado are neither; their minds spin upon themselves without reference to practical reality or moral truth, like the mind of the author of the *Tale*, or the body of the Spider in the *Battle*. The excessive intellectualism of the Flying Island (which is itself a symbol of its inhabitants' remoteness from actuality) leads to separation from the real world. In the countries visited by Gulliver later in the third voyage this impression of the meaningless, sterile, fantasy-world man can create for himself to live in is deepened and darkened. From the comic Lagado he and we go to Glubbdubdrib, a land of sorcerers and ghosts, and then to a still more sombre place, Luggnagg, where Gulliver is brought face to face with man's final illusion, only to have it broken before him. This is the illusion which leads us to a forgetfulness of the last reality, that all our efforts will be closed by the weakness of age and finally by death. In Luggnagg every so often is born an immortal; and in an intensely moving passage Gulliver daydreams about the noble life of increasing wisdom such people must live, only to find that to an immortal, immortality is as horrifying as death is to us, and that endless time may mean endless time to develop our innate vices rather than, as Gulliver supposes, to develop our virtues and knowledge. At the end of the third book reality, which throughout has been avoided by the people of Laputa and the other countries, is brought before us with a dreadful and inescapable vividness.

This moving and horrifying experience which we share with Gulliver should prepare us for the steady gaze which in the fourth voyage Swift turns upon the inevitable situation of mankind. Gulliver goes to an island inhabited not by large or small or even distorted men but by rational horses who live a pastoral life with other creatures subject to them as in our world animals are subject to the only rational creature, man. One of the subject species is, as Gulliver slowly realises with horror, physically a grosser, hairier, dirtier version of man, but it is apparently not man, since it has no reason and no speech, the utterance of the rational mind.[31] Swift's subject, the investigation of the nature of man, is embodied not in the Yahoos alone or the Houyhnhnms alone, nor even in Gulliver alone, though Gulliver (along with the Portuguese sailors who rescue him) is the only representative of man in this voyage. The subject is embodied in the inter-relation of all the figures in a beautifully constructed fiction, in which Gulliver stands as it were at the centre with on one side of him the highly rational Houyhnhnms, and on the other the Yahoos, who are all body and bodily passions with no reason to control them. Swift is here writing in a very ancient tradition revived at the Renaissance, that which considers man in relation to the other animals (for man, whatever else he may be, is certainly an animal), seeks to define him in relation to them, and often compares him unfavourably to them in respect of certain qualities. The tradition therefore involves philosophic satire of man's nature, and it is this that we find in Swift's fourth voyage. That a 'travel book' should be the vehicle for such satire was by no means new; 'satiric voyages' and 'philosophic voyages' had been written for centuries, and in seventeenth-century France more than one had been written which described the visit of the hero to a race of men more rational and more virtuous than European man, reason being traditionally that which in man inclines him to virtue and which should keep in order the unruly passions which are always striving to overthrow it. Differences in interpretation of the fourth voyage turn upon the question how far Swift may have supposed man to be capable of becoming a rational and virtuous being. One might look at the fourth voyage as an examination of the ancient definition of man, 'animal rationale'. In logic books of the time and earlier, comparison with the horse as a representative of animals was a usual part of the syllogistic definition of man,[32] and the fourth voyage, with its three neatly differing creatures (the rational Houyhnhnms, the merely physical, passionate, and irrational Yahoos, and Gulliver who as a man has both reason and bodily passions), could be seen as a kind of extended and fictionalized syllogism. Our decision on Swift's meaning depends on the way in which we work out the definition. Gulliver works it out in a particular way, but the opinions of Swift's personae are not necessarily to be taken at their face value. They are commonly themselves satirised, and Gulliver's own reactions to what he has seen and heard—in the second voyage, for example—have been far from reliable; so our interpretation of the meaning of Gulliver's adventures will not necessarily be the same as Gulliver's own. Gulliver, like the Houyhnhnms and the Yahoos, is a character in the satiric fiction, part of the material which Swift manipulates in the service of meaning.

The Yahoos are the first creatures Gulliver sees on the island, and he loathes them. He does not recognize that they are in degraded, brutalized human form, but we recognize it from his description. Swift stresses very strongly the physical unpleasantness of the Yahoos and their habits, which are cruder versions of our own passion for jewels and gold, our own avarice, jealousy, and the rest. In terms of the philosophy of Swift's time they are close to the warlike 'state of nature' envisaged by Hobbes, in which every man's hand is against every other. And the Hobbesian state of nature is nearer to the Christian tradition of the fall of man than are the more optimistic theories of the nature of man also current at the time. The Yahoos are that in man which, in Christian terms, is fallen, the corrupt passions, in their case entirely divorced from the reason which should control those passions and turn them, wherever possible, to good. The Houyhnhnms, on the other hand, are almost wholly rational; as Gulliver puts it:

> As these noble *Houyhnhnms* are endowed by Nature with a general Disposition to all Virtues, and have no Conceptions or Ideas of what is evil in a rational Creature; so their grand Maxim is, to cultivate *Reason*, and to be wholly governed by it. Neither is *Reason* among them a Point problematical as with us, where Men can argue with Plausibility on both Sides of a Question; but strikes you with immediate Conviction; as it must needs do where it is not mingled, obscured, or discoloured by Passion and Interest.[33]

As rational creatures whose reason is unclouded by passions, and who have no conception of what is evil in rational creatures like themselves, the Houyhnhnms are rather sharply differentiated from man, who is not 'endowed by Nature' as they are. The Houyhnhnms' name for themselves means *'the Perfection of Nature'*, and clearly a Houyhnhnm really fulfills man's traditional definition for himself, 'animal rationale', a rational animal. Their reason is as unclouded and unerring as is instinct in other animals, and all their attributes and actions as reported by Gulliver testify to the untroubled predominance of reason in them. They feel a universal benevolence for all of their species, and no particular indulgence for their own kin, they choose their mates on rational, not passionate grounds, they have no fear of death, and since their speech is the direct utterance of reason, they not only do not lie but do not know what a lie is, or what its purpose can possibly be. That speech could be meant to conceal or deceive, rather than to communicate truth, is beyond their comprehension, and Gulliver's master Houyhnhnm has to express this new concept in a clumsy phrase, telling Gulliver that he *'said the thing which was not'*.[34] The Houyhnhnms regard Gulliver as a Yahoo, but as one with 'some Glimmerings of Reason'[35] which the Yahoos of their country do not possess. It is the master's conclusion that men are 'a Sort of Animals to whose Share, by what Accident he could not conjecture, some small Pittance of *Reason* had fallen, whereof we made no other Use than by its Assistance to aggravate our *natural* Corruptions, and to acquire new ones which Nature had not given us'.[36] (The good King of Brobdingnag had come to a similar conclusion.)

Gulliver, for some time, will not recognize his likeness to the repulsive Yahoos, and he clings to his clothes as the differentiating factor between himself and them, but his master discovers his secret. Clothes, of course, are unknown to all the creatures of Houyhnhnmland, and the master Houyhnhnm's uncomprehending comment is perfectly appropriate to his nature, that of a naturally rational animal. Gulliver has asked, using a familiar circumlocution, not to be compelled to 'expose those Parts that Nature taught us to conceal'. The Houyhnhnm replies that 'he could not understand why Nature should teach us to conceal what Nature had given'.[37] Of course the virtuous Houyhnhnm cannot understand our necessity to cover our bodies, traditionally a result of the fall; it was when Adam first knew sin that he also knew shame. The Houyhnhnms know neither, and so are unable to understand man, who is to be defined not as an animal to whom 'some small Pittance of *Reason*' had accidentally come, but as a rational creature who has fallen from his original state and whose reason is therefore weakened and his passions strengthened.

Throughout Gulliver's stay with the Houyhnhnms severe satire on human irrationality, foolishness, and wickedness arises out of Gulliver's account of conditions in England and the master Houyhnhnm's comments on them, and on their likeness, in more sophisticated form, to the doings of the Yahoos. These rational and nonhuman creatures provide an admirable satiric position from which to show human activities freshly in all their irrationality, for they look at us from a point of view even more remote than that of a giant; humanity is utterly strange to them, and from the standpoint of pure reason there is little that can go uncondemned. There is no doubt that Gulliver, and we, should be impressed by the Houyhnhnms' clear sight of our errors in government and law (neither of which exists in Houyhnhnmland, since 'Reason alone is sufficient to govern a Rational creature')[38] and in so many of our customs and institutions. The only question is whether Gulliver is right to accept also the Houyhnhnm view of man as nothing but a more sophisticated Yahoo, and to change as a result from a good-humoured man, rather fond of his fellow-humans, to a shuddering misanthrope who sickens at the human smell. Gulliver, set adrift at sea, is found by a group of humane Portuguese sailors who, thinking his reason is disturbed, take him despite his entreaties to their captain, Pedro de Mendez, a good and compassionate man who helps him despite his churlishness and insists that he ought to go back to his own people and family. Even Gulliver has to give him some grudging praise : for example, he had 'very good human Understanding'.[39] Clearly Gulliver has come to see all human beings, however kindly, as Yahoos except himself, and himself as a kind of honorary Houyhnhnm. This attitude is maintained when he returns home, where he swoons with horror at the touch of 'that odious Animal,' his wife, and cannot tolerate the smell of her or his children for a year after his return. 'To this Hour they dare not presume to touch my Bread, or drink out of the same Cup.' [40] The reference to the communion service can hardly be accidental; Gulliver's surely almost insane pride and disgust is contrasted with a Christ-like humility, companionship, and love. And he closes his book with the statement that shows his own addiction to the particular vice which, above all, he castigates : 'and therefore I here intreat those who have any Tincture of this absurd Vice [pride], that they will not presume to appear in my Sight'.[41] It would appear that the attempt of Gulliver, a human being, to identify himself with the nonhuman Houyhnhnms, has led him only to pride and misanthropy, and we should not be too quick to think that his misanthropy is Swift's too. Possibly Gulliver has once again failed quite to see the meaning of his own adventures, and has not seen that an attempt to live a Houyhnhnm life in isolation from one's fellows may not be the best way to attain human virtue. Gulliver is right to condemn much of human life, but his insistence that all human beings are merely Yahoos causes him to dismiss *all* humanity as worthless and disgusting. It is perhaps relevant to think, in this context, of Gulliver's maker's profession of hating abstractions like 'man' but loving individuals. For Gulliver has met several good human beings on his voyages, apart from the inhuman, rational horses, and he obliquely reminds us of this when he thinks once more of the Brobdingnagians, 'least corrupted' of Yahoos.

Thus through relations of the various species—Houyhnhnm, Yahoo, and man—Swift creates a satire on the ways and institutions of Europe which is also an investigation of that which lies behind habits, institutions, ways of writing and thinking, and behind the things he had been satirizing all his life: the unchanging nature of man. Swift's friends thought of the *Travels* as a perfectly successful comedy; but already others were denouncing it as 'degrading human Nature' (Swift makes Gulliver use this phrase in his letter to Sympson) and as time went by this came to be the predominant opinion. Now, whatever our decision as to Swift's meaning, we are ready once more to perceive in the *Travels*, as in his other works, Swift's comic art, his rhetorical skill, his brilliance in adopting a persona whose very style is part of his characterization. Whatever else it is, *Gulliver's Travels* is a work of great intellectual force: not the outburst of a disappointed misanthrope but the complex, precisely thought out and precisely shaped work of a learned and experienced writer at the height of his powers, giving us, through his persona's travels into four exactly imagined lands, his considered views on the nature and life of man.

1. A disease of the inner ear which produces deafness and faulty balance.

2. By an ancient law, clergymen paid to the crown certain fees called the First Fruits, and Queen Anne had agreed that this money should be used instead by the Church of England to improve certain poorly paid livings. It was now hoped to gain the same concession for the sister Church of Ireland.

3. *Works*, ed. Herbert Davis, Oxford, 1959, vi. 55–56.

4. Its full title is *A Compleat Collection of Genteel and Ingenious Conversation, According To the most polite Mode and Method, now used at Court, and in the best Companies of England. In several Dialogues* (1738).

5. *The Correspondence of Jonathan Swift*, ed. H. Williams, Oxford, 1963, iii. 103.

6. 'Verses on the Death of Dr. Swift,' ll. 313–14.

7. *Ibid.*, ll. 207–8.

8. *Ibid.*, ll. 115–16.

9. See, for Swift's rhetorical skills, the books by Bullitt and Beaumont cited in the bibliography.

10. *A Tale of a Tub*, ed. A. C. Guthkelch and D. Nichol Smith, Oxford, 1920, p. 208.

11. *Ibid.*, p. 148.

12. *Ibid.*, p. 83.

13. Swift also attacks doctrines like that of transubstantiation in a way that had often been used in seventeenth-century polemical writing. See the book by Phillip Harth cited in the bibliography.

14. *Ibid.*, pp. 252–53.

15. *Ibid.*, p. 232.

16. Davis, ii. 27.

17. *Ibid.*, p. 31.

18. Deism was a particular form of theism which grew up in the seventeenth and eighteenth centuries, and was seen by Christian divines as a grave danger. The Deists claimed that man was capable, through his reason alone, of knowing the existence of God, the immortality of the soul, and the necessity of following certain moral rules, and that this knowledge was enough for salvation. This meant, of course, that the revelation made to man through the Bible and through the life of Christ, and indeed Christ's death and atonement itself, was not necessary to man's salvation. Thus though not anti-religious, Deism was certainly an anti-Christian philosophy.

19. Davis, ii. 33.

20. Davis, xii. 1–12.

21. The economic situation behind the idea is put in mercantilist terms in Swift's *Maxims Controlled in Ireland*:

It is another undisputed Maxim in government, that people are the riches of a nation; which is so universally granted, that it will be hardly pardonable to bring it in doubt. And I will grant it to be so far true, even in their island, that, if we had the African custom or privilege, of selling our useless bodies for slaves to foreigners, it would be the most useful branch of our trade, by ridding us of a most unsupportable burthen, and bringing us money in the stead. But, in our present situation, at least five children in six who are born lie a dead weight upon us for want of employment. And a very skilful computer assured me, that above one half of the souls in this kingdom supported themselves by begging and thievery, whereof two thirds would be able to get their bread in any other country upon earth. (Davis, xii. 135–6).

22. Davis, xi. 30. (The text of vol. xi cited here is the repaginated edn of 1959.)

23. *Ibid.*, p. 43.

24. This incident, like much else in the first voyage, which is by far the most topical, politically, of the voyages, has reference to events of Swift's time, but the topical references do not constitute the most important aspect of the political and moral allegory and there is no space to deal with them here.

25. Davis, xi. 58.

26. *Ibid.*, pp. 135–6.

27. *Ibid.*, p. 132.

28. *Ibid.*, p. 107.

29. *Ibid.*, p. 292.

30. *Ibid.*, pp. 183–4.

31. Gulliver comes to believe that Yahoo and man are the same, and some critics have thought that he was right, and that the fourth voyage is simply a satiric attack on man as Yahoo, contrasted with what man *could* be (a Houyhnhnm) if he used his reason. Examples of this interpretation will be found in books cited in the bibliography.

32. On this and related topics see R. S. Crane, 'The Houyhnhnms, the Yahoos, and the History of Ideas,' *Reason and the Imagination*, ed. J. A. Mazzeo, New York, 1962, pp. 231–53.

33. Davis, xi. 267.

34. *Ibid.*, p. 235.

35. *Ibid.*, p. 235.

36. *Ibid.*, p. 259.

37. *Ibid.*, pp. 236–7.

38. *Ibid.*, p. 259.

39. *Ibid.*, p. 288.

40. *Ibid.*, pp. 289–90.

41. *Ibid.*, p. 296.

BIBLIOGRAPHY

I *Editions*

Swift's prose is best read in the 14 volume edition cited above, ed. Herbert Davis, Oxford, 1939–62. Several of the volumes have very helpful introductory material. Other authoritative texts are:

A Tale of a Tub, to which is added The Battle of the Books and The Mechanical Operation of the Spirit, ed. A. C. Guthkelch and D. Nichol Smith, Oxford, 1920, second edition 1958. This is annotated in great detail.

The Poems of Jonathan Swift, ed. Sir Harold Williams, 3 vols., Oxford, 1937, second edition 1958.

The Correspondence of Jonathan Swift, ed. Sir Harold Williams, 5 vols., Oxford, 1963–65.

The Journal to Stella, ed. Sir Harold Williams, 2 vols., Oxford, 1948.

Useful working Collections are:

Gulliver's Travels and Other Writings, ed. Louis A. Landa, Cambridge, Mass., 1960.

Gulliver's Travels and Selected Writings in Prose and Verse, ed. John Hayward, London, 1934.

Jonathan Swift, A Selection of his Works, ed. Philip Pinkus, Toronto, London, and New York, 1965.

Satires and Personal Writings, ed. W. A. Eddy, London, 1932.

Swift on his Age, Selected Prose and Verse, ed. Colin J. Horne, London, 1953.

Collected Poems, ed. Joseph Horrell, 2 vols., London, 1958.

II *Biographical Studies*

Ehrenpreis, Irvin, *Swift, The Man, His Works, and the Age*. Vol. I, *Mr. Swift and His Contemporaries*, London, 1962. Vol. II, *Doctor Swift*, 1967. The most dependable biography; two of the projected three volumes so far published.

Ehrenpreis, Irvin, *The Personality of Jonathan Swift*, London, 1958. A collection of biographical and critical essays.

Jackson, R. Wyse, *Jonathan Swift, Dean and Pastor*, London, 1939. Concentrates on Swift's life and work as clergyman.

Landa, Louis A., *Swift and the Church of Ireland*, Oxford, 1954. An excellent but specialized study of Swift's work for and in relation to the Church of Ireland.

III *Critical Studies*

General

Beaumont, C. A., *Swift's Classical Rhetoric*, Athens, Georgia, 1961. Closely examines several shorter satires; demonstrates Swift's skilful use of formal classical rhetoric.

Bullitt, John M., *Jonathan Swift and the Anatomy of Satire*, Cambridge, Mass., and London, 1953. Good general treatment of satiric methods.

Davis, Herbert, *The Satire of Jonathan Swift*, New York, 1947. Essays on the literary, political, and moral satire.

Ewald, W. B., *The Masks of Jonathan Swift*, Cambridge, Mass., and Oxford, 1954. Detailed examination of the satiric personae.

Ferguson, Oliver W., *Jonathan Swift and Ireland*, Urbana, Illinois, 1962. A useful setting of the Irish satires into their historical background.

Jeffares, Alexander Norman, ed., *Fair Liberty was All His Cry: A tercentenary Tribute to Jonathan Swift, 1667–1745*. London, 1967.

Price, Martin, *Swift's Rhetorical Art*, New Haven, 1953. A valuable and readable general study.

Quintana, R., *The Mind and Art of Jonathan Swift*, London and New York, 1936; London, 1953. A very inclusive treatment of life as well as works.

—— *Swift, An Introduction*, London, 1955. Very useful introductory short study; essays on various aspects of Swift's work, covering his entire career.

Rosenheim, Edward R., *Swift and the Satirist's Art*, Chicago, 1965.

Tuveson, Ernest, ed., *Swift: A Collection of Critical Essays*, (Twentieth Century Views), Englewood Cliffs, New Jersey, 1964. Some of the most important essays previously published in journals.

Voigt, Milton, *Swift and the Twentieth Century*, Detroit, 1964. A survey of major modern developments in criticism, biography, and textual studies.

Williams, Kathleen, *Jonathan Swift and the Age of Compromise*, Lawrence, Kansas, 1958; London, 1959.

The Battle of the Books

Jones, Richard Foster, *Ancients and Moderns, a Study of the Background of the Battle of the Books*, St. Louis, Missouri, 1936. Valuable study of the Ancients and Moderns controversy.

A Tale of a Tub

Harth, Phillip, *Swift and Anglican Rationalism. The Religious Background of A Tale of a Tub*, Chicago, 1961. Relates *Tale* to seventeenth-century religious controversy.

Paulson, Ronald, *Theme and Structure in Swift's Tale of a Tub*, New Haven, 1960. A fine discussion of the complex methods of the *Tale* as embodying Swift's criticism of man.

Starkman, Miriam K., *Swift's Satire on Learning in A Tale of a Tub*, Princeton, 1950. Examines the sources Swift drew upon for the Digressions.

Gulliver's Travels

This is extensively treated in all the general works. Specialized studies are:

Case, Arthur E., *Four Essays on Gulliver's Travels*, Princeton, 1945. Partly critical; also discusses the establishing of the correct text.

Eddy, William A., *Gulliver's Travels, A Critical Study*, Princeton, 1923. Includes discussion of sources and influences.

Nicholson, Marjorie, and Mohler, Nora M., 'The Scientific Background of Swift's voyage to Laputa,' *Annals of Science*, ii (1937); reprinted in M. Nicholson, *Science and Imagination*, Ithaca, New York and London, 1956. Examines Swift's handling of his sources in the Transactions of the Royal Society.

Williams, Harold. *The Text of Gulliver's Travels*, Cambridge, 1952. Wholly bibliographical study.

3

ALEXANDER POPE

Roger Lonsdale, Balliol College, Oxford

Among the neglected minor verse of Pope's early years is 'The
Alley', an imitation of Spenser, which is usually mentioned if
at all as somewhat dubious evidence of Pope's interest in Elizabethan literature. The joke of this parody no doubt lies in the
contrast of the naïve, diffuse, archaistic style with its unpleasant
content, a description of the slums close to the Thames. Yet
parody often contains the involuntary expression of deeper
interests: what is striking in 'The Alley' is its concluding assertion, after fifty lines of insistently sordid detail, that such low
life lies behind the façade of all the towns along the river:

> Ne Village is without, on either side,
> All up the silver *Thames*, or all a down;
> Ne *Richmond*'s self, from whose tall Front are ey'd
> Vales, Spires, meandring Streams, and *Windsor*'s tow'ry Pride.
>
> (51–4)

The suddenly expanded perspective is felt as a welcome release
from the sordid alley: what is also conveyed, of course, is the
stylish escapism of this pastoral vision and the precariousness
of the dignified, civilized façade of Richmond and Windsor ('At
once the Monarch's and the Muse's Seats', as Pope later wrote).

Too much must not be made of a minor poem, but in some
ways it seems to embody incidentally Pope's vision of the
aspirations and limitations of Augustan society, to which his
own relationship, for all that he is so often taken to be its
spokesman, was basically an ambivalent one. His father, a
prosperous merchant and Roman Catholic convert, had retired
from business in 1688, the year of the Glorious (i.e. Protestant)
Revolution and of the poet's birth. Pope's religion, never perhaps
deeply felt but never disowned, was to limit his educational op-
portunities and exclude him from public office. He was taught
largely by private tutors or, as he preferred to think, by his
own voracious reading and by constant imitation of classical

poetry. He also believed that his perpetual studies helped to ruin his health[1] : tubercular and crookbacked by adolescence, he was never more than four feet six inches tall, plagued throughout his life by illness.

His religion, his education, his deformity were eventually to be excluding, isolating, sensitising factors, but Pope set out as something of an idealist. When he emerged in about 1705 from a boyhood of Catholic piety and relentless reading in Windsor Forest (the family had moved there in about 1700), he met in London a circle of older, more sophisticated literary men, mostly friends of the late John Dryden : Wycherley and Congreve, Betterton the actor, Granville and Garth the poets, William Walsh, gentlemanly poet and critic. These friendships remind us of Pope's literary relationship with the Restoration period. From these writers, as well as from other poets of their generation, such as Oldham, Rochester and the great Dryden himself, Pope learned much that he would put to immediate or future use. William Walsh soon gave the young Pope an often quoted piece of advice :

> He encouraged me much, and used to tell me that there was one way left of excelling, for though we had had several great poets, we never had any one great poet that was correct —and he desired me to make that my study and aim.[2]

If such encouragement was important, the advice was perhaps unnecessary : from the beginning, the drive to whatever was perfectible was intense in the crippled youth. No one considered 'correctness' to be the highest attribute of poetry but it seemed a significant condition of poetic success, a tangible aspect of the 'refinement' attained after the barbarism of the early seventeenth century. In so far as it involved clarity, conciseness, elegance, metrical and musical smoothness, Pope had the temperament and the ear to attain it to an unprecedented degree. His *Pastorals* (written 1704–7, published 1709) were soon being passed round by admiring friends. Many of the rhetorical niceties of his couplet versification are here already displayed : antithesis and parallel, pleasing repetitions and syntactic patternings, alliteration and assonance, sweet metrical variations of pause and cadence and smooth vowel sounds.

Normally indignant at the mere thought of poetic sheep and shepherds, even Dr. Johnson admitted to enjoying Pope's pastoral versification.[3] Yet the *Pastorals* offer an experience which is entirely literary. Pope's prefatory 'Discourse' (not published till 1717) is conscientiously aware of recent French critical debate about the true nature of pastoral and the poems themselves exist largely by graceful reference to Theocritus, Virgil and Spenser. The 'simplicity' of experience admissible in the depiction of man in the Golden Age, the self-conscious 'delicacy', the bemusing orchestration of amorous moods solaced by a sympathetic Nature, convey a sense of innocence not so much lost as irrelevant.

The confrontation of Pope's technique, disciplined and enriched in these early years by constant translation and imitation of earlier poets, with the witty but careless excesses of the Restoration was curiously enacted in his touchy correspondence with the elderly Wycherley, whose verses he had been invited to 'correct' for publication.[4] In his imitations of Chaucer's *Merchant's Tale* and *Wife of Bath's Prologue* (c. 1704) (imitating in themselves Dryden's enthusiasm for Chaucer), both the brilliance and the limitations of Pope's early 'correctness' are again revealed. Impatient with Chaucer's garrulity and slackness, Pope compresses wherever possible and supplies his own epigrammatic, antithetic wit:

> The children of Mercurie and of Venus
> Been in hir wirkyng ful contrarius;
> Mercurie loveth wysdam and science,
> And Venus loveth ryot and dispence.
> And, for hire diverse disposicioun,
> Ech falleth in otheres exaltacioun.

> > (Chaucer, 697–702)

> Love seldom haunts the Breast where Learning lies,
> And *Venus* sets ere *Mercury* can rise:
> Those play the Scholars who can't play the Men;
> And use that Weapon which they have, their Pen ...
> > (Pope, 'The Wife of Bath Her Prologue', 369–72)

Yet where Chaucer probes human experience of time and passion more searchingly, Pope's elegance seems perfunctory and his interference with the original merely impertinent.

Literature and literary society usually provided the experience which Pope felt most confident about exploring early in his career. His *Essay on Criticism* (written by 1709, published 1711) can be related to earlier Restoration verse treatises on poetry but the ultimate model was Horace's *Ars Poetica*, the 'irregularity' of which Pope himself professed to imitate.[5] On one level he was aiming at a synthesis of the most valuable critical precepts since Aristotle and his modern editors have fully demonstrated his debts to Rapin, Boileau, Dryden and other recent critics. Yet the poem is much more than the 'mere versification, like a metrical multiplication-table, of common-places the most mouldy with which criticism has baited its rat-traps' condemned by De Quincey.[6] Its three sections deal in turn with general critical principles (founded in the intelligible moral order of Nature, and accessible through her high priests the ancient poets, and the 'rules' formulated from their art), the faults of bad critics, and the virtues of good ones, and each ends with a passage of elevated rhetoric, at once a poetic climax and a thematic summary of what has preceded. For all its debts, moreover, the *Essay*'s broader concerns are deeply personal: the state of literature in Pope's own age, the relationship of poet and critic, the damage done by irresponsible criticism, the quarrels of wits and poets and of Ancients and Moderns, the virtues of self-knowledge and humility and charity which the critic needs in addition to intellect, learning and taste.

At times Pope decisively elevates true poetic genius above the critics, especially the failed creative writers who can swarm in an insect-like confusion anticipating the later Dunces (36–45). Yet his ultimate aim is reconciliation of the critical and creative capacities, of Judgement and Wit, of Art and Nature, of the 'rules' and genius, of the energy of the individual talent and a fruitful sense of the past. The faults of the bad critic described in the middle section of the poem—failure to see the whole because of preoccupation with the parts, to penetrate surface distractions to the basic truths of Nature, to attain self-knowledge and to shun pride—are primarily literary shortcomings, although the moral implications are increasingly stressed as the poem proceeds. But these same failings will recur in Pope's later poetry in larger contexts and gloomier perspectives, lamented as inherent in human nature in the *Essay on Man*, derided as the perversions of Dulness in the *Dunciad*.

In another sense the *Essay on Criticism* is modestly but firmly personal. The young poet himself intervenes at crucial moments: to assert his own allegiance to the ancient poets (195–200), or to make his friendship with William Walsh the conclusion of his compressed history of literary criticism (729–44), so that the whole poem becomes an embodiment of the fruitful relationship of poet and critic it recommends. Pope's technical virtuosity confronts the reader repeatedly in his confident willingness to parody the mechanical versification or cold correctness he condemns, just as his own paradoxes and rhythmic freedom, for example, mime the 'happy Boldness' which he commends as beyond the domain of criticism:

> Great Wits sometimes may *gloriously offend*,
> And *rise* to *Faults* true Criticks *dare not mend*;
> From *vulgar Bounds* with *brave Disorder* part,
> And *snatch* a *Grace* beyond the Reach of Art,
> Which, without passing thro' the *Judgment*, gains
> The *Heart*, and all its End *at once* attains.

$$(152-7)$$

Pope's imagery is also significant: drawn from all aspects of contemporary life, military, artistic, sexual, religious and sartorial, it helps to project the poet as an urbane, level-headed observer of his age. This impression, blending with Pope's expressions of allegiance to the classical poets, helps to support his implicit reconciliation of the quarrel of the Ancients and Moderns which had absorbed the previous generation. Similarly, Pope's frequent use of the word 'wit' is notoriously ambiguous in this poem, with a spectrum of meanings from smart, flashy ingenuity to a penetrative intelligence and creativity amounting to genius.[7] Pope himself lays claim to a range of the most acceptable senses, reconciling in his own flexible tones familiarity with the knowing conversation of the coffee-house and the inventive faculties of the true poet.

Pope aims in the *Essay* primarily at the familiar, conversational but judicious 'Horatian' style. But there are passages of fervent elevation and at other moments something like the animated conviction of his later satiric mode emerges. In a paragraph on the bad critic, alliteration underlines contempt, references to real persons and places give concreteness to the portrait, and the intonations of speech and rhythmic flexibility impart a sudden aggressive edge to the verse:

> The Bookful Blockhead, ignorantly read,
> With *Loads* of *Learned Lumber* in his Head,
> With his own Tongue still edifies his Ears,
> And always *List'ning to Himself* appears.
> All Books he reads, and all he reads assails,
> From *Dryden's Fables* down to *Durfey's Tales*.
> With *him*, most Authors steal their Works, or buy;
> *Garth* did not write his own *Dispensary*.
> Name a new *Play*, and *he's* the Poet's *Friend*,
> Nay show'd his Faults—but when wou'd Poets mend?

No Place so Sacred from such Fops is barr'd,
Nor is *Paul's Church* more safe than *Paul's Church-yard*:
Nay, fly to *Altars*; *there* they'll talk you dead;
For *Fools* rush in where *Angels* fear to tread.

(612–25)

The complementary portrait of the good critic (631–6) may seem abstract by comparison. Yet the parallels, antitheses and balanced syntax of Pope's couplets enact the moral and intellectual discipline and discrimination essential in the true critic, as he picks his way through alternating temptations of narrowness and pride.

Aware of the disparity between the quarrels of the modern Mount Parnassus and an idealized classical world (for which the irascible John Dennis's furious attack on the *Essay on Criticism* soon provided new evidence), Pope was still essentially optimistic about the civilizing potential of his age. In other contexts the celebration of reconciliation and harmony was still his aim. In 1713 he hailed the approach of the Peace of Utrecht with an expanded version of his *Windsor-Forest* (begun 1704) which he now dedicated to George Granville, Lord Lansdowne'[8] As a poet himself and as a Tory minister involved in the peace negotiations, Lansdowne focused for Pope the poetic and political associations of the landscape which he describes. Pope was not aiming at faithful and fresh depiction of nature nor to affect us with scenes nostalgically remembered or revisited. Historically, it is no saner to look for Tintern Abbey in Pope's Windsor Forest than it would be geographically. The poem is related to the kind of topographical poetry which had emerged in the seventeeth century, notably in Denham's *Cooper's Hill* (1642), in which the landscape provided the poet with the occasion for generalized description and reflection on its moral, literary or political associations. Thus, all the main themes of *Windsor-Forest* are expounded in lines 1–42 in terms of the landscape: underlying all its features are the divine principles of diversity and order, harmonious variety and ordered strife, which reflect and correspond to the harmonious confusion of God's newly created world. Through the fertility of the scene and the joyful swain (a recurrent point of reference in the poem), Pope moves from the universal to the political implications of the landscape, which manifests the plenty and industry resulting from the peaceful reign of the Stuart monarch, Queen Anne. The details of the landscape, the arts (notably, painting) which contribute to the description, the political situation of

England and the universe all manifest the same principles of diversity, design and harmony.

In this way the poem transcends its function as propaganda for the Tory Peace. Thereafter the landscape gives rise to a series of episodes, contrasting in their brilliant descriptive effects and in their moods of desolation, fierce energy and repose, but each taking its place in the ultimate harmony which is the poem's theme. Geographically, the poem moves gradually from the Forest, along the Thames past Windsor and on to London and the outer world. So Pope reaches a last triumphant statement, voiced by Father Thames himself, of his principle of harmony and reconciliation in a vision of world peace :

> The Time shall come, when free as Seas or Wind
> Unbounded *Thames* shall flow for all Mankind,
> Whole Nations enter with each swelling Tyde,
> And Seas but join the Regions they divide;
> Earth's distant Ends our Glory shall behold,
> And the new World launch forth to seek the Old.
> Then Ships of Uncouth Form shall stem the Tyde,
> And Feather'd People crowd my wealthy Side,
> And naked Youths and painted Chiefs admire
> Our Speech, our Colour, and our strange Attire!
>
> (397–406)

Pope borrows from Isaiah and from Virgil's celebration of the reign of Augustus but there is a note of convincing personal fervour in his vision of a world from which conquest, slavery and the baser passions have been banished. By contrast with his bitterly satiric later poetry, *Windsor-Forest* may appear naïvely idealistic. Pope's own career supplies the missing irony. The nature of that final pessimism can be better understood from this colourful, dynamic and expansive (if sometimes self-consciously literary) vision of a society which reflects the principles of a benevolent and harmonious universe.

For all his optimism, contemplation of the cycles of human history and, in particular, reverent meditations on the vanished grandeurs of classical civilization can often give rise to an elegiac strain in Pope's early verse. The vulnerability of human achievements to time's destructive powers is a theme of *The Temple of Fame* (written c. 1711, pub. 1715), a free imitation of part of Chaucer's *Hous of Fame*, his 'Epistle to Mr. Addison, Occasion'd by his Dialogues on Medals' (c. 1713; pub. 1720) and his 'Epistle to Mr. Jervas' (1716). *The Rape of the Lock*, the supreme achievement of Pope's early career, is complicated by this elegiac mood. In other ways *The Rape* is related to Pope's recent poetry : in its imitative 'literariness', here however taking the ironic and exploratory form of mock-heroic, in its amused recommendation of 'good Sense and good Humour'[9] (the modes of harmony and reconciliation appropriate to polite society) and in its fascination with the fashionable female world. Pope no doubt benefited from the recent depiction of female affectations and frivolities in *The Tatler* and *The Spectator* but in his 'Epistle to Miss Blount, With the Works of Voiture' (1710) he had already written of the constraints imposed by 'Custom' and 'Form' on female instincts, had asserted that only 'Charms' based on 'Good Humour' could survive 'Age, or Sickness', and had celebrated the power of Art, in this case Voiture's, to preserve female beauty and wit.

All these themes are woven together in the scintillating tapestry of *The Rape of the Lock*. First published in 1712 in two Cantos (only 334 lines long), the poem was occasioned by Lord Petre's bold theft of a lock of hair from the head of the beautiful Arabella Fermor. Pope was asked to write a poem to 'make a jest' of the incident and reconcile the quarrelling Catholic families of the two protagonists in the affair.[10] To provide a good-humoured and sensible perspective on the incident Pope used the mock-heroic form, most notably developed for him in Boileau's *Le Lutrin* (1674) and Garth's *Dispensary* (1699). (The influence of Dryden's *Mac Flecknoe* will be more apparent in the *Dunciad*.) The original poem is a brisk narrative describing the foolish episode in the poetic language associated with heroic deeds and passions, and imitating epic conventions and situations, mainly by allusion to or parody of Homer, Virgil, *Paradise Lost* and Dryden's *Aeneid*.

The additions which more than doubled the length of the poem in 1714 skilfully reinforced the mock-heroic element (e.g. the card-game in Canto III, the visit to the underworld in Canto IV) but also diversified and complicated Pope's method and interests. Not surprisingly, the narrative coherence of the final version of *The Rape of the Lock*, its delicacy of perception and imaginative exuberance, have made it the most continuously admired of his major poems. But critical emphases have inevitably shifted. For Hazlitt, it was 'the most exquisite specimen of *fillagree* work ever invented. It is admirable in proportion as it is made of nothing.'[11] This approach culminated in Edith Sitwell's hypnotic account of it as 'a poem so airy that it might have been woven by the long fingers of the sylphs in their dark and glittering Indian gauzes, floating like a little wind

among the jewelled dark dews on the leaves of the fruit-trees.' [12]
At the other extreme are recent, more morose interpretations, extracting from Belinda confessions of pride, hypocrisy and blasphemy under the harsh light of close verbal analysis.

The truth is that Pope's intense imaginative engagement with Belinda's world balances and complicates his sense of its short-comings. His ironic, highly allusive style, now first fully achieved, involving in the trivial events of Belinda's fashionable day a wealth of literary experiences—heroic resonances, pastoral delicacies, colloquial intonations—and bringing to bear on the heroine religious and sexual perspectives which she herself can hardly acknowledge, certainly lends itself to interpretations of differing emphasis. Pope's handling of the mock-heroic itself reflects the complexity of his attitude. The self-important 'heroic' roles in which Belinda and the Baron cast themselves may be deflated as self-delusion; juxtaposition with the lofty, dignified and ritualistic can reveal the trivial, low and modern for what they are. Yet we are left with no simple exposure of Belinda's world, as Johnson recognized : 'we feel all the appetite of curiosity for that from which we have a thousand times turned fastidiously away.' [13] The heroic perspective bestows as well as denies; mystery and fine formality fall on the ceremonies of the dressing-table, card-game and coffee-drinking which correspond to its own religious or military rituals and feasts. This glittering, richly concrete diminution of the epic world no doubt afforded imaginative relief and release to an age strained by the disparity between its heroic ideals and mundane realities. Again, Pope's repeated allusions to the *Aeneid* may contrast Belinda's prudish tantrums with Dido's tragic grief for Aeneas. But the reader's satisfaction also springs not merely from the literary pleasure of recognizing the presence of Virgil but from the resulting perspective on Dido, as well as on Belinda. Pope's prefatory letter sanctioned this reaction : 'the ancient Poets are in one Respect like many modern Ladies; Let an Action be never so trivial in itself, they always make it appear of the utmost Importance.'

Pope admitted in 1714 to the ambivalence of his 'whimsical' poem :

> at once the most a satire, and the most inoffensive, of anything of mine. People who would rather it were let alone laugh at it, and seem heartily merry, at the same time that they are uneasy. 'Tis a sort of writing very like tickling. [14]

Uneasiness might well have tickled the reader of the description of Belinda's toilet (i. 121–48) as 'the sacred Rites of Pride'. The religious diction suggests a society in which the ritual of self-adoration has subverted more serious values. Yet to emphasize these implications in isolation is to coarsen the meaning, for Pope is still celebrating the power of Belinda's beauty, founded as it may be in vanity and improved by cosmetic art. This astonishing metamorphosis of the dressing-table to a temple and next to a huge geographical perspective contracts eventually to the depiction of Belinda as epic hero arming for battle. There are many other indications (e.g. ii. 23–8 and the card-game) that what Belinda has in fact been dedicating herself to, with religious earnestness, is provocation of the male, her own kind of aggression.

In this way Pope makes his point about the self-deception in Belinda's later outraged reaction to the loss of the Lock. And, since the sun-like beneficence of her beauty and gaiety in her little world is carefully established in Canto II, he can also skilfully combine compliment and criticism in his hyperbolic account in Canto IV of the damaging effects on 'half the world' of her prudish spleen at the Baron's prank. Umbriel's visit to the Cave of Spleen is a grotesquely humorous representation of the spiritual disorder and frustration underlying Belinda's prudery. Yet Belinda is not merely the victim of self-deception: Pope sees her also as the victim of the conventions, inhibitions and frivolities of her own society, which are wittily and gracefully explored through the machinery of the sylphs added in 1714. Through this cunning travesty of the preoccupation of the Rosicrucian sylphs with the preservation of chastity, Pope not merely gave himself the opportunity for some of his most imaginative descriptive verse but extended his poem to an examination of the whole code of female sexual decorum invoked in the quarrel. Ariel's opening speech (his appearance as a 'Birth-night Beau', in parody of divine manifestations in epics, is a prompt index to the values of Belinda's world) blandly identifies female 'Honour' as mere coquetry and levity. It is not honour or chastity which preserve female virtue but the giddy multiplicity of surrounding temptations and the vanity at the heart of coquetry (i. 99–100).

In such a society, the loss of 'reputation' is as serious as real loss of honour: both are as frail as a China jar which one flaw renders valueless; as external and easily stained as a new brocade (ii. 105–7). Even more ominous to the sylphs is the threat of real emotion. When Ariel detects the lover in Belinda's heart (the Baron himself?), he loses his power to protect her. Pope's attitude to her predicament in a society where young women must attract men without losing reputation and without expressing true feelings is sympathetic. The aged, frustrated spinsters lurking in the background of the poem point to the fate which awaits Belinda if she try either too hard or not hard enough.

The last complication of Pope's attitude to Belinda is the pathos associated with her beauty and vulnerability to time. The ultimate enemy is neither the aggressive male nor the scandalmonger. Like the sun with which she is repeatedly associated, her beauty is powerful but transient. In the face of an outrage much more shocking than anything the Baron's scissors can inflict, Clarissa's speech (v. 9–34; added in 1717) recommends a flexible and good-humoured wisdom. The mock-heroic perspective (Pope is parodying his own translation of Sarpedon's famous exhortation to Glaucus in the *Iliad*, Book XII)[15] acknowledges the limitations of some of Clarissa's values (heroic fame is replaced by the 'Glories' of male admiration). Yet that ancient magnanimity in the face of death imparts to the confidential female intonations of Clarissa's advice a wise and generous realism in the face of time :

> Oh! if to dance all Night, and dress all Day,
> Charm'd the Small-pox, or chas'd old Age away;
> Who would not scorn what Huswife's Cares produce,
> Or who would learn one earthly Thing of Use?
> To patch, nay ogle, might become a Saint,
> Nor could it sure be such a Sin to paint.
> But since, alas! frail Beauty must decay,
> Curl'd or uncurl'd, since Locks will turn to grey,
> Since painted, or not painted, all shall fade,
> And she who scorns a Man, must die a Maid;
> What then remains, but well our Pow'r to use,
> And keep good Humour still whate'er we lose?
> And trust me, Dear! good Humour can prevail,
> When Airs, and Flights, and Screams, and Scolding fail.
>
> (v. 19–32)

The mock-heroic battle which follows rehearses the gaiety and aggression, pleasure and earnestness, flirtation and affectation, of the sex-war itself, a last reminder to Belinda of the inappropriateness of her own reaction. Yet neither victim nor aggressor (and part of Pope's point is that Belinda and the Baron could both be either) now possess the Lock itself. Pope entertains the possibility that it has joined all the human follies preserved in Ariosto's 'lunar Sphere' (v. 113–22), which would dismiss the whole episode as mere triviality and affectation. But the last of the many metamorphoses of the poem expresses the real significance of the Lock: transformed to a star by the Muse, the Lock is ultimately preserved against time and given meaning only by Pope's poetic art itself:

> For, after all the Murders of your Eye,
> When, after Millions slain, your self shall die;
> When those fair Suns shall sett, as sett they must,
> And all those Tresses shall be laid in Dust;
> *This Lock*, the Muse shall consecrate to Fame,
> And mid'st the Stars inscribe *Belinda*'s Name!

(v. 145–50)

The Rape of the Lock, poised and yet also delighted, embodies the good humour and good sense which can too often seem merely the cold and narrow ideals of Pope's age. Biographically, the poem may represent an exertion of supreme imaginative mastery on Pope's part over a female world from which he himself was inevitably excluded. His triumph was to make it more, and more than an ambivalent tribute to the precarious but attractive surface of the fashionable life of his time. The poem celebrates and mourns the power and vulnerability of human beauty itself, at once a compliment, a critique and an elegy. Hazlitt observed that in reading the poem 'You hardly know whether to laugh or weep'.[16] If he had pondered the reasons for that response, he might have found it harder to make his earlier assertion that the poem 'is admirable in proportion as it is made of nothing'.

II

Pope's ideals of moderation and his professions of political impartiality were put under increasing strain as his literary acquaintance grew. Literature and politics were closely and dangerously entangled. For a time, Pope was flattered by the attentions of Joseph Addison, who was trying to attract talented writers into political journalism: he contributed to *The Spectator* and *The Guardian*, became acquainted in 1712/13 with the Whig writers surrounding Addison at Button's Coffeehouse, and wrote a prologue for Addison's famous *Cato* (1713). Yet by 1712 Pope had probably also met most of the men who within a year had formed the celebrated and unambiguously Tory Scriblerus Club: Swift, Arbuthnot, Parnell, Gay and the Earl of Oxford,

the Lord Treasurer. The primary aim of the Club was to com-
pile the satirical *Memoirs* of Martinus Scriblerus, the representative of all contemporary critical and pedantic abuses and
fatuities. Although regular meetings of the Club ended with the
Queen's death in 1714 (the unfinished *Memoirs* were not published until 1741), its ideals and satiric vigour had by then contributed to a series of memorable works: *Gulliver's Travels*,
the *Dunciad* and *The Beggar's Opera*, as well as many minor
works which show its influence.[17]

Pope's new Tory friends inevitably drew him away from
Addison's circle and the complex political, literary and personal
factors involved made trouble inevitable. Pope's brilliantly
ironic praise of Ambrose Philips's *Pastorals* in *Guardian* no. 40
in 1713 was a small instance of the competition in a confined
and often irritable literary world which led to the steady
deterioration in Pope's relations with Addison. The real break
was a result of the translation of Homer which was to absorb
most of Pope's poetic energies for a decade. The subscription
list opened in October 1713 and the first Books of the *Iliad* appeared in 1715. Thomas Tickell's rival translation of Book I
of the *Iliad*, sponsored and, as some believed, actually written
by Addison, was published two days later. Pope's version was
preferred but if his way thereafter was unimpeded by competitors, he was from this period to become all too familiar
with the journalistic abuse of his person, character and art to
which he eventually replied in the *Dunciad*.

Pope was at first haunted by the fear that his classical learning was insufficient for his task. Thirty years later he could still
dream of 'being engaged in that translation and got about half
way through it, and being embarrassed and under dreads of
never completing it.'[18] In 1714 he contrasted himself with his
friend Parnell, who was assisting him: 'I a Hackney Scribler,
You are a Grecian & bred at a University, I a poor Englishman of
my own Educating'.[19] Yet, although he could later say that it
was 'purely the want of money'[20] that led him into the undertaking, he was in fact sustained by the conviction that his age
needed a translation of Homer to complement Dryden's noble
Aeneid and by his ultimate confidence in his ability to meet the
poetic challenge he had to face. The emphasis, in his 'Preface'
(1715) to the *Iliad*, on Homer's 'Invention' and powerful poetic
imagination, the repeated oppositions of nature and art, genius
and rules, poetical fire and mere correctness, dictate the terms
in which he himself wished to be judged. For all its elaborate
scholarly apparatus, the main concern of his translation was to

avoid painful literalism and to transfuse the 'original Spirit' and 'Fire' of Homer.

Pope's *Iliad* now seems emphatically Augustan in its stress on design and clarity of outline, its sententious pointing up of the epic's 'moral', its allusiveness to the epic tradition since Homer, and its stylistic adherence to restrictive and questionably relevant concepts of epic decorum. Pope himself was concerned about the stylistic problem, aware at least of the dangers of an elevation disproportionate to the subject matter, of aspirations to sublimity which could seem merely strained, of 'choiceness' in diction and 'propriety' in sentiment which lose more than they gain. Even contemporaries expressed doubts about the appropriateness of his neat couplets and the general 'politeness' of the translation to the violent Homeric world.[21] Yet Pope's reinterpretation of Homer achieved at times an impressive lucidity, energy and pictorial splendour and, in that it embodied many of the ideals of an age which cared deeply about Homer, its own coherence. Johnson thought it the 'noblest' of all translations and for Coleridge it remained an 'astonishing product of matchless talent and ingenuity'.

By the time the *Iliad* was completed in 1720, Pope was disillusioned about recent political developments and weary of literary animosities and virulences. The translation had already won him financial independence for life, which was to set him free from subservience either to aristocratic patrons or the increasingly powerful booksellers. 'The life of a Wit is a warfare upon earth', he had remarked in 1717 in the 'Preface' to his collected *Works*, in which he wrote with gentlemanly superiority and pained regret of the literary world. To Parnell at this time he described this volume as containing 'all I ever intend to give . . . you must look on me no more a poet'.[22] Some failure of creativity after years of translation may be reflected : between 1714 and 1726 Pope's original verse was written mostly for social reasons (epistles, prologues, epitaphs) or for amusement.

The exceptions in the 1717 volume were 'Eloisa to Abelard' and the 'Elegy to the Memory of an Unfortunate Lady', which were to be among Pope's most admired writings later in the century. 'Eloisa' in particular imitates the basic situation and the style of Ovid's heroic epistles. In his passionate heroine, secluded in the convent founded by her now castrated lover Abelard, Pope dramatized what his 'Argument' calls 'the struggles of grace and nature, virtue and passion'. At times, as in the opening lines, Pope seems to try to override the couplet's tendency to neatness and self-enclosing conciseness. Yet its genius for antithesis in fact lends itself to the depiction of the multiple conflicts in Eloisa's heart which pervade the texture of the verse and dictate the larger organization of the poem : between love for Abelard and duty to God, passion and chastity, earth and heaven, instinct and conscience, life and death, the light and warmth of love and the cold, dark covent. The subtlest aspect of the poem is the way in which Abelard and God are not merely opposed but are repeatedly merged and confused in Eloisa's heart. Rhetorical, melodramatic, at times over-schematic, 'Eloisa to Abelard' still has a surging eloquence, and the passages of melancholy natural description, the controlled fluctuations of mood and often subtle tumult of passions retain considerable power. The 'Elegy', similarly Ovidian and melodramatic, is alternately more lyrical and more satiric than 'Eloisa', but it also depicts the frustration of passion and ends by turning to the poet himself. Fragments of evidence survive to connect 'Eloisa' at least with Pope's passion at this time for the remarkable Lady Mary Wortley Montagu. The intensity of his later dislike of her could have originated in the rejection which would inevitably follow any declaration of his vulnerable feelings towards her.

In 1719 Pope and his mother (his father had died in the previous year) settled in the villa at Twickenham where he was to live for the rest of his life in gentlemanly detachment from the 'great world' of London, making summer visits to the growing number of his upper-class friends. In 1718, now aged thirty, he had spoken of himself as 'One that had been a Poet, was degraded to a Translator, and at last thro' meer dulness is turn'd into an Architect'.[23] His interest in gardening and building was to be given scope not merely in his own assiduously nurtured five acres but in the magnificent grounds of his aristocratic acquaintance. In this way his influence on the development of English gardening was to be a significant one.[24] In the early 1720s, by another 'due gradation of dulness', he became 'a mere editor'.[25] In 1722 he published the *Poems* of Parnell and in 1723 the *Works* of his friend John Sheffield, Duke of Buckingham, although this edition was temporarily suppressed on a charge of Jacobitism. Later projects led to even more trouble. Pope had by now undertaken to translate the *Odyssey* with the collaboration of two minor poets, William Broome and Elijah Fenton, the secrecy of the scheme leading in the end to public denunciation by Pope's enemies and private recriminations from

Broome and Fenton. Pope himself profited by some £5000 from the translation (published 1725–26). Finally, his edition of Shakespeare, which appeared in March 1725, failed to live up to the scholarly standards expounded in its interesting Preface. Its shortcomings were revealed a year later in Lewis Theobald's relatively informed and by no means violent *Shakespeare Restored*.

Other literary figures—unscrupulous publishers, malicious journalists and scurrilous pamphleteers—had also been qualifying for a decade for admission to the imminent *Dunciad*. By October 1725 Pope had been contemplating a satire 'to correct the Taste of the town in wit and Criticisme'.[26] Swift's visits to England in 1726 and 1727 no doubt heartened Pope for the inevitable conflict. The return to England in 1725 of another friend, the once-powerful Henry St. John, Lord Bolingbroke, whom Pope had also met at the time of the Scriblerus Club and who had been in exile for a decade, was probably just as significant. Bolingbroke was now to be an increasing influence on Pope's thought, no doubt helping to confirm his pessimistic conviction that under the government of Robert Walpole some radical degeneration in society was taking place. Bolingbroke's periodical *The Craftsman* began to appear in December 1726. The *Dunciad*, perhaps completed by early 1727, finally appeared in three Cantos in May 1728, but Pope had probably planned from the beginning the new edition which followed in April 1729. The *Dunciad Variorum* added an elaborate mock-scholarly apparatus of prefaces, notes and appendixes (to which several friends seem to have contributed), which served various functions. Apart from parodying contemporary scholarly excesses in the Scriblerian manner—including, needless to say, those of Theobald, the poem's hero—the annotation gave a great deal of information (sometimes distorted) to justify Pope's derision of his obscure literary enemies as well as his depiction in the poem of a debased, quarrelsome, malicious literary world. In contrast, Pope himself is projected as a modestly virtuous man and brilliant poet, concerned only to protect the public from the scurrilous 'weekly riff-raff railers and rhymers'[27] who had plagued him.

The apparatus also helps to clarify Pope's larger intentions. While the notes draw attention to specific allusions to the *Aeneid*, 'Martinus Scriblerus, of the Poem' emphasizes the broader relationship to Virgil of the *Dunciad*'s '*one, great and remarkable action*':

the introduction of the lowest diversions of the rabble in *Smithfield* to be the entertainment of the court and town; or in other words, the Action of the Dunciad is the Removal of the Imperial seat of Dulness from the City to the polite world; as that of the Æneid is the Removal of the empire of *Troy* to *Latium*.[28]

Unlike *The Rape of the Lock* which has its own coherent narrative, the *Dunciad* thus parodies the action of a specific epic. Aubrey Williams's *Pope's Dunciad* (1955) illuminatingly explores this level of epic parody in the poem by means of which Pope depicts Dulness's progress from the lower classes to the irresponsible aristocracy, supported geographically by the fact that the Dunces follow the route from the commercial City to fashionable Westminster taken by the Lord Mayor's procession on the day of his election. The triumph of Dulness's empire is thus displayed simultaneously in the literal procession across London, in the spread of a debased theatrical taste, in the travesty of the *Aeneid*, in parallels with Satan's plot to replace order and light by Chaos and Darkness in *Paradise Lost*, and, especially in Book III, in the explicit relationship of the action to the repeated triumphs of destructive ignorance over civilization in the history of mankind.

The trouble is that what should be mutually intensifying levels of action are sensed only with variable clarity and intensity, sometimes only as amusing hints or allusions, sometimes swamped by the greater immediacy of the local satirical material. Heroic and modern, so perfectly blended in *The Rape of the Lock*, often remain as distinct in the poetry of the *Dunciad* as do the Virgilian parallels and the Dunce-biographies in the footnotes. The relative passivity of Theobald-Aeneas and the dominance of the Goddess also tend to blur the mock-heroic level. As a result, the reader's attention tends to be divided between Pope's fascination with the denizens of Grub Street, the grotesque modern *Aeneid* and the exuberant Scriblerian notes.

Another dichotomy may be sensed between Pope's professed concern for declining standards in the literary world—in publishing, patronage, journalism, criticism and the theatre—and the personal animus behind the satire. Johnson has not been alone in doubting 'that the design was moral, whatever the author might tell either his readers or himself.'[29] Even so, there is more good humour and detached amusement in the poem than has often been allowed, even in the mud and excrement of the mock-heroic games in Book II. Yet Pope's victory over the Dunces must be experienced ultimately in the triumph of his artistry and imagination over his dull and unpleasant material : in, for example, the brilliant depiction of the chaotic breeding-ground of literary dullness in Book I, the strange grandeur of the urinatory contest between the booksellers, the muddy beauty of Smedley's underwater adventures in Fleet Ditch, the melodiously somnolent description of the critics' contest in Book II.

Martinus Scriblerus claimed that the poem moved from dealing with bad poets in Book I to the wider literary scene in Book II, and that Book III 'if well consider'd, seemeth to embrace the whole world'.[30] Certainly, mock-heroic parallels do little to lighten the gloomy eloquence of certain passages in this vision of collapsing civilizations (e.g. 1729 text, iii. 75–92). Yet the debased theatrical tastes of the decade which Pope goes on to describe, even if transformed with brilliant wit and imagination into symbols of chaos and blasphemy, hardly seem grave enough to carry the threat to traditional civilized values that Pope foresees in the superb closing vision of the final triumph of Dulness. Pope's consciousness of the disparity may be sensed in a footnote which emphasizes that this is only a prophecy, although he warns the reader not to 'rest too secure in thy contempt of the Instruments for such a revolution in learning' (iii. 337n.). Book IV, added in 1742, was to contain a much more sustained and far-reaching argument for the imminence of such a collapse of civilized values than a vogue for John Rich's pantomimes.

III

Satisfying as his spirited rout of his literary enemies must have been, Pope knew that many friends and admirers did not find the *Dunciad* particularly elevating. By November 1729 he was committed to a more edifying project, described to Swift as 'a system of Ethics in the Horatian way' and again, in the summer of 1730, as 'a book, to make mankind look upon this life with comfort and pleasure, and put morality in good humour'.[31] Now, presumably, Pope 'stoop'd to Truth, and moraliz'd his song'.[32] He was planning an elaborate series of ethical poems, in which what later became the *Essay on Man* was 'to be to the whole work what a scale is to a book of maps', merely the first of four books.[33] Although the scheme as a whole had in effect been abandoned by the mid-1730s, the four *Moral Essays* were to have appeared in Book II of the 'Ethic Epistles', from which material was also later salvaged for Book IV of the *Dunciad*. At the end of his life he was still planning to use material from Book III in his epic 'Brutus'.

The *Essay on Man* was to provide the intellectual framework of the great plan. Its philosophical background and content, and the theological controversy in which it was eventually involved, can hardly be discussed in detail here.[34] It is compounded of diverse and hardly reconciled elements: Renaissance Platonism, Newtonian science, traditional theodicy (the explanation of the existence of evil in a benevolent universe), and the ideas of Pope's philosopher friend Lord Bolingbroke (although the old belief that Pope merely versified Bolingbroke's prose arguments is no longer taken seriously). Underlying and unifying the poem is the venerable, Platonic concept of the Great Chain of Being, the vast, perfectly ordered, all-inclusive hierarchy of created things, rising from inanimate matter, through insects and animals, to man, the angels and God. If Pope is denied this premise, his whole argument about man, society and the universe totters or serves only to elaborate a myth of dubious potency. For Johnson, Pope's 'metaphysical morality' was at best 'the talk of his mother and his nurse' happily disguised. Hazlitt commented of Pope's professed aim that 'All that he says . . . would prove just as well that whatever is, is *wrong*, as that whatever is, is *right*.'[35]

Whatever its philosophical shortcomings the *Essay* has a careful organization which can be in itself aesthetically attractive. Its importance to an understanding of Pope lies in the fact that it is a solemn, climactic expression of themes found throughout his poetry in submerged or allusive forms. Man's fixed place in the Chain of Being is viewed in a series of perspectives. In Epistle I the emphasis is on man's pettiness, blindness and pride in questioning divine, beneficent purposes beyond his comprehension. Epistle II stresses both man's divided and ambiguous nature, placed as he is between the beasts and the angels, and God's power to turn this faulty nature to good, reconciling the apparently opposed drives of self-love and reason through the Ruling Passion. Epistle III applies to the evolution of human society the consequences of the pervasive principle of love in the Chain of Being, which reconciles human self-love and the apparently opposed social instinct. In Epistle IV Pope defines happiness as dependent precisely on man's capacity to discipline himself into accepting humbly what the poem has established: his limited place in God's providential purposes, the frailty of his nature, and the necessity of fulfilling God's providence through benevolence and charity.

The argument, such as it is, and the poetic energy of the *Essay* exist in an unpredictable relationship. Pope himself told Spence that his real problem lay 'not only in settling and ranging the parts of [the *Essay*] aright, but in making them agreeable enough to be read with pleasure.' His remarks on 'The Design', added to the poem in 1734, also recognize the danger of becoming 'dry and tedious' in such a poem, but equally claim the impossibility of treating philosophical material 'more *poetically*, without sacrificing perspicuity to ornament, without wandring from the precision, or breaking the chain of reasoning'.[36] One of the poetic problems Pope failed to solve was that of tone. The conversational, urbane but earnest, Horatian voice of the opening and closing passages of personal address to Bolingbroke is not sustained. More often Pope is driven towards either strident, exclamatory, didactic tones, scornfully denouncing human pride and frailty, or the complacency of a man who (paradoxically, in view of the poem's argument) is admitted to confident knowledge of God's purposes. As one critic has suggested, Pope tends to assume the role and tone of God himself.[37]

Much of the rhetoric of the poem springs from the sometimes laborious irony with which Pope contrasts God's power and wisdom with man's ignorance and weakness : 'Tho' Man's a fool, yet GOD IS WISE' (ii. 294). Man's contradictory nature in itself can be impressively dissected by means of antithesis, paradox and bathos, as in the wellknown lines at the beginning of Epistle II. Elsewhere there is occasional scope for Pope's delicacy of perception and power of imaginative metamorphosis, as in the lines on man's desire for keener senses :

> Say what the use, were finer optics giv'n,
> T' inspect a mite, not comprehend the heav'n ?
> Or touch, if tremblingly alive all o'er,
> To smart and agonize at ev'ry pore ?
> Or quick effluvia darting thro' the brain,
> Die of a rose in aromatic pain ?
> If nature thunder'd in his op'ning ears,
> And stunn'd him with the music of the spheres,
> How would he wish that Heav'n had left him still
> The whisp'ring Zephyr, and the purling rill ?

(i. 195–204)

The description of the hierarchy of the senses in the animals shows how even the remote notion of the Chain of Being could be treated with sensitive particularity (i. 207–18). Later, Pope evokes the relationship of part and whole, the change and stability of nature, with sustained energy in one long unbroken paragraph which, overriding all antitheses and connecting all extremes, convincingly enacts his positive affirmation (i. 267–80).

If Pope has his successes, awkward shifts of tone and perspective still occur as he turns from praising God's wisdom to jeering at man's folly. When the perspectives are mingled, poetic and philosophic interests can seem to diverge, as in the analogy which Pope offers to illustrate God's benevolent concealment from man of all but his 'present state':

> The lamb thy riot dooms to bleed to-day,
> Had he thy Reason, would he skip and play?
> Pleas'd to the last, he crops the flow'ry food,
> And licks the hand just rais'd to shed his blood.
>
> (i. 81–4)

Officially, no doubt, the reader should recognize an implicit *contrast* between God's attitude to man and man's to the lamb. Poetically and in its context, the analogy suggests that God *is* to man as the butcher to the lamb, so that man becomes a slaughtered lamb in God's merciless hands. Even the famous lines on the 'poor Indian' (i. 99–112), complicate rather than illuminate Pope's argument: once more the divine and human perspectives (man is frail and yet a manifestation of God's power) seem imperfectly focused or opportunistically exploited.

Spasmodically, but increasingly in Epistle IV, the contemplation of human folly and unhappiness offered richer scope for Pope's characteristic blend of moral concern with compressed, ironic analysis:

> Honour and shame from no Condition rise;
> Act well your part, there all the honour lies.
> Fortune in Men has some small diff'rence made,
> One flaunts in rags, one flutters in brocade,
> The cobler apron'd, and the parson gown'd,
> The friar hooded, and the monarch crown'd.
> 'What differ more (you cry) than crown and cowl?'
> I'll tell you, friend, A Wise man and a Fool.
> You'll find, if once the monarch acts the monk,
> Or, cobler-like, the parson will be drunk,
> Worth makes the man, and want of it, the fellow;
> The rest is all but leather or prunella.
>
> (iv. 193–204)

The anonymous publication of Epistles I–III in March 1733 (Epistle IV in January 1734) meant that for a time Pope could enjoy the unguarded acclaim of the literary world, including that of several old enemies. If in this way Pope managed to prove something to himself and his contemporaries, he seems also to have learned his own lesson from the *Essay on Man*: his own 'proper study' was going to be man himself, scrutinized more closely than these vast philosophic perspectives had permitted. As early as 1732 he had told Swift: 'I know nothing that moves strongly but Satire'. By the end of 1734 he was admitting: 'Imagination has no limits . . . but where one is confined to Truth . . . we soon find the shortness of our Tether.' [38]

Pope's real concerns at this period had already been appearing in his four *Moral Essays* [39] (1731–35), which he himself at first wished to be related to his larger project, rather than 'ignorantly look'd upon one by one'.[40] Yet increasingly Pope's poetic imagination was responding to deviations from the natural order, to perversions of his aesthetic or social ideals, to the frailty and vice lurking behind façades of virtue, beauty or piety —the 'slums' behind the façade of his society. From now on, Pope found man's restless, self-destructive impulses more inevitable, as if the harmony and order he affirmed as universal principles were more precarious than he admitted. Undoubtedly Pope's growing pessimism was deeply influenced by Bolingbroke's long campaign against the government, in which Walpole's administration by patronage and bribery was condemned as merely a prominent manifestation of the fraud and corruption of the new capitalistic economic system which had developed since 1688. To Bolingbroke and Pope, as to Swift and Gay, economic individualism and opportunism were undermining the traditional social order and all the older humanistic values. The South Sea Bubble of 1720 had symbolized the social disorder involved in the new commercialism. The elegiac strain in Pope's earlier poetry turns now to a gloomier conviction that what seemed the total degradation of public life under Walpole closely paralleled the decline of Roman civilization; that the new Augustan age was similarly doomed. Pope's poetry from this period is never far, explicitly or implicitly, from what has been called 'the politics of nostalgia', the appeal to vanishing social and political ideals in the face of a new and inevitable order.

The *Moral Essays* are Horatian epistles and the tone is now usually adjusted sensitively to the addressee, who in himself will embody the values Pope is recommending. As Reuben

Brower has pointed out,[41] the tone of polite, Roman cultivation in the *Epistle to Lord Burlington* (1731) is appropriate to this nobleman who was publishing Palladio's *Designs* at this time and was himself an important figure in English neo-classical architecture. The simple, functional grandeur of the architecture, and the close cooperation of Art and Nature in the landscape gardening, approved by Pope and Burlington are the poem's unifying ideals. True taste based on an intelligent, cultivated sensitivity to the order and processes of Nature ('good Sense') is steadily related to wider moral and social concerns. The lines on the destruction of Sabinus' 'growing woods' by his son's 'finer Taste' invoke values which are more than horticultural:

> The thriving plants ignoble broomsticks made,
> Now sweep those Alleys they were born to shade.
>
> (97–8)

The characteristic compression only stresses the shocking reduction of the thriving plants to broomsticks, a shock reinforced by the suggested social degradation ('ignoble', 'born to shade'). Within this single couplet aesthetic sensibility, filial piety, aristocratic dignity, the social order and the vital processes of nature are all violently affronted.

Wider moral and social values are similarly involved in the superb account of Timon's villa (99–176), which offends all the principles of taste established earlier in the poem. The huge house is proudly disproportionate to its puny owner, the elaborate gardens coldly formal, a sterile perversion of the natural order. The tastelessness is closely related to the intellectual vacuity of the library, the inappropriately festive chapel and the solemn, inhospitable rites of the dining-hall. The disproportion and disorder are described in vivid and amusing, but always pointed detail. Pope's own positive beliefs are presented less convincingly in his final assertion that Timon's vain extravagance turns ultimately to social good (such are the ways of Providence) than in his brief but compelling vision of the ultimate triumph of a fruitful, resurgent, regal nature over Timon's barren luxury:

> Another age shall see the golden Ear
> Imbrown the Slope, and nod on the Parterre,
> Deep Harvests bury all his pride has plann'd,
> And laughing Ceres re-assume the land.
>
> (173–6)

The closing lines relate Pope's views on taste to social ideals consciously opposed to what he felt to be the growing self-interest and prodigality of the age. The virtues of the good land-owner radiate out to the benefit of society as a whole (181–90); and Burlington's own architectural plans are seen as potentially serving society and the nation in the glorious and patriotic functions of building harbours, bridges and churches.

These lines have a classical dignity and expansiveness which Pope was hardly to recapture. His darkening vision was not lightened by the malicious identification of Timon as his friend the Duke of Chandos. To avoid misconstructions, he resolved to use real names in future in his satires, to refuse a comfortable separation of life and art, a practice he later justified as follows:

> To attack Vices in the abstract, without touching Persons, may be safe fighting indeed, but it is fighting with Shadows. General propositions are obscure, misty, and uncertain, compar'd with plain, full, and home examples: Precepts only apply to our Reason, which in most men is but weak: Examples are pictures, and strike the Senses, nay raise the Passions, and call in those (the strongest and most general of all motives) to the aid of reformation.[42]

The *Epistle to Lord Bathurst* (1733) dissects the *actual* operations of man and society with uncompromising directness, focusing on, and now naming, the financiers, misers, prodigals, and speculators whose antithetically arranged portraits occupy much of the poem. There are passages of humorously inventive, richly allusive fantasy even on the subject of the corrupting power of gold and paper money (35–78). Yet Pope himself significantly spoke of the poem as a sermon [43] and Christian allusions and undertones are unusually pervasive. The assertion, explicitly carried over from the *Essay on Man*, that Heaven turns all evil to good (161–78) might seem to absolve man from any moral responsibility. Yet when he is closer to the actual workings of society, Pope's conviction that man must co-operate actively with Providence is explicit. The meekly pious bishop who leaves the poor only 'Providence's care' (108) is as despicable as Old Cotta the miser, whose life is described, partly by skilful allusion, as a travesty of a virtuous retirement from the world and as an abnegation of all traditional social responsibilities. Cotta likewise declines to 'take the Poor from Providence' (188).

Bathurst himself embodies for Pope a practical ideal of

liberality and charity, which is emphasized by the balance and sanity of the couplets as a classical mean between the extremes of avarice and prodigality (219–28). Yet Pope felt obliged to go further and to depict in the Man of Ross (249–82) a transcendental charity, which combined aspects of Moses and Christ in its creative, harmonizing beneficence. The conscious exaggeration of the virtues of the real John Kyrle [44] is betrayed in the uneasy pastoral effects, the hyperbole and the somewhat predictable rhetorical strategy. The following lines on Hopkins the miser, whose 'end' is contrasted with that of the Man of Ross, have a compressed subtlety denied to the affirmation of Christian charity:

> When Hopkins dies, a thousand lights attend
> The wretch, who living sav'd a candle's end:
> Should'ring God's altar a vile image stands,
> Belies his features, nay extends his hands;
> That live-long wig which Gorgon's self might own,
> Eternal buckle takes in Parian stone.
>
> (291–6)

The blasphemously obtrusive effigy of the miser ironically extends its hands in a way Hopkins had never done in charity, but all too faithfully fixes the ancient wig he had meanly refused to replace in ironically 'eternal' buckle. These lines are followed in turn by the superb transition to the powerful rhythms and dramatic syntax of the description of the deathbed of the wastrel Duke of Buckingham.

The *Epistle to Lord Cobham* (1734) again carries over a principle from the *Essay on Man*. Yet when Pope at last triumphantly produces the Ruling Passion as the key to the various contradictions in human character he has been describing, it turns out to have little to do with its original providential function of reconciling discordant impulses in man. The solution (the lust for praise) to the puzzle of Wharton's extravagant, self-defeating character (180–227) seems insignificant by comparison with Pope's relentlessly precise definition of the puzzle itself. The sketches which conclude the epistle purport to show the Ruling Passion surviving to the moment of death, yet once again the effect may be more complex than Pope intended. These snatches of conversation, ironically placed by Pope's diction in an eternal perspective, in their very incomprehension of what death involves, convey a strangely pathetic sense of the tenacity with which men cling to life:

> The frugal Crone, whom praying priests attend,
> Still tries to save the hallow'd taper's end,
> Collects her breath, as ebbing life retires,
> For one puff more, and in that puff expires.
>   'Odious! in woollen! 'twould a Saint provoke,
> (Were the last words that poor Narcissa spoke)
> No, let a charming Chintz, and Brussels lace
> Wrap my cold limbs, and shade my lifeless face:
> One would not, sure, be frightful when one's dead—
> And—Betty—give this Cheek a little Red.'

(238–47)

The intimate, apparently casual but always purposeful opening of the *Epistle to a Lady* (1735) perfectly illustrates Pope's tactful ability to adapt his tone to his addressee (in this case his old friend Martha Blount). Much of the poem is devoted to a series of female character sketches of increasing scope and severity, the first sequence culminating in the account of the self-destructive aggression and energy of Atossa (115–50). The character sketches are explicitly offered as portraits and Pope makes good use of the painting metaphor in this gallery of female poses. Deftly blending fragments of behaviour, descriptive detail, impersonation and psychological and emotional insight, these characters add up to a searching exposure of the trivial hypocritical or self-deceiving values of fashionable female society.

If the poem has any relationship with the *Essay on Man*, it lies less in the attempt to adapt the theory of the Ruling Passion to women (207–18) than in the implicit demonstration that virtue and happiness are identical. All the folly and lack of self-knowledge Pope has been describing are summarised in one of his finest passages in which he exposes with surgical attentiveness the fate which awaits such women:

> As Hags hold Sabbaths, less for joy than spight,
> So these their merry, miserable Night;
> Still round and round the Ghosts of Beauty glide,
> And haunt the places where their Honour dy'd.
>   See how the World its Veterans rewards!
> A Youth of frolicks, an old Age of Cards,
> Fair to no purpose, artful to no end,
> Young without Lovers, old without a Friend,
> A Fop their Passion, but their Prize a Sot,
> Alive, ridiculous, and dead, forgot!

(239–48)

The closing lines take their meaning largely from the contrasting tone in which Pope addresses Martha Blount, easy but respectful, affectionate yet earnest. In this way she becomes a fully realized embodiment, in contrast with the preceding unhappy poseurs, of the practical virtues of equanimity, good sense, self-discipline and tact which alone bring contentment and an ability to come to terms with the processes of time.

The *Moral Essays* reveal all the characteristics of Pope's mature verse, in which the power and conviction lie less in the direct assertion of positive values than in the very texture of the verse itself, in the inescapable sense of an extraordinarily alert moral intelligence, which is hardly to be separated from the concentration, discipline and incisiveness of the couplets. Here is the true 'living variety' [45] of Pope's poetry: not merely the variety of subject matter he can now turn to his purposes, but the versatility of his rhetorical resources in the handling of the couplet, increasingly flexible in rhythm, in range of allusion, in the blend and contrast of ironic, fervent and tender tones, in the wealth of witty and surprising imagery, in incisive analysis or the play of humorous imagination.

IV

The casual and rapid manner in which Pope wrote the first of his *Imitations of Horace* (*Satire* II. i.) during an illness early in 1733 might seem to justify Johnson's description (if not the implicit evaluation) of them as 'relaxations of his genius'.[46] Yet, far from remaining a digression from his great ethical scheme, the Horatian poems were to become Pope's main literary mode later in the 1730s. In turning to the form of the explicit Imitation, adapting classical masterpieces to modern circumstances, which had become a recognized genre in the later seventeenth century, Pope was merely taking his lifelong poetic interest in classical literature to its logical, formal conclusion. His aim was not merely to achieve witty parallels or ironic disparities between ancient Rome and modern Britain. He began writing the *Imitations* because of the 'clamour' which greeted his *Moral Essays*: '*An Answer from* Horace *was both more full, and of more Dignity, than any I cou'd have made in my own person*'.[47] To imitate and adapt Horace was to claim a place in the long tradition of satirists who had been driven to justify their indignation at contemporary evils, to relate his own immediate conflict to a timeless confrontation of virtue and vice.

Pope no doubt also realized that the Imitation, which by its nature might seem to guarantee a degree of detachment from his material, in fact allowed him to be more deeply personal than any other extended form his age offered him. Yet the way in which he blends his own voice with that of Horace is complex: personal passages in the *Imitations* should not be taken as either complacent autobiography or as the assertions of a purely fictional character. If the satirist's idealism is reinforced by the classical authority and dignity of Horace, the direct relationship with the poet's own life at the same time insists on its contemporary relevance. Pope's quiet retreat at Twickenham from the corruption of the great world, his friends' and his own isolation from power, his uncompromising art, operate with the immediacy of fact and the suggestiveness of symbol in these poems.

While each of Horace's satires and epistles gave Pope a 'form' to work in or against, their relatively naturalistic or informal organization sanctioned a variety of subjects, moods and tones within the same poem. As recently as 1730 Pope had spoken of the importance of correctness, decorum and consistency within the different poetic kinds:[48] some instinct had in fact been drawing him to a form which encouraged informality and variety. Pope often uses the urbane, good-humoured, gracefully ironic 'Horatian' tone to gain the confidence and amused sympathy of his readers at the opening of a poem:

> There are (I scarce can think it, but am told)
> There are to whom my Satire seems too bold,
> Scarce to wise *Peter* complaisant enough,
> And something said of *Chartres* much too rough.
> The Lines are weak, another's pleas'd to say,
> Lord *Fanny* spins a thousand such a Day.
> Tim'rous by Nature, of the Rich in awe,
> I come to Council learned in the Law.

> (*Sat.* II. i. 1–8)

By the end of the poem Pope's voice is vibrant with a characteristic combination of moral fervour and contempt. The measure of this dramatic development is the difference between the ironic meekness of line 7 above and his angry defiance of the 'rich or noble knave' in 118–24.[49] Such developments are often assisted by the use of dialogue with a cautious friend or adversary, whose 'good sense', by contrast with the satirist's fearless integrity and idealism, steadily comes to seem expediency or willingness to compromise.

Whereas in the *Moral Essays* Pope's addressees had dictated the tone and embodied the values of the poem, Pope now centres in the satirist himself (Horace-Pope) the courage and virtue he is commending, and the satirist's own tone is crucial in defining these qualities. In *Satire* II. i. 105ff. Pope adapts to himself the virtues attributed by Horace to the satirist Lucilius. In *Satire* II. ii. 129–60 the poet himself once more claims the old-fashioned virtues attributed in the original to Ofellus, whose career Pope parallels with the various troubles of his own lifetime. The simplicity, moderation, and independence of his life at Twickenham, as described here, were no doubt intended to contrast with the corruption and luxury of which Pope, like Bolingbroke, was accusing the Court and Government. But the detailed references to his garden, his hospitality, his friends, the sense of involvement with the local community in this passage, relate to the wider ideals of social responsibility, and of the necessary union of use and beauty, stressed in the *Epistle to Burlington*. The verse, shunning all formality or pretentiousness, in itself guarantees the poet's integrity, a preference of moral to literary harmony made almost monosyllabically explicit in *Epistle* II. ii :

> Well, on the whole, *plain* Prose must be my fate :
> Wisdom (curse on it) will come soon or late.
> There is a time when Poets will grow dull :
> I'll e'en leave Verses to the Boys at school :
> To Rules of Poetry no more confin'd,
> I learn to smooth and harmonize my Mind,
> Teach ev'ry Thought within its bounds to roll,
> And keep the equal Measure of the Soul.

> (198–205)

The three paragraphs which follow these lines (206–29) illustrate most of the possibilities the Horatian Imitation offered Pope : the variety of tones, the skilful transitions between them, the colloquial metrical flexibility, and the introduction of bitterly satiric allusions or episodes springing from little or nothing in Horace. If, as has been suggested, Pope tends to lose Horace's more serious or noble tones, there are still passages which have a weight and resonance hardly to be found elsewhere in his poetry :

> Years foll'wing Years, steal something ev'ry day,
> At last they steal us from our selves away;
> In one our Frolicks, one Amusements end,
> In one a Mistress drops, in one a Friend :
> This subtle Thief of Life, this paltry Time,
> What will it leave me, if it snatch my Rhime?
> If ev'ry Wheel of that unweary'd Mill
> That turn'd ten thousand Verses, now stands still.
>
> (*Epistle* II. ii. 72–9)

Yet the spare, plain, apparently improvised style remains the norm : elevated tones tend to be ironic, as most notably and, in the end, explicitly at the conclusion of *Epistle* II. i. ('To Augustus').

The most powerful of Pope's 'Horatian' poems dispense with specific models. The *Epistle to Dr. Arbuthnot* (1735), ostensibly an exercise in self-defence against attacks on '*not only my Writings . . . but my* Person, Morals, *and* Family',[50] becomes a potent affirmation of the integrity and dignity of his life and art, and an incisive indictment of corruption and degradation in the literary world of his day. The colloquially dramatic opening lines, the rueful humour at his predicament as he is besieged by mad, bad poets at home and at church, gain our confidence, while steadily defining the persistent menace he faces. The shift in tone whenever Arbuthnot is directly addressed, the implied sincerity and depth of this friendship, has an important normative function in a poem so concerned to expose insincerity, flattery and malice. Arbuthnot's role as Pope's doctor also permits the recurrent contrast of Pope's ill-health and physical vulnerability with his moral energy and courage.

Pope eventually embarks on a long justification of his literary career, in which the reader's responses are skilfully manipulated. (Johnson commented that 'In this poem Pope seems to reckon with the publick.'[51]) His enemies are repeatedly associated with disease and dirt, insects and animals, a process which reaches its climax in the portrait of Sporus (305–33). This startling passage cannot simply be reduced to the level of Pope's quarrel with Lord Hervey. In its context this portrait of the speciously beautiful but insidious, morally and sexually ambiguous, tempter and corrupter of the Court contains the final definition of the evil Pope is denouncing. Poetically, what matters is 'the wonderful play of fancy' in these lines, which Byron cited to illustrate Pope's 'teeming . . . *imagination*'[52] : the intensity of the rapid succession of animal images, the harsh diction and taut versification, the paradoxes which trans-fix the elusive evil of Sporus in the final couplet.

The earlier portrait of Addison as Atticus (193–214) works quite differently. The long conditional sentence, with its anti-thetic clauses, conveys at once Pope's professed regret at Addi-son's weaknesses and the intonations of the malicious reserve and insecurity which undermined Addison's candour and good nature. Memorable as these portraits are, however, they must be read in the context of the fluctuating tones and moods of the poem, ranging from patient good humour and humility to bitterness and moral fervour, and of the repeated confrontations between good and evil which give the poem its structure.

The *Imitations* written in 1736–38 reflect Pope's increasingly explicit involvement through Bolingbroke in the Opposition's unsuccessful efforts to depose Walpole's government. Pope was now moving steadily away from the acceptable 'raillery' which his age thought was all the more effective if it never lost an urbane self-control.[53] In some ways the Horatian balance and moderation had always been under strain from Pope's more intense and aggressive moral concern, his fascination with the dark, grotesque details of the evil he had been deploring. More than one contemporary in fact detected the influence of an-other Roman satiric model in his *Imitations*.[54] The contrast of Horace's 'agreeable Mixture of good Sense, and of true Pleas-antry' with Juvenal's 'Anger, Indignation, Rage, Disdain, and the violent Emotions, and vehement Style of Tragedy' was fami-liar to the age. Dryden, in his *Discourse Concerning Satire* (1693), had implied that Horace's urbanity was close to insipidity and servility and had preferred Juvenal.[55]

By the time of the first *Dialogue* (1738) of the *Epilogue to the Satires* equanimity and detachment had become for Pope luxuries that the satirist could hardly afford. The insidious 'Friend' actually contrasts Horace's tactful, oblique satiric man-ner with Pope's embarrassingly blunt and intense mode (19–22). Maynard Mack has described the social concensus which usually lies behind satire, its tendency to promote the assurance that life does make moral sense, its emphasis on social solidarity rather than the lonely values of the tragic hero.[56] In that case the *Epilogue to the Satires* leans towards the tragic mode, as Pope's dramatised satirist adopts a stance of isolated, desperate, heroic opposition to contemporary corruption. That despera-tion no doubt reflects the particular frustrations of the Opposi-tion party, but also Pope's deeper disillusion at the apparent collapse of so many early ideals. As he wrote in 1738:

I can but Skirmish, & maintain a flying Fight with Vice; its Forces augment, & will drive me off the Stage, before I shall see the Effects complete, either of Divine Providence or Vengeance; for sure we can be quite Saved only by the One, or punishd by the other: The Condition of Morality is so desperate, as to be above all Human Hands.[57]

This is the mood of the *Epilogue to the Satires*. *Dialogue I* works through preliminary ironic manoeuvres towards the bitter concluding vision of the triumphant procession of Vice. The only artistic strategy Pope is left with in the end is the stark, abstract definition of this total and startling subversion of values (160, 170), and the lonely defiance of his own satire. In *Dialogue* II he develops his own self-dramatising definition of Virtue. A new intensity enters the verse at line 171, with the extraordinary simile in which Pope compares certain 'Courtly Wits' to 'hogs in Huts of *Westphaly*'. The disgust which some readers have shared with the 'Friend' at this protracted image is precisely what Pope hoped to arouse:

> This filthy Simile, this beastly Line,
> Quite turns my Stomach—*P*[*ope*]. So does Flatt'ry mine. . . .

In this artistically risky, almost desperate, way, Pope hoped to convey the violent moral revulsion which he himself felt.

If Pope's final lonely, fervent moralizing seems harsh and eccentric, that oddness only reinforces the satirist's isolated refusal to join in the knavery or slavery to which the rest of society had assented (197–219). At the very end Pope at last attains something like the true heroic tones after which his generation had always hankered—but ironically only in a vision of the collapse of Augustan ideals. The satirist has now dramatized society into his own tragic universe:

> Yes, the last Pen for Freedom let me draw,
> When Truth stands trembling on the edge of Law:
> Here, Last of *Britons!* let your Names be read;
> Are none, none living? let me praise the Dead,
> And for that Cause which made your Fathers shine,
> Fall, by the Votes of their degen'rate Line!

> (248–53)

The shocked 'Friend' ends by urging Pope to write more *Essays on Man*: more reassuring, optimistic theorising about the benevolent purposes of the universe, turning evil in man's nature and society to good. Even if Pope was not retracting his earlier theories, he was bitterly aware of the disparity between that generalized vision and the evils in contemporary society which now flooded his senses.

There were other reasons for Pope's growing sense of isolation. Gay and Arbuthnot had died earlier in the decade. Swift in Dublin was in his seventies, less and less communicable with, soon to be thought mad. From about 1740 Pope became increasingly dependent on William Warburton, an intelligent, if ambitious and arrogant, clergyman, who had voluntarily defended the *Essay on Man* against Continental attacks on its heterodox and fatalistic implications. Before long Warburton ('the greatest general critic I ever knew',[58] Pope called him) was assisting the poet with the definitive edition of his works which now preoccupied him. It was apparently Warburton who encouraged him to add a new Book to the *Dunciad*. To some extent Pope could draw on material once intended for the 'Ethic Epistles', described in 1736 as dealing with the 'Extent and Limits of Human Reason, and Science', and the use of the arts and learning, which concluded with 'a Satire against the misapplication of all these, exemplify'd by pictures, characters, and examples'.[59] The *New Dunciad*, as it was called, appeared in March 1742 and was followed in October 1743 by a revised edition of the whole poem.

Colley Cibber's *Letter to Mr. Pope* (1742), protesting against Pope's frequent satiric references to him, had by then conveniently provided a replacement for Theobald as the poem's hero. The vain and blandly ingenuous Cibber was a much more appropriate symbol of Pope's developing definition of Dulness. An incompetent poet, acclaimed as an actor mainly for his foppish roles, a supporter of the Government, as Poet Laureate identified with the Court, Cibber's career to that appointment precisely embodied the process in the *Dunciad* by which Pope believed debased literary taste had spread upwards through a degenerating society. The change gave added point to the theatrical material in the poem and permitted new references to the Court (e.g. i. 213–4, 299–318).

Although Pope revised and expanded Books I–III, the greater scope and seriousness of the new Book IV still set it apart. Pope himself admitted in a note that: 'This Book may properly be distinguished from the former, by the Name of the GREATER DUNCIAD, not so indeed in Size, but in Subject'. Partly due to Warburton's influence, the notes have a more ponderous religious and philosophical emphasis. The mock-heroic action has virtually ended, although recurrent allusions to *Paradise Lost* impart a new diabolic urgency to the Dunces' dedication to chaos and disorder. After a single reference (iv. 20), Cibber as hero disappears. Dulness herself and the triumph of her empire are unambiguously the main subjects. The vaguely defined setting is some sort of royal drawing-room, where the goddess receives her suitors and eventually bestows her degrees upon them. The main figures in each episode, though amusingly dramatized as individuals, are basically representative of some radical subversion of nature, reason or order. As a result the satire has a deeper seriousness and lacks the sense of personal animus or over-reaction at merely literary offences in the earlier books. Pope himself was ruefully conscious of the different impact of Book IV: 'my Poem . . . dealing much in General, not particular Satire, has stirrd up little or no Resentment. Tho it be leveld much higher than the former, yet Men not being singled out from the Herd, bear Chastisement better'.[60]

Pope's references to Book IV as 'higher' or 'greater' than Books I–III point partly to the higher social sphere he was now concentrating on, as he admitted in 1742, when he contrasted 'the whole polite world' with the 'Dunces of a lower Species' he had satirized in 1728. He was also conscious of a loftier moral purpose, of 'a Good Conscience, a bold Spirit, & Zeal for Truth, at whatsoever Expence, of whatever Pretenders to Science, or of all Imposition either Literary, Moral, or Political'.[61] Yet the split between Books I–III and Book IV is by no means total. Book IV exploits climactically various images and processes associated with Dulness from the beginning: images of literary, social and moral disorder and negation, of mist, shadow and darkness swallowing up light, of sleep overpowering intelligence and reason, of jabbering, braying or stupefying noise, of perverted language, of formless, irresistible crowds or swarms, such as the seething chaos of the debased literary breeding-ground (i. 51–70, 121–6), the flow of the Dunces across London and the grotesque, if menacing, black crowds drawn to Dulness in Book IV (73–80, 189–92, 397–400).

Pope was now anxious to present Dulness as more than mere inert stupidity. Cibber's mixture of pert vivacity with stupidity (i. 109n., 111–12) had helped to qualify him as hero and a new note to Book I carefully identified Dulness as a busy, bold, agressive unreason (i. 15n.), 'a ruling principle not inert, but turning topsy-turvy the Understanding, and inducing an Anarchy or confused State of Mind'. Many images help to define the formidable momentum of Dulness as a sinister, thriving, swelling, monstrous disorder, seeking to fulfil itself in the triumph of darkness and chaos.

Expectations based on Books I–III, and the grotesque poetic imagination which animates the satire, have tended to obscure Pope's basic concern in Book IV with the extended process by which he believed the upper classes were being trained to play a passive part in a corrupt and cynical society. Dr. Busby proudly relates the narrow, sterile education with which he stifled Fancy and Wit in his boys at Westminster School; Dr. Bentley boasts of the meaningless pedantry of the universities (iv. 139–274). One of Pope's most brilliant passages then describes the modern travesty of the Grand Tour which had traditionally completed a humane education, the civilizing and reverent journey in scholarly company through the relics of classical civilization. In verse of appropriately decadent pastoral beauty, Pope wittily and allusively dwells on the triviality and depravity which are the only outcome of the complacent tour of his 'young Aeneas' through a charmingly degenerate modern Europe:

> Intrepid then, o'er seas and lands he flew:
> Europe he saw, and Europe saw him too.
> There all thy gifts and graces we display,
> Thou, only thou, directing all our way!
> To where the Seine, obsequious as she runs,
> Pours at great Bourbon's feet her silken sons;
> Or Tyber, now no longer Roman, rolls,
> Vain of Italian Arts, Italian Souls:
> To happy Convents, bosom'd deep in vines,
> Where slumber Abbots, purple as their wines:
> To Isles of fragrance, lilly-silver'd vales,
> Diffusing languor in the panting gales:
> To lands of singing, or of dancing slaves,
> Love-whisp'ring woods, and lute-resounding waves.
>
> (iv. 293–306)

The returned tourist and his kind, the irresponsible, bored upper classes, remain the chief concern of Pope and the goddess for the rest of the work (cp. iv. 337–46). Her next suppliants are those who further her cause by providing fashionable hobbies trivial or misleading enough to occupy the idle young: the agent for bogus antiques, the numismatist, the botanist and the natural scientist. In this way the somnolent young are drawn into pursuits precisely expressive of their own dull, bewildered intellects:

The common Soul, of Heav'n's more frugal make,
Serves but to keep fools pert, and knaves awake:
A drowzy Watchman, that just gives a knock,
And breaks our rest, to tell us what's a clock.
Yet by some object ev'ry brain is stirr'd;
The dull may waken to a Humming-bird;
The most recluse, discreetly open'd find
Congenial matter in the Cockle-kind;
The mind, in Metaphysics at a loss,
May wander in a wilderness of Moss . . . .

(iv. 441-50)

Such pursuits, concentrating on the part and the surface, obscuring the whole and God's larger purposes, advance the cause of Dulness. This deeper concern, closely related to the arguments of the *Essay on Man*, leads to a passage on free-thinkers as a related manifestation of Dulness: in this very different context, we meet again that arrogance and pride which lead man to an inflated sense of his importance in the universe and to an account of nature from which God is excluded (iv. 453-86). For Pope, literary, religious and political ideals were hardly separable in his vision of an ideal order, whose subversion he was now climactically describing. The end-product of this perverted educational process, 'A trifling head, and a contracted heart' (iv. 504), is ripe for exploitation by political tyranny, dramatized in the old wizard (Walpole) and his cup of self-love (iv. 517-28). By now the definition of Dulness covers the decay of private and public morality, and the spread of political and financial corruption. After conferring her degrees and titles, the goddess gives her final charge and blessing in a vision of grotesque chaos in the social hierarchy (iv. 579-604).

In the climactic vision of negation, which begins with the goddess's yawn (iv. 605), sleep and darkness spectacularly spread across land and sea. The poet makes one last epic gesture (see iv. 620n.), an ironically conventional appeal for aid to the Muse, but both 'the Poet and the Song' must also travel into the all-consuming darkness, as he had earlier forecast (iv. 1-8), a darkness which is overpowering imagination, wit, the arts and sciences, philosophy, religion and morality. It is no doubt wiser, certainly more comfortable, to read Book IV as a lament for a lost political and social order, for supposedly irrecoverable humanistic values, rather than as an assertion of the totally unregenerate nature of man and society. Pope's actual views were not entirely negative, as the implicit parallels with his more positive writings, as well as his letters, might indicate. The fact remains that, as in the *Imitations of Horace*, it is the negative vision which can inspire in Pope verse of a heroic, tragic grandeur which was not convincingly available to him elsewhere. Ironically enough, one of the few verse fragments which survive from the very last years of Pope's life, was the opening of the blank-verse epic 'Brutus' which he had long planned to write. Not surprisingly, this tentative fumbling in an unfamiliar verse-form for an expansive tone in which to celebrate 'Britain's Glory' was not continued beyond the first eight lines.[62]

In January 1743 Pope wrote: 'I have seen and heard, what makes me shut my Eyes, & Ears, and retire inward into my own Heart . . . I have lost all Ardor and Appetite, even to Satyr, for no body has Shame enough left to be afraid of Reproach, or punish'd by it.'[63] His last years were devoted to the definitive edition of his works, and to making additions to the ornamentation of the grotto which led to his garden at Twickenham, dedicated, as his graceful 'Verses on a Grotto' (1740) claim, to 'Great NATURE' and those 'Who dare to love their Country, and be poor'. He died in May 1744, amused to compare himself to Socrates distributing morality on his deathbed, as he sent the new edition of his *Moral Essays* to his friends. Spence's fragmentary notes on the days preceding the poet's death movingly evoke the conversation and reactions of Pope and his friends.[64]

In his later career, Pope repeatedly insisted that he wished to be judged as a virtuous man and as a moralist, rather than as merely a poet. It is a judgement from which many modern admirers have been concerned to protect him. Even into the present century his deformity, rather than his idealism, seemed to some hostile critics a sufficient explanation of his satiric intensity. Recent biographical revelations about, for example, his devious machinations to ensure the publication of his letters in his lifetime have not made him more appealing to others. Critical attention now tends to focus properly on the artistry on which his greatness rests: on the subtle and intricate texture of his verse at its best, on the 'nervous precision' of statement admired by his contemporaries, on the inimitable mastery of his couplet technique, on the delicacy or grotesque power of his imagination, on the poise and allusive complexity of his tone. Of course, as Thomas Gray, the dominant poet of the next generation, wrote in 1746.

it is natural to wish the finest Writer, one of them, we ever had should be an honest Man. it is for the interest even of that Virtue, whose Friend he profess'd himself, & whose Beauties he sung, that he should not be found a dirty Animal.[65]

Yet the emotional, dramatic morality conveyed in Pope's mature verse need not be undermined by what we know of Pope the man, agressive and vulnerable, idealistic and fallible as he may have been. The discipline of his art is in itself the most convincing assertion of the ideal of order and civilized intelligence with which he opposed the forces of darkness, an ideal to which he himself at least aspired, and which he depicted in his verse as the unending struggle of 'The clearest Head, and the sincerest Heart' against 'The dull, the proud, the wicked and the mad'.[66]

1. Joseph Spence, *Observation, Anecdotes and Characters of Men*, ed. James M. Osborn, Oxford, 1966, i. 6, 29–30. (This work is hereafter cited as Spence.)

2. Spence, i. 32.

3. Samuel Johnson, *Lives of the Poets*, ed. G. Birkbeck Hill (Oxford, 1905), iii. 224–5. (Hereafter cited as Johnson, *Lives*.)

4. See Spence, i. 227; and *Correspondence of Alexander Pope*, ed. G. Sherburn, Oxford, 1956, i. 34, 86. (This work is hereafter cited as *Correspondence*.)

5. Spence, i. 227.

6. *Collected Writings*, ed. D. Masson, London, 1890, xi. 29–30 (cited by E. Audra and A. Williams, Twickenham Edition of Pope, i. 208).

7. See William Empson, 'Wit in the *Essay on Criticism*,' *Hudson Review*, ii (1950), 559–77, reprinted in *The Structure of Complex Words*, London, 1951, pp. 84–100 and *Essential Articles for the Study of Alexander Pope*, ed. M. Mack, London, 1964, pp. 198–216.

8. According to Pope himself the addition began at l.291.

9. See Pope's prefatory letter to Arabella Fermor.

10. Spence, i. 43–4.

11. William Hazlitt, 'On Dryden and Pope,' *Lectures on the English Poets*, 1818, in *Complete Works*, ed. P. P. Howe, 1930–34, v. 72.

12. Edith Sitwell, *Alexander Pope*, London, 1930, p. 89.

13. Johnson, *Lives*, iii. 234.

14. *Correspondence*, i. 211.

15. See *The Poems of Alexander Pope*, ed. John Butt, 1963, pp. 61–2. (Hereafter cited as *Poems*.)

16. See note 11.

17. These would include Pope's *Key to the Lock* (1715), the farce *The What D'Ye Call It* (1717), apparently of joint authorship like the *Miscellanies* (1727–32), in which many minor works were collected, included *Peri Bathous: or The Art of Sinking in Poetry*, which was being compiled as early as 1714.

18. Spence, i. 83.

19. *Correspondence*, i. 226.

20. Spence, i. 82.

21. Joseph Spence, *An Essay on Pope's Odyssey* (1726), pp. 119–34; G. Sherburn, *The Early Career of Alexander Pope*, Oxford, 1934, p. 264.

22. *Correspondence*, i. 396.

23. *Correspondence*, ii. 23.

24. For Pope's views on gardening and building, and for his own garden and grotto, see Spence, i. 249–56; F. Bracher, 'Pope's Grotto: The Maze of Fancy,' *Huntington Library Quarterly*, xii (1949), 140–62, and A. L. Altenbernd, 'On Pope's "Horticultural Romanticism,"' *Journal of English and Germanic Philology*, liv (1955), 470–7 (both

reprinted in *Essential Articles*, ed. Mack, pp. 97–121, 136–45); and M. Mack, 'A Poet in his Landscape,' in *From Sensibility to Romanticism*, ed. F. W. Hilles and H. Bloom, New Haven, 1965, pp. 3–29 and ' "The Shadowy Cave": Some Speculations on a Twickenham Grotto,' in *Restoration and Eighteenth Century Literature*, ed. C. Camden, Chicago, 1963, pp. 69–88. Several of these writers find parallels between Pope's practice as gardener and as poet.

25. *Correspondence*, ii. 140.

26. *Correspondence*, ii. 332.

27. 'Testimonies of Authors Concerning our Poet and his Works,' *Poems*, p. 333.

28. *Poems*, p. 345.

29. Johnson, *Lives*, iii. 241. Aaron Hill, in a letter to Pope, 28 Jan. 1731, write of 'that Emotion and Bitterness, wherewith you remember Things which want Weight to deserve your Anguish,' *Correspondence*, iii. 167.

30. *Poems*, p. 345.

31. *Correspondence*, iii. 81, 117.

32. *Epistle to Dr. Arbuthnot*, 341.

33. Spence, i. 129.

34. See Maynard Mack's valuable introduction to the poem in the Twickenham Edition, III. i.

35. Johnson, *Lives*, iii. 242–3; Hazlitt, *Complete Works*, ed. P. P. Howe, v. 76.

36. Spence, i. 129–30; *Poems*, p. 502.

37. T. R. Edwards, *This Dark Estate*, Berkeley, 1963, pp. 30–1.

38. *Correspondence*, iii. 276, 445.

39. Warburton's collective title (1751) is usually preferred to Pope's own *Epistles to Several Persons*.

40. *Correspondence*, iii. 348.

41. Reuben Brower, *Alexander Pope: The Poetry of Allusion*, Oxford, 1959, p. 244.

42. Letter to Arbuthnot, 26 July 1734, *Correspondence*, iii. 419. Though probably a 'forgery', published in 1737, the value of the statement of Pope's views is not lessened.

43. *Correspondence*, iii. 345.

44. *Ibid.*, iii. 290.

45. W. P. Ker, *The Art of Poetry*, Oxford, 1923, p. 109.

46. Spence, i. 143–4; Johnson, *Lives*, iii. 241.

47. 'Advertisement' (1735), *Poems*, p. 613.

48. Spence, i. 171.

49. See M. Mack, 'The Muse of Satire,' *Yale Review*, xli (1951), 80–92, reprinted in *Discussions of Alexander Pope*, ed. R. A. Blanchard, Boston, 1960, pp. 99–106.

50. 'Advertisement,' *Poems*, p. 597.

51. Johnson, *Lives*, iii. 177.

52. Byron, 'Some Observations upon an Article in *Blackwood's Magazine*,' *Works*, ed. R. E. Prothero, iv (1900), 489.

53. See Peter Dixon, *The World of Pope's Satires*, London, 1968, pp. 25, 30.

54. Aaron Hill to Pope, 31 July 1738, *Correspondence*, iv. 112; Joseph Warton, *Essay on the Genius and Writings of Pope*, ii (1782), 338. In the 1730s Pope also revised and published his two *Satires of Dr. John Donne* (written *c.* 1713), which allowed a more direct and impatient tone.

55. John Dennis, 'To Matthew Prior, Esq; Upon the Roman Satirists' (1721) in *Critical Works*, ed. E. N. Hooker, Baltimore, 1939–43, ii. 219; John Dryden, *Of Dramatic Poesy and Other Critical Essays*, ed. G. Watson, London, 1962, ii. 129–30.

56. See note 49 above.

57. *Correspondence*, iv. 109.

58. Spence, i. 217.

59. *Correspondence*, iv. 5.

60. *Ibid.*, iv. 396.

61. *Ibid.*, iv. 377.

62. 'Fragment of Brutus, an Epic,' in *Poems*, p. 836 (first printed in 1919, not 1954 as stated by Butt).

63. *Correspondence*, iv. 437.

64. Spence, i. 257–70.

65. *Correspondence*, ed. P. Toynbee and L. Whibley, 3 vols., Oxford, 1935, i. 229–30.

66. *Essay on Criticism*, 732; *Epistle to Dr. Arbuthnot*, 347.

BIBLIOGRAPHY

I *Editions*

(a) The definitive edition, with valuable introductions and annotation, is *The Twickenham Edition of the Poems of Alexander Pope:*

I *Pastoral Poetry and An Essay on Criticism*, ed. E. Audra and Aubrey Williams, 1961.

II *The Rape of the Lock and Other Poems*, ed. Geoffrey Tillotson, 1940, 1954, 1962.

III i *The Essay on Man*, ed. Maynard Mack, 1950, 1958.

III ii *Epistles to Several Persons (Moral Essays)*, ed. F. W. Bateson, 1951, 1961 (revised).

IV *Imitations of Horace*, ed. John Butt, 1939, 1953.

V *The Dunciad*, ed. James Sutherland, 1943, 1953, 1963.

VI *Minor Poems*, ed. Norman Ault and John Butt, 1954.

VII–X *The Iliad and The Odyssey of Homer*, ed. Maynard Mack and others, 1967.

Other editions include:

The Poems of Alexander Pope, ed. John Butt, London, 1963. The best one-volume edition, based on the text of the Twickenham edition, with a selection of the annotation.

The Poetical Works of Alexander Pope, ed. Herbert Davis, Oxford, 1966 (Oxford Standard Authors).

Alexander Pope: Selected Poetry and Prose, ed. W. K. Wimsatt, New York, 1951. A useful selection, including the prose *Peri Bathous*, with a valuable introduction.

(b) *Other Works:*

Correspondence, ed. George Sherburn, 5 vols., Oxford, 1956. An indispensable tool.

Literary Criticism of Alexander Pope, ed. B. A. Goldgar, Lincoln, Nebraska, 1965.

(c) *Bibliography:*

R. H. Griffith, *Alexander Pope: A Bibliography*, 2 vols., Austin, Texas, 1922–7. Out-of-date, but not yet superseded.

II *Biographical Studies* (see also Rogers, and Nicolson and Rousseau in Section III):

Ault, Norman, *New Light on Pope*, London, 1949. Contains information about many aspects of Pope's life and poetry.

Quennell, Peter, *Alexander Pope: The Education of Genius, 1688–1728*, London, 1968. A readable, if popularized, account of Pope to the age of forty.

Root, R. K., *The Poetical Career of Alexander Pope*, Princeton, 1938. A still useful biographical and critical survey.

Sherburn, George, *The Early Career of Alexander Pope*, Oxford, 1934, 1968. A scholarly biography to 1728, still unsuperseded.

Sitwell, Edith, *Alexander Pope*, London, 1930.

Spence, Joseph, *Observations, Anecdotes and Characters of Books and Men*, ed. James M. Osborn, 2 vols., Oxford, 1966. The definitive edition of the record of Pope's conversation preserved by his friend.

III *Critical Studies:*

(a) General :

Adler, Jacob A., *The Reach of Art: a Study in the Prosody of Pope*, Gainesville, Florida, 1964.

Audra, Emile, *L'Influence Française dans l'Oeuvre de Pope*, Paris, 1931.

Boyce, Benjamin, *The Character Sketches in Pope's Poems*, Durham, N. C., 1962.

Brower, Reuben A., *Alexander Pope: The Poetry of Allusion*, Oxford, 1959. An important study of the major poems in terms of Pope's use of classical literature.

Discussions of Alexander Pope, ed. R. A. Blanchard, Boston, 1960. Excerpts from Pope's early critics and some important modern essays, including Maynard Mack's 'The Muse of Satire'.

Edwards, Thomas R., *This Dark Estate: A Reading of Pope*, Berkeley, 1963. A short and often perceptive interpretation.

Essential Articles for the Study of Alexander Pope, ed. Maynard Mack, London, 1964; 2nd edn., expanded, Hamden, Conn., 1968. Not all 'essential' for the general reader, but these essays illustrate every aspect of recent Pope scholarship and criticism.

Goldstein, Malcolm, *Pope and the Augustan Stage*, Stanford, 1958.

Jack, Ian, *Augustan Satire*, Oxford, 1952. Chs. v–vii on Pope.

Knight, G. Wilson, *Laureate of Peace*, London, 1955 (re-issued 1965 as *The Poetry of Pope*). Unpredictable insights.

Nicolson, Marjorie and G. S. Rousseau, *'This Long Disease, My Life'*: *Alexander Pope and the Sciences*, Princeton, 1968. Pope's medical history and interest in scientific discoveries.

Parkin, Rebecca P., *The Poetic Workmanship of Alexander Pope*, Minneapolis, 1955. Over-schematic but helpful study of many aspects of Pope's poetry.

Pope and his Contemporaries: Essays Presented to George Sherburn, ed. J. L. Clifford and L. A. Landa, Oxford, 1949. Contains several essays on Pope, including Maynard Mack's 'Wit and Poetry and Pope.'

Price, Martin, *To the Palace of Wisdom*, New York, 1964, Ch. v on Pope.

Tillotson, Geoffrey, *On the Poetry of Pope*, Oxford, 1938 (2nd edn., 1950). A still helpful pioneer work in the modern appreciation of Pope.

—— *Pope and Human Nature*, Oxford, 1958.

Trickett, Rachel, *The Honest Muse: A Study in Augustan Verse*, Oxford, 1967. Ch. vi on Pope, with emphasis on his relationship to Restoration predecessors.

Warren, Austin, *Alexander Pope as Critic and Humanist*, Princeton, 1929. Out-dated in some aspects, but still a useful survey of Pope's reading and scholarship.

Rogers, Robert W., *The Major Satires of Alexander Pope*, Urbana, 1955. A valuable biographical and critical study of Pope's later career (after the period covered by Sherburn).

(b) *Individual Works:*

Cunningham, J. S., *The Rape of the Lock* (Studies in English Literature), London, 1961. A stimulating critique.

Dixon, Peter, *The World of Pope's Satires: An Introduction to the Epistles and Imitations of Horace*, London, 1968. An attempt to relate the poetry to the thought and assumptions of its age.

Knight, Douglas, *Pope and the Heroic Tradition: A Critical Study of his 'Iliad,'* New Haven, 1951.

The Rape of the Lock: A Selection of Critical Essays, ed. John Dixon Hunt, London, 1968. Includes Pope's *A Key to the Lock* and contemporary reactions, as well as important modern essays.

Wasserman, Earl R., *Pope's 'Epistle to Bathurst': A Critical Reading with an Edition of the Manuscripts*, Baltimore, 1960.

Williams, Aubrey L., *Pope's 'Dunciad': A Study of its Meaning*, London, 1955. A short but constantly illuminating interpretation.

4

ADDISON, STEELE AND THE PERIODICAL ESSAY

F. W. Bateson, Corpus Christi College, Oxford

I

The crucial innovations in a literature occur when some sub-literary form—such as the folk-song, the popular sermon, the melodramatic romance, to give three familiar examples—ceases to be 'trash' and becomes the vehicle of aesthetic experience. The ultimate causes of such a metamorphosis are usually trace-able to some cataclysm in the particular society where it occurs, or at any rate in some change in its ruling class or dominant groups. But between the social revolution and the emergence of the new literary form which is its by-product a temporal interval must apparently occur. Augustan satire was essentially an after-effect on the literary plane of what might be called the Royalist resistance movement to the Commonwealth; but though its political sources go back to the 1640s the satire it-self does not find effective literary expression before Butler's *Hudibras* (Part I, 1662). Restoration comedy, which came to its maturity in the 1670s, was the product of a second wave in the anti-Puritan reaction that followed the return of Charles II from France. The eighteenth-century periodical essay, on the other hand, was the result of a reaction *against* that reaction. Addison and Steele were both Whigs, and the emergence of *The Tatler*, twenty years after the Glorious Revolution that had expelled the Stuarts and established a constitutional monarchy, was its aesthetic after-product. The sub-literature out of which the periodical essay evolved was, of course, the polemical jour-nalism of the later seventeenth century. But the political func-tion of that journalism had ceased with the discrediting of the Jacobite cause. The stage was now set, therefore, for a higher journalism, which could rebuke or reform the individual rather than the nation, one that was moral and social in its objectives rather than political, and with some innocent entertainment not altogether precluded. And under these new conditions the sub-literature of Restoration journalism became Augustan literature. Steele may be called the engineer of the transition—though there had been one or two periodicals of amusement before *The Tatler* (those of Ned Ward and Peter Motteux, for example, and the curious 'Scandal Club' in Defoe's *Review*)—but its hero, its genius, was Addison.

II

The quality that immediately differentiates Joseph Addison (1672–1719) from all the rest of the Queen Anne's men is an elusive, perverse, Ariel-like refinement. 'Who would not weep', Pope asked in the *Epistle to Dr. Arbuthnot* at the end of his brilliantly plausible caricature, 'if Atticus were he?' But Addison was *not* Atticus, even if Pope has done his malicious best to make us think he was. Somehow a rarer dimension in the man, of which Pope was only partly conscious, had got left out. The Victorians, who preferred him to Pope, were apt to identify Addison's refinement with their own gentility. Macaulay's long and still very readable essay [1] consists, apart from the biographical sections, of a series of testimonials to the *morality* of Addison's satire—'the moral purity, which we find even in his merriment', respectability somehow combined with a 'wit more sparkling than the wit of Congreve, and . . . humour richer than the humour of Vanbrugh'. The last sentence of Macaulay's essay sums up the whole Victorian attitude. Addison, we are told, was the 'great satirist, who alone knew how to use ridicule without abusing it, who, without inflicting a wound, effected a great social reform, and who reconciled wit and virtue, after a long and disastrous separation, during which wit had been led astray by profligacy, and virtue by fanaticism.' And Thackeray's 'Congreve and Addison' in *The English Humourists of the Eighteenth Century* (1853) is to the same general effect, if there is rather more emphasis on Addison's naturalness and gaiety and rather less on his morality. To both, however, his special distinction is to have rescued English humour from the obscenity of Restoration comedy. Addison's fun, they insist, was clean. What they did not ask, or if they did it was only intermittently and superficially, was whether the fun was more than a rescue operation.

The question was asked again some forty years ago by Bonamy Dobrée in a substantial essay [2] that is probably the best criticism we have of Addison, and the answer suggested that there is something unpleasant, almost neurotic, in his sense of humour because of the prevailing if unconscious condescension. In other words, Addison was too self-centred to be a true satirist. Atticus, according to Pope, 'without sneering' used to 'teach the rest to sneer'. According to Dobrée, however, Addison himself is continually sneering—not perhaps at single identifiable individuals perhaps but at anybody and everybody, at the whole human race (especially that half of it that Addison called 'the fair sex'). And why? Simply because they have not had the supreme good fortune apparently to be—Joseph Addison.

Dobrée, who was of the school of Lytton Strachey, made out a morally damning case against 'The First Victorian', as he calls Addison. A small but very effective point in that case was to point to the curious habit Addison had of inserting the epithet *secret* when there seems to be no real justification for it in the context: *secret joy, secret pleasure, secret satisfaction, secret pride, secret approbation,* and so on. The attitude to his contemporaries suggested by this recurrent stylistic *tic* is not an attractive one. Addison seems to be preening himself on being a sort of psychological know-all, an observer of his contemporaries who knows all *their* secrets—especially the discreditable ones that the human object under observation is unaware of himself. In the quarrel with Pope we find ourselves decidedly on Pope's side.

Addison's claim upon our critical attention is not, however, as the Victorians (and Dobrée too) tended to think, because of his personality but in spite of his personality. Nor does it rest primarily upon the brilliance of his satirical humour. As a humourist he is no better really than his school-fellow and coadjutor Steele, who in founding *The Tatler* in 1709 provided Addison with the ideal medium for the exhibition of his one supreme talent, which was the ability to write excellent English. Addison's prose style is probably the best, considered simply as style, in the whole range of English literature —more consistently excellent even than Shakespeare's, Dryden's, Sterne's, Matthew Arnold's, Bernard Shaw's or George Orwell's. And although, measured in the number of its words, a *Tatler* or a *Spectator* may not seem very long, it must be remembered that Addison's perfection of style in *The Spectator*, where it is most brilliant, had to be maintained three or even sometimes six times a week.

Johnson, who practised a prose style very different from

Addison's, has said what is still *faute de mieux* the last word on this matter :

> His prose is the model of the middle style; on grave subjects not formal, on light occasions not groveling; pure without scrupulosity and exact without apparent elaboration; always equable, and always easy, without glowing words or pointed sentences. Addison never deviates from his track to snatch a grace; he seeks no ambitious ornaments, and tries no hazardous innovations. His page is always luminous, but never blazes in unexpected splendour . . .
> Whoever wishes to attain an English style, familiar but not coarse, and elegant but not ostentatious, must give his days and nights to the volumes of Addison.[3]

What is this middle style in which Addison excelled? There is no text-book definition, but Johnson was presumably applying to prose the neo-classic gradation applied by critics such as the elder Scaliger to Greek and Latin poetry. The most highly respected genres—the epic, tragedy and the 'great ode' (such as Pindar's)—demanded a high or 'sublime' style, because they described the actions and conversations of princes and nobles. Next to them came comedy and satire, which were supposed to be restricted to the depiction of the urban middle class. The lowest form of drama or poetry in Renaissance critical theory, because it was theoretically limited to the description of farm-workers like shepherds, was the pastoral. Applied to prose the high style is characterized linguistically by long sentences, with many subordinate clauses, a polysyllabic vocabulary, and a general suggestion of artifice. The low style, on the other hand, was essentially colloquial. The period immediately preceding Addison and Steele had in fact been dominated by this 'pert' style, as Pope called it, which even penetrated into literary criticism in Thomas Rymer's vigorous attacks on Elizabethan drama (including *Othello*), and Jeremy Collier's pious onslaught on Restoration comedy. A popular preacher like Bunyan and a journalist like Defoe never employed anything but the low style, which is lively and immediately intelligible but without much subtlety.

Addison's middle style must be presumed to have combined in the eyes of Johnson the virtues of both the high and the low styles. It was not an accident that he was by birth of the upper-middle class (his father, Lancelot Addison, was a successful High Churchman who finally became Dean of Lichfield), even if by marrying in middle age the dowager Countess of Warwick he finally penetrated into the aristocracy. The special fascination however that Addison's style still exerts has never been satisfactorily explained. Macaulay was no doubt right in saying that 'the mere choice and arrangement of his words would have sufficed to make his essays classical', but as criticism the dictum does not take analysis very far. What is there specifically 'classical' about either Addison's choice of words or their arrangement? The eulogy floats ineffectively in the air.

The most elaborate of the eighteenth-century criticisms of Addison's style is that in Hugh Blair's *Lectures on Rhetoric and Belles Lettres* (1783), in which the first four of the essays in *The Spectator* on the pleasures of the imagination are subjected to a prolonged scrutiny. But Blair's method is to proceed sentence by sentence and either improve on it, as he imagined, or else pronounce it unimprovable and 'elegant'. Blair was the Professor of Rhetoric at Edinburgh and spoke broad Scots, as we know from Boswell, and his comments need not therefore be taken very seriously. It is precisely in the *clash* between colloquial speech and 'learned' English, or more strictly, by the exploitation of such verbal clashes, that Addison's stylistic brilliance seems to consist, just as his 'delicacy'—a term that he borrowed from his favourite French critic Bouhours—lies in his refusal to over-exploit such contrasts.

A few examples will illustrate the point. A characteristic passage in *The Tatler*, no. 116, concludes (after poking fun at some contemporary extravagances of feminine fashion such as the hooped petticoat):

> I consider woman as a beautiful romantic animal, that may be adorned with furs and feathers, pearls and diamonds, ores and silks. The lynx shall cast its skin at her feet to make her a tippet; the peacock, parrot, and swan shall *pay contributions* to her muff; the sea shall be searched for shells, and the rocks for gems; and every part of nature furnish out its share towards the embellishment of a creature that is the most consummate work of it.

Here the ambivalence of Addison's attitude to women, which is similar to that of Pope in *The Rape of the Lock*, is reflected in the mocking contrast between the elaborate paratactic clauses and their homely objects—a tippet and a muff. A woman is an animal, a sub-human creature, but 'a beautiful romantic animal', an animal who is also the lovely princess in a romance. The clash between compliment and disparagement is epitomized in the two words *animal* (colloquial) and *romantic* (a non-popular word only introduced into the language in 1650, which had already bifurcated into a eulogistic sense, 'exciting like a romance', and a dyslogistic sense, 'impossible to credit like a romance'). The 'delicacy' of the passage lies in its equipoise of statement and irony. Addison does not commit himself one way or the other and the two antithetic connotations are allowed to add piquancy to each other.

The description of Will Wimble in *The Spectator*, no. 108, is a stylistic masterpiece in another genre. Will's letter to Sir Roger de Coverley is blunt and particularized. Later on in the essay we are provided with other similar concrete details such as the tulip-root in his pocket, the puppies that he exchanges, and the garters that he knits for the mothers or sisters of his friends. But the particularity is again given piquancy by the elaborateness of the syntax, as in the following passage :

> He hunts a Pack of Dogs better than any Man in the Country, and is very famous for finding out a Hare. He is extremely well versed in all the little Handicrafts of an idle Man : He makes a *May*-fly to a Miracle; and furnishes the whole Country with Angle-Rods.

On the one hand we are presented with convincingly concrete details of country life. A real river still runs at the bottom of the rectory garden in Wiltshire where he was born and grew up, and the flies and fishing rods that Will makes are clearly drawn from the life. On the other hand, the verbal skill Addison displays in finding a different formula for praising each of Will Wimble's several activities is breath-taking (in 'He makes a *May*-fly to a Miracle' alliteration is added to variation). A brilliant rhetorician is unostentatiously at work as well as a man with his eye firmly fixed on rural objects. The two approaches are not strictly compatible with each other; the fascination lies in this persuasive incompatibility.

Addison was much more of a poet in his prose than in his poems. *The Campaign* (1705), the poem written to celebrate Marlborough's victory at Blenheim, is unreadable today, its simile of the angel and the storm, which was greatly admired at the time, surviving, in so far as it survives at all, as a characteristic specimen of the bogus neo-classicism of the period. *Cato* (1713), Addison's Racinian tragedy, is better but it is still at best second-rate. Matthew Arnold's notorious pronouncement that 'Dryden and Pope are not classics of our poetry, they are classics of our prose' [4] might be inverted in Addison's case. He is a classic of our poetry by virtue of his prose. What we are aware of in Addison's best prose is not the subject-matter but the inevitable, apparently effortless sequence of the best words in the best order. But considered simply *as* subject-matter what the modern reader is most conscious of in Addison's essays is their triviality. Their author had an uninteresting mind. Although the illusion of thinking, the parade of philosophy, is frequently proffered—especially in the Saturday essays in *The Spectator*, which were intended to provide edifying matter for the following Sunday—the barrenness of the thought-processes is distressingly evident. Addison discusses almost every subject under the sun and he has nothing original or stimulating to say about any of them. But, as far as his literary status is concerned, does this ultimately matter? Ought it to matter?

The proper critical approach to the problem set by the best of Addison's *Spectator* essays is that adopted by T. S. Eliot in *What is a Classic?* Macaulay had used the term, but he had failed to define it. Eliot, however, has suggested four criteria that a work of literature must satisfy if it is to be admitted into the rank of the classics. The relevance of the four tests to the difficulties that the modern reader unquestionably has in not *liking* Addison is that they are essentially extra-personal. Eliot demands 'maturity of mind, maturity of manners, maturity of language and perfection of the common style' in his ideal literary classic, but the crux of his argument is that these qualities must reside in a society rather than in any one member of it. In the long history of English literature such a society has only existed once, according to Eliot—and its representative individual *ought* to be Pope. But Pope won't do because of the limitations of his verse, and Eliot has to content himself with the lame conclusion that in England 'we have no classic age and no classic poet', though Pope is as it were a near-miss for one.[5]

Addison's name only occurs once in Eliot's essay, which was primarily concerned with 'What is a Classic?' in poetry. But if classical prose is included, as it clearly must be in any adequate definition, Addison is a much more plausible representative of the English classic moment than Pope. If, as Eliot asserts, 'the realization of classical qualities by Pope was obtained at a high price—to the exclusion of some greater potentialities of English verse',[6] the objection does not apply equally to Addison's prose *considered simply as a medium*. Eliot's further point that the nearest thing we have in English to the perfection of a common style in poetry comparable to Dante's or Racine's is again Pope is also challenged by Addison. Eliot's criterion for such a common style is 'one which makes us exclaim, not "this is a man of genius using the language" but "this realizes the genius of the language"'. And this is exactly the impression that Addison's prose gives. This is a prose style that does *realize* the potential genius of the English language.

But to Eliot's four criteria a fifth may be added, whether it is a question of classical poetry or of classical prose. The fifth criterion can only be applied with the hindsight of literary history, but it is none the less crucial—more important perhaps in the long run than any of Eliot's tests. A classical style must look backwards to earlier styles in the language and cognate tongues (Latin, for example), but it must also look forward—and this is where an individual writer's stylistic genius or intuition becomes relevant—to what is to come in the immediate future. The seeds of the future were in Addison's loins; in Pope, on the other hand, the early pre-romantic aspirations were crude and melodramatic, as he came to recognize himself :

> Soft were my Numbers; who could take offence
> While pure Description held the place of Sense?

To a literary critic what is of special interest about Addison is the degree to which he seems to anticipate almost all the significant developments of the next hundred and fifty years of English literature. The prose style, as it detaches itself from both its author and its content, almost jumps a century and a half to *la poésie pure*. As Walter Pater recommended, it has begun to aspire to the condition of music. But his boldest critical gesture was to take up the cause of the popular ballad. The essays on 'Chevy Chase' (*The Spectator*, nos. 70, 74) are a milestone in the history of literary taste. The contrast between them and the eighteen papers on *Paradise Lost* (beginning with no. 267) is between the forward-looking and the backward-looking mode of criticism. Addison is accomplished at both. As a critic of Milton Addison was applying at length if in a more readable form the commonplaces of French criticism, particularly those of Le Bossu, which were themselves derived from the sixteenth-century Italian commentators on Aristotle's *Poetics*. Addison, who had read almost everything, quotes the inevitable tribute from Sir Philip Sidney's *The Defence of Poesy* : 'Certainly I must confess mine own barbarousness; I never heard the old song of Percy and Douglas that I found not my heart moved more than with a trumpet. . . ." There is no doubt a similar theoretical contradiction between Sidney's neo-classicism and what he looked into his heart and read. But in Sidney the rude style of the blind minstrel to which he responded with such surprising intensity is an incidental lapse from the central argument; with Addison two whole essays are devoted entirely to 'Chevy Chase', and although some parallel passages are cited from the *Aeneid* there is no suggestion that the noble 'simplicity' of the ballad is inferior to Vergil. An even bolder essay in rehabilitation is *The Spectator*, no. 85 on 'The Babes in the Wood', which Addison calls 'The Two Children in the Wood'. Although the ballad, which is now classified as a broadside or street ballad and is excluded as such from Child's great collection, is not actually quoted by Addison as 'Chevy Chase' had been, it is described as 'a plain simple Copy of Nature' exhibiting genuine and unaffected sentiments that are able 'to move the Mind of the most polite Reader with inward Meltings of Humanity and Compassion'. What could be less neo-classic? The fact that Wordsworth quoted a stanza from this ballad in the preface to the second edition of *Lyrical Ballads* is a striking confirmation of the incipient Romanticism in Addison. The gap between him and a typical Augustan is indicated by Gay's Bowzybeus, the drunken protagonist in the 'Saturday' of his *The Shepherd's Week* (1714). Bowzybeus is about as 'low' a figure as any in Augustan satire and two of the songs he sings when drunk are 'The Children in the Wood' and 'Chevy Chase', both of which are paraphrased in some detail. What was pathetic and even 'noble' to Addison was merely ridiculous to Gay, Swift and Pope. Swift, it may be remembered, wrote a number of ballads, but their initial assumption was always that a ballad degrades whatever it describes. The critical *volte face* that Addison's admiration for the popular or street ballad implies—and that was to make possible not only Percy's *Reliques of Ancient English Poetry* (1765) but also 'The Ancient Mariner' and 'La Belle Dame Sans Merci'—was revolutionary in its consequences.

Addison's 'Romanticism' can also be detected in his interest in the creative imagination, in which he is the tentative precursor of Coleridge, though *The Spectator*, no. 411, which initiates the series on the pleasures of the imagination, refuses to distinguish between imagination and fancy ('which I shall use promiscuously'). The use of dreams, notably in the Vision of Mirza (*The Spectator*, no. 159), as a literary genre also makes Addison a precursor of De Quincey. By restricting 'imagination' to the visual imagination Addison is also in effect an enthusiastic prophet of 'the picturesque', including even landscape gardening (no. 414). And the predilection for 'amiable' humour rather than satire made him an important influence, especially through the de Coverley series (*The Spectator*, nos. 106 ff.), on the nineteenth-century novel. (Sir Roger paradoxically was a Tory whereas Addison was a prominent Whig.)

In spite of an unattractive personality, then, Addison retains his place in English literature by virtue of his brilliant prose style. His importance in English literary history is also assured: English Romanticism was, it is not too much to say, almost his invention. Or, if that *is* an overstatement, at least the progress to Romanticism in England was decidedly facilitated by his influence.

Until wine had loosened Addison's tongue his contemporaries —he had no intimate friends, though he had many protégés —found it impossible to penetrate his reserve. The marriage late in life to the Countess of Warwick was a disastrous failure. Even Steele, who had thought himself a friend (they had been at Charterhouse and Oxford together) quarrelled with him in the end. A statement made by Pope to Spence in April 1739 may partly explain the psychological problem Addison's character poses. According to Spence what Pope said was this:

> Addison and Steele [were] a couple of H—s. I am sorry to say so, and there are not twelve people in the world that I would say it to at all.[7]

By 'H—s' Pope seems to have meant 'hermaphrodites', the usual term in the eighteenth century for a homosexual. The fact, if it is a fact, may explain the curious animus against women, except as objects of ornament, to which Dobrée has called attention. 'His intuition' Dobrée writes, 'warned him against commerce with the fair sex, which, however, he never ceased to ridicule or try to improve. For although he knew their nature was antipathetic to his, it was not altogether foreign; some effeminacy in his own nature made them strangely fascinating to him; he could not leave them alone in his essays.' Dobrée's essay incidentally was published some forty years before Spence's note was made public. Another modern commentator has called attention to the apologies with which Addison tempers his misogyny: 'It is as if this misogyny of Addison's was pathological, the product not of conviction but of some psychological 'fault', and that Addison himself, in his waking moments, was dismayedly conscious of the exaggerations he could not help falling into.'[8] The neurotic element in Addison's psyche provides for the literary critic one more link between the 'pure poetry' of his essays and the subjectivism of the typical Romantic. The pearls presuppose a morbid secretion in the originating shell-fish.

It is difficult to believe that Sir Richard Steele (1672–1729) was a 'H—'. Spence's editor refers us to the angry interchange with Addison in *The Old Whig* and *The Plebeian*, two rival short-lived periodicals that the old collaborators conducted in 1719, primarily, it would almost seem, to throw mud at each other in public. In the second number of *The Plebeian* Steele significantly introduced a digression on the homosexual ephors of Sparta, though, as he at least asserts, without intending 'the least appearance of personal reflection.'

The innuendo is typical of Steele's heavy-handed methods. There is nothing Addisonian here, or indeed, except superficially, in anything else that he wrote. His letters to his 'Prue' (whose real name was Mary) convince us that he was an affectionate husband. That she was an heiress—as his first wife had also been, who died only two years after she had become Mrs. Steele—and a 'cried-up beauty' (as Kneller's portrait demonstrates) must be conceded. And the interval between the death of the first wife and the marriage to the second was perhaps too short (about six months). But the long series of letters now in the British Museum to his 'absolute governess' show that the absence of subtlety and refinement was compensated for by a natural sincerity and kindness of heart. Steele is much more likeable than Addison; he is not in the same class as a writer. And he is quite without the fineness of touch and delicacy of feeling, both as man and as writer, that characterize Addison.

It may seem paradoxical to accuse Steele of coarseness, since he was continually pounding the moral drum. But there is a crudity in the critical gospel that he preaches that convicts him of a lack of literary sensibility. The paper on Etherege's *The Man of Mode* (*The Spectator*, no. 65) is a typical Puritan denunciation; it concludes as follows:

> To speak plainly of this whole Work, I think nothing but being lost to a Sense of Innocence and Virtue can make any one see this Comedy, without observing more frequent Occasion to move Sorrow and Indignation, than Mirth and Laughter. At the same time I allow it to be Nature, but it is Nature in its utmost Corruption and Degeneracy.

Steele's sentimental comedies—of which the first, *The Funeral* (1701), is much the best—are practical dramatic applications of this formula. Everything possible is done to gloss over the corruptness of human nature, and the spectators are incited to enjoy their tears over any corruptions that remain.

Steele's place in the text-books is probably a higher one than he deserves. If he is to be defended the merit to insist on is a certain sturdy independence. The kind of sentimental comedy that he practised is different from that of his immediate predecessors—Colley Cibber's, for example, or George Farquhar's —because it is clearly not motivated by mere box-office considerations. Steele wanted to *say* something. Unfortunately he had not the specific literary talent required to develop his intuitions; his last comedy, *The Conscious Lovers* (1722), is undoubtedly his worst just as the later essays are also inferior to the early ones.

But Steele did invent the periodical essay. Addison was in Ireland, the secretary of the Lord Lieutenant, when Steele launched *The Tatler* (no. 1, 12 April 1709) and he has no share in the innovation on the exploitation of which his own reputation now rests. If Steele owed anything to anybody—apart from his own nose for a possibly profitable speculation (the furnaces that he built a few years earlier to produce a 'philosopher's stone' had not been profitable)—it was to Swift. The first number like all the succeeding numbers is headed 'By Isaac Bickerstaff Esq.re' and the connection with Swift's *Bickerstaff Papers* (1708–9), is explicitly made in its section headed 'From my own Apartment', which ends with this advertisement :

> 'A Vindication of ISAAC BICKERSTAFF, Esq. against what is objected to him by Mr. *Partridge* in his Almanack for the present year 1709.' By the said ISAAC BICKERSTAFF, Esq. London, printed in the year 1709.

The pamphlet advertised was the last of Swift's Bickerstaff papers and demonstrated in his best ironical manner that Partridge (whose death on March the 29th 1708 had been foretold in the first Bickerstaff pamphlet) was really dead in spite of Partridge's own protests that he was still alive. Steele also paid a special tribute, in the preface to the fourth volume of *The Tatler*, to Swift 'whose pleasant writings, in the name of BICKERSTAFF, created an inclination in the town towards any thing that could appear in the same disguise.' He admitted a further debt 'at my first entering upon this work' to 'a certain uncommon way of thinking, and a turn in conversation peculiar' to Swift that 'rendered his company very advantageous to one whose imagination was to be continually employed upon obvious and common subjects.' The 'uncommon way of thinking' was a more important stimulus than the persona of the astrologer.

Swift's voice is continually making itself heard in the early numbers of *The Tatler*, which bear something of the same relation to the newspapers of the time that Bickerstaff's *Predictions for the Year 1708* bear to the contemporary almanacs. The dry ironic tone is as unmistakable as the continuous suggestion of parody. It must be remembered that the original sheets of *The Tatler* looked exactly like the common-or-garden newspaper. Like *The Daily Courant*, *The Observator* and *The Flying Post*, it was printed in double columns on both sides of a single folio sheet of paper. It came out, like *The Evening Post*, *The Post Boy* and Defoe's *Review*, three times a week—on Tuesdays, Thursdays and Saturdays. If there was any difference it was that *The Tatler* was more carelessly printed and on even worse paper than its less literary competitors.

The disguise of a mock-newspaper has all the outward signs of Swift's satiric technique. The title may even be due to Swift. To *tattle* meant more at the time than to gossip; it included the probability that the gossip was false and malicious—a sense immortalized in Mr. Tattle of Congreve's *Love for Love* (1695), one of the most popular plays of the period and, as it happens, one specially commended by Steele in no. 1. To Swift the news reported in newspapers was precisely *tattle*, whereas Steele, much of whose income at this time was derived from his official post as Gazeteer or editor of *The London Gazette*, can hardly have been as sceptical of the contents of newspapers. Elsewhere too, in these early numbers, though the pen was always Steele's, the words are sometimes Swift's. The promise made in no. 4 to publish a treatise against operas, with 'a very elaborate digression upon the London cries, wherein he [a great critic] has shown from reason and philosophy why oysters are cried, card-matches sung, and turnips and all other vegetables neither cried, sung nor said but sold with an accent and tone neither natural to man or beast' has been identified by Swift's latest editor as essentially Swiftian. The list could easily be extended.

There are good things in the early numbers of *The Tatler*, but it is formless and too heterogeneous in its subject-matter. The initial formula was to use White's Chocolate-House as the source of 'accounts of gallantry, pleasure and entertainment', with Will's Coffee-House, where Dryden had lorded it ten years earlier, for poetry, the Grecian in the Strand for learning, and St. James's Coffee-House for foreign and domestic news. And 'what else I shall offer' from Mr. Bickerstaff's own apartment. Steele was living at the time in Bury Street, Piccadilly, with all the coffee-houses at a convenient distance. He was of the genial, sociable temperament that one associates with those of Anglo-Irish origin (he was born in Dublin), and a coffee-house (where stronger liquors than coffee or chocolate were also obtainable) was his natural element. But the retailer of coffee-house news was finding it difficult to double the part with that of Bickerstaff, the eccentric astrologer (who has a familiar spirit called Pacolet in his service). It was fortunate that Addison came to his rescue at this point.

Addison penetrated Bickerstaff's disguise on reading the sixth number. Steele had repeated there an observation made to him by Addison himself many years before to the effect that Virgil had shown his discrimination in not calling Aeneas *pius* or *pater*, the standard epithets, in the cave episode with Dido where he substituted *dux Trojanus* instead, 'for he very well knew a loose action might be consistent enough with the usual manners of a soldier, though it became neither the chastity of a pious man nor the gravity of the father of a people'.

Addison's first contribution to *The Tatler* was the account of 'the Distress of the News-Writers' in no. 18. The exact number of papers or parts of papers for which he was responsible is not known. It was certainly more than the 62 papers (out of a total of 271) printed by Tickell, Addison's literary executor, in the collected edition of Addison's writings that was published in 1721, immediately after his death. Nevertheless, measured quantitatively *The Tatler* is undoubtedly mainly Steele's. It also includes most of his best writing, such as the touching account of his father's death in no. 181 :

> The first sense of sorrow I ever knew was upon the death of my father, at which time I was not quite five years of age; but was rather amazed at what all the house meant, than possessed with a real understanding why nobody was willing to play with me. I remember I went into the room where his body lay, and my mother sat weeping alone by it. I had my battledore in my hand, and fell a-beating the coffin, and calling Papa; for, I know not how, I had some slight idea that he was locked up there. My mother catched me in her

arms, and, transported beyond all patience of the silent grief she was before in, she almost smothered me in her embraces and told me in a flood of tears, 'Papa could not hear me, and would play with me no more, for they were going to put him under ground, whence he could never come to us again.' She was a very beautiful woman, of a noble spirit . . .

Such autobiographical passages are unfortunately rare, and most of the essays—on duelling, on fashionable visits, on the education of girls, on the evils of drinking—now have a merely historical interest. Addison's beneficent influence can be recognized in the trend away from disconnected episodes based on the separate coffee-houses and with each number now becoming a single coherent essay. But for the modern reader there is too much Steele, especially too much of Steele the moralist, and too little of Addison and Swift.

Between Steele's terminating *The Tatler* (2 January 1711) and the first number of *The Spectator* (1 March 1711) the interval in time was short. The crucial difference—apart from the change from three numbers a week to six—was that the supply of 'copy' was now divided equally and on equal terms between Addison and Steele, instead of Steele paying Addison for whatever material he provided. Altogether there were 555 numbers to 6 December 1712, the last number being again signed by Steele who pays a proper tribute to Addison in it, though again as in the last paper of *The Tatler* without mentioning his name. Addison contributed 251 essays; Steele's total is also 251 essays. (Friends and correspondents, some of them not identifiable now, provided the other 53 papers.) Qualitatively, however, Steele's essays are not in the same class. The coarseness of spiritual fibre almost always present in Steele's work is exemplified in three heavy-handed essays in the Sir Roger de Coverley series. The perverse widow (no. 113) who still fascinates the elderly Sir Roger is drawn with spirit, but the comedy is much too obvious. In no. 118 Steele returns to her and the dangerous influence of confidants, but here the point has to be reinforced by Sir Roger's game-keeper who is discovered sitting by the side of his inamorata by 'a transparent fountain' in which his Betty is reflected. Sir Roger and the Spectator overhear the game-keeper addressing the reflection :

Oh thou dear Picture, if thou could'st remain there in the Absence of that fair Creature whom you represent in the Water, how willingly could I stand here satisfied for ever. . . .

And so on for half an unconvincing page. Apparently Betty had been listening to the spiteful gossip of Kate Willow about the game-keeper and Susan Holliday. The modern reader cannot help comparing Sir Roger's pompous game-keeper with the idiom of Lady Chatterley's lover.

Steele shows himself a competent enough journalist in *The Spectator*, but rarely much more than that. The moralizing is what *The Tatler* has prepared us for—the art of pleasing, the right choice in marriage, the relationship between parents and children, and similar topics—and though Steele's attitude is always humane the actual presentation shows no advance. Steele had been deprived of his Gazeteership by Harley and the items of foreign news that are a distracting element in *The Tatler* were no longer available for *The Spectator*. Their place tends to be taken, however, by letters sometimes written by Steele himself and sometimes—to judge by specimens still extant at Blenheim Palace—by genuine letters from readers that Steele has touched up. As literature most of the numbers for which he was responsible are at best second-rate. *The Spectator* survives in spite of Steele and because of Addison. The judgement is one that it would be futile to question.

IV

The periodical essay was an immediate success as a literary genre. Between the first number of *The Tatler* and the end of the eighteenth century no less than 314 imitations made a longer or shorter appearance (excluding *The Spectator* itself). And the editor/authors included such eminent literary or political figures as Swift, Lord Bolingbroke, Fielding, Lord Chesterfield, Christopher Smart, Smollett, John Wilkes, 'Junius', Burke, Boswell, Canning and Coleridge. But only two or three series merit special discussion or reference in this chapter.

The Guardian was the immediate successor of *The Spectator* with Steele again the nominal editor, and only 51 of its 175 numbers were by Addison. The lesser contributors included Berkeley, already established as the most original philosopher of the age, and Young, the future author of *Night Thoughts*. But only one essay in *The Guardian* is still remembered. This is Pope's devastating mock-eulogy of the pastorals of Ambrose Philips, a special favourite of Addison's, which is accompanied by a mock-depreciation of his own pastorals that had been pointedly ignored by Tickell, another Addisonian, in an earlier series of papers on the pastoral. The essay (no. 40) needs to be read in its entirety for its comic impudence to be appreciated. Steele did not, apparently, realize the hilarious implications of the 'simplicity' Pope professed to be praising.

The Guardian ran from 12 March to 1 October 1713. On 18 June 1714 Addison revived *The Spectator* for a further 80 numbers, but this time without Steele who was now deeply engaged in politics. Addison's twenty-five essays are pleasantly written, as indeed are those in *The Guardian*, but they cannot compete with the best essays in *The Spectator*.

Addison's immediate successors in the periodical essay suffer from being too Addisonian. The elegance of the middle style has been diluted in the process of imitation. It is only with the arrival of *The Rambler* in 1750 that a new note is to be heard. But what is of most interest in *The Rambler* does not come from what it owes to the periodical essay tradition but to its idiosyncratic author. *The Rambler*, as well as *The Adventurer* (1752–4) and *The Idler* (1759), and Johnson's contributions to miscellaneous periodicals are therefore discussed in a later chapter.

The case of Oliver Goldsmith (1730?–1774) is different. In the words of Johnson's Latin epitaph on his friend and protégé there was nothing Goldsmith touched that he did not adorn. This is not the place to discuss *The Vicar of Wakefield* or the two comedies or the poems, but admirable though these all are in their several ways he was not primarily a novelist, a dramatist or a poet so much as a general man of letters, a professional writer who could turn his pen to anything—from the review to the text-book, from the anthology to the potted biography. To such a man's mill the periodical essay was obvious grist and Goldsmith contributed essays in Addison's manner to at least eight journals between 1759 and 1773. But the essays are generally discontinuous, more prophetic of Lamb and Hazlitt than reminiscent of Addison and Steele. The exception is the 119 'Chinese Letters' that appeared in *The Public Ledger* between 24 January 1760 and 14 August 1761 and were reprinted separately in 1762 as *The Citizen of the World; or, Letters from a Chinese Philosopher, Residing in London, to his Friends in the East*. This series has *dramatis personae* who reappear regularly in the manner of Sir Roger, Sir Andrew Freeport, Will Honeycombe, Captain Sentry and the other members of Mr. Spectator's Club.

The Chinese element in *The Citizen of the World* is the least successful part. The device of a visiting Oriental who writes letters home describing the curious habits of Europe was a favourite of the French *philosophes* (Montesquieu's *Lettres Persanes* [1721] is the masterpiece of the genre), although Goldsmith's immediate source seems to have been an anonymous pamphlet by Horace Walpole on the trial of Admiral Byng which uses Chinese correspondents with names similar to his. But all this, as Austin Dobson put it in an excellent essay on *The Citizen of the World*, is 'practically dead wood'.[9] Goldsmith's real advance on Addison and Steele is to use the periodical form as essentially a novel in instalments. The best of the essays are those describing the comic adventures and misadventures of such characters as the eccentric Man in Black and a certain Beau Tibbs, who is really a pathetic lower-middle-class aspirant to being a 'dog'. And the reader is left at the end of each essay wondering what odd or paradoxical situation he will find the familiar figures in next.

The Citizen of the World is an embryonic Dickens novel. Take Letter LXXI. Although it is 'From Lien Chi Altangi, to Fum Hoam, first president of the Ceremonial Academy at Pekin, in China', the reader finds it difficult to remember that the 'I' is either Chinese or a philosopher. He and the Man in Black, Mr. Tibbs and his wife ('in flimsy silk, dirty gauze instead of linen, and an hat as big as an umbrella'), and a pawnbroker's widow have made up a party to visit Vauxhall Gardens. After the supper Mr. Tibbs tries to persuade his affected wife 'to favour the company'. But at first Mrs. Tibbs cannot be persuaded : ' "for you know very well, my dear, says she, that I am not in voice today, and when one's voice is not equal to one's judgment, what signifies singing?" ' And, in the context of such realistic comedy as this, what signifies style?

It is all very good fun, but the formal structure of the essay has been stretched to its limits. Even the most realistic of the Coverley series remained within the conceptual confines originally determined by Montaigne and Bacon. It is true that Goldsmith was also interested in intellectual problems, but even in treating them the tone is noticeably different. Goldsmith 'plays' with ideas; his Chinese philosopher is not concerned with their logical validity, but with the humour he can derive from the paradoxes he picks up in the streets of London.

The periodical essay survived Goldsmith's attempts—which were largely unconscious, of course—to pervert it from its Addisonian norm. The collections with such titles as *The British Essayists* by Harrison (1796–7), Drake (1811), Chalmers (1808, 1817, 1823), Ferguson (1819) and Lynam (1827), many of them in thirty or forty volumes, prove the continuing popularity of the genre at the beginning of the nineteenth century. And series like Henry Mackenzie's *The Mirror* (1779–80), Richard Cumberland's *The Observer* (1785), Vicesimus Knox's various lucubrations and even *The Microcosm* (1786–7, conducted by George Canning and Hookham Frere while they were still schoolboys at Eton), or *The Loiterer* (1789–90, in which two of Jane Austen's brothers had a hand when Oxford undergraduates), still make pleasant bed-side reading. In these series the middle style does survive. But it is not the classical middle style of Addison, a style that looks forward to the nineteenth century, but a conservative, regressive, monotonous style, because (as Eliot emphasizes in *What is a Classic?*) 'the resources of the language have, for the time at least, been exhausted'. Goldsmith, who 'wrote like an angel' (according to Garrick), was almost alone in the premonitions he offered of the future of the English essay. But angels prefer *not* to write in the middle style. Or so the example of Oliver Goldsmith would suggest.

NOTES

1. 'The Life and Writings of Addison,' *Edinburgh Review*, lxxviii (July, 1843), 193–260.

2. 'The First Victorian,' in *Essays in Biography 1680–1726*, London, 1925, pp. 197–345.

3. *Lives of the English Poets*, ed. G. B. Hill, 3 vols., Oxford, 1905, ii. 149–50.

4. 'The Study of Poetry' (1880) in *Essays in Criticism. Second Series*, London, 1888, pp. 41–2.

5. *What is a Classic?*, London, 1945, pp. 16, 17.

6. *Ibid.*, p. 22.

7. Joseph Spence, *Observations, Anecdotes and Characters of Books and Men*, ed. J. M. Osborn, 2 vols., Oxford, 1966, i. 80.

8. F. W. Bateson, 'The *Errata* in *The Tatler*,' *Review of English Studies*, v (1929), 11.

9. 'The Citizen of the World,' *Eighteenth Century Vignettes*, London, 1892, p. 117.

BIBLIOGRAPHY

I *Editions*

Donald F. Bond's elaborate edition of *The Spectator*, 5 vols., Oxford, 1965, supersedes its many predecessors. In addition to a long and judicious introduction there are footnotes explaining topical or learned allusions.

Professor Bond is preparing a similar edition of *The Tatler*: the best edition to date is that by John Nichols and others, 6 vols., London, 1786.

There is no scholarly edition of *The Guardian* but a number of Steele's minor periodicals have been edited: *The Englishman* (1713–14), ed. R. Blanchard, Oxford, 1955; *Richard Steele's Periodical Journalism 1714–16*, ed. R. Blanchard, Oxford, 1959; and *The Theatre* (1720), ed. J. Loftis, Oxford, 1962.

There are modern editions of three of Fielding's series of essays: *The Covent Garden Journal*, ed. G. E. Jensen, New Haven, 1915; *The Voyages of Mr. Job Vinegar from The Champion* (1740), ed. S. J. Sackett (Augustan Reprint Society no. 67, 1958); and *The True Patriot* (a facsimile text), ed. M. A. Locke, Alabama Univ., 1964.

The Citizen of the World will be found with the rest of Goldsmith's essays in the definitive edition of his *Works*, ed. Arthur Friedman, 5 vols., Oxford, 1966.

For a general view of the essay-periodicals it is still necessary to use such collections as that by Alexander Chalmers, 45 vols., London, 1808, 1817 and 38 vols., London, 1823.

II *Modern Surveys*

Walter Graham, *English Literary Periodicals*, New York, 1930; reprinted 1966. The standard work.

Bonamy Dobrée, *English Literature in the Early Eighteenth Century*, Oxford, 1959; vol. vii of *The Oxford History of English Literature*. Has lengthy sections on Addison and Steele and useful bibliographies. As criticism the section on Addison is inferior to the discussion in his *Essays in Biography 1680–1726*, London, 1925.

POETRY 1700–1740 [1]

Charles Peake, Queen Mary College, University of London

The date 1700 had no special historical or literary significance, although it happened to be the year in which Dryden, the last great seventeenth-century poet, died. But although the accidents of the calendar have no bearing on historical process, people often behave as though they had, and at the end of a century, as at New Year, tend to survey the past and formulate hopes for the future. Such reviews and hopes cannot bring about change, but they often express and encourage a mood conducive to it.

Dryden, out of favour and deprived of his laureateship, looked back with a sour and tired eye, and concluded 'The Secular Masque' (1700),

> 'Tis well an Old Age is out,
> And time to begin a New.

Matthew Prior, whose rising reputation had been founded on a ridicule of Dryden, devoted his *Carmen Seculare for the Year 1700* to a eulogy of William III and an opulent vision of the future, begging the god Janus,

> Be kind, and with a milder Hand,
> Closing the Volume of the finish'd Age,
> (Tho' Noble, 'twas an Iron Page)
> A more delightful Leaf expand,
> Free from Alarms, and fierce BELLONA'S Rage.

> (337–41)

The two poets—the one old, disillusioned and satirical, the other in his prime, optimistic, panegyrical—agreed at least in hoping that the new century would be very different from the last.

There is a similar note in most of the retrospective or prospective views of the time; after the disruptions of the seventeenth century people hoped for a more peaceful era. In 1700, an old man like Dryden could easily remember the Civil War and the Commonwealth, the Restoration, the Plague, the Great Fire, the Dutch invasion of the Medway, the Popish Plot, the danger of civil war at the time of the Exclusion Bill crisis, the accession of a Roman Catholic king, the Monmouth rebellion and its bloody suppression, the deposition of James II and the summoning of a Dutchman to the throne of England, a long succession of foreign wars and bitter political and religious dissensions—all these during an age of rapid and fundamental social, economic and intellectual development. It was not surprising that the change most people hoped for was to a more stable period when change should be less unpredictable, less violent, less destructive.

This desire for stability was a factor in most of the activities of the early eighteenth century, but it should not be confused with hostility to anything new or original. If people feared revolution, they had no wish to repeat the mistakes of their fathers: if the writers admired what they took to be the establishment of polite literature in seventeenth-century England, their admiration was not uncritical. To Dryden, the pre-Civil War period was

> A very Merry, Dancing, Drinking,
> Laughing, Quaffing, and unthinking Time.
>> (*The Secular Masque*, 39–40)

Pope condemned the 'obscenity' of the Restoration wits—

> In the fat Age of Pleasure, Wealth and Ease,
> Sprung the rank Weed, and thriv'd with large Increase—

and was even more caustic about the reign of William III, when

> ... Witt's *Titans* brav'd the Skies,
> And the Press groan'd with Licenc'd *Blasphemies*.
>> (*Essay on Criticism*, 534–5, 552–3)

What the past century had to offer to the poets of Queen Anne's reign were exemplars: Waller for sweetness, Denham for strength, Milton for sublimity, Cowley for wit, Dryden for energy and mastery of modern idiom. But the first two were rather remote figures, moving in the courts of the Stuarts[2]: the new poets could learn from them, but what they learned would have to be used in a different spirit. Similarly, although a few of Milton's early poems suggested possible variations, poets more concerned with their own society than with the Miltonic cosmos could do little with his blank verse except parody it for fun, as in John Philips's humorous poem, *The Splendid Shilling* (1701). To make use of the lofty manner of *Paradise Lost*, a poet needed not only to have digested thoroughly Milton's diction and rhythms but to have a subject of comparable sublimity, as Thomson was to demonstrate in 1726. Cowley's so-called 'Pindaric Odes' (1656) had popularized a literary kind which was frequently, though not often successfully, practised, but critics were already complaining that he had sacrificed too much to ingenuity. Dryden alone was close in tone and spirit, yet even his works were severely criticized for structural defects, poorly sustained fable, too much involvement in transient controversy, and too much license in versification. Those who could not match him in genius might excel him in the design, coherence and correctness of their poems. The aesthetic principle of the new age was summed up in Pope's praise of Windsor Forest, a principle which reflected the cosmic views of the time, whether religious or scientific, and was related to the social and political hopes:

> Where Order in Variety we see,
> And where, tho' all things differ, all agree.
> *(Windsor-Forest, 15–16)*

The other great exemplars were the classical authors, especially those of Augustan Rome. The classics were, in literary terms, the very symbols of stability, and declared by their example that poetry, if it is to last, must deal with what is fundamental and permanent in human nature and experience, and must be carefully wrought to discover order and coherence in the incoherent disorder of life. Yet, even in their handling of the classical forms and themes, the eighteenth-century poets were not content merely to copy.

This is particularly clear in their treatment of the pastoral or eclogue, a form which had the prestige of a tradition, stemming from Theocritus and Virgil, renewed in the Renaissance, especially by Spenser, 'the father of English poetry', and used in the Restoration period for sentimental or gallant erotic verse. It had been adopted for expressions of love, grief, and piety; its familiar conventions had been borrowed in prose fiction, drama and masque; and an important critical controversy had developed in France between those who insisted that it must have rural simplicity of diction and thought, and those who argued that the pastoral's shepherds and shepherdesses, since they were not farm-labourers but belonged to the Golden Age, might be as eloquent as the poet chose.

Pope began the prefatory 'Discourse' to his *Pastorals*,

> There are not, I believe, a greater number of any sort of verses than of those which are called Pastorals, nor a smaller, than of those which are truly so.

He set out to correct irregularities in earlier usage, and to re-establish the classical kind, by eliminating from it what might be thought improper, and by reconciling in his practice the views of opposing critics. It is remarkable how well he succeeds within the inhibiting patterns, but the question remains: were these traditional patterns at all appropriate to what an eighteenth-century poet might have to say? Most of the important poets and critics from Swift and Gay (and Pope in his maturer years) to Dr. Johnson and Crabbe believed that they were not. There were attempts to salvage the pastoral with new subject-matter or new diction. Ambrose Philips (1709) attempted an appropriately simple style, and Thomas Purney (1717) tried a pseudo-rustic dialect, but the simplicity of style often exposed inanity of content. William Diaper, in his *Nereides: or Sea-Eclogues* (1712), transferred the scene to the ocean-bed, and replaced swains, nymphs and flocks by tritons, mermaids and fish: his poem is accomplished and colourful, but offers no lasting solution to the problems of the pastoral. These and such later attempts as William Collins's *Persian Eclogues* (1742) were the dying gasps of the tradition: in so far as it survived into the nineteenth century, it did so in the specialized elegiac form descending from *Lycidas* to Shelley's *Adonais* and Arnold's *Thyrsis*.

A form so artificial and easily recognizable attracted parody and burlesque. Even when mock-pastoral was intended primarily to amuse, some criticism of the form was generally implied, since the introduction of humour into the idealized stereotypes underlined their unreality. In this, mock-pastoral differed from mock-epic or mock-georgic where the classical parallels offered a commentary on modern life without damage to the forms imitated.

In Swift's 'Pastoral Dialogue' (1732) there is no apparent satirical purpose besides the comic exposure of the form. The poem begins in the feeble traditional way:

> Sing heavenly Muse in sweetly flowing Strain,
> The soft Endearments of the Nymph and Swain.

> (7–8)

But it turns out to be a lover's tiff between two Irish labourers, Dermot and Sheelagh, who follow the echoic patterns of the eclogue but little else:

> When you with *Oonah* stood behind a Ditch,
> I peept, and saw you kiss the dirty Bitch.
> *Dermot*, how could you touch those nasty Sluts!
> I almost wisht this Spud were in your Guts.

> (37–40)

The violence with which the convention is rejected is typical of Swift. To him it was useful only for the ironic presentation of the squalid or the absurd. He begins a poem, 'A Beautiful Young Nymph Going to Bed' (1734),

> *Corinna*, Pride of *Drury-Lane*,
> For whom no Shepherd sighs in vain,

and at once the stock pastoral names and terms are appropriately perverted for the description of a decayed prostitute, like so many nymphs before her, destroyed by love, but this time physically and piecemeal. Swift's inventiveness in discovering new uses for the ruins of the traditional form is illustrated not only in his own poems but in his suggestions that Gay should write a Quaker pastoral ('The Espousal') and a Newgate pastoral (*The Beggar's Opera*).

These suggestions were probably occasioned by his recognition that Gay was a specialist in mock-pastoral, whose reputation had begun with the publication of *The Shepherd's Week* (1714), a learned mockery of the form. In his 'Proeme' Gay claims to be restoring true Theocritean rusticity, and promises the reader 'a picture, or rather lively landscape of thy own country', all written in a language which never has nor will be spoken, 'it having too much of the country to be fit for the court, too much of the court to be fit for the country; too much of the language of old times to be fit for the present, too much of the present to have been fit for the old, and too much of both to be fit for any time to come.' He laughs at both Pope and Ambrose Philips, and achieves his mockery through a comic but detailed presentation of ordinary country-life. Thus, when Bumkinet and Grubbinol mourn the death of the peerless Blouzelinda, the stock pastoral lament becomes both humorous and pathetic, since they remember her, not brushing the dewy lawn, but making butter, skimming cream, feeding hogs and poultry, or hay-making. Moreover, the intrusion of real occupations brings with it a more down-to-earth view of human nature : the pastoral vows of eternal constancy are made, though ludicrously, but are succeeded by a more sceptical notion of the duration of a lover's grief :

> Thus wail'd the louts in melancholy strain,
> 'Till bonny *Susan* sped across the plain;
> They seiz'd the lass in apron clean array'd,
> And to the ale-house forc'd the willing maid;
> In ale and kisses they forget their cares,
> And *Susan Blouzelinda*'s loss repairs.
>
> ('Friday; or, The Dirge', 159–64)

Reaction against the conventional artificialities thus permitted a more realistic view of country-life and country-people. Similarly, when in *Baucis and Philemon* (1709), Swift transferred to a Kent village the Ovidian story of the old couple who gave hospitality to the gods and were rewarded by having their cottage transformed into a temple and they themselves into its priest and priestess, the moral of the story as well as the setting is changed : the gods become two hermits, 'Saints by Trade', suspiciously like canting beggars, and the old peasants are not improved by conversion into a greedy and obsequious parson and his place-proud wife.[3]

However, there are fairly narrow limits to the response to rural life that can be presented in burlesque or parody, and there were other well-established traditions much closer to the eighteenth-century poet's experience of the countryside. There was, for instance, the praise of rural retirement. But, in general, poets modelled themselves less on the sensuous example of Marvell's 'The Garden' or 'Upon Appleton House' than on a more practical pattern derived from Horace in his 'Second Epode' and the 'Sixth Satire of the Second Book'. John Pomfret in *The Choice* (1700) describes in detail the estate he requires for retirement, and adds such extras as a good library, a sufficiency of money, a cellar stocked with the best wines, and the presence in the neighbourhood of 'some Obliging, Modest Fair', whose company he might seek, without spoiling 'By a too frequent, and too bold an Use'. The popularity of this poem was no doubt largely due to the graceful way in which it disguised the Englishman's dream of the easy life of a country-gentleman as a piece of

Roman simplicity; many other followers of Horace were less discreet. Swift, for instance, is blunt and specific:

> I often wish'd, that I had clear
> For Life, six hundred Pounds a Year,
> A handsome House to lodge a Friend,
> A River at my Garden's End,
> A Terras Walk, and half a Rood
> Of Land set out to plant a Wood.
>
> ('Horace, Lib. 2. Sat. 6', 1–6)

Much the most agreeable poem in this vein is Matthew Green's *The Spleen* (1737). Green is as specific as Swift in his wishes ('Two hundred pounds half-yearly paid'), but combines wit, commonsense and self-mockery, with a genuine affection for country life. He can fix in a brief, vivid image those who attend the levees of the great—

> And hungry hopes regale the while
> On the spare diet of a smile,—
>
> (442–43)

and suggest in simple language, but subtle rhythms, an easy acquaintance with the life he desires:

> A pond before full to the brim,
> Where cows may cool, and geese may swim;
> Behind, a green like velvet neat,
> Soft to the eye, and to the feet.
>
> (648–51)

Yet his emphasis, like that of most poets in this Horatian mode, is on the comforts and repose of retirement, rather than on any passionate response to natural beauty.

An exception has to be made for Lady Winchilsea's 'Petition for an Absolute Retreat' (1713), where there is a sensitive feeling for the variety of trees and plants in her desired garden, but Lady Winchilsea was a poet who sought to be different and often succeeded:

> My Hand delights to trace unusual Things,
> And deviates from the known, and common Way.
>
> ('The Spleen', 83–84)

Her best-known poem, 'A Nocturnal Reverie' (1713), though in a tradition of nocturnals which went back to 'Il Penseroso', is without the gloomy meditations usually associated with that tradition and is concerned mainly with the beauty of falling night,

> When freshen'd Grass now bears it self upright,
> And makes cool Banks to pleasing Rest invite,
> Whence springs the Woodbind, and the Bramble-Rose,
> And where the sleepy Cowslip shelter'd grows;
> Whilst now a paler Hue the Foxglove takes,
> Yet chequers still with Red the dusky brakes....
>
> (11–16)

Parnell's 'Night-piece on Death' (1722), has a briefer but evocative night-scene, but depends less on natural imagery than on the fine ordering of all the elements in the poem. The action is simple : the poet leaves his books, wanders by a lake to a churchyard, imagines ghosts and hears the voice of Death. An informal opening is followed by a hushed image of the lake mirroring the night-sky. Then, in the churchyard, more emphatic rhythms and more forceful language are used as the poet distinguishes between the graves, from the nameless mounds of the poor to the marble tombs and vaults,

> Whose Pillars swell with sculptur'd Stones,
> Arms, Angels, Epitaphs, and Bones.
>
> (41–42)

The cry of the visionary ghosts, 'Think, Mortal, what it is to die', seems like a climactic *memento mori*, but a counter-movement begins as Death eloquently reproaches men for frightening themselves with ghostly images and funeral paraphernalia, instead of recognizing that to die is to escape from suffering,

> Clap the glad Wing, and tow'r away,
> And mingle with the Blaze of Day.
>
> (89–90)

The theme of the poem is resurrection, rather than mortality, and the beauty of it derives from the poetic process which integrates argument, action, language, imagery to lead the reader into darkness and gloom only to raise him suddenly at the end into 'the Blaze of Day'. The setting of the poem is both effective and relevant but, as in most nocturnal verse, the natural scene is firmly subordinated to the moral or spiritual argument.

Similarly, in the poems about a specific locality, of which Denham's *Cooper's Hill* (1642) was the exemplar, the features of the view are employed to lead, as Pope put it, 'into some Reflection, upon moral Life or political Institution'.[4] Pope's own descriptive passages in *Windsor-Forest* (1713) are brilliant and diversified, but are in a sense decorative, like illuminations in a manuscript; they adorn, and emphasize and link together a complex poem which has more important matters in hand. But in Dyer's 'Grongar Hill' (1726) the description is the primary source of interest and unity, and it is the moral aphorisms which seem like inserted ornaments. Dyer sets out to 'Draw the Landskip bright and strong', and his sensuous response to its colours and forms constitutes the essence of the poem. The scene itself changes little, although the poet's view of it varies as he climbs the hill or turns round on the summit, but Dyer's fondness for terms of motion give excitement and liveliness to the poem :

> Rushing from the Woods, the Spires
> Seem from hence ascending Fires!

(51–52)

There is an immediacy which was rarely present in poems where natural description was subordinated to argument. When Pope said that in his own early poems 'pure Description held the place of Sense', he showed how far he and most of his contemporaries were from perceiving that description was a form of sense—that a poet selecting, ordering, and evoking his vision of a landscape might be dealing as directly with human nature and experience as when he was writing moral verse.

The complexity of the experience presented must obviously vary with the complexity of the description. In Ambrose Philips's 'Epistle to the Earl of Dorset' (1709), describing the brittle, frozen landscape of Denmark, it is only the aesthetic response to a brilliant and strange scene that is involved; in 'Grongar Hill' Dyer is responding not only to the beauty of the scene but to its combination of grandeur and familiarity. But in *The Seasons* (1726–30), Thomson is much more variously and profoundly involved in the natural world, as indeed his Preface to *Winter* indicates :

I know no subject more elevating, more amusing; more ready to awake the poetical enthusiasm, the philosophical reflection, and the moral sentiment, than the works of Nature. Where can we meet with such variety, such beauty, such magnificence? All that enlarges and transports the soul!

Thomson was an innovator, although he was careful to establish his literary ancestry by mentioning the *Georgics*, acknowledging the example of John Philips's *Cyder*, and using a manner reminiscent of Milton, for a 'great and serious' subject. Many earlier 'physico-theological' poems had praised God and his created universe, but there had been nothing comparable in scale or quality to *The Seasons*, nothing of comparable range and variety.

Instead of painting the natural world as a backcloth to human activities, Thomson presents a living universe ('Full nature swarms with life') in which man is part of a universal, but not always apprehendable, harmony:

> Thus the glad skies,
> The wide-rejoicing earth, the woods, the streams
> With every life they hold, down to the flower
> That paints the lowly vale, or insect-wing
> Waved o'er the shepherd's slumber, touch the mind,
> To nature tuned, with a light-flying hand
> Invisible, quick-urging through the nerves
> The glittering spirits in a flood of day.
>
> ('Spring') [5]

The Seasons contains passages of moralizing and philosophising, but the unifying conception is that experience of nature can be inspiriting, uplifting and instructive, so that whether Thomson is celebrating the divine benevolence or drawing a moral or giving a scientific explanation of some phenomenon or telling a story or describing a scene, everything is equally part of a complex exploration of man's response to a world which delights him, dwarfs him, and sometimes terrifies and destroys him. To recreate in verbal sound and movement the sounds and movements of nature contributes to the instructive as well as the delighting function of poetry: it puts the reader imaginatively in the presence of nature and shapes his apprehension of it. Sometimes one may feel that Thomson is encumbered with remnants of stock diction, but more often he is astonishingly precise and evocative. He can suggest the jerky hopping of a robin, or the swirling flight of sea-birds:

> The cormorant on high
> Wheels from the deep, and screams along the land.
> Loud shrieks the soaring hern; and with wild wing
> The circling sea-fowl cleave the flaky clouds.
>
> ('Winter', 144–47)

Or he can capture much larger and vaguer movements involving a whole landscape—the ripple of light and shade across a cornfield on a windy day, the hesitant descent of a light fall of snow, or the erratic course of a stream as it pours from the mountains, and spreads over a valley, until, reaching a narrow pass, 'It boils, and wheels, and foams and thunders through'. The precise control of sound and movement in Thomson's verse is a long way from description as decoration : it is one of the chief methods by which he creates a poetic vision of a world in which everything, from the scum on ponds to thunderstorms, is a manifestation of natural energy. In such a vision, old assumptions about man's place in the universe are implicitly challenged, and celebrations of the creative benevolence are balanced against episodes in which man, like every other creature, is overwhelmed by forces beyond his understanding.

The importance of Thomson's achievement was less that it extended the subject-matter of poetry than that it developed a new vocabulary capable of expressing a poet's deepest intuitions, uncertainties or obsessions. Thus Richard Savage's *The Wanderer* (1729), though it plainly owes much to Thomson, presents a very different world shaped by and expressive of the poet's own romantic, egocentric personality, while in *The Chacé* (1735), Somerville uses Thomson's vocabulary to describe the extrovert delights of hunting. However carefully critics have traced Thomson's borrowings from other poets and from scientists, philosophers and theologians, in the end one has to agree with Dr. Johnson :

As a writer he is entitled to one praise of the highest kind : his mode of thinking and of expressing his thoughts is original.[6]

To the new reading-public, largely collected in cities, the poetry of Thomson and his imitators offered an imaginative escape from the squalor and congestion of the streets, and an escape that neither offended their sense of reality nor required the financial resources of a country-gentleman. The country was always near at hand; merchants and comfortably-off tradesmen could live on the fringes of the city; Sunday excursions into the countryside were becoming a favourite recreation; and most of those who could read Thomson were able to practise first-hand the sensitivity to and interest in nature which he fostered.

Yet these new readers wanted more than a literary compensation for the disadvantages of town-life. They wanted, also, a literature which would reflect and comment on their daily lives, concerns, and environment, and would relate them to the permanent elements in human experience recorded in the literature of the past. Plain realists like Defoe were popular, but at the cost of being regarded as uncultivated; *The Tatler* and *The Spectator*, on the other hand, mirrored contemporary life with a colouring of classical culture. In poetry, the presentation of urban life was usually combined with imitation of a classical form—pastoral (as in the town eclogues of Gay and Lady Mary Wortley Montagu), georgic (as in Swift's 'Description of a City Shower' or Gay's *Trivia*) or epic (as in Garth's *Dispensary* or Pope's *Rape of the Lock*). The most obvious function of such mock-forms was to ridicule the contemporary world by the ludicrous discrepancy between form and subject-matter, but, in good hands, they served much more complex purposes. *The Rape of the Lock* (1712), for instance, mocks the triviality of polite society by the implied heroic contrast, and yet, at the same time, bestows a delicate and refined grace on that frivolous world. Similarly, though less subtly, Swift laughs at the squalor of London in 'A Description of the Morning' and 'A Description of a City Shower', but, in doing so, presents the life of the streets so vividly and humorously that the total image is of a city full of grotesque vitality.

Gay acknowledged that *Trivia, or the Art of Walking the Streets of London* (1716) was indebted to Swift for 'several hints', but his mock-georgic has a far greater variety of scene and incident, attitude and tone, than any other verse-portrait of the city. Gay has all the gifts of a great poet except the highest intensity of passion and imagination; he is intelligent, witty, humorous, sensuous and shrewd, and whether one reads *Rural Sports* (1713), *The Shepherd's Week* (1714), *Trivia*, town eclogues, epistles, fables, songs or ballad-operas, one finds a consistently high level of brilliant and conscientious craftsmanship and an unfailingly sensitive control of rhythm and diction. In *Trivia*, where he found a subject entirely suited to his genius, the diversity of the scene is equalled by the variety of his verse. It labours when describing the muddy streets in autumn—

> When late their miry sides stage-coaches show,
> And their stiff horses through the town move slow—
>
> (i. 25–26)

or jars discordantly when the subject is a traffic-jam—

> Here laden carts with thundring waggons meet,
> Wheels clash with wheels, and bar the narrow street;
> The lashing whip resounds, the horses strain,

And blood in anguish bursts the swelling vein.

> (ii. 229–32)

A humorous but exact verb can imply a parallel between the proud and the milk-sellers' asses:

> Before proud gates attending asses bray,
> Or arrogate with solemn pace the way.

> (ii. 13–14)

Or an equally evocative verb, supported by alliteration, can express a vigorous contempt:

> There flames a fool, begirt with tinsell'd slaves,
> Who wastes the wealth of a whole race of knaves.

> (ii. 581–2)

Although the avowed theme of the poem is the difficulties and dangers of walking the London streets, Gay urges the pedestrian not to envy the beaux in their carriages—

> In gilded chariots while they loll at ease,
> And lazily insure a life's disease.

> (i. 69–70)

For all the complaints, the poem conveys the poet's enjoyment of the congestion that fills the street with unending variety of sights, smells, sounds and incidents, and celebrates city-life with a gusto that matches the more exalted enthusiasm of the nature-poets.

Many other poems appeared praising or criticizing London but none of comparable merit. Even Dr. Johnson, whose love of the city was at least equal to Gay's, and whose poetic gift was more powerful, if less flexible, falls far short. *London, a Poem in Imitation of the Third Satire of Juvenal* (1738) presents the capital as 'The common shore of Paris and of Rome', a hot-bed of vice and corruption where 'All crimes are safe, but hated poverty'. The uncharacteristic hostility may be blamed on Juvenal, or on the fact that in 1738 Johnson was still wretchedly poor, but the more important objection to his poem is that, apart from a few nominal references, the satire could be as easily directed against any large city. There is no apprehension of the individuality of London, no sense of the confused liveliness to which Swift and Gay had responded and which Johnson himself was later to enjoy. But although one cannot apply to *London* the terms Johnson applied to *Trivia*—'sprightly, various and pleasant' [7]—it has, on the other hand, passages of intense moral seriousness and weighty eloquence beyond Gay's range. Moreover, it belongs to a different kind : *Trivia* is a mock-georgic with satirical episodes; *London* is a satire.

In a period so concerned with the instructive and social functions of literature, satire stood high in the literary hierarchy as the most direct way of influencing moral and cultural standards. When Defoe began his Preface to *The True-Born Englishman* (1701), 'The end of satire is reformation', he was re-asserting the accepted critical justification of satire. But there were many theoretical corollaries. If the end was reformation, one should not attack a man for faults he could not correct, such as innate stupidity : but if the fool pretended to be wise (as most fools do), he could be exposed. A vicious man might be beyond reformation : could he then escape satire? No, Dryden had said, because ' 'Tis an action of virtue to make examples of vicious men'.[8] Swift went further and added that it was as much a duty to warn people against evil men as to warn them of the presence of a savage animal in the neighbourhood.[9] A dead man could not be reformed nor constitute a public menace, but Swift declared that '*De mortuis nil nisi bonum*' was a foolish precept : men too powerful to be attacked while alive should be attacked after death, since 'although their Memories will rot, there may be some Benefit for their Survivers, to smell it while it is rotting'.[10] Yet despite such extensions to the simple moral purpose of reformation, the satirist could still hold a lofty notion of his role as moral arbiter, and could still regard satire as a literary kind that demanded the highest exercise of his talents. (Later in the century, when moralists like Cowper could describe satire as character-assassination, the loss of moral authority was accompanied by a deterioration in the formal qualities of the verse, and perhaps it is significant that the only major poet of the nineteenth century to devote a large part of his poetic energy to satire was Lord Byron, who believed that 'the highest of all poetry is ethical poetry' and regarded Pope as the great master of it.)

In the period 1700–1740 the literary prestige of satire was such that nearly all poets of stature (Thomson is the obvious exception) at one time or another turned their hands to it, and poems not essentially satirical (like *Trivia* or *An Essay on Man*) would be enriched with passages of satirical eloquence. But the first two satires of any account in the eighteenth century are notable neither for moral passion nor poetic art. Defoe's *The True-Born Englishman*, like Dryden's political satires, is concerned with a specific issue of the time—the hostility shown against the Dutchmen whom William III had brought with him to England; while Mandeville's *The Grumbling Hive* (1705) appears to teach an immoral rather than a moral lesson, by a fable which shows that a successful society is dependent on private vices, and that a sudden conversion to virtue would ruin a state. Whether these compositions are to be called poems, or, as some critics have said, merely verses is a matter of terminology : both have distinct flavour and interest. Defoe and Mandeville were men of varied talents and forceful personalities, and both had a command of lively colloquial idiom. Mandeville's poem (later the foundation of *The Fable of the Bees*) has greater economy and firmer design, and can still surprise with the boldness and force of its criticism of ordinary moral assumptions, but Defoe's has more native energy and humour, and, despite its particular occasion, has commonsense relevance to xenophobia wherever and whenever it appears. To those who complained of the new influx of foreigners, Defoe replied by showing the meaninglessness of the claim to be true-born Englishmen, enumerating the often unsavoury ingredients blended to form the nation from the time of the Britons and Romans to the more recent introductions of Charles II :

> The royal refugee our breed restores,
> With foreign courtiers and with foreign whores,
> And carefully repeopled us again,
> Throughout his lazy, long, lascivious reign.

> (i. 231–34)

Some literary historians have said that Defoe and Mandeville are closer to seventeenth- than to eighteenth-century satire, and naturally enough, their manners in some ways resemble those of their predecessors. But eighteenth-century verse satire must not be identified with Pope. He is the master, but by far the greater part of his satirical work was in the second quarter of the century. At least two satirical traditions co-existed—the homely, vigorous, but comparatively unrefined kind exemplified by Defoe, and a more urbane, stylish kind based usually on a classical model. (Walter Harte in his *Essay on Satire* (1730) makes in fact three categories of satire : epic satire, like the *Dunciad*; 'rugged' satire where the verse 'rolls with Vehemence and Force'; and satire which 'nicely pointed in th'Horatian way/Wounds keen'.)

To his last category belongs Samuel Garth's *The Dispensary*, first published in 1699 but frequently revised and brought up to

date, a mock-heroic account of a current dispute between phy-
sicians and apothecaries, which owed its popularity to Garth's
skill in varying the couplet and in deploying his classical learning. Edward Young's *The Universal Passion* (1725–28, collected
as *The Love of Fame* in 1728) has more serious moral content,
and in the way it traces the prevalent love of fame through a
variety of satirical episodes and character-studies foreshadows
Pope's method in the *Moral Essays*. Young lacks Pope's ima-
inative agility or penetration, but his satire is well-directed and
often enlivened with neat, amusing and observant couplets, as
in the lines on pride of birth :

> They that on glorious ancestors enlarge,
> Produce their debt, instead of their discharge.
>
> (i. 147–48)

Of the major poets, Pope clearly belongs to the polished
classical tradition, and so does Gay, though his classicism is
tempered by native humour. Swift, however, fits neither category, or rather combines both. Sometimes he believed in the
efficacy of satire and sometimes doubted it, and sometimes was
concerned mainly with personal satisfaction : 'I will kill that
Flea or Louse which bites me, though I get no Honour by it'.[11]
Consequently, during most of his long career he was producing
satirical verse, ranging from topical lampoons to general ridicules of folly and pretence, from street-ballads to imitations of
Horace.

The fertility of his mind in producing 'lucky hints' for poems
was equalled by his extraordinary ingenuity in the exploitation
of such hints. Because he was so often engaged in stripping off
pretence, his characteristic manner is based on the deflating misuse of the stock conventions of form, imagery and diction. If
he wants to compare the greed of Marlborough to that of
Midas, he ensures that the general derives no accidental elevation from the mythical comparison by telling the classical
story with belittling colloquial realism : 'The Golden Scurf peels
off his Limbs' (*The Fable of Midas*, 1712). He takes the familiar
parallel between a chaste and beautiful woman and the moon
and discovers unsuspected justification for it :

> When first Diana leaves her Bed
> Vapors and Steams her Looks disgrace,
> A frouzy dirty colour'd red
> Sits on her cloudy wrinckled Face.
>
> ('The Progress of Beauty', 1–4)

This is only the beginning of a hundred-line exploration of the similitude, imitating the idiom of romantic love to present a sordid reality.

The blunt unpleasantness of image and language in such poems is sometimes attributed to an obsessive hatred of the body and its functions but it can be more reasonably explained in terms of Swift's satiric purpose. In 'Strephon and Chloe' (1734), for instance, the argument of the poem is that the inflated romantic nonsense, represented by the praise of Chloe as a goddess of 'taintless body', is bound to collapse under the strain of married intimacy and leave only disillusion and disgust : if it is proper for the language to imitate romantic affectation, it is equally proper for it to express, in contrast, the consequent physical disgust, just as it is proper to shift to a balanced and moderate tone for the concluding advice :

> On Sense and Wit your Passion found,
> By Decency cemented round;
> Let Prudence with Good Nature strive,
> To keep Esteem and Love alive.
>
> (307–10)

Swift's gift of mimicry enabled him to invent appropriate styles to ridicule many different affectations—of astrologers, lawyers, hack-poets, society-ladies, tradesmen and courtiers— and also to vary his style within a poem for more serious moral purposes. In 'A Satirical Elegy on the Death of a late Famous General' (1722), he begins with an imitation of the back-biting with which those who had obsequiously lauded Marlborough receive the first news of his death, and then shifts to a darker and bitterer tone as the funeral passes, accompanied neither by 'widow's sighs nor orphan's tears' :

> But what of that, his friends may say,
> He had those honours in his day.
> True to his profit and his pride,
> He made them weep before he dy'd.
>
> (21–24)

And the poem concludes in a quite different manner, an eloquent address to all the creatures of kings to 'Come hither, and behold your fate' in this vision of the great man 'Turn'd to that dirt from whence he sprung'.

In this, as in many of Swift's poems, mounting passion is expressed by a darkened tone, retardation of the verse-movement, heavy stressing, thumping alliteration and a long suspension of syntax until the accumulated energy falls with overwhelming emphasis on a single word or expression. In *On Poetry: A Rhapsody* (1733) there is an even clearer example of this accumulation where Swift, having declared in an extended sentence that no human activity requires such 'heavenly influence' as the writing of poetry, follows it at once with a sentence of parallel construction describing the poet's social situation:

> Not Beggar's Brat, on Bulk begot;
> Not Bastard of a Pedlar Scot;
> Not Boy brought up to cleaning Shoes,
> The Spawn of Bridewell, or the Stews;
> Not Infants dropt, the spurious Pledges
> Of Gipsies littering under Hedges,
> Are so disqualified by Fate,
> To rise in Church, or Law, or State,
> As he, whom Phebus in his Ire
> Hath *blasted* with poetick Fire.

(33–42)

Equally characteristic is the prevailing irony, often implicit in the very idea or structure of a poem, and often very complex. For instance, the *Verses on the Death of Dr. Swift*, written in 1731, seem intended as an expansion of La Rochefoucauld's irony: 'In the Adversity of our best Friends, we find something that doth not displease us'. Swift takes the cynicism even farther—not only are we pleased by our friends' misfortunes but we are displeased by their successes. He proceeds to illustrate this by abusing Pope for his wit, Gay for his humour, Arbuthnot for his irony, and St. John and Pulteney for their prose:

> If with such Talents Heav'n hath blest 'em
> Have I not Reason to detest 'em?

(65–66)

Now the irony is devouring its own tail, because under the pretence of jealous complaint Swift is publicly celebrating his friends' talents. Yet the contradictions do not cancel out; they combine in an image of human friendship more truthful and more complex than the simplifications either of commonplace moralists or of La Rochefoucauld.

Swift rightly acknowledged Pope's supremacy in verse, but not even Pope is more varied in satirical method. The occasions which provoked some of Swift's best poems (like 'The Legion Club') were local and ephemeral, but what he called 'my own hum'rous biting Way' was an original and impressive achievement.

What was achieved in the kinds which were at the top of the literary hierarchy, epic and tragedy, was much less substantial. The epic conventions were based on assumptions about the nature of the universe, of society, of man, which had little relevance to the world the poets lived in. Homer could be praised, translated, analysed, parodied, but not successfully imitated. Sir Richard Blackmore continued the laborious heroic poems he had begun writing in the 1690s, and later in the period Richard Glover's *Leonidas* (1737) was overpraised for its rhetorical patriotism. Other, briefer attempts were made, as in Addison's *The Campaign* (1705), to give heroic stature to contemporary events, but it proved difficult to praise a modern general, far from the fighting, as though he were Agamemnon, without a note of incongruity : when we are told that, amid the slaughter of battle, Marlborough 'In peaceful Thought the Field of Death survey'd', callousness seems as much implied as heroic calm, and Addison has to shift from reality to the elevated image of the general as the angel who 'Rides in the Whirl-Wind, and directs the Storm'. In 1735, the critic, Thomas Blackwell, shrewdly pointed out that the life and language of eighteenth-century England differed in kind from those of Homer's Greece, and that the truly elevated contemporary poetic manners were those of *The Rape of the Lock* and *The Seasons*.[12]

In tragedy, too, the sublime was much less common than the pompous or sentimental. Addison's *Cato* (1713) is well-constructed, and a certain stiffness in the language can be seen as appropriate to the rigid Roman virtue of its hero, but it is hard to resist Johnson's verdict that it is 'rather a succession of just sentiments in elegant language than a representation of natural affections'.[13] Most tragedies of the time are peopled with 'tragic figures', rather than men and women, who tell each other about the 'grief', 'horror' and other emotions which they claim to be experiencing. Nicholas Rowe's *Jane Shore* (1714) and some of Thomson's tragedies can still be read with interest and occasional pleasure, but it is very unlikely that they will ever be revived in the theatre, save, perhaps, as historical curiosities.

The early eighteenth century was witnessing the emergence of commonplace, unheroic, modern society, and this seems to have encouraged the mock-heroic style, while forcing those poets who attempted heroic verse, tragedy or the Pindaric Ode to strain away too strongly from the contamination of common speech. For prolonged and genuine elevation of language one has to turn to *The Seasons*, where the subject is the sublimity of Nature, or to the tragic universal triumph of Dulness at the end of the *Dunciad*.

At the other end of the scale was verse which purported to be no more than a memorable and attractive way of conveying information or opinion. A modern reader may be puzzled by the nature of the subject-matter. What audience was there for John Philips's *Cyder* (1708) with its information about apple-growing and cider-making? The fact is that the technical advice is there less for its intrinsic usefulness than because such material is necessary if one is to write a georgic, just as the Miltonic verse and diction is intended to provide an English equivalent for Virgilian dignity and sonority. The popularity of *Cyder* was not due to an intense interest in horticulture, but to enjoyment of the poet's skill in giving to an English scene and English occupations a classical aura.

Cyder, then, is less didactic in purpose than it pretends. The instructive function, however, was more seriously undertaken in areas where a poet might claim special insight. Yet, even here, it is necessary to bear in mind the distinction between a poem and a treatise. A treatise should offer reasoned and systematic argument or analysis: a poem offers a way of looking at a subject, a projection of the poet's temperament, passions and imagination as well as of his reason. One should not turn to Pope's *Essay on Criticism* (1711) for brand-new critical ideas or specific analyses, or to his *Essay on Man* (1733–34) or Prior's 'Solomon' (1718) for the kind of satisfactions one finds in Locke or Hume. But they are not merely ornamented summaries of other men's ideas: they are representations of the poet's total response to some question, and this response is variously articulated in the language as well as the structure of the poem, in imagery and emotion as well as in reasoning. The superiority of the *Essay on Criticism* to the numerous critical poems of the period—among the most interesting are Parnell's *Essay on the Different Styles of Poetry* (1713), Walter Harte's *Essay on Satire* (1730) and James Miller's *Harlequin-Horace, or the Art of Modern Poetry* (1731)—is not in its containing more original critical notions, but in the superior quality and coherence of Pope's response to literature, and his far greater power to organize and express the thoughts, intuitions and feelings involved in that response.

Such didactic poems show most clearly the current concept of the social usefulness of verse. There was no feeling that verse should be reserved for exalted experiences. The notion that the poet should pour out his private emotions with no responsibility save to his inspiration and his art, and that humanity might benefit, as it were accidentally, from his effusions was hardly conceivable. The task of the poetic genius was to think deeply and feel deeply, and then to use his personal insights to explore or serve the permanent concerns of all mankind.

Consequently religious poetry expressed communal rather than private belief. The emphasis tends to be less on Christ than on God the benevolent creator, the omnipotent planner, the divine scientist whose last apostle was Newton. The poetry is usually more expressive of awe and admiring wonder than of love; Addison's great hymn is typical:

> The Spacious Firmament on high,
> With all the blue Etherial Sky,
> And spangled Heav'ns, a Shining Frame,
> Their great Original proclaim.

It is the same theme as that of the physico-theological poets and Thomson. Isaac Watts, more than any other poet of the time, appears to write from personal religious experience, but his most famous hymn, 'Our God, our Help in Ages past', is, like Addison's, praise of the Almighty Power that rules the universe; and, even in his more passionate and specifically Christian hymns, such as 'When I survey the wond'rous Cross', the emotion is sufficiently generalized to stand for all Christians' humility in face of the crucifixion. A congregation can stand up and sing the hymn, with each person believing that he is expressing his own feelings, not those of Isaac Watts. Thus, although the early eighteenth century has nothing to compare with the private religious intensity of the Metaphysicals, poets like Watts and the Wesleys contributed some of the finest expressions of communal worship.

What is true of the religious poetry is also generally true of the love-poetry of the period. Apart from 'Eloisa to Abelard', most attempts to explore or express the passion swell into bombast or dwindle into conventional poeticisms. The more successful love-poetry generally adopts the detached elegant manner and the witty compliments, persuasions and reproofs of poets like Prior and Congreve, or the 'manly' jocular vein of some of the songs in *The Beggar's Opera*—for instance, 'How happy could I be with either,/Were t'other dear charmer away' or 'Before the barn-door crowing,/The Cock by Hens attended'. Prior's special gift was his mastery of the tone of playful irony, a suggestion of intelligence smiling at its own pretences. The light self-mockery is evident in the polite dissembling of 'The Merchant, to secure his Treasure', and explicit in the poem, 'A Better Answer to "Cloe Jealous"', where the poet defends himself against his mistress's jealousy of the other women whose praises he has sung:

> What I speak, my fair Cloe, and what I write, shews
>   The Diff'rence there is betwixt Nature and Art:
> I court others in Verse; but I love Thee in Prose:
>   And They have my Whimsies; but Thou hast my Heart.
>   (13–16)

Prior's cool affection is about as personal a manner as one finds in the love-poetry of the period—with one exception, and that in poems not initially intended for publication, and addressed to a friend, not a mistress. In 'Cadenus and Vanessa' Swift showed that he could manage a graceful compliment, though his elaborations tend towards social satire, but in the verses written for 'Stella' Johnson a deep personal relationship is unaffectedly and convincingly expressed. Some verses are teasing, some are very moving, as when Swift, knowing that Stella was ill, thanked her for attending his sick-bed, and concluded with a warning to her to be careful of her own health:

> For such a Fool was never found,
> Who pull'd a Palace to the Ground,
> Only to have the Ruins made
> Materials for an House decay'd.
> ('To Stella, Visiting me in my Sickness', 1720, 121–24)

But the best of the poems is that entitled 'Stella's Birthday, Written A.D. 1720–21', where Swift begins by comparing the entertainment of Stella's company to that of 'the true old Angel-Inn', teasingly compares her face to the inn-sign ('An Angel's Face, a little crack't), and then turns to address the young woman who has hopes of supplanting Stella as a hostess, in a long sentence of mounting emotion, which concludes,

> No Bloom of Youth can ever blind
> The Cracks and Wrinckles of your Mind,
> All Men of Sense will pass your Dore
> And crowd to Stella's at fourscore.
>
>   (55–58)

Swift's tone of intense private emotion is something which the poetry of the period mainly lacks, although it has an abundance of easy and urbane epistles and addresses to friends. Whether Stella was friend or lover is irrelevant: as Swift wrote, when he was tormented by the fear that Stella was dying, 'Believe me that violent friendship is much more lasting, and as much engaging, as violent love'.[14]

When poetry and society are so closely related as in the early eighteenth century, private passion has to be, for the most part, transmuted and sublimated into terms of general reference, while the most passionate verse may occur in the more public form of moral indignation at social follies and corruptions. Poetry seems to be addressed to its readers, rather than overheard by them, and conversely the social influences on poets and their work are especially direct and powerful. In an essay of this length it is impossible even to mention all the influences and achievements in forty years of poetry: what I have tried to emphasize is that the period, like any other period, was not one of complacent uniformity. If there were strong forces making for stability and conformity, there were equally powerful forces making for change and experiment. It was a period when Addison could declare,

> It is impossible, for us who live in the latter Ages of the World, to make Observations in Criticism, Morality, or in any Art or Science, which have not been touched upon by others. We have little else left us, but to represent the common Sense of Mankind in more strong, more beautiful, or more uncommon Lights.[15]

But it was also a period when Swift could describe 'a true genius' as

> one, who upon a deserving Subject, is able to open new Scenes, and discover a Vein of true and noble Thinking, which never entered into any Imagination before: Every Stroke of whose Pen is worth all the Paper blotted by Hundreds of others in the Compass of their Lives.[16]

NOTES

1. As Pope's poetry is discussed separately, it is here referred to only in passing.

2. Born 1605, Waller did not die until 1687 and published his *Divine Poems* in 1685. However, his characteristically 'smooth' manner was achieved well before the middle of the century.

3. The point of the conversion is clearer in Swift's autograph version (*Poetical Works*, ed. Herbert Davis, Oxford, 1967, pp. 61–66) than in the version published (*ibid.*, pp. 77–82).

4. *The Iliad of Homer*, xvi. 466 n.

5. These lines were omitted from the 1744 edition of *The Seasons*: see *The Complete Works of James Thomson*, ed. J. L. Robertson, Oxford, 1908, 1951, p. 51.

6. *Lives of the English Poets*, ed. G. B. Hill, Oxford, 1905, iii. 298.

7. *Ibid.*, ii. 283–4.

8. 'A Discourse Concerning the Original and Progress of Satire,' in *Of Dramatic Poesy and Other Critical Essays*, ed. G. Watson, London, 1962, ii. 126.

9. *The Examiner* no. 38, 26 April 1711, in *The Examiner and Other Pieces Written in 1710–11: The Prose Works*, ed. Herbert Davis, Oxford, iii (1940), 141.

10. *An Answer to a Paper, call'd 'A Memorial,'* in *Prose Works*, ed. Herbert Davis, Oxford, xii (1955), 25.

11. Letter to Rev. Thomas Sheridan, 25 Sept. 1725, *The Correspondence of Jonathan Swift*, ed. Sir Harold Williams, Oxford, 1963–65, iii. 101.

12. *An Enquiry into the Life and Writings of Homer*, pp. 33–35.

13. *Lives of the English Poets*, ed. G. B. Hill, ii. 132.

14. Letter to Rev. James Stopford, 20 July 1726, *Correspondence*, ed. H. Williams, iii. 143.

15. *The Spectator*, no. 253, 20 Dec. 1711.

16. *A Proposal for Correcting, Improving and Ascertaining the English Tongue*, in *Prose Works*, ed. Herbert Davis, Oxford, iv (1957), 19.

BIBLIOGRAPHY

I *Editions* (*in chronological order of poets*)

Prior, Matthew, (1664–1721) *Complete Works*, ed. H. Bunker Wright and M. K. Spears, 2 vols., Oxford, 1959.

Swift, Jonathan (1667–1745) *Poems*, ed. H. Williams, 3 vols., Oxford, 1937, rev. 1958; *Poetical Works*, ed. H. Davis, Oxford, 1967 (*Oxford Standard Authors*). (See also chapter 2.)

Philips, Ambrose (1675?–1749) *Poems*, ed. M. G. Segar, Oxford, 1937.

Philips, John (1676–1709) *Poems*, ed. M. G. Lloyd Thomas, London, 1927.

Gay, John (1685–1732) *Poetical Works*, ed. G. C. Faber, Oxford, 1926 (*Oxford Standard Authors*).

Diaper, William (1686?–1717) *Complete Works*, ed. Dorothy Broughton, London, 1951.

Pope, Alexander (1688–1744) *Poems*, ed. John Butt, London, 1963. (See also chapter 3.)

Savage, Richard (1697?–1742) *Poetical Works*, ed. C. Tracy, Cambridge, 1962.

Thomson, James (1700–48) *Poetical Works*, ed. J. L. Robertson, Oxford, 1908, 1951 (*Oxford Standard Authors*).

Johnson, Samuel (1709–84) *Poems*, ed. D. Nichol Smith and E. L. McAdam, Oxford, 1941; ed. E. L. McAdam and G. Milne, New Haven, 1964. (See also chapter 10.)

Minor Poets of the Eighteenth Century, ed. H. I'A. Fausset, London, 1930 (*Everyman's Library*). Contains the collected poems of the Countess of Winchilsea (1666–1720), Thomas Parnell (1679–1718), Matthew Green (1696–1737), John Dyer (1700?–58) and William Collins (1721–59).

II *Selections:*

The following anthologies include a selection of poems of the period:

The Oxford Book of Eighteenth Century Verse, ed. D. Nichol Smith, Oxford, 1926. This useful collection has the whole of Pomfret's *The Choice* and some poems or excerpts by most of the poets referred to in this article.

Early Eighteenth Century Poetry, ed. James Sutherland, London, 1965. Includes many of the poems referred to in this article, besides the whole of *The Rape of the Lock* and *Winter* (1726). The poems are fully annotated.

Poetry of the Landscape and the Night, ed. Charles Peake, London, 1967. Includes the whole of *Cooper's Hill* and *Windsor-Forest* and many poems of natural description, with annotation.

English Satiric Poetry: Dryden to Byron, ed. James Kinsley and J. T. Boulton, London, 1966.

Selected Poems of Johnson and Goldsmith, ed. A. Rudrum and P. Dixon, London 1965. Contains an annotated text of *London*.

III *Critical and Historical Studies* (see also Bibliography to chapter 11):

The following books have chapters on the period and the first two contain lists of recent studies of particular authors and subjects:

Bonamy Dobrée, *English Literature in the Early Eighteenth Century 1700–1740*, Oxford, 1959. (*Oxford History of English Literature*, vol. vii.)

George Sherburn, *The Restoration and Eighteenth Century 1660–1789* in *A Literary History of England*, ed. A. C. Baugh, 1948; rev. by Donald F. Bond and separately printed, London, 1967.

From Dryden to Johnson, ed. B. Ford, London, 1957. (*Pelican Guide to English Literature*, vol. iv.)

Butt, John, *The Augustan Age*, London, 1950.

Humphreys, A. R., *The Augustan World: Life and Letters in Eighteenth-Century England*, London, 1954.

Jack, Ian, *Augustan Satire, 1660–1750*, Oxford, 1952.

Røstvig, Maren-Sofie, *The Happy Man: Studies in the Metamorphosis of a Classical Ideal*, vol. ii, *1700–1760*, Oslo, 1958.

Sutherland, James, *A Preface to Eighteenth-Century Poetry*, Oxford, 1948.

6

DRAMA FROM 1710 TO 1780

Ian Donaldson, Australian National University, Canberra

Ian Donaldson

The age is one which may well seem remarkable less for the distinction of its dramatic writing than for the oddity of its dramatic taste. It is an age which could strain at *The Way of the World* and *The Good Natur'd Man* and yet swallow Mrs. Centlivre's *The Busy Body* and Hugh Kelly's *False Delicacy*. It is an age, Fielding's Luckless remarked in *The Author's Farce*, which 'would allow Tom Durfey a better poet than Congreve or Wycherley'. Its successful dramatists might be gentlemanly part-timers, men like Dr. Benjamin Hoadly, F.R.S., physician to the households of the King and of the Prince of Wales, who in 1747 found time to write his popular comedy, *The Suspicious Husband*, or like General Burgoyne, whose comic operas and melodramas, written to lighten the tedium of a military career, occupied the boards of Drury Lane thirty years later. Variety was much in demand : pantomime, tumbling, rope-dancing, puppets; even the most sombre of tragedies enlivened by a brisk entertainment between the acts or by a farcical afterpiece to round the evening off. Countless theatrical transplants were maladroitly carried out. Shakespeare, Jonson, Wycherley, Vanbrugh, Molière, Voltaire, Kotzebue all underwent surgery :

> Small thanks to France, and none to Rome or Greece,
> A past, vamp'd, future, old, reviv'd, new piece,
> 'Twixt Plautus, Fletcher, Shakespear, and Corneille,
> Can make a Cibber, Tibbald, or Ozell.[1]

It was an age in which even the most eminent of literary figures passed judgements on theatrical matters which are likely continually to surprise us. Pope could dismiss the plays of Ben Jonson as 'Trash', yet profess to find in Aaron Hill's *Athelwold* (a piece he claimed to have read no less than six times) a perfection flawed by 'Nothing but Trifles';[2] Congreve, asked if he thought *The Beggar's Opera* was likely to succeed, dared to commit himself only to a prophecy of Sibylline ambiguity ('It would either take greatly, or be damned confoundedly'); Dr. Johnson could admire the tragedies of Nicholas Rowe, and tolerate Nahum Tate's emasculation of *King Lear*. To modern eyes, the principal characteristic both of the drama and of the dramatic criticism of the age is uncertainty.

The uncertainty is well revealed in the century's most common theatrical joke: that it was difficult nowadays to know whether a play was meant to be tragic or comic. 'Pray do me the favor, Sir, to inform me; Is this your Tragedy or your Comedy?' is a quip which Pope attributed to the theatre-manager John Rich;[3] and Pope's own Goddess of Dulness was to behold in the *Dunciad* 'How Tragedy and Comedy embrace' (i. 69). The joke is at least as old as the prologue to *The Rehearsal*: 'Our Poets make us laugh at Tragoedy/And with their Comedies they make us cry'. 'What is this *Historical Register*? Is it a Tragedy? or a Comedy?' asks one player of another in Fielding's burlesque play of the same name; 'Upon my word, Sir, I can't tell.' '*Laugh—if you can—if you cannot laugh—weep*', is the invitation extended in Mr. Trapwit's prologue at the rehearsal of his comedy in Fielding's *Pasquin*. The well-worn joke is still going strong later in the century. One of the characters in Act III of Hugh Kelly's *The School for Wives* (1773), asked if she finds no modern comedy to her liking, replies demurely, 'O yes; some of the sentimental ones are very pretty, there's such little difference between them and tragedy.' Six years later, Sheridan brings it out once more in *The Critic*:

> *Dangle*: [*Reading*] 'Bursts into tears, and exit.' What, is this a tragedy?
> *Sneer*: No, that's a genteel comedy, not a translation—only *taken from the French*; it is written in a style which they have lately tried to run down; the true sentimental, and nothing ridiculous in it from the beginning to the end.

But it was John Gay who exploited the joke more subtly than any other dramatist of the century. His 'Tragi-Comi-Pastoral Farce', *The What D'Ye Call It* (1714/15) gravely asks the essential question in its very title. '*The whole Art of* Tragi-Comi-Pastoral Farce,' he explains patiently in his Preface to the play, '*lies in interweaving the several Kinds of the Drama with each other, so that they cannot be distinguish'd or separated.*' On the first night that this little burlesque play was performed, the audience's reaction—to Gay's and Pope's delight—was one of extreme emotional confusion : there was laughter, 'sedateness', and tears.[4]

Why was the joke so tenacious? Partly, it was a perfectly simple joke at professional incompetence, aimed at the writer (or actor) who bored or amused his audiences in the wrong places. Eighteenth-century audiences could be quick to applaud plays which they admired, and equally quick to damn those which they did not. It is clear that a good many tragedies fared unhappily in the theatre. At a performance of Charles Johnson's *Medea* in 1730, for instance (the year of *Tom Thumb*), we learn that 'the house was in one continued roar of laughter from the beginning of the 3d act to the end of the 5th.'[5] It was an old story that went back at least to the time of Dryden : Lisideius in *An Essay of Dramatic Poesy* had complained that 'in all our tragedies, the audience cannot forbear laughing when the actors are to die; 'tis the most comic part of the whole play.'[6] But new questions were now being asked about the nature of tragedy. Might not Dryden actually have intended his tragedies to be seen as rather funny? asked Colley Cibber in the fifth chapter of his *Apology* in 1740, pointing out that there were moments even in Shakespearian tragedy when 'it is impossible not to be transported into an honest Laughter', and that he had finally won Addison himself round to his own view that certain passages in *Cato* 'might admit of a *Laugh* of *Approbation*'. (Certain passages in *Cato* were to draw less generous laughter when they were parodied in *Tom Thumb*.) Tragedy, other writers were prepared to argue, might also be allowed to end happily; and comedy, according to another powerful school of thought, might legitimately move an audience not to laughter but to tears. Yet while the neo-classical principles began to break up, these new principles were far from being universally accepted; the joke that we have observed indicates the depth of the eighteenth-century uncertainty about the aesthetic premises of dramatic criticism. Protests were registered. In the past, wrote John Dennis in 1722, 'the tragick and comick Poets frequently borrow'd their Hints from one another', yet—unlike the moderns—they took 'Care to do it with Judgement, and not to intrench upon each other's Province.'[7] Goldsmith in his celebrated *Essay on the Theatre* in 1773 appealed in a similar way to the traditional notion that the dramatic kinds were not to be confused : 'Since the first origin of the Stage, Tragedy and Comedy have run in different channels, and never till of late encroached upon the provinces of each other.'[8] Reading through many of the dramatic experiments of the age, we are likely to feel an instinctive sympathy for the commonsensical protests of Dennis and Goldsmith, and to want to dismiss such plays as mere sports and aberrations ('mulish productions', was Goldsmith's term). In a great many cases this instinct is perfectly justifiable. Yet it is worth remembering that in some respects history has been on the side of the experimenters. It has been respectably argued by more than one modern critic that Dryden probably did intend parts of his heroic plays to be regarded humorously; we find no difficulty in accepting the idea that Shakespeare's most profound tragedies contain a 'comedy of the grotesque'; and it is an obvious fact that in the modern theatre, as in modern criticism, the traditional categories of tragedy, comedy, and tragi-comedy have been found steadily less and less serviceable. Apollinaire was speaking for more than one generation of writers in 1918 when, in discussing the subject of tragedy and comedy in the Preface to *Les Mamelles de Tirésias*, he predicted that no future audiences would be 'able to endure, without impatience, a play in which these elements are not balanced against each other'. Here—as so often—one glimpses the real interest of many of the dramatic experiments of the eighteenth century, which, for all their occasional naïveté, were often made in response to moral, social, and artistic pressures which we continue to feel and to respect to this day.

The merging of the dramatic kinds in this period means that any grouping of eighteenth-century plays must necessarily be a little arbitrary and artificial, yet I shall look, in turn, at some of the principal developments in the field of comedy, in that of tragedy, and finally in that of burlesque. Goldsmith in 1773 declared that there were two principal types of comedy : sentimental comedy and laughing comedy. Although in practice it is often exceedingly difficult to distinguish these two types, Goldsmith's statement provides a useful point of entry into the central problem of eighteenth-century comedy. Certainly it is true that the sentimentalists tended to regard laughter with a grave suspicion. In the year that Goldsmith's *Essay on the Theatre* appeared in *The Westminster Magazine*, the newly-founded *Sentimental Magazine* boasted modestly in its first number that while 'Our Ancestors placed their Amusement in Laughter, we place ours in Chastity of Sentiment.' Uneasiness about the propriety of laughter—as in part we have already seen—was characteristic of the century. Lord Chesterfield, as is well known, advised his son that laughter was a habit to be avoided, and in thinking this way he was not alone. Dr. Johnson tells us that Swift 'stubbornly resisted any tendency to laughter', and that 'by no merriment, either of others or of his own, was Pope ever seen excited to laughter'. Johnson himself, who was said to have a laugh 'like a rhinocerous', declared elsewhere that 'To laugh is good, as to talk is good', but added sensibly that there were as many ways of laughing as of talking, and that one should have a care on such matters.[9] Addison prefaced a *Spectator* paper (no. 240) on the subject of laughter with a significant tag from Menander : 'Unseasonable laughter is a grievous ill'. In their very different ways, such comments and observations are evidence of the growing eighteenth-century awareness of the demands of politeness, an awareness that was of crucial importance to the development of comedy in the period. Once again, the jokes alert us to what is happening. 'But there is nothing more unbecoming a Man of Quality than to Laugh', said Lord Froth in Congreve's *The Double Dealer* (I.i), ''tis such a Vulgar Expression of the Passion!' Swift in his *Compleat Collection of Genteel and Ingenious Conversation* ironically declared that one of the characteristics of 'Politeness' was a knowledge of 'how often and how loud to laugh'. Yet it was an unease not only about matters of social decorum, but also about the possible psychological origins of laughter. Hobbes's view that laughter represented an act of 'sudden glory' over one's fellows was well known in the early part of the eighteenth century, when various attempts were made to posit alternative theories. Shaftesbury in his *Sensus Communis : An Essay on the Freedom of Wit and Humour* (1709) was intent, like so many writers of the period, to point out the various possible kinds of laughter : 'There is a great difference between seeking how to raise a laugh from everything, and seeking in everything what justly may be laughed at'; and he went on to argue that laughter may be not only a sign of an individual triumph, but also of a triumph for the good sense of society as a whole, over individual gravity and imposture.[10] Sir Richard Steele in the same year argued along very similar lines in *Tatler*, no. 67 that laughter need not arise 'out of the ordinary Motive, viz. Contempt and Triumph over the Imperfection of others', but might have its origins rather in a feeling of 'general Benevolence'. Steele also obviously had had Hobbes in mind when he wrote in his epilogue to *The Lying Lover* a few years earlier that 'Laughter's a distorted Passion, born/Of sudden self Esteem, and sudden Scorn'. (The notion that laughter caused either physical or emotional 'distortion' was common, and appeared in both Addison's and Chesterfield's discussions of the subject.) Steele announced that *The Lying Lover* had not been intended to raise laughter, but quite different emotions: 'generous Pity' and 'pure Joy'. Pity, the emotion which Aristotle had said was aroused by the representation of tragedy, is officially declared to be one of the principal emotions which might be aroused by comedy. Laughter is relegated to a secondary position. Sentimental comedy is under way. Steele found a model for non-laughing comedy in the work of Terence; writing in *The Spectator*, no. 502, in 1712, he said approvingly of *The Self-Tormentor*: 'I did not observe in the Whole one Passage that could raise a laugh. How well disposed must that People be, who could be entertained with Satisfaction by so sober and polite Mirth!'

'Sober and polite mirth': the formula does not sound altogether promising. Ten years later, in *The Conscious Lovers* (1722), Steele tried to put the formula into operation, going, not surprisingly, to Terence for his source: this time to *Andria*. *The Conscious Lovers* turns on a situation which was to be very popular in the sentimental comedy of the century: it might be called the delicate deadlock. Bevil Junior is about to marry Lucinda, daughter to the great merchant Mr. Sealand. Lucinda is in fact in love with Bevil Junior's friend, Myrtle; and Bevil Junior is in fact in love with Indiana, an apparent orphan, whom he has met in Toulon and brought to England, with her aunt. Bevil Junior is nevertheless pushing ahead bravely with the idea of marrying Lucinda, as he feels it is what his father wants. Bevil Senior feels the marriage must be what his son wants; so considerate are father and son to each other's feelings that 'their fear of giving each other Pain, is attended with constant mutual uneasiness.' Bevil Junior also respects the delicate situation in which Indiana is placed, and will not tell her that it is she whom he really loves (such matters are hardly in doubt in *Andria*, where Indiana's counterpart is in advanced pregnancy when the play opens, and gives birth before the end of the last act). 'Habitually to enjoy feelings without acting upon them', wrote Jacques Barzun, 'is to be a sentimentalist'; and his aphorism is particularly suggestive in relation to a play such as *The Conscious Lovers*.[11] Bevil is a man of feeling, but does not act spontaneously upon his feelings; instead, restraint sharpens his sensibilities. Restraint wins another victory in the scene of which Steele was most proud, where Bevil refuses a duelling challenge from his hot-headed friend Myrtle, who has (understandably enough) become suspicious of the nature of Bevil's relationship with Lucinda. In an exclamatory and absurd denouement, the obstacles to the desired attachments are rapidly swept away, and it is revealed that Indiana is in fact the long-lost daughter of Mr. Sealand. The ending of the play, Steele later wrote in his Preface, aroused in playgoers 'a Joy too exquisite for Laughter, that can have no Spring but in Delight'. Laughter, the most spontaneous of emotions, is replaced by another more sensitive and exquisite kind of feeling. John Dennis pointed out very sensibly, though at great length, that the denouement was full of absurdities, and that the idea of a comedy too exquisite for laughter was anyhow a contradiction in terms. Comedy—and Dennis called Jonson and Molière to witness—had always been intended to deal with the ridiculous and to arouse laughter in its audiences.[12] Colley Cibber (according to his son) had been shown an earlier version of The Conscious Lovers which he considered 'rather too grave for an English audience', and added a number of comic touches of his own to the play, persuading Steele at the same time to write in the minor parts of Tom and Phyllis, the mildly engaging pair of amorous servants.[13] Laughing comedy was always likely to find a way in through the back door. And there is little doubt that the real, though lightweight, talents of Steele (and indeed of Cibber himself, most of whose comedies fall just outside our period) are to be found not in the scenes of tender and tearful passion, but rather in those of freer comedy in the style of Vanbrugh and Farquhar. The best things in The Conscious Lovers run agreeably against the main current of the piece:

Mrs Sealand: Oh, Cousin *Cimberton*! Cousin *Cimberton*! How abstracted, how refin'd is your Sense of Things! But, indeed, it is too true, there is nothing so ordinary as to say in the best govern'd Families, My Master and Lady are gone to Bed; one does not know but it might have been said of one's self.

[*Hiding her Face with her Fan.*]

Cimberton: *Lycurgus*, Madam, instituted otherwise; among the *Lacedaemonians*, the whole Female World was pregnant, but none, but the Mothers themselves knew by whom; their Meetings were secret and the Amorous Congress always by Stealth; and no such professed Doings between the Sexes, as are tolerated among us, under the audacious Word, Marriage (III. i).

It is as well to remember how varied the work of individual comic dramatists in this period could be. We may think of Henry Fielding, for instance, as a dramatist firmly in the school of laughing comedy, recalling his complaint in *Tom Jones* (v. i) that 'the modern judges of our theatres' have ousted everything that is 'low' from modern comedy, 'by which they have happily succeeded in banishing all humour from the stage, and have made the theatre as dull as a drawing-room!' Fielding's burlesque and rehearsal plays (which we shall look at a little later) may indeed be thought his most attractive, but the range and variety of his comic writing should not be forgotten. *Rape Upon Rape*, otherwise known as *The Coffee-House Politician* (1730), is probably the gayest of his other pieces and the most likely to succeed with a modern audience (it has in fact been recently revived as a musical, under the title *Lock Up Your Daughters*). Politic, the 'coffee-house politician' who is too engrossed in national affairs to know or worry about the amorous escapades of his daughter, is a nice comic creation who stands mid-way between Jonson's Sir Politic Would-Be and Dickens's Mrs. Jellaby. Fielding's touch throughout is light and ironical, somewhat in the style of John Gay. 'Rape and murder, no gentlemen need be ashamed of', says the warder Mr. Staff consolingly to two of his gentlemen prisoners, arrested for rapes they did not commit, 'I have ravished women myself formerly: but a wife blunts a man's edge' (III. iv). In his other comedies Fielding can be more serious. *Love in Several Masques* (1728) and *The Temple Beau* (1730) move along briskly rather in the manner of Wycherley or of Mrs. Centlivre—assignations in darkened rooms, concealments in closets, multiple intrigues, duping of husbands and fathers—yet they also have a more serious streak. In the first play a 'plain honest man' from the country named Wisemore stolidly resists the blandishments of a rich town widow who invites him to consider adopting more 'modern notions' of love ('Generous, worthy man!' she exclaims in an aside, as he stands firm); and an over-hasty suitor finds himself rebuked by the young heroine for his impetuosity; 'Why what have we here?' he says in surprise: 'Seneca's morals under a masque!' (IV. iii). Seneca's morals also lurk beneath the gay surface of the second play, where one lover solemnly and successfully lectures his rival on the importance of basing love not upon 'brutal appetite' but upon mutual affection. *The Modern Husband* (1732) has a deeper and more central seriousness. Once again, it is 'modern notions' which are under attack: Mr. Modern allows Lord Richly to sleep with his wife, in return for any favours which his lordship may want to bestow. The easiness of Mrs. Modern on such matters is contrasted with the rectitude of Mrs. Bellamant, who steadfastly refuses to give in to Lord Richly's advances, even though she is aware that her husband is doing his best to carry on with Mrs. Modern. In its celebration of wifely fidelity the play is recognizably on the same pattern as Colley Cibber's *The Careless Husband* (1704), and Cibber himself contributed an admiring epilogue; in its gravity and in its theme the play also anticipates Fielding's novel *Amelia* (1751). *The Modern Husband* had an excellent cast when it was first performed at Drury Lane, but was nevertheless an utter failure. It is not hard to guess at the reasons for its failure. Like Steele, Fielding had quite deliberately tried to write a comedy which aroused a more thoughtful emotion than laughter : 'Though no loud laugh applaud the serious page/ Restore the sinking honour of the stage!' is the appeal of his prologue. 'I hate your dull writers of the late reigns', says Lord Richly in a scene (II. v) within the play which is clearly intended to hint at Fielding's own larger intentions : 'The design of a play is to make you laugh; and who can laugh at sense?' Noone, to be sure, seems to have laughed at *The Modern Husband*. When Fielding abandoned the idea of laughing comedy, he was seldom at his best.

Happily, his ideas about laughter soon changed. In the Preface to *Joseph Andrews* (1742) and in his *Essay on the Knowledge of the Characters of Men* Fielding set forth his ideas about laughter and comedy in greater detail. He argued the importance of the element of ridicule in comedy, and pointed, as John Dennis had done, to the example of Jonson. At the same time, Fielding countered Hobbes's idea that laughter was an act of sudden glory, arguing that it was often strongly tempered by compassion. 'Good humour', Fielding conceded, was often 'nothing more than the triumph of the mind, when reflecting on its own happiness, and that, perhaps, from having compared it to the inferior happiness of others'; but good humour was not to be confused with what he called *good nature*, 'that benevolent and amiable temper of mind which disposes us to feel the misfortunes, and enjoy the happiness of others.' This notion of good nature, deriving in part from Shaftesbury, is of some importance in eighteenth-century comedy. The good-natured man is a recurrent figure in the drama; sometimes he appears as an exemplar, sometimes as a warning, sometimes as a mixture of both these things. Mr. Boncour in Fielding's *The Fathers, or, the Good Natured Man* carries his good nature to excess. He is so obliging that he will never speak his mind; so permissive that he lets his children do what they will; so kindly that he allows them to betroth themselves to partners who are simply after the family's cash. Boncour's brother, Sir George, takes matters in hand. He puts it about that Boncour has become bankrupt: the suitors drop off, the children instantly rally around father. 'Good nature!', exclaims Sir George, 'damn the word! I hate it!—they say it is a word so peculiar to our language that it can't be translated into any other—Good nature!' (III. iii). Such scoffing is clearly in large measure affectionate, as the neat assertion about the Englishness of good nature would alone show; and the play ends, after all, with a demonstration of the way in which good nature does operate both in Boncour's children and in Sir George himself.

The Good Natur'd Man (1768) by Oliver Goldsmith (1730?–74) shows very much the same kind of affectionate criticism. (There is no question of influence here: Fielding's play, written in the early 1740s, was lost for many years and was only recovered well after Fielding's death; it was pulled into shape by Garrick and Sheridan and not finally staged until 1778, at Drury Lane.) Goldsmith's Mr. Honeywood, like Fielding's Mr. Boncour, is so excessively dedicated to promoting the happiness of other people that he becomes a nuisance to himself, and, ironically, to them as well. He is lavish with his loans, even when he has debts of his own to meet; he tries to help a couple who wish to elope, and gives them a bill which is not honoured. The open-hearted man is forced to become a hypocrite: to conceal from his friends the fact of his bankruptcy, he dresses the bailiffs who come to his house in such clothes of his own as he has not yet given away to the poor, and passes them off as his guests. Yet *The Good Natur'd Man* is not altogether the play one might expect the advocate of laughing comedy to have written. Honeywood's good nature is not entirely a laughing matter; and the attitude the play invites us to take up is not simple. 'What a pity it is, Jarvis', says Honeywood's uncle Sir William, who plays a watchful role very like Fielding's Sir George Boncour,

> that any man's good will to others should produce so much neglect of himself, as to require correction. Yet, we must touch his weaknesses with a delicate hand. There are some faults so nearly allied to excellence, that we can scarce weed out the vice without eradicating the virtue (Act I).

Here, as so often in his work, Goldsmith returns to that most teasing and recurrent of eighteenth-century dilemmas: how to balance benevolence with prudence, without looking rather less than Christian.

The Good Natur'd Man plays an ironic variation upon the theme of the delicate deadlock: Honeywood is in love with Miss Richland, as she is with him, yet when asked by a friend (to whom Honeywood erroneously believes himself to be indebted) if he will pay suit to Miss Richland on his behalf, Honeywood is too good-natured to refuse. A curious courtship scene ensues, fraught with misunderstandings. A more elaborate series of variations upon the theme of the delicate deadlock is to be found in a play which opened at Drury Lane six nights before the first performance of *The Good Natur'd Man* at Covent Garden—*False Delicacy*, by Goldsmith's fellow-country-man, Hugh Kelly (1739–77). (It was a great century for Irish comic dramatists: Farquhar, Steele, Sheridan, and Bickerstaffe were also from Ireland.) In conception, *False Delicacy* is quite ingenious: instead of the traditional apparatus of 'comedy of mistaking' (twins, disguises, darkness), Kelly substitutes delicacy. The mistakes of the play arise entirely out of the characters' excessive anxiety not to hurt each other's feelings. Lord Winworth has proposed to Lady Betty, who has declined him; she thinks, with pleasure, that he is about to propose again—an act he is too tactful to dream of indulging in—only to find that he wants her to assist him in another suit, for the hand of her ward, Miss Marchmont, and in the circumstances Lady Betty can hardly refuse to help him. Miss Marchmont herself is in love with Sidney, but does not want to displease Lady Betty by refusing the suitor whom she commends to her; Sidney himself loves Miss Marchmont, but is on the point of marrying Miss Rivers, because Miss Rivers' father wishes the match; Colonel Rivers wishes the match because he thinks it is what the young couple want, although Miss Rivers is actually in love with Sir Harry Newburg. It is a card-house of delicate misunderstandings. While Kelly is certainly inviting us to see the humorous aspect of these misunderstandings, it is a little difficult to see the play as a sustained satire upon false delicacy; like Fanny Burney in her novels, Kelly fully exploits the notion of social embarrassment, but allows his comedy to remain some-where just below the threshold of laughter. 'What a ridiculous bustle there is here about delicacy and stuff!' says the sensible old bachelor Cecil, who is to be found at other points of the play wiping the tears from his eyes, and who—with the vulgar maid, Mrs. Harley—contrives finally to push these willing-yet-unwilling lovers together. At the end of the play, the wild Sir Harry is suddenly reformed, and Colonel Rivers sums up the significance of the play in a few words:

> . . . the principal moral to be drawn from the transactions of today is, that those who generously labour for the happiness of others, will, sooner or later, arrive at happiness themselves.

The role of Cecil and Mrs. Harley is here curiously ignored; and it is assumed that Providence is automatically well-disposed to help the tongue-tied. The same trust had been shown in the concluding tag of *The Conscious Lovers*:

> Whate'er the generous Mind it self denies
> The secret Care of Providence supplies.

Goldsmith's play, on the other hand, ends rather as *Tom Jones* does, with a sharp reminder of the need to look after oneself: 'Henceforth, nephew, learn to respect yourself.'

Goldsmith's second major play, *She Stoops to Conquer* (1773), is more decisive in its ridicule of sentimentalism. 'The undertaking a comedy, not merely sentimental, was very dangerous', Goldsmith later wrote in his dedication of the play to Dr. Johnson; yet his way had been eased a little by the appearance at the Haymarket just one month earlier of Samuel Foote's burlesque of sentimental drama (and of Richardson's *Pamela*), *The Handsome Housemaid, or Piety in Pattens*. The success of *The Good Natur'd Man* had only been mild; the success of *She Stoops to Conquer* was overwhelming; both in England and abroad it was soon—as one contemporary writer put it—happily 'raising the *laughing standard*'.[14] Goldsmith once again ridicules delicacy as a ludicrous source of error and misunderstanding. In Young Marlow, delicacy is simply 'the Englishman's malady' of acute shyness: Marlow is gay and confident with the girl he takes to be the chambermaid, and paralyzed with shyness with the same girl when he knows she is of his own class. The interviews between the tongue-tied Marlow and Miss Hardcastle are quite similar to those between the equally tongue-tied Lord Winworth and Lady Betty in Kelly's play, but, unlike Kelly, Goldsmith leaves us in no doubt as to what we are to think about such delicacy. The over-sensitive man can become a kind of hypocrite, altering his behaviour too readily to suit the social context; even Miss Neville (according to Tony Lumpkin) has a mild form of the same complaint, being 'sensible and silent' before company, wild and mischievous out of it. The over-sensitive man literally cannot see things as they are: Young Marlow is too nervous to look Miss Hardcastle in the face and recognize her as the very girl with whom he has just been flirting. The fault lies in education: 'My life has been chiefly spent in a college, or an inn, in seclusion from that lovely part of the creation that chiefly teach men confidence', Marlow confesses to Hastings. Tony Lumpkin, too, has been spoilt, though in quite a different way, by a sentimental education: 'Ecod, mother, all the parish says you have spoil'd me, and so you may take the fruits on't', is his parting shot after one of his elaborate practical jokes. Yet the high spirits of Lumpkin form the emotional centre of *She Stoops to Conquer*. There is no question of reforming Lumpkin at the end of the play, as Sir Harry Newburg was reformed at the end of *False Delicacy*; rather it is the sentimentalists who must reform, and that will be helped by 'an hour or two's laughing'.

Richard Cumberland (1732–1811), grandson of the famous Dr. Bentley and the unfortunate original of Sir Fretful Plagiary in Sheridan's *The Critic* (in which Cumberland's tragedy of *The Battle of Hastings* is mercilessly ridiculed) is often grouped with Kelly as a sentimental dramatist, but this reputation is not fully deserved. *The Brothers* (1769) is a tale of filial intrigue, seduction and abandonment, privateering, shipwrecks and earthquake, and coincidental reunions, helped along by creaking soliloquies and rounded off with an improbable reformation; some of its absurdities are certainly sentimental in nature, but the portrait of the breezy sea-captain Ironsides —an entertaining chip off the block of Smollett's Hawser Trunnion in *Peregrine Pickle*—shows what Cumberland was capable of doing in a different comic vein. Cumberland's best comedy, *The West Indian* (1771), has no very marked connexion with sentimentalism (although there is an interesting passage in which tribute is paid to the sensibility of Laurence Sterne). The 'strong animal spirits' of Belcour, a lively variation on the type of the good-natured prodigal, animate this comedy as surely as those of Tony Lumpkin did *She Stoops to Conquer*. If Belcour likes the look of a girl, he tells her so at once; he confesses his faults readily; he is easily fooled by duplicity. Cumberland contrasts in the play two different ways of life, rather as Wycherley had done in *The Plain Dealer*: that of the West Indies, 'that warm sunny region, where naked nature walks without disguise', and 'this cold contriving artificial country' of England, inhabited by such Puritans as Sir Oliver Roundhead, who 'was never seen to laugh himself, nor ever allowed it in his children.' The comedy allows victory to the forces of spontaneity and laughter.

The Rivals (January 1775) by Richard Brinsley Sheridan (1751–1816) appears to aim a more calculated blow at 'The Goddess of the woeful countenance—/The sentimental Muse!' *The Rivals* was Sheridan's first play, written in a couple of months shortly after his romantic elopement with Elizabeth Linley from Bath; the scene in King's Mead Fields at the end of the play is almost certainly a playful reminiscence of Sheridan's own recent duels with rival suitors in Bath (though it is possibly a literary reminiscence as well, of the farcical 'duels' between Viola and Aguecheek in *Twelfth Night*, and between Daw and La Foole in Jonson's *Epicoene*). The first night of *The Rivals* was a disaster, owing partly to the incompetence of the actors—Shuter as Sir Anthony did not know his lines, and Lee as Sir Lucius was finally pelted with apples, and had to expostulate with the audience in his rich Irish brogue : 'By the pow'rs, is it *personal*?—is it me, or the matter?' [15] The fault did in some way lie with 'the matter' as well as with the actors; for one thing, the play ran for four hours, at least an hour longer than any other piece then on the stage. The story of Sheridan's deft and rapid revision of the play, and of its successful return to the stage eleven days later, is well known. [16] Today the most surprising feature of the story is that even on the first night the scenes between Julia and Faulkland should have been so warmly praised; Julia was actually described as 'an honour to the drama'. The sub-plot of *The Rivals* today presents a minor problem of interpretation a little like that of *False Delicacy* : how far is the author really laughing at his sentimentalists? The relationship between Julia and Faulkland is, of course, often undermined by parody : Julia's gratitude to Faulkland for having saved her from drowning is, for instance, an ironic memory of a device that goes back at least to Otway's *Venice Preserv'd*, in which Belvidera feels a 'nobler gratitude' to Jaffeir for having rescued her from 'the saucy waves'. Violetta in Cumberland's *The Brothers* feels the same way towards Belfield :

> . . . can I forget, when the vessel, in which I had sail'd from Portugal, founder'd by your side, with what noble, what benevolent ardour you flew to my assistance? regardful only of my safety, your own seem'd no part of your care (I. v).

'Why, a water-spaniel would have done as much!' remarks Sheridan's Lydia coolly; 'Well, I should never think of giving my heart to a man because he could swim!' (I. ii). The parody in the sub-plot does not always cut as surely as this; Sheridan was not yet confident enough to attack the dramatic foibles of the time as decisively he was later to do in *The Critic*, yet one can already see him enjoying, in a Wildean way, the ironic manipulation of stock dramatic clichés. Sheridan's writing is often at its swiftest and best when he moves frankly into the realm of farce, as he does in the rapid pile-up of imminent calamities at the end of *The Rivals*:

> *Mrs. Malaprop*: So! So! here's fine work!—here's fine suicide, paracide, and simulation going on in the fields! and Sir Anthony not to be found to prevent the antistrophe!
> *Julia*: For Heaven's sake, Madam, what's the meaning of this?
> *Mrs. Malaprop*: That gentleman can tell you—'twas he enveloped the affair to me.
> *Lydia*: Do, Sir, will you, inform us. [*To Fag*.]
> *Fag*: Ma'am, I should hold myself very deficient in every requisite that forms the man of breeding, if I delayed a moment to give all the information in my power to a lady so deeply interested in the affair as you are.
> *Lydia*: But quick!, quick, Sir!
> *Fag*: True, Ma'am, as you say, one should be quick in divulging matters of this nature; for should we be tedious, perhaps while we are flourishing on the subject, two or three lives may be lost!
> *Lydia*: O patience!—Do, Ma'am, for Heaven's sake! tell us what is the matter?
> *Mrs. Malaprop*: Why! murder's the matter! slaughter's the matter! killing's the matter!—but he can tell you the perpendiculars (V. i).

On the page, such dialogue looks sketchy; on the stage, it can succeed wonderfully because of Sheridan's control of speed and timing: as the events and the anxieties increase in scale, so too does the agonising verbosity of the would-be rescuers—the effect is like trying to run in a nightmare.

The sketchiness of Sheridan's writing is not always so successful. *St. Patrick's Day, or, The Scheming Lieutenant* (1775) has comic possibilities, but is undeniably thin, and some of its scenes simply trail away. Most of Sheridan's work has rather the air of being dashed off, though we know that his best work did cost him considerable pains. It is understandable that Byron admired him so warmly, though few people would probably agree with his extravagant praise of Sheridan's comic opera, *The Duenna* (1775), a piece that might not have greatly taxed the powers of Mrs. Centlivre. *The School for Scandal* (1777), Sheridan's most polished and considered work, is of quite a different order. The germinal idea of the play, the scandal club, may remind us of Congreve's *The Way of the World* (I. i), where Lady Wishfort's cabal 'come together like the Coroner's Inquest, to sit upon the murder'd Reputations of the Week'; and possibly also of the college of censorious ladies in Jonson's *Epicoene*. *The School for Scandal* is perhaps the only comedy of the century which one can confidently compare with the mature work of Congreve and of Jonson, yet Sheridan's language is never as dense or as intricate as that of the two earlier dramatists. Here is Sheridan's Sir Benjamin Backbite:

Nay, now, Lady Sneerwell, you are severe upon the widow. Come, come, 'tis not that she paints so ill—but when she has finished her face, she joins it so badly to her neck, that she looks like a mended statue, in which the connoisseur sees at once that the head's modern, though the trunk's antique (II. i).

This is enjoyable enough as a conversational stroke, but it hardly has the sophisticated inventiveness of Lady Wishfort's 'Let me see the Glass—Cracks, say'st thou? Why I am arrantly flea'd—I look like an old peel'd Wall' (*The Way of the World*, III. i), nor the chilling precision of Clerimont's description of Lady Haughty at her toilette:

There's no man can bee admitted till shee be ready, now adaies, till shee has painted, and perfum'd, and wash'd, and scour'd, but the boy, here; and him shee wipes her oil'd lips vpon, like a sponge (*Epicoene*, I. i).

Yet Sheridan's light, rapid, conversational style carries supremely well in the theatre, where *The School for Scandal*—unlike *Epicoene* and *The Way of the World*—has always enjoyed great success. The laughter and applause which greeted the famous 'screen' scene when the play was first performed were said to exceed anything in living memory. The play is the climactic eighteenth-century treatment of the theme of the good-natured man, and Charles Surface's genealogy can be traced back through Cumberland and Goldsmith to Fielding: the original audiences probably glimpsed somewhere behind Charles and his hypocritically sententious brother the figures of Tom Jones and Blifil (and Fielding had actually paired a good-natured and a hypocritical brother even earlier, in *The Temple Beau*). The comedy does not stress, as *The Good Natur'd Man* had done, the virtues of prudence, but instead freely celebrates the virtues of generous spontaneity; sententiousness is thrown out the window:

> *Rowley*: I never will cease dunning you with the old proverb—
> *Charles*: 'Be just before you're generous.'—Why, so I would if I could; but Justice is an old lame hobbling beldame, and I can't get her to keep pace with Generosity for the soul of me.
> *Rowley*: Yet, Charles, believe me, one hour's reflection—
> *Charles*: Aye, aye, it's all very true; but hark'ee Rowley, while I have, by Heaven I'll give; so damn your economy, and now for hazard (IV. i).

Spontaneity, curiously enough, manages to redeem even the scandal-mongers themselves, and it is hard to be convinced by Maria as she stands on the side-lines, mildly deploring their energetic and inventive gossip. In the final act of the play the rumours concerning the pistolling (or sword) duel between Sir Peter Teazle and Charles (or Joseph) Surface accumulate with a farcical speed which recalls the speed of the last act of *The Rivals*. With *The School for Scandal* laughing comedy reached its eighteenth-century zenith. Not until the time of Shaw and Wilde—two more Irishmen—was such comedy to be seen again in the English theatre.

II

Sentimental comedy, as we have seen, grew up in a time of new ideas on matters of social behaviour. Other social changes left just as clear a mark upon both comedy and tragedy in the period. As the composition and social background of the London audiences began to change gradually in the early years of the century, so too (only rather more slowly) did the dramatic stereotypes carried over from the Restoration period. The treatment in the drama of characters from the city and from the country, for instance, underwent constant and significant change in the early eighteenth century.[17] The presence of certain well-defined social groups in the audience led to the creation of some new and flattering stereotypes. One obvious such stereotype is that of the gallant, though often somewhat impoverished, soldier, such as Lord Hardy in *The Funeral* (1702):

> But what will become of me? How shall I keep my self even above Worldly want? Shall I live at Home a stiff, Melancholy, Poor man of Quality, grow uneasy to my Acquaintance as well as my self, by Fancying I'm slighted where I am not; with all the Thousand particularities which attend those whom low Fortune and high Spirit make Male-contents? No! We've a Brave Prince on the Throne, whose Commission I bear, and a Glorious War in an Honest Cause, Approaching [*Clapping his Hand on his Sword*], in which this shall Cut Bread for me, and may perhaps Equal that Estate to which my Birth Entitled me (II. i).

Such a passage seems calculated to raise a ready patriotic cheer; and it should be remembered that not only was Steele (like Vanbrugh and Farquhar) himself an officer, but further, that as fighting was still a seasonal business, officers and men home from their summer campaigns could attend the winter seasons of the playhouses, and hear their profession praised in this way.[18] Two more important social groups deserve to be noticed here; like the soldiers, they were often directly addressed and directly praised in the theatre, and the changes that were affecting their status are to be felt both in the comedy and in the tragedy of the period. These are the women, and the merchants.

It is clear that women were frequent visitors to the theatre during the Restoration period; often they went because they had a serious interest in the drama, and sometimes they even went without male escorts.[19] In the early years of the eighteenth century the practice of women wearing vizard-masks to the theatre was forbidden by law, and the number of women-visitors at the same time began to increase; their presence in the theatre was clearly felt to be a new and genuine attraction. Steele remarks with pleasure in *The Spectator*, no. 270, that on a recent visit to the theatre he found the boxes filled with ladies (like 'Beds of Tulips'), and in an earlier paper (no. 51) he complains of the way in which the ladies' modesty must be offended by the way in which the actresses so blatantly displayed their bodies in the theatre: 'I, who know nothing of Women but from seeing Plays, can give great Guesses at the whole Structure of the fair Sex, by being innocently placed in the Pitt, and insulted by the Petticoats of their Dancers; the Advantages of whose pretty Persons are a great help to a dull Play.' And the presence of growing numbers of women in the playhouses did indeed begin to change the style and tone of much eighteenth-century drama. The pressures came, of course, from outside the theatre as well as from within. Jeremy Collier in 1698 had directed one of his major charges against the way in which women were represented in modern plays, and his complaints were kept vigorously alive throughout the first quarter of the century.[20] It is also relevant to remember that these were years in which the subject of women's rights was being actively debated. In 1694 Mary Astell had written her *Reflections on Marriage* and *A Serious Proposal to the Ladies*, and in 1697 Defoe had proposed in his *Essay on Projects* the foundation of an academy for women. The accession of Queen Anne in 1702 appeared to lend strength to the cause of women's rights, and the subject frequently appears in the drama of the period. 'Were I born a humble Turk, where Women have no Soul nor Property', says Mrs. Sullen in Farquhar's *The Beaux Stratagem* (1707), 'there I must sit contented—But in *England*, a Country whose Women are it's Glory, must Women be abused, *where Women rule, must Women be enslav'd?*' In Addison's *The Drummer* (1715/16), likewise Lady Truman and Abigail tease the foppish freethinker Tinsel for his opinion that women have no souls; and in the comedies of Mrs. Centlivre the same flattering appeal to the Englishness of the feminist movement is again heard. In *The Busy Body* (1709) Sir Jealous Traffick admires the Spanish habit of keeping wives and daughters safely under lock and key, but his daughter forces him to respect the principles of English liberty: 'Sir, 'tis not the Restraint, but the Innate Principles, secures the Reputation and Honour of our Sex'. In *The Wonder: A Woman Keeps a Secret* (1714) Mrs. Centlivre sets the action in Lisbon, and allows her heroine to speak freely about the way in which they order matters better in England:

> Ah, *Inis*! What pleasant Lives Women lead in *England*, where Duty wears no Fetter but Inclination: The Custom of our Country inslaves us from our very Cradles, first to our Parents, next to our Husbands; and when Heaven is so kind to rid us of both these, our Brothers still usurp Authority, and expect a blind Obedience from us; so that Maids, Wives, or Widows, we are little better than Slaves to Tyrant Man . . .

Later in the century James Beattie, in striking anticipation of Meredith's more famous views, was to argue in his 'Essay on Laughter and Ludicrous Composition' (begun 1764) that the superiority of English comedy over that of other nations was due to the position of freedom which women enjoyed in Eng-

lish society, and to the development of English 'Gallantry':
'by which I here understand those generous and respectful attentions we pay to the Fair Sex'.[21] In other societies, such as
Greece, Italy, Germany, and Asia, he argued, women have been
secluded and treated rather as slaves than as equals; in England
the equality of the sexes had led to the flowering of the comic
genius. However doubtful such an argument may appear to be
in general terms—one notes that the emancipated and independent lady continues to be an object of comic ridicule even
in the enlightened eighteenth century—it is important that
contemporaries thought that such a change was actually occur-
ring.

A change in the status of women was reflected, too, in the
tragedy of the period. The tragedies of Nicholas Rowe, Poet
Laureate and first editor of Shakespeare, seem at first to be
primarily concerned with moralizing over female frailty. Calista
in *The Fair Penitent* (1703), seduced by Lothario while
betrothed to Altamont, stabs herself at the end of the piece, and
we are reminded of the dangers of unlawful love, and of the
fact that virtue is the universal bond. *The Tragedy of Jane
Shore* (1714) climaxes with a scene of somewhat sentimental
marital reconciliation and another pious moral: 'Let those, who
view this sad Example know,/What Fate attends the broken
Marriage Vow.' Yet in Rowe's tragedies, as in Defoe's novels,
the ostensible moral often obscures what is often a fairly complex and sympathetic treatment of the problems involved in
being a woman—the double sexual standard, the subordination
of men to women, and so on. 'How hard is the Condition of
our Sex/Thro' ev'ry State of Life the Slaves of Men' is a complaint which is heard in *The Fair Penitent*, and which forms
a ground-swell in Rowe's tragedies. Despite his theme, Rowe is
unlikely to find many admirers today. For modern tastes,
his tragedies glide all too easily to their wild and extravagant fifth-act climaxes: Calista in her room hung with black, a
skull, a book, a corpse beside her; Jane Shore at the point of
insanity and death, turned away from her rival, Alicia's, door,
like another Mrs. Yeobright; Lady Jane Grey, preparing to meet
her death at '*a Scaffold hung with Black*', distributing her possessions amongst her attendant women—the pathos is always
a little too palpably engineered. Rowe's blank verse can achieve
a pleasing enough firmness in the more neutral passages of
dialogue, but tends to disintegrate under any sort of stress.
Here, for instance, is how Guildford tells Lady Jane Grey in
Act II that if she feels upset about marrying him on the very

day of Edward's death, then he is quite prepared to sleep elsewhere for the night :

> Nay, coud'st thou be so cruel to command it,
> I will forgo a Bridegroom's sacred Right,
> And sleep far from thee, on the unwholsom Earth,
> Where Damps arise and whistling Winds blow loud.
> Then when the Day returns come drooping to thee,
> My Locks still drizzling with the Dews of Night,
> And chear my Heart with thee as with the Morning.

Though *Lady Jane Grey* was never a popular favourite, Rowe's
other 'she-tragedies'—the term was his own—were well thought
of in their day, and the fashion for tragedies of feminine distress continued down the century : Ambrose Philips's *The Dis-
trest Mother* (1712), James Thomson's *Sophonisba* (1730), and
Dr. Johnson's *Irene* (1749) are amongst the best known examples
of the genre. Charles Johnson's *Caelia: or, the Perjur'd Lover*
(1733) is a typical, and undistinguished, tragedy after the same
style, telling the story of a girl who is abducted by a Lothario-
like figure named Wronglove, who tires of her as soon as she
is pregnant, and abandons her to a brothel (which Caelia at
first believes to be a midwife's establishment); when the brothel
is raided by constables, Caelia is taken off to prison, where she
finally dies of a broken heart. The play was damned for the
ludicrous sprightliness of its brothel scenes, yet it shares with
Rowe's *The Fair Penitent* the small historical honour of having
partly inspired Samuel Richardson's *Clarissa*. If the new genre
of tragedy, praised by Dr. Johnson as being 'easily received by
the imagination, and assimilated to common life',[22] produced
no masterpiece of its own, it was at least partly responsible for
the appearance of one of the great masterpieces of English
prose fiction.

The other major social shift which finds its reflection in the
drama of the time is the rise to power of the merchant-class.
The formal praise of the trading-merchant becomes a regular
topos of eighteenth-century drama. Here is Mr. Barter in Gay's
The Distress'd Wife (1734) speaking out for the dignity of his
profession :

> Is the Name then a Term of Reproach?—Where is the Pro-
> fession that is so honourable?—What is it that supports every
> Individual of our Country?—'Tis Commerce.—On what de-
> pends the Glory, the Credit, the Power of the Nation?—On
> Commerce.—To what does the Crown itself owe its Splendor

and Dignity?—To Commerce.—To what owe you the Revenues of your own half-ruin'd Estates? To Commerce: and are you so ungrateful then to treat the Profession with Contempt by which you are maintain'd? (II. xvi).

Mr. Sealand in *The Conscious Lovers* and Mr. Stockwell in *The West Indian* praise the merchant's calling in similar terms. Even in Garrick and Colman's *The Clandestine Marriage* (1766), which shows the struggles of the newly-rich merchant to put his new landscape-garden in order and to marry his daughter to the right titled gentleman of the town, such satire as there is is gentle and on the whole affectionate, and the play ends with a happy liaison between peer and merchant. The merchant also plays an important role in eighteenth-century tragedy. Thorowgood in George Lillo's *The London Merchant* (1731) praises the profession as follows:

The populous East, luxuriant, abounds with glittering Gems, bright Pearls, aromatick Spices, and health-restoring Drugs: The late found Western World glows with unnumber'd Veins of Gold and Silver Ore.—On every Climate and on every Country, Heaven has bestowed some good peculiar to it self. —It is the industrious Merchant's business to collect the various blessings of each soil and climate, and, with the product of the whole, to enrich his native Country (III. i).

One's first reaction is to assume that the passage is simply a dramatically gratuitous compliment to the well-to-do merchants in the house, yet it is rather more than this. *The London Merchant* is a simple tale of a London 'prentice who is seduced by a courtesan, persuaded to murder his uncle to obtain his cash, and who finally meets death at the gallows. 'Tradesman's Tragedy' was Goldsmith's sneer at this new dramatic form (he was quoting Voltaire),[23] and there were probably many people who shared his prejudice. The basic Aristotelian tenet of tragedy was that it should concern the fall of a great man; how (it might reasonably be asked) could one be interested in the fall of a London 'prentice? Dryden's Dollabella states the classic viewpoint in *All For Love* when in Act III he contrasts his own sufferings with those of Antony:

But yet the loss was private that I made;
'Twas but my self I lost: I lost no Legions;
I had no World to lose, no peoples love.

Lillo's first counter to such a prejudice is to be found in his dedication to *The London Merchant*, where he argues (rather as Steele had done in *The Tatler*, no. 172) on somewhat Benthamite grounds that this new kind of tragedy is likely to affect more people than did the old, exclusive kind of tragedy which concerned itself with the fate of princes. In some ways Lillo's argument anticipates that of a modern writer of tragedy, Arthur Miller, who has pointed out that Aristotle's precepts were directed to a particular kind of society, the lowest stratum of which consisted of slaves, and that tragedy must always adapt itself to the society from which it emerges. Yet Lillo does more : by his praise of the merchant-class he suggests that although Barnwell is a humble man, his profession gives him a certain dignity and importance. The play opens with an (apparently quite unhistorical) account of the way in which the international fraternity of merchants have exerted their authority in order to prevent the invasion of England by the Spanish. Lillo attempts to give his tragedy a further resonance by bringing in a number of echoes of other famous tragedies : *Othello*, *Macbeth*, *Dr. Faustus*, *Venice Preserv'd*.[24]

Eighteenth-century tragedy is much preoccupied by scenes which depict a man preparing to meet his death. The fifth act of Addison's *Cato* (1713) shows Cato before his suicide, 'solus, *sitting in a thoughtful posture: In his hand* Plato's *book on the Immortality of the Soul. A drawn sword on the table by him.*' Two years later, Rowe had shown that a woman might encounter death with equal dignity; Lady Jane Grey is also found reading before her death :

> 'Tis *Plato's Phaedon*,
> Where Dying *Socrates* takes leave of Life,
> With such an easy, careless, calm Indifference,
> As if the Trifle were of no Account,
> Mean in it self, and only to be worn
> In honour of the Giver.

Lillo shows that an apprentice, too, has his own dignity : Barnwell is also found reading shortly before his execution; he reads not Plato, but the scriptures, and meets his death not with Cato-like stoicism, but with tears of joy and repentance. In his dying words, Barnwell asks that his audience might, in turn, spare him '*a pitying tear*', and the request was evidently well heeded throughout the century and well into Victorian times. It became traditional to present the play every Christmas and Easter for the entertainment and instruction of the apprentices; and later in the eighteenth century the dramatic historian Thomas Davies records that one Dr. Barrowby was called to attend a young apprentice whom he found 'extremely indisposed and low-spirited', and discovered that 'his distemper was owing to his having lately seen the tragedy of George Barnwell.' [25]

Lillo's *Fatal Curiosity* (1736) has never enjoyed the reputation of *The London Merchant*, yet it is likely to lay a firmer hold upon the modern reader. Its didacticism is less obtrusive, its story swift and simple. Young Wilmot, missing for many years and presumed drowned at sea, returns to his home in Penryn, Cornwall, from the East Indies, where he has made his fortune in trading. (A significant change from Lillo's source, where Wilmot made his money through piracy.) Tanned 'like a sunburnt *Indian*' and dressed in Indian attire, Young Wilmot is not recognized by his parents, at whose house he lodges. The parents, who have fallen on hard times, murder their lodger to obtain the casket of jewels he has asked them to look after; learning, too late, of his identity, they kill themselves in despair. The story is based on an allegedly true incident reported in a pamphlet of 1618, but analogues have been found in many parts of the world: recently, Albert Camus in *Le Malentendu* (1944) has given a version of the same story.[26] The power of the play no doubt arises very largely out of the somewhat legendary and archetypal nature of this story: one's mind is likely to turn to Oedipus's unwitting murder of his father, and to Pandora's similar 'fatal curiosity' in opening a forbidden casket. Henry Fielding, who presented the play at the Little Theatre in the Haymarket in 1736, later declared in *The Champion* (26 February 1740) that it gave Lillo 'a title to be call'd the best Tragic Poet of his Age', and reckoned that it was 'inferior only to Shakespear's best pieces'. The reader who has been scouring the unrewarding field of eighteenth-century tragedy may at least feel inclined to agree with Fielding that *Fatal Curiosity* is 'a Master-Piece of its kind'. The play was later adapted by both George Colman and by Henry Mackenzie, the novelist, and was much read and imitated in Germany in the early nineteenth century.

Eighteenth-century tragedy is often acutely money-minded. The industry and thrift of the merchant forms one of its major themes; the extravagance of the gambler forms another, complementary, one. Aaron Hill's and Joseph Mitchell's *The Fatal Extravagance* (1721) is a typical if unimpressive example of this small but popular sub-genre of gambling tragedies. Bellmour, ruined by gambling, decides to poison his family in order to spare them further misery: his wife's uncle, by a lucky stroke, learns of his intentions and swaps the poison phial for a harmless one. The family is saved, but Bellmour, deep in remorse, has already plunged a dagger to his heart. Edward Moore in *The Gamester* (1753) uses the same simple elements—the despairing gamester, the black-hearted friend who brings about his ruin, the patient wife, the convenient uncle, the phial of poison—yet manages to shape them into a quick-moving melodrama which enjoyed considerable success in the latter half of the century. Gambling was a popular theme in eighteenth-century comedy, too: Mrs. Centlivre in *The Gamester* and *The Basset Table* (both 1705) and Cibber in *The Lady's Last Stake* (1707) had both dealt with the subject. One of the weaknesses, indeed, of several of the tragedies just discussed is that they might be converted into comedies with only the slightest twist of the plot: if only word had got through a few minutes earlier, all would have been well. There is, of course, the best of precedents for a tragedy which depends upon an accident of timing (Sophocles' *Antigone*; *Romeo and Juliet*), and in the hands of a skilful dramatist, the tragic effect can be heightened by ironic reminders that things might easily have been otherwise. *Fatal Curiosity* has some of the traditional elements of comedy: the reunion, after long separation, of parents and child; the son's wish 'to improve/Their pleasure by surprise'; the presence of the casket, a ubiquitous property in eighteenth-century comedy (to be found in *The Beaux Stratagem*, *She Stoops to Conquer*, *The West Indian*), used as an identifying device in comedy since at least the time of Plautus' *Cistellaria* (*The Casket Comedy*). Yet Lillo exploits the irony of this situation with confidence:

> How near is misery and joy ally'd!
> Nor eye, nor thought can their extreams divide:
> A moment's space is long, and light'ning slow
> To fate descending to reverse our woe,
> Or blast our hopes, and all our joys o'erthrow.
>
> (II. iii)

With lesser dramatists such as Hill and Mitchell, the easy interchangeability of events may make the tragedy look frankly ludicrous. One is apt to remember Mr. Bayes's brisk confidence in converting his plays: 'I'll make it to a tragedy in a trice'. As we have already seen, the border-line between eighteenth-century comedy and tragedy was seldom drawn with great confidence.

III

If it was a short step from tragedy to comedy, it was an equally short step from tragedy to burlesque. Since the re-discovery of Longinus—*Peri Hupsous* was first translated into English in 1652—*sublimity* had been a much talked-of literary ideal; yet it was an ideal (as many writers recognized) which carried its own hazards. In 1711 Samuel Werenfels wrote his dissertation upon the subject of 'False Sublimity', and a few years later in *Peri Bathous* (1715, published 1728) Pope and other members of the Scriblerus Club humorously outlined their 'Art of Sinking in Poetry', drawing several of their ex-amples from dramatic writing: 'Whoever is conversant in modern plays', they wrote, 'may make a most noble collection of this kind.' Writing in his treatise on acting in 1755, John Hill pointed out that not only the writer but also the actor was exposed to the dangers of false sublimity: 'The excess of sub-limity is bombast', he wrote; 'Force, up to a certain degree, is strength and beauty, but carried a little farther, it converts tragedy into farce.' [27] 'An author, who would be sublime, often runs his thought into burlesque', wrote Oliver Goldsmith in his essay on 'The Characteristics of Greatness'; 'True Genius walks along a line, and, perhaps, our greatest pleasure is in seeing it so often near falling, without being ever actually down.' [28]

The burlesque plays of John Gay could certainly be said to walk 'along a line' in this way. In *The What D'Ye Call it* (1715), one of the most delightful and neglected of the minor dramatic pieces of the century, Gay subtly weaves in amongst his literary parody and social satire a light but quite discernible thread of genuine pathos. A play is being presented in a country hall for the entertainment of three Justices of the Peace: the absurdi-ties and injustices depicted in the inner play gently suggest the existence of similar absurdities and injustices in the society of which these three J.P.s are overlords. The worlds of the inner and outer plays merge when the steward's daughter Kitty is married by a real chaplain (whom the spectators assume to be a stage-play chaplain) to Squire Thomas, the son of one of the J.P.s, by whom she is in fact really pregnant. The 'mad scene' in the play-within-the-play in which Kitty appears '*with her Hair loose*' veers delicately between pathos and bathos, moving to a climax in a parody of Belvidera's famous 'mad' speech at the end of *Venice Preserv'd*:

> [*They throw Water upon her.*
> *Kitty*: Hah!—I am turn'd a Stream—look all below;
> It flows, and flows, and will for ever flow.
> The Meads are all afloat—the Haycocks swim.
> Hah! who comes here?—my *Filbert*! drown not him.
> Bagpipes in Butter, Flocks in fleecy Fountains,
> Churns, Sheep-hooks, Seas of Milk, and honey Mountains.
>
> (II. viii)

The parody is often grave and half-affectionate in a way that the parody in *The Rehearsal* or *The Critic* is not. The same is true of *The Beggar's Opera* (1728). There is little doubt that Gay, like Swift and Pope, considered the contemporary infatuation with Italian opera to be both ludicrous and sentimental, and a number of features of *The Beggar's Opera* point to direct parody of the genre: the poisoned cup offered by Lucy to Polly in Act III, for instance, seems to ridicule a favourite device of Handelian opera;[29] the fact that Lucy's and Polly's parts are almost exactly equal in size is an ironical glance at the recent squabbles between two famous prima donnas, Faustina and Cuzzoni, over the question of which of them was to take the larger part; and it was obviously amusing to substitute for the castrato of Italian opera a philanderer such as Macheath, who, by the end of the play, has scattered his image freely through the town. Yet these touches of parody, like the parody of Shakespeare, Dryden, and Otway elsewhere in the play, have the curious effect of heightening rather than subverting the play's emotional effects, often setting up a series of literary echoes which increase its total suggestiveness. (It is rather like the effect which Lillo was to try to capture by his literary echoes in *The London Merchant*.) 'By the assumed licence of the mock-heroic style', wrote Hazlitt in a brilliant insight, Gay 'has enabled himself to *do justice to Nature.*'[30] The parting-scene between Polly and Macheath at the end of the first act is certainly intended to mock the over-familiar parting-scenes of heroic and sentimental drama, yet the total effect is very different from the more obvious mockery of such scenes which Cibber had already gone in for in his *The Comical Lovers* in 1707; there is a bizarre poignancy, as well as pure absurdity, about the way in which Polly and Macheath seem to be playing at being Belvidera and Jaffeir, Isabel and Richard II. The tolling bell which summons Macheath to the gallows through Air LXVIII, '*Would I might be hang'd!*', was likewise a hackneyed device whose use as 'a mechanical help to the Pathetic' was soon to be ridiculed by

216

Pope in the third book of the *Dunciad*, as it had been already by Addison in *The Spectator*, no. 44; yet as many generations of playgoers have found, it is a 'mechanical' device that still carries some force. At the first performance of the play, the audience was in some doubt as to whether they liked the piece until the point at which Polly pleaded with her parents (Air XII):

> *Oh, ponder well! be not severe;*
> *So save a wretched wife!*
> *For on the rope that hangs my dear*
> *Depends poor Polly's life.*

Even without the benefit of Mr. Empson's virtuoso explication of the play's central, merging, images of the lover's and the hangman's knots, the original audience evidently enjoyed the word-play of the song's last two lines, being—as Boswell relates —'much affected by the innocent looks of Polly, when she came to those two lines, which exhibit at once a painful and ridiculous image'.[31] The innocent, the painful, and the ridiculous are indeed closely interwoven throughout the play. Eighteenth-century performances, like those in our own time, sometimes stressed one element, sometimes another. Nigel Playfair's famous revival of the play in the 1920s (adaptation by Arnold Bennett, music arranged by Frederick Austen, design by Claud Lovat Fraser) aspired to a light and somewhat saccharine Gilbert-and-Sullivan prettiness; Bertolt Brecht's adaptation of 1928, *Die Dreigroschenoper*, emphasized the play's harsher social realities. The original *Beggar's Opera* 'walks along a line' with a poise that is lacking in both these adaptations: the pretty and the harsh, the innocent and the ironic, the pathetic and the bathetic are held in fine balance. That balance has been lost in Gay's *Polly* (1729), the sequel to *The Beggar's Opera*, in which Macheath has been transported to the West Indies, and has married Jenny Diver and turned pirate. The praise of the Indians ('How happy are these Savages!') is surprisingly sentimental, and the play lacks Gay's characteristic deftness and complex irony. It ends with the remarkable spectacle of a Polly in boy's clothing capturing Macheath (his face blackened to look like a 'Neger') as he runs away from a band of Indians: this time he is sent off to execution in no uncertain manner, with no chance of reprieve.

Most of the little plays that followed in the immediate wake of *The Beggar's Opera*, such as Charles Coffey's *The Beggar's Wedding* (1729), Essex Hawker's *The Wedding* (1729), and George Lillo's *Silvia, or the Country Burial* (1730) make disappointing reading today. Henry Fielding's *Tom Thumb* (April 1730, revised as *The Tragedy of Tragedies*, March 1731) does not. The play is still recognizably within the tradition of Scriblerian humour—Fielding learnedly annotates the play after the manner of the 1729 *Dunciad Variorum*, writes in his Preface of 1731 that 'Tragedy hath, of all writing, the greatest share in the Bathos; which is the profound of Scriblerus', and signs himself H. Scriblerus Secundus. *Tom Thumb* is broader, more farcical, frankly funnier than any of Gay's plays, or, for that matter, than *Peri Bathous*—Swift laughed at seeing the play, though he is said to have laughed only twice in his entire life. Yet Fielding has not quite mastered the quiet and complex style of the older generation of Tory wits: he does not try to walk the line between sublimity and burlesque with the same grave attention as Pope or Gay, and as a result the play lacks something in the way of subtlety. The play is really closer to *The Rehearsal* (by then sixty years old, though still performed regularly) than it is to *The Beggar's Opera*; and it is noteworthy that the main target of Fielding's ridicule is heroic tragedy of the age of Dryden.[32] Fielding may have taken his starting-point for the play from Addison's discussion of the conventions of heroic tragedy in *The Spectator*, no. 42 :

> The ordinary Method of making an Heroe, is to clap a huge Plume of Feathers upon his Head, which rises so very high, that there is often a greater Length from his Chin to the Top of his Head, than to the Sole of his Foot. *One would believe, that we thought a great Man and a tall Man the same thing.*

A few years after *Tom Thumb*, in his 'Modern Glossary' (*Covent Garden Journal*, no. 4), Fielding was to define the word 'Great' as follows : 'Applied to a Thing, signifies Bigness; when to a Man, Often Littleness or Meanness'. The hit was obvious enough at a time when Robert Walpole was popularly known as 'the Great'. Fielding's creation of a pygmy hero in *Tom Thumb* nicely catches contemporary uncertainty, inside the theatre and out, about the precise nature of what Fielding called 'True Greatness'. The chaotic events of the play—'heaven and earth in wild confusion'—mirror what Fielding sees as the confusion of England itself in 1730.

Like Pope,[33] Fielding continued to draw elaborate comparisons between the confused state of the theatre and the confused state of the nation. *The Author's Farce*, presented a few weeks before *Tom Thumb* in 1730, veers rather inconsistently between gloomy, *Dunciad*-like lamentations over the philistinism of the age—'when party and prejudice carry all before them; when learning is decried, wit not understood, when the theatres are puppet-shows and the comedians ballad-singers'—to the gay and farcical conclusion in which the unfortunate author Luckless is found to be the long-lost son of the King of Bantam. Things seldom end too unhappily in Fielding's work. The play allows some interesting glimpses into the plight of the poor writers of the time, but as a satire it is finally rather muddled: is Luckless a mere scribbler, or is he a genius whose work is neglected because of the ignorance of the theatre-managers and book-sellers of the day? Fielding never clarifies this central point. *Pasquin* (1736) is a double rehearsal-play, the first half being a rehearsal of a comedy called *The Election*, which satirizes corruption in a country election, the second half being a rehearsal of a tragedy called *The Life and Death of Common Sense*, in which Queen Ignorance invades the country from Europe with her 'singers, fidlers, tumblers, and rope-dancers', and puts to death Queen Common Sense. Once again, political satire lurks behind what is ostensibly mere theatrical burlesque, and the play ends with a dark prophecy from the dying Queen about the advent of an age of further and deeper disorders within the kingdom. At other times Fielding's political thrusts were bolder and more open. In *The Welsh Opera*—rewritten as *The Grub-Street Opera* in 1731—Fielding had attacked not only both political parties, but also the Royal Family itself; in *Don Quixote in England* (1734) he had again attacked electioneering. But it was in *The Historical Register for 1736* (1737), a clever and thorough-going attack on the Walpole administration, and in *Eurydice Hissed*, played as an afterpiece to *The Historical Register*, that Fielding's harrassment of the government at last became in-tolerable. It was not, however, a play of Fielding's but an anonymous and scurrilous play called *The Golden Rump* which finally provoked Walpole to bring in his Licensing Act of 21 June 1737,[34] which brought the theatre under the direct control of the Lord Chamberlain—a control finally lifted in England only in 1968.

The Licensing Act is conventionally represented as being a highly tyrannical and unpopular measure. No doubt most people at the time felt that it was just that. Yet it should be remembered that as far back as 1732 Fielding in *The Modern Husband* had satirized those who thought that theatrical control was unnecessary: it was the unspeakable Lord Richly who declared that 'It wou'd be very fine, truly, if men of quality were confin'd in their taste; we should be rarely diverted, if a set of pedants were to licence all our diversions; the stage then wou'd be as dull as a country pulpit' (II. v); and that, only five years after the passing of the Act, Fielding was to have Parson Adams protest (*Joseph Andrews*, III. vii) that it was scandalous that the government allowed plays to be performed which brought the clergy into contempt. Clearly the question of censorship was far from simple; and recently John Loftis has suggested (in *The Politics of Drama in Augustan England*) that the Licensing Act came into being in response to a fairly widespread feeling that there ought to be more, rather than less, control over theatrical matters. Although the Licensing Act managed to curb the grosser kinds of political satire in the theatre, theatrical burlesque nevertheless continued to flourish in the second half of the century. *Tom Thumb* and other plays of Fielding's were still performed after the passing of the Act. The little plays of Samuel Foote, one of the most feared of theatrical figures in Garrick's time, continued to mimic and to ridicule well-known figures of the day—Macklin, Tate Wilkinson, Thomas Sheridan, even Garrick and Dr. Johnson were amongst those either attacked or threatened; and R. B. Sheridan wrote what is probably the funniest of the century's burlesque plays, *The Critic*. The Licensing Act is often held responsible for the decline of English drama in the eighteenth century. 'Fielding, driven out of the trade of Molière and Aristophanes, took to that of Cervantes; and since then the English novel has been one of the glories of literature, whilst the English drama has been its disgrace.' So Bernard Shaw wrote in 1898 [35]; such a view exaggerates the quality of the drama of Fielding's age, and undervalues the quality of that in the age of Goldsmith, Garrick, and Sheridan. Yet it contains an element of truth. Although the new form of the novel did not supplant the drama, it is important to recognize the extent to which it evolved out of it: all the major novelists of the century—Fielding, Richardson, Sterne, Smollett—were to a greater or a lesser extent influenced by techniques which they had learnt from the theatre, and theatrical conventions are prominent in the English comic novel at least until the time of Dickens. The Licensing Act undoubtedly accelerated the growth of the new form. Whether he knew it or not, Robert Walpole was helping one of the major cultural shifts of the eighteenth century.

NOTES

1. Pope, *Dunciad,* i. 183–6.
2. Joseph Spence, *Observations, Anecdotes, and Characters of Books and Men,* ed. James M. Osborn, Oxford, 1966, i. 184; and *The Correspondence of Alexander Pope,* ed. George Sherburn, Oxford, 1956, iii. 200, 209.
3. *Correspondence,* i. 71.
4. *The Letters of John Gay,* ed. C. F. Burgess, Oxford, 1966, p. 19.
5. *Lord Hervey and his Friends, 1726–38,* ed. Earl of Ilchester, London, 1950, p. 61.
6. *Of Dramatic Poesy and Other Critical Essays,* ed. G. Watson, London, 1962, i. 51.
7. *Critical Works of John Dennis,* ed. E. N. Hooker, Baltimore, 1939–43, ii. 259.
8. *Collected Works,* ed. A. Friedman, Oxford, 1966, iii. 211.
9. *Lives of the English Poets,* ed. G. B. Hill, Oxford, 1905, iii. 56, 202; *Boswell's Life of Johnson,* ed. G. B. Hill, rev. L. F. Powell, Oxford, 1934–50, ii. 378, i. 449.
10. *Characteristics,* ed. J. M. Robertson, London, 1900, i. 85.
11. *Classic, Romantic, and Modern,* New York, 1961, p. 75.
12. *Critical Works,* ed. Hooker, ii. 251–74.
13. Theophilus Cibber [and Robert Shiels], *Lives of the Poets,* 1753, iv. 120.
14. See *Collected Works,* ed. Friedman, v. 92.
15. *The Life and Times of Frederick Reynolds, Written by Himself,* London, 1826, ii. 227–8.
16. See R. L. Purdy's edition of the first version of the play (Oxford, 1935) for details of Sheridan's revisions.
17. See John Loftis, *Comedy and Society from Congreve to Fielding,* Stanford, 1959.
18. See John Loftis, *The Politics of Drama in Augustan England,* Oxford, 1963, pp. 35 ff.
19. Emmett L. Avery, 'The Restoration Audience,' *Philological Quarterly,* xlv (1966), 54–61.
20. See J. W. Krutch, *Comedy and Conscience after the Restoration,* New York, 1924, pp. 264–70.
21. *Essays,* Edinburgh, 1776, p. 469.
22. *Lives of the English Poets,* ed. Hill, ii. 67.
23. *Collected Works,* ed. Friedman, iii. 211.
24. Many of these are pointed out by W. H. McBurney in his edition of the play (see Bibliography).
25. *Dramatic Miscellanies,* 1783–84, iii. 62.
26. W. E. A. Axon, 'The Story of Lillo's *Fatal Curiosity*,' *Notes and Queries,* 6th series, v (1882), 21–23; Reino Virtanen, 'Camus' *Le Malentendu* and some Analogues,' *Comparative Literature,* x (1958).
27. *The Actor,* 1755, p. 262.
28. *Collected Works,* ed. Friedman, i. 429.

29. See B. H. Bronson, 'The Beggar's Opera,' in *Studies in the Comic*, University of California Publications, 1941, pp. 197–231.

30. *Complete Works*, ed. P. P. Howe, London, iv (1930), 65.

31. *Life of Johnson*, ed. Hill, rev. Powell, ii. 368.

32. This matter is discussed in some detail by J. H. Hillhouse in his edition of the play (see Bibliography).

33. See George Sherburn, 'The Dunciad, Book IV,' *Texas Studies in Literature and Language*, xxiv (1944), 174–90.

34. A succinct account of the events leading up to the Licensing Act is given by Phyllis Hartnoll in 'The Theatre and the Licensing Act,' in *Silver Renaissance, Essays on Eighteenth Century English History*, ed. Alex. Natan, London, 1961, pp. 165–186; for a fuller account see Watson Nicholson, *The Struggle for a Free Stage in London*, Boston, 1906.

35. Preface to *Plays Unpleasant*, in *The Complete Prefaces of Bernard Shaw*, London, 1965, p. 720.

BIBLIOGRAPHY

I *Editions*

There are still large editorial gaps in this field. Amongst the most useful editions of individual authors are :

The Miscellaneous Works of *Joseph Addison*, ed. A. C. Guthkelch, 1914, 2 vols. (Vol 1 contains the plays.)

Henry Fielding, *The Tragedy of Tragedies*, ed. J. T. Hillhouse, 1918; ed. L. J. Morrissey, Edinburgh, 1970.

Collected Works of Oliver Goldsmith, ed. Arthur Friedman, 5 vols., Oxford, 1966. (Vol. 5 contains the plays.)

Four Comedies by Charles Macklin, ed. J. O. Bartley, 1968.

Three Plays by Nicholas Rowe, ed. J. R. Sutherland, 1929.

The Plays and Poems of R. B. Sheridan, ed. R. Crompton Rhodes, Oxford, 1928, 3 vols. (Vols. 1 and 2 contain the plays).

R. B. Sheridan, *The Rivals* (first version), ed. R. L. Purdy, Oxford, 1935.

The Plays of Richard Steele, ed. S. S. Kenny, Oxford, 1970.

Major editions of the plays of Gay and Fielding are now in preparation. *Three Hours After Marriage*, by Gay, Pope, and Arbuthnot, has been edited by R. Morton and W. M. Peterson, Painsville, Ohio, 1961, and by John Harrington Smith for the Augustan Reprint Society (Publication No. 91–2, Los Angeles, 1961). Also available in the Augustan Reprint Society series are Mrs. Centlivre's *The Busie Body* (Series V, No. 3, 1949), ed. Jess Byrd, and Edward Moore's *The Gamester* (Series V, No. 1), ed. Charles H. Peake. The Regents Restoration Drama Series (general editor John Loftis) provides convenient annotated single-text editions : the following eighteenth-century titles in this series have appeared so far : Richard Steele, *The Conscious Lovers*, ed. S. S. Kenny, 1968, *The Tender Husband*, ed. Calhoun Winton, 1967; Nicholas Rowe, *The Fair Penitent*, ed. M. Goldstein, 1969; John Gay, *The Beggar's Opera*, ed. E. V. Roberts, 1969; Mrs. Centlivre, *A Bold Stroke for a Wife*, ed. T. Stathas, 1969; George Lillo, *The London Merchant*, 1965, and *Fatal Curiosity*, 1967, both edited by William H. McBurney; Henry Fielding, *The Author's Farce*, ed. Charles B. Woods, 1967, *The Historical Register for 1736* and *Eurydice Hissed*, ed. William W. Appleton, 1968, *The Grub St. Opera*, ed. E. V. Roberts, 1969. The following anthologies of eighteenth-century drama are available : Everyman (818), World's Classics (292, 603), and Modern Library (T80) editions, and G. H. Nettleton's and A. E. Case's *British Dramatists from Dryden to Sheridan*, Boston and London, 1939.

II *Critical and Historical Studies*

F. W. Bateson, *English Comic Drama 1700–50*, 1929. A lively and informative critical account.

M. M. Belden, *The Dramatic Works of Samuel Foote*, Yale Studies in English no. 80, New Haven, 1929.

A. V. Berger, 'The Beggar's Opera, the Burlesque, and Italian Opera', *Music and Letters*, xvii (1936), 93–105.

Ernest Bernbaum, *The Drama of Sensibility*, Boston and London, 1915. Still worth consulting, though in many ways superseded by Arthur Sherbo's more recent study (see below).

J. W. Bowyer, *The Celebrated Mrs. Centlivre*, Durham, N. C., 1952.

V. C. Clinton-Baddeley, *The Burlesque Tradition in the English Theatre after 1660*, London, 1952. Very readable.

R. S. Crane, 'Suggestions Towards a Genealogy of the "Man of Feeling"', *ELH*, i (1934), 205–30.

Bonamy Dobree, *Restoration Comedy 1660–1720*, Oxford, 1924; *Restoration Tragedy 1660–1720*, Oxford, 1929.

J. W. Draper, 'The Theory of the Comic in Eighteenth-Century England,' *JEGP*, xxxvii (1938), 207–23.

J. P. Emery, *Arthur Murphy*, Philadelphia, 1946.

William Empson, *Some Versions of Pastoral*, London, 1935. Ch. VI contains a brilliant analysis of *The Beggar's Opera*.

E. McA. Gagey, *Ballad Opera*, New York, 1937.

W. F. Gallaway, 'The Sentimentalism of Goldsmith,' *PMLA*, xlviii (1933), 1167–81.

B. L. Joseph, *The Tragic Actor*, London, 1959.

J. W. Krutch, *Comedy and Conscience after the Restoration*, New York, 1924.

John Loftis, *Comedy and Society From Congreve to Fielding*, Stanford, 1959. Skilful analysis of the social context of early eighteenth-century comedy. *The Politics of Drama in Augustan England*, Oxford, 1963. A valuable, though more specialized (and, for the general reader, somewhat less accessible) study than the previous one.

The London Stage 1660–1800, Part II, 1700–29, ed. Emmett L. Avery, Carbondale, Illinois, 1960; Part III, 1629–47, eo. Arthur H. Scouten, 1961; Part IV, 1747–76, ed. G. W. Stone, Jr., 1962. Indispensable and encyclopaedic. Valuable introductions, and detailed accounts of performances, casts-lists, etc., throughout the period.

J. J. Lynch, *Box, Pit and Gallery*, Berkeley and Los Angeles, 1953. Audiences and their behaviour.

Allardyce Nicoll, *A History of English Drama 1660–1900*, Vols. II and III, Cambridge, 1925, 1927. A mine of information.

Ronald Paulson, *Satire and the Novel in Eighteenth Century England*, New Haven and London, 1967. Contains a good account of Fielding as dramatist.

H. W. Pedicord, *The Theatrical Public in the Time of Garrick*, New York, 1954.

Ricardo Quintana, 'Goldsmith's Achievement as Dramatist,' *UTQ*, xxxiv (1965), 159–77.

C. J. Rawson, 'Some Remarks on Eighteenth Century "Delicacy," With a Note on Hugh Kelly's *False Delicacy* (1768),' *JEGP*, lxi (1962), 1–13.

Allan Rodway, 'Goldsmith and Sheridan: Satirists of Sentiment,' *Renaissance and Modern Essays*, ed. G. R. Hibbard, 1966, pp. 66–72.

W. E. Schultz, *Gay's Beggar's Opera*, New Haven and London, 1923. A compendious account of the play's genesis and history.

Arthur Sherbo, *English Sentimental Drama*, Michigan, 1957. One of the best major studies of the drama of this period.

E. P. Stein, *David Garrick, Dramatist*, 1938.

Dane Farnsworth Smith, *Plays About the Theatre, From The Rehearsal in 1671 to the Licensing Act in 1737*, London and New York, 1936. A thorough if at times pedestrian survey.

G. Wilson Knight, *The Golden Labyrinth*, 1962. Ch. VIII gives a brilliant and concise account of the drama of the period.

7
DEFOE AND RICHARDSON—Novelists of the City

Mark Kinkead-Weekes, University of Kent

Defoe became a novelist at almost sixty, Richardson in his fifties.[1] One had been a failed merchant turned journalist, pamphleteer and secret agent; the other a successful printer. They had spent hardworking lives in 'the City', not 'the Town'; and in imaginative terms too their work belonged to the other side of Temple Bar from the Augustan gentlemanly culture. Indeed, part of their value for us is the mapping of new territory in the new kind of literature they invented. We watch 'the City' becoming imaginatively aware of itself and trying to analyse its particular problems. We turn to common men working in an upstart medium (not the poetry, drama, and witty satire of polite literature) for insight into the human implications of a new kind of society.

Both men were not only rooted in the 'middle class',[2] but also in its puritan past. Defoe was born in 1660, the year of undoing for the revolution of the 'saints' and the year in which John Bunyan went to prison. Richardson was born in 1689, the year after the bloodless revolution that ushered in the new era and saw Bunyan's death. In Bunyan's allegories we can already detect the imaginative world of the defeated 'saint' turning into that of the bourgeois merchant in an allegorical landscape. For Christian in the first part of *The Pilgrim's Progress*, 'the City' can only be the City of Destruction or Vanity Fair. Life, eternal life, can only begin with headlong flight, fingers in ears, from his family and a godless society, and be won after incessant battling against the seductions and challenges of the world and the devil. In the second part of the *Progress*, however, there is a tenderness and warmth of relationship in the pilgrimage of Christiana and her children, a renewed sense of the society which can extend—though still sundered from the City of Destruction—through the Christian

226

family into a community of believers, even inside the walls of Vanity Fair. In *The Life and Death of Mr. Badman* the Christian conscience faces the challenge of conceiving the good life within the world of business and commerce itself. Defoe was a Dissenter like Bunyan, Richardson was not, but in their later situations and their different ways, both share Bunyan's puritan concern with personal salvation, and with the tensions between commerce and conscience, economic individualism and human fellowship. Behind their novels lies not a literary tradition, but the puritan inheritance of domestic, devotional and instructive writing, which sought to accommodate Christian the pilgrim with Mr. Goodman the upright merchant.

So we turn to 'that fellow who was pilloried', whose name Swift affected never to remember, and to the timid Fleet Street printer whose fear of noblemen's servants so amused Dr. Johnson, for new kinds of awareness: of the fiercely competitive and acquisitive world of 'the City'; of the poverty, dependence, and crime that lay just beneath the prosperous surface; of the challenge to integrity and human relationship from economic individualism.

Inevitably, new awareness demanded a new literary medium, and if we talk of 'the novel' we at least pay some tribute to the inventiveness this required. We do not, however, grasp the value of Defoe and Richardson as imaginative explorers until we begin to value them separately as the inventors of two quite different new ways of writing. (As a critical term 'the novel' is little more than a convenient collective noun for many different kinds of 'fiction in prose of a certain extent'.)[3] Indeed, a preoccupation with literature as a social register tends to make one disregard what is really the essence of the literary work: what Coleridge called the 'shaping spirit of imagination', and Wallace Stevens, more accurately, 'the maker's rage to order words'. The primary value of any writer lies in his ability to embody and explore in words a unique informing vision. His reactions to society will be part of this, and he will be affected by his lifetime's experience, but no writer can reflect social reality. Each conveys a kind of 'reality' defined by a personal vision, a process of selection, a peculiar ordering of words. There are as many 'realities' as there are ways of 'seeing' with imaginative coherence and verbal control; and we cannot hope to understand how a writer sees society until we understand how he sees. The imagination, however, always tends to explore beyond the conscious awareness of the man who holds the pen. How much, it may be asked, did Defoe or Richardson know what they were doing in their new ways of writing? Or is this an irrelevant question?

I

Defoe's fiction begins at his own name, with its suggestion of upper-class ancestry, bearing eloquent witness both to the experience of being an outsider, and to the determination to make himself a success in spite of it, which are also the mark of the Defoe protagonist. He was born Daniel Foe, son of a dissenting tallow-chandler in Cripplegate, low on the social scale, and barred by his religion from the schools and universities which opened into the higher professions. James Foe wanted his son to become a minister, and had him educated at a notable school for Dissenters, Charles Morton's Academy at Newington Green, but the young Defoe realized that the key to the success, security, and gentility he wanted was money, and he set up as a merchant. Fortunately (from our point of view) the future author of *The Complete English Tradesman* (1725, 1727) was a sad failure in business, going bankrupt in 1692 to the extent of £17,000. He was to be haunted by creditors for much of his life. Yet his fascination with trade remained the central thread in the varied and colourful tapestry of his career, and the central theme of his voluminous writings. It was through trade that he gained so wide and diverse a knowledge of life. His journeyings as a merchant, as well as his later expeditions as a confidential political agent, laid the foundations of that indispensable sourcebook for the economic and social historian, *A Tour through the Whole Island of Great Britain* (1724–27). It was his devotion to the advancement of trade that first took him into politics in the cause of King William, and then provided (along with his extreme financial insecurity) at least some consistency behind his turncoat service as agent and spy for opposed Ministries. In the *Review*, the periodical which he wrote single-handed for the moderate Tory Harley between 1704 and 1713, we can see that what he really cared about remained the initially Whig conception of England as a trading nation. It was through his understanding of the implications of trade that he acquired his insight into the essentially commercial nature of English society after 1688. It was because of his own failure and insecurity that he came to understand what it meant to be poor, dependent, underprivileged, desperate, in a society based on money and property. He knew all about bailiffs, and the spectre of destitution. He had been pilloried, and imprisoned in Newgate, for publishing *The Shortest-Way with the*

228

Dissenters (1702), the most traumatic event in his life. Though he was clearly in one sense a spokesman for the post-Restoration middle-class, his experience gave him an imaginative insight into the plight of the poor man and the outsider which is by no means characteristic of the bourgeois—for example in *The Poor Man's Plea* (1698).

The puritan side of Defoe is, however, no less constant than his fascination with trade. He chose to be a merchant rather than a minister, but all his life he remained a Dissenter and suffered for it. He was of course no saint, even in the seventeenth-century sense. The puritanism of his time had lost revolutionary ardour and spiritual passion, and had become more concerned with practical morality. Defoe's commercial and political conscience does not seem to have been over-sensitive, and his religious thought and sensibility were neither deep nor subtle. Yet he firmly held to puritan articles of faith which he returned to over and over again in his work, and a good deal of his voluminous output, like *The Family Instructor* (1715) and *Religious Courtship* (1722), was in the direct tradition of puritan instructive writing. Above all, his sense of the perilous insecurity of the human condition had a religious as well as an economic basis. It is Defoe's unique matter-of-factness that gives the *Journal of the Plague Year* (1722) its curious power. He is imaginatively absorbed in circumstantial detail and verisimilitude, so that it is the situation itself that holds his fascinated eye, and ours. But part of the matter-of-factness is the straightforward certainty that the disease is the visible Hand of God, a 'fact' that can be recorded with the same chilling simplicity as all the other 'facts'. The book deeply influenced Camus, but there is none of the metaphysical questioning and argument of *La Peste*; Defoe is more perturbed about the implications of quarantine than he is about the implications of his belief in the direct intervention of Providence. Yet it would be we who were simple-minded if we were to take this unembarrassed certainty as evidence that Defoe's religion was perfunctory. The challenge is rather to see how the situations of his other fictions brought the otherworldly and the worldly side of his imagination into greater and greater tension.

The description of Crusoe landing on his island may serve as a convenient example of one kind of imaginative vision in Defoe. If we compare William Golding's Pincher Martin landing on his rock, we have both an interesting case of the relativity of 'realism' as a critical term, and an indication of just what it is that Defoe's imagination seizes as significant—how he orders his prose to do something very different from Golding's attempt to bring home to us what the experience would 'really' feel like. Golding's language works on the sensory imagination; we are inside a head, we are eyes recovering focus, a consciousness becoming aware of fear and pain; the sensation of recovering from drowning is created by rivetting our attention on what it is that the man sees, and feels. Defoe's passage is dominated by the personal pronoun. He keeps our attention fixed on the man, so that although the sea threatens to overwhelm him, we never doubt that he is in control. The verbs accumulate to establish our response; for a while they belong to the sea, but the loose syntax turns, the object becomes the subject and the passive the active. Crusoe is hurried, landed, dashed, left senseless and helpless, beaten, until 'I must have been strangled in the water'; but I recovered, I resolved, I held, I clambered up, and 'sat me down . . . quite out of reach of the water'. This is the essential movement of the prose. We may note that the nouns are things with no resonance in themselves; things that the 'I' and the actions deal with. If we then try to describe the kind of imaginative vision that is operating, from the kind of selection made by the style, we would surely say that this is an imagination essentially concerned with the successful struggle of the individual to dominate his environment. It is hardly concerned with the particular character of the individual or his particular consciousness, nor is it much more concerned with the particularities of the environment; it is taken up with the way in which they act on each other. Action, consequently, is by far the most important mode. A typical Defoe paragraph is made up of a succession of actions—this happened, then that, then this—in a very loose and episodic agglomeration; for it is not the relation between the actions that is important, but the way that in a succession of them the key pattern is continually established and re-established. This imaginative vision sees the world as one of objects for humans to act on; objects dangerous, or useful, or not useful like those famous shoes that are so denuded of pathos by the automatic recording that they are not a pair. If one can see what critics mean by comparing Defoe with law-court evidence, it is not that such a style can give us 'the truth, the whole truth, and nothing but the truth'. It is rather that the account is stripped down to reveal the essential pattern of action, stripped of complexities like the worlds of private sensation and consciousness, and (as we shall see) of human relationship. Defoe's vision is extraordinarily selective, so that the experience of reading him excludes a number of ways in which we experience life ourselves, but this is because his imagination is so taken up with what he sees as the basic human condition, archetypally.

What the passage did in miniature, the book does as a whole. Crusoe is Everyman, isolated on his desert island in order to reveal Man as he 'really' is to Defoe's imagination: alone, faced by a hostile environment, forced to make his way against it, shape it to his will, or be crushed. He is driven on, however, by an energy which impels him always to move forward from apparent security and pit himself against the unknown, but which also enables him to cope with challenges and overcome. When the protections as well as the complexities of society are ripped away, it is Everyman's nature to know terrible fear; but the 'I' at the heart of him is resilient, energetic, resourceful, determined to survive.

Defoe's imagination soon moves beyond survival, however, to expansion. Robinson Crusoe is alone but he is not naked; he is given the most complete collection of tools and supplies ever assembled for a castaway, and his island soon becomes less a desert island than an estate crying out for development. Again it is the way that the imagination strips away our normal consciousness that makes it so fascinating. We see every object that comes from the wreck with new eyes, because we appreciate its vital importance to the lonely human being in his archetypal struggle. We experience for the first time the true difficulty and grandeur of each of the steps and processes by which economic progress is made—processes which economic specialization hides from us in everday life. We get in fact a kind of synoptic economic history of man, imaginatively concentrated in the twenty-eight years of Crusoe's life on the island. First there is the cave-man stage, where the basic necessities are shelter, fortification, hunting. Then Crusoe learns how to make his environment serve him in the agricultural and herding stage. He learns to grow food, manufacture utensils, enclose and cultivate the land, acquire, domesticate and tend livestock. Gradually to the 'castle' is added the 'summer residence', the 'estate', the growth of economic civilization based on labour (which is neither moral duty, nor burdensome necessity, but the outcome of Everyman's restless energy) and the exploitation of natural resources by human ingenuity.

The significance of desert islands for dreamers is the freedom to create an idyll, selecting from real life what is basically the heart's desire. The significance of Defoe's made-up world, as opposed to the imaginative reconstruction of an historical event in the *Journal*, is that it should allow us to see not only how capitalist his imaginative vision was, but also what is involved in capitalist expansion under ideal conditions, outside society. Crusoe steadily reduces human relationships to economic ones. The arrival of Man Friday provides additional manpower, but in a classically paternalist form. Crusoe gives a master's affection, but in return for the bond-servant's absolute submission, loyalty, and labour. He does not ask Friday his name or try to learn his language; he gives him a name which sounds like a ledger entry, and teaches him enough pidgin English to convey what Crusoe thinks he needs to know. (More simply, he had sold Xury, the boy who helped him to escape from slavery.) He ties later arrivals down by contracts ensuring complete autocracy. The island is his absolute property, he becomes first the Governor, then the absentee landlord of a colony. The struggle for survival concludes with magnificent profit. We find a basic imaginative force, not in anything we could usefully describe as 'realism', but in a vision so selective, so intensely archetypal, that we are driven to see it as one of the most powerful European *myths*. Defoe is not concerned with intricacies of character. The world of the senses is missing also; the novel is crammed with objects, but we see only their utility, and the island never composes a landscape. The world of consciousness is attenuated to a point that is psychologically unrealistic. Actual castaways were degraded by fear and loneliness and sank, within a far shorter time than Crusoe's twenty-eight years, to the level of animals. Crusoe spends twenty-four years on the island before he voices any heart-felt longing for companionship, and never expresses any longing for women at all, in stark contradiction to the most common form of desert island daydream. When companions do arrive, human relationship is reduced to economic relationship, colonists' wives are eventually chosen on economic criteria. Yet the selectiveness and the freedom from normal social conditioning are also the source of real imaginative power. *Robinson Crusoe* is both 'the City's' mythic celebration of economic man, his power to dominate and profit from his environment; and also a revelation of some of the implications of economic individualism.

With another part of his mind, however, Defoe sees a no less archetypal vision of sinful man brought to regeneration by divine grace. Crusoe disobeys his earthly father in running away to sea, and the echoes of the prodigal son and the story of Jonah make it clear that this is a sin against the Divine Father too. The young Kreutznaer, fool of the cross, refuses to heed the clear warning of the storm on his first voyage, and his compounded disobedience lands him in enslavement. He fails to grasp the real meaning of his miraculous preservation on the island, or of the 'accidental' sowing of the seed in the one place where it will grow. He draws only practical inferences from the threat of lightning to his gunpowder, and the comment of the earthquake on his attempts to barricade himself from external danger. Realization that the remotest corner of the universe is ruled by divine power and providence comes to him only in illness, when (like Balaam) he is visited by the terrible apparition of God's angel. Through grace and the neglected Bible in his sea-chest, he is regenerated. He learns to see the hand of providence, as puritans did, in casual openings of the scriptures and in the insistent correspondence of the dates of his disasters and escapes. He remains a fearful and a rash man, but he learns to cope better with his terrors and his impulsiveness, and to be grateful for God's mercy and care. When he comes to instruct Friday in the faith, he instructs himself, and this is the one place where Friday is admitted, as *noble* savage, to human equality. Moreover Crusoe's musings on cannibalism (once his horror and murderous rage are under control), and the experience of instructing Friday, give rise to quite serious reflections on the distinction between natural and divine law, and the inability of natural religion to progress to divine religion without revelation. Defoe is concerned with the state of nature in religious and moral ways as well as economic ones.

Only, how are we to relate the vision of *homo economicus* to the vision of sinful Adam? The ungovernable impulse that sends Crusoe to sea is his original sin, but it is the same impulse that makes him a hero. Can his restless energy, his refusal to be limited by circumstances, his determination to take on challenges, be *sinful*, when the imaginative zest and power of the book suggest that Defoe himself approved of them? Yet we cannot dismiss the religious pattern as merely Defoe's conventional side, or a gesture to a middle-class audience suspicious of the moral validity of 'stories'.[4] It is too insistent for that.

It is true that Defoe's style seems oddly capable of holding apparent contradictions without discomfort. When Crusoe finds money in the wreck, for instance, the puritan's imagination suddenly collides with the merchant's. Crusoe's plight makes money worthless, and he apostrophises the gold as Spenser, Milton or Bunyan might have done. Then in almost the same breath, he proceeds to take it anyway, in the trader's knowledge that it might well come in useful later on. Yet there is no conscious irony, for still another part of Defoe's mind is already busy with the story-teller's interest in getting his hero off the wreck before a storm breaks. The passage is made up as it goes along. The opposite ways of looking at the money are only part of a much longer and rambling syntactical unit, whose loose connections and bustling pace allow very different elements to rub along together quite easily. The homeliness of the style makes one feel close to the situation, momentarily interested (as Defoe is) in each of the three things in turn, but it does not encourage one to explore, far less resolve, any potential conflict. There is this, and that, and also this; the style is essentially episodic and works by addition; and what the style is in miniature the book is as a whole. Moreover, Defoe did not think of his novels as 'literature', requiring care and polish. He wrote at tremendous speed, and without revision, as the presence of many factual inconsistencies betrays.

Yet there is a more significant imaginative factor to be taken into account. Defoe is not interested in character, he is interested in action—but he always sees action in terms of *situation*. To understand this is to appreciate why Crusoe's conversion is not a radical change of character, any more than his sin was a character flaw. His conversion is, precisely, a vision, an opening of his eyes to a more accurate reading of the human situation. Once he has understood the nature of the universe, the same energies which had led to disaster when God's messages were ignored, can lead to success when they are heard and understood, and divine vengeance gives way to grace and mercy. Conversion does not make Crusoe less worldly, it makes him more effective in the world. Similarly, if we look through Defoe's eyes, it is simply the case that money is both useless on the island and useful if Crusoe ever gets back to civilization. It all depends on the situation, and since the situation includes the gathering storm, it is right to take the coins, though it might be wrong if the gold were in heavy bars, which would take time to load and might upset the raft. Crusoe is an erring economic man who becomes a God-fearing economic man and is blessed with success. Defoe as yet saw no serious contradictions in these terms. When the desert island myth is replaced in society, however, the implications of his peculiarly selective vision become both more obvious and more disturbing.

Moll Flanders begins her life in a state of isolation; only now the hostile environment against which Everywoman battles for survival is the economic nature of society itself. The key fact about this society is that its money economy is made for and

234

directed by the male. A moneyless female may survive by selling herself into servitude, but against this the child heroine instinctively rebels, demanding for herself the independence she calls being a 'gentlewoman', and this is what makes her heroic. In a man's society, however, most kinds of profitable work are closed to the gentlewoman. She may make a precarious living by sewing or washing, but at the cost of the quality of life that Everywoman demands. Her only economic weapons are her sex, her wits, her courage and resourcefulness. Her main hope is marriage, but marriage is an economic institution in which most of the cards are in the hands of the male. Outside marriage there is, for a lonely would-be gentlewoman without money, only the choice of poverty, or prostitution, or crime.

This is the situation in which the five phases of Moll's life are played out. The first—her girlhood, seduction, and the first two marriages—shows an innocent learning the economic facts of life. The second phase is concerned with her struggle to maintain herself through a succession of economico-sexual contracts. All but one of these are called 'marriages' and are thought to be so by the male, and all aim at permanence, but none can be legal, and all are precarious in various ways. The third phase, after the death of her banker 'husband', shows her reduced to exactly the same economic position as when the second began, with one crucial difference: her looks have gone. Without them and without money, she can no longer hope for any permanent sexual bargain, and grim economic necessity drives her to crime. But in society as it is, this can have only one outcome; and the fourth phase places Moll in Newgate. The prison is Moll's hell, and in some ways Defoe's also, one that he had experienced traumatically, but it is significant to notice what makes it hellish. It is an apotheosis of destitution; it is first of all a slum, with the noises, the dirt, the smell, the disorder of a slum, and its spectres of human degradation. It is also an apotheosis of absolute passivity and inaction. The death-cell is the place where the human being experiences complete aloneness, and becomes the absolutely helpless victim of forces outside any possibility of control; and this death-in-life leads straight to the horror of the scaffold where the life force itself is finally extinguished. Moll is saved by her repentance, and the consequent efforts of the minister on her behalf, but it is money in the hands of her faithful governess that allows her to redeem herself from servitude in Virginia, and start life afresh in the New World on a sound economic footing. In the last phase, to her who has, more is given: the restoration of the 'husband' she has cared for most, the rediscovery of a son, the possession of large estates and wealth in her hands, and under her control.

So we have another myth of the archetypal human condition, of Everywoman in society this time, and another expression of Defoe's faith in the power of the human being to survive. Again, however, the shaping vision is concerned not only with survival, but with expansion, exploitation and profit; not only with individualism but with capitalism. The little girl who longs to be a gentlewoman is concerned with more than independence; the arch-criminal is only initially driven to her career by necessity; and the full success in the New World is the rich imaginative enjoyment of profits. At the end of each economic transaction Moll balances her books for us; but we are not only fascinated and involved with the graphic curves of her battle against the terrors of poverty in an economic world, we experience also the fascination of the acquisitive instinct for its own sake.

At the same time we are even more aware of the extreme selectivity of the imaginative vision than we were in *Robinson Crusoe*, because the myth has been replaced in society. We are as involved as before with the enjoyment of the protagonist's resourcefulness and courage, and there is an important new factor: an irrepressible cheerfulness that often issues in wry, shrewd humour. But because Moll battles in a world of human beings, not a world of wild nature including some savages, the human implications of the vision come home to us more sharply than before. Again we confront a world crammed with objects, and again we see them anew, in the sharp spotlighting of necessity; but we become more aware of how emptied they are of sensuous qualities because they are far more sophisticated objects. Brocades and laces, rings and jewels, furniture and plate—to see these purely in the light of economic value is to be even more aware of how much of our normal vision is missing. Only in Moll's state of innocence is there sexual excitement, and even there it is oddly fused with the guineas in the hand and the purse in the bosom; but the fact that it has been present at all points up the extent to which the economic nature of her world banishes the sensual as well as the sensuous. We detect more sharply how the basic criteria for success involve complete freedom from family, social and moral ties. The novel is crammed with 'relationships', but what we think of as human relationship is even more radically reduced to contracts and profit and loss accounting. Husbands become ordinal numbers, children are abandoned and forgotten, what human beings mean to Moll is primarily dictated by economics.

Here the value of grasping Defoe's overriding concern with situation becomes apparent, for not only do Moll's responses to others ebb and flow according to economic pressures, but she is a chameleon herself. We never know her real name. She always takes on the shape that the situation demands for her advantage; and in the key criminal phase when we see the implications of her world most nakedly, she has a different dress, accent, appearance and behaviour in every episode, to the point of passing as a man. But even when the pressure of necessity is removed the position is the same. She seems radically incapable of showing herself truly to anyone, right to the end. She is always strategic, always playing a part in which what she is, and says, and feels, will be to her maximum advantage. It is not that she is incapable of strong or genuine feeling; but we are always aware that the relationship of what she can allow herself to feel to the contingencies of the situation is more direct and determined than it is in the world in which we ourselves live. In one situation she can afford to feel nothing whatsoever about the abandonment of a child so that it is hardly mentioned. In another she can afford compunction, but cannot afford to act on it. In yet another she can give herself the relief and satisfaction of expressing a mother's feelings to a high and even exaggerated degree—not unaccompanied however by an alert response to the dampness of the ground. What is true of feeling is true also of moral consciousness. Moral reflections occur, not only in the commentary of the old woman who remembers, but also at the time. However, they are either sited at moments when there is nothing to be done, periods of stasis either disastrous or safe; or when they occur in the heat of the struggle they have no effect on what Moll actually does. Dislocation between thought and action is constant. And if there is a kind of intelligence in Moll's ability to think out, often at lightning speed, what a situation is and what moves it demands of her, there is no life of the mind, no bringing a situation to fully human consciousness for its own sake.

When the replacement of the myth in society shows up implications such as these in Defoe's overriding concern with situation, there is bound to be a far more radical discrepancy between the economic vision, and the religious paradigm of sin, conversion and redemption, than there was in *Robinson Crusoe*. This involves more than the dislocation between thought and action that occurs in the younger Moll; the commentary of the old woman looking back over her career raises the question even more insistently. We may take as read the practical instructiveness Defoe claims in his preface, the useful lessons in foresight and prudence that could be learnt from Moll's history. We can take wholly seriously the sharp insight into the ways in which Moll is determined by her situation. But how seriously can we accept her repentance, and her self-evaluation? On the few occasions when her judgement goes to the heart of things, this simply throws into relief her normal superficiality. When Moll is abandoned by her Bath lover, it is clear enough that genuine penitence must involve not only a break with previous failings, but a remorseful reaction to accomplices in sin. But the old woman never realizes how totally this undermines the 'religious' account of her own repentance. The only time her realization of wrong results in such a response is over her incest, where she feels that human nature itself cries out against the act. Yet the quality of her genuine remorse is perhaps even more disturbing than her inability to feel it elsewhere, for she ceases to be able to regard her brother humanely at all, the language she subsequently uses of him is brutal, and her later accounts of the affair are untrue. Her repentance in Newgate affects neither her relationships nor her later behaviour. It never suggests any idea of restitution, or enquiry after her only true husband and her abandoned children; and her new life is built solidly, as are the lives of the 'repentant' governess and the 'repentant' Jemmy, on the criminal foundations of the old. To the end she remains incapable of truth, her reformation is purely the effect of fear, and virtually ceases when the fear does.

So we seem to respond to the novel in quite different ways. With one eye, as it were, we respond to a heroic energy, a cheerful indestructability, a testament of Defoe's faith in the capacity of Everywoman to cope with her situation in an economic society. With the other eye we see what purports to be a moral and religious evaluation, but the more we grasp the implications of Moll's career and the selectivity of the vision we have experienced, the more inadequate that self-evaluation must seem, and the more sobering the exposure of an economic society. Yet we cannot but admit how perfectly Moll is adjusted to the necessities of her world, and how curiously we enjoy watching her.

To what extent, we may ask, was Defoe aware of how far he had been led by his sense of the way that situation determines behaviour? One kind of criticism points to evidence that suggests rapid and piecemeal composition and a lack of awareness of what he was doing : the rambling and episodic style that permits a high degree of inconsistency and narrative incoherence; and a frequent discontinuity between episode and episode. The logical end of this would be to call his stature as a major artist in question. An opposite view sees the confusions in Moll's narrative as a realistic creation of the disorganizations of her life; a sharp perception of what her social situation has done to her as a human being. The logical end of this would be to claim an awareness subtle enough to employ artlessness, and even apparent carelessness, as a triumph of expressive art. The first view tends to identify Defoe with Moll, the second insists on their separation. A third approach denies that the question of Defoe's awareness is really relevant. The contradictions in the novel force us to read it ironically. What the experience is, amounts to the delightful counterpointing of incompatible orders of behaviour, which can co-exist only in the hypocrisy or at least obtuseness of the heroine. If Defoe did not see the ironies himself, then they include him as well as Moll.

There is, clearly, a degree of conscious artistry and of conscious irony in *Moll Flanders*. Yet most readers are also hard put to it to know whether they can properly describe much of their response in sentences beginning 'Defoe . . .' Nor is it easy to argue that this does not matter, if art is produced by a *shaping* spirit of imagination and a maker's rage to *order* words.[5] A critic can hardly make high claims for a work by implying that his own sensitivity is greater than the author's. There ought to be a distinction between an ironic object (easily produced by an energetic writer unaware of the implications of what he is saying) and a work of ironic art which implies a considerable controlling awareness. Yet we cannot make the value of all kinds of art depend entirely on the author's conscious awareness at every stage.

It does seem that the power and value of Defoe's novels comes from his ability to throw himself into the imagined situation of his protagonists. The very energy of this self-projection exposes a discord between the two sides of his mind which a smaller writer could not have achieved; and when one realizes the weight of social experience behind the fiction, one is not perhaps inclined to be too high-mindedly aesthetic in judging it. Nevertheless the same energetic self-projection does work against the sensitivity to implications characteristic of a great writer. One must concede that the conditions under which Defoe wrote, his own attitude to his fictions, and the simple first-person narrative form he chose, were not such as to encourage a full exploration and comprehension of the tensions he was so remarkably successful in revealing. His vision, and the language and style which embody it, are an art of exposure rather than an art of analysis. Yet, if we bear in mind the intense difficulty of self-awareness in a new milieu and a new dimension of literature, we shall not undervalue 'the City's' first real leap of energetic imagination.

II

Compared with Defoe's various career, Richardson's seems humdrum. He was the son of a London joiner and like Defoe was destined for the ministry, but his father could support him at school only until he was fifteen or sixteen. He then chose to be apprenticed as a printer. He was a solemn, even priggish boy, nicknamed 'Serious' and 'Gravity', and a model apprentice. He became an overseer, then set up for himself and prospered steadily. He made two advantageous but apparently harmonious marriages, and achieved the tradesman's ambition of a thriving business near Fleet Street and a 'country house' in the outskirts. By 1754, when he was elected Master of the Stationers' Company, he had become one of the most successful and respected men in his trade. Not the least surprising aspect of his sudden emergence as a novelist fourteen years earlier, at the age of 51, and his authorship thereafter of two of the longest novels in English, is how he found the time.

We have only hints of the inner development behind this hardworking outer life. He chose to be a printer, with boyish naïveté, because he thought he might have scope for his passion for reading. At ten he anticipated his future as both novelist and moralist by impersonating a much older character in a letter of reprimand to a local backbiting gossip; and he was sought after by school friends as a storyteller (whose stories always had a moral). At a demure thirteen he was writing love-letters for several young women. The young apprentice had a friendship and correspondence with an older man, 'a Gentleman greatly my superior in Degree, & of ample Fortunes, who, had he lived, intended high things for me',[6] and we can detect here, as also perhaps in his interest in plays, the opportunity for imaginative insight into worlds and values very different from his own. Later, there was to be a dimension of private tragedy behind the business success. All six of his sons died in infancy, though two daughters survived. Richardson was a domestic man

240

as Defoe was not, and at one stage he suffered eleven family bereavements in rapid succession. To the shock of this he traced the nervous debilities of his later years.

By the 1730s he had acquired among fellow-tradesmen a modest reputation for 'elegant disquisitions in prose', as one of them put it.[7] Towards the end of the decade two booksellers asked him to compose a model letter-writer, to which he characteristically decided to give a moral turn. As he worked on these *Familiar Letters on Important Occasions* (1741) which posed a challenge to put himself into the minds and the language of different people, and began to suggest how subtly letters could be used to indicate character, the idea of his first novel took shape. The possibilities of a correspondence between a daughter, whose master has tried to seduce her, and her father, were too fascinating to be confined to the letter-writer. He laid it aside for the moment, and in two months of intense creativity among all his everyday business he finished *Pamela: or, Virtue Rewarded*, and published it anonymously in 1740.

The basic situation has affinities with Moll's: a girl on the edge of an abyss of poverty which terrifies her; willing to be a servant as Moll was not, but nevertheless making the same basic demand to be a self-determining individual. Pamela too is isolated, forced to fend for herself in a man's world where money and position are the sources of power; and her story also reaches its nadir in imprisonment, albeit in Mr. B.'s country house rather than Newgate. Moreover the story is again not only concerned with the girl's survival as an independent individual; she is 'rewarded' for her struggles with wealth, security, and status.

Richardson, it is true, insists as Defoe does not that it is her exemplary virtue which is rewarded. Yet for many readers this merely points up again the tension between individualism and morality, and raises questions about the moral awareness of the author. The novel was an enormous success and even earned the rare distinction, in an age when fiction was morally suspect, of being recommended from a London pulpit. Yet, from the beginning, other voices attacked its heroine as a hypocrite whose moral pretensions cover self-seeking strategy—most memorably in Fielding's very funny and slanted parody *Shamela* (1741).[8] This kind of criticism, still common, assumes the imaginative identification of author and character, and confronts us again with an ironic object rather than a work of irony. The author looks on Pamela as a moral paragon; the reader remembers Mrs. Peachum's advice that 'by keeping men *off*, you keep them *on*', and sees Pamela's morality as, at best, self-deception by author and heroine, or, at worst, as a hypocrite's weapon in a war of sex, economics and status.

Of course the experience of reading *Pamela* is also very unlike the experience of reading *Moll Flanders*. Richardson is intensive, Defoe extensive. Defoe is concerned with the way situation determines action, and in his imagination the worlds of feeling, consciousness and reflection are secondary to, dependent on, and sometimes even excluded by the demands of economic behaviour. Richardson takes us inside, there is very little action, and situation is only the means of exploring personality, character, and consciousness, in depth.

Hence critics are driven to say that Pamela, however hypocritical, is also intensely lifelike in a new way. Richardson is the beginning of the psychological novel, and moral accusation can be taken up into praise of psychological realism or psychological analysis of Richardson himself. On the other hand, the consciousness revealed by both author and character is still the product of society: Pamela displays not only Richardson's own confusions but a typical ambivalence in the contemporary feminine code of value. As Steele had pointed out, both prude and coquette have 'the distinction of sex in all their thoughts, words and actions' [9]—this is why the values of Pamela and her creator can be open to either interpretation. The novel becomes, in various ways, a case-study.

As soon as we look closely, however, the assumption that Richardson can be identified with his heroine, and is wholly unconscious of the criticisms that can be levelled against her, becomes untenable. A scene like the 'clothes-scene' of Letter 24, when Pamela dresses in the simple outfit she has prepared for going home, requires to be read from four points of view, though it is told only from Pamela's. We see through her eyes, but we also become aware of how Mrs. Jervis and Mr. B. see her, and when we have absorbed this cross-lighting our own inclusive point of view becomes clearly distinct from Pamela's, and must involve criticisms of her as well as of the others. We see more, and more truly, than any participant. Pamela's consciousness is highly complex: moral satisfaction at having made the choice the clothes symbolize, of poverty rather than wrong; feminine vanity in also looking very pretty in them; the desire to be praised which sends her to Mrs. Jervis; and the unconscious attraction to Mr. B. (of which we have had several hints before) which explains why she allows herself to be shown off to him against her better judgement. Mrs. Jervis shows one kind of blindness in her insensitivity to the moral implications of Pamela's clothes. Mr. B. shows another, in his automatic reference of them to concepts of sex-war. But Richardson is also clearly aware of the possibility of hypocrisy in Pamela, since he proceeds to make Mr. B. voice the charge that she has set out to entice him sexually, and yet hypocritically pretends that the sexual consequences repel her. Pamela is punished for her vanity by being made to see the sexual implications of taking pleasure in her own 'attractiveness', and by the conversion of her robes of purity into their opposite. But the charge of hypocrisy is confuted. Mr. B. becomes aware for the first time of the genuine nature of her moral feeling; and the result is the beginning of real conflict in him which opens up the possibility of moral change. Only, to see this is to become aware of a blindness in Pamela to the complexity of others; and of her dangerous suspicion and self-righteousness. We may or may not find the scene satisfactory, but Richardson is clearly not 'unconscious' of defects in his heroine, and cannot be identified with her.

Pamela is prentice-work. Sometimes the writing is comically crude, but for all that, the art is already far more complex than it looks and it demands the closest attention. As against Defoe's 'X-ray' vision, which renders shadowy much of the 'body' of human experience in order to spotlight the essential structure of an archetypal human condition, we have an exploration of the complexity of motivations and relationships, and of the process of inner development. The protagonists grow and alter as we watch. What Richardson invented in *Pamela* and developed to a high degree in *Clarissa* was the dramatic novel. The device of writing in letters was a means not an end. He himself called his invention 'writing to the moment'; the epistolary technique is a way of involving us in a 'now' which is happening or has only just happened, a substitute for the immediacy of the stage and its direct experience without a narrative filter. The letters give us dialogue, action and gesture, dramatic scene; they also give us immediate self-analysis, like extensions of soliloquy. The author moreover creates as the dramatist does, not in his own voice, but by projecting himself into all his characters and playing them off against one another on a stage where he does not appear. On the other hand, the dramatic novel in letters allows us to pause for thought as the stage does not, though the author cannot tell us what to think. He may be closer to one character than to others, but he cannot and must not be identified with any or the nature of the experience will be distorted. The reader too must guard against acceptance of a single point of view; he must enter each imaginatively, and also measure all against one another, diagnosing and understanding as the characters cannot. He must be alive to the implications of what is said, done and thought. He must be ready to pick up hints of what the characters do not yet know about themselves, for letters written 'to the moment' can be very revealing. He has to respond to significant variations of style, for to Richardson 'styles differ, too, as much as faces, and are indicative, generally beyond the power of disguise, of the mind of the writer'.[10]

Above all, Richardson's dramatic novel is an art of discovery. Even in prentice-work like *Pamela* the value lies precisely in the exploratory criticism of its heroine. We must not make him too 'conscious', he may never have fully realized where his art had taken him; nevertheless a steady critical investigation is characteristic of him from the start. The assumption that he is unconscious of what he is doing has led to serious neglect of the novel's structure. An exploratory author cannot have a predetermined route, though he may know what the end of the story will be; he imagines from situation to situation. Nevertheless Richardson's progress is methodical and his scenes are carefully related. In the first movement, for example, up to Pamela's abduction, he is concerned to create the day-to-day fluctuations of her struggle with Mr. B., but the scenes are not episodic, or the product of unconscious imagination; we are constantly invited to relate them to one another in a cumulative act of judgement. So we should balance the 'clothes scene' of Letter 24 against the gift of clothes with which the novel opens, and with Mr. B.'s parody in *his* 'clothes scene' of Letter 27, and that again with Pamela's 'bundle scene' in Letter 29; we should compare the 'judgement scene' that precedes Letter 24 with the 'judgement scene' that follows; we should weigh the crisis of Letter 24 against the crisis which leads to the abduction—to cite a few examples. Richardson obviously uses Pamela's moral values to expose the amoral world of pride and power that Mr. B. inhabits, but in the process he discovers and steadily explores the weaknesses of his heroine too. Hypocrisy is not one of them, but her motives are very mixed, and she understands neither herself nor her persecutor. She is vain, and finds it difficult to achieve real humility, social, moral, or spiritual. And, significantly, Richardson exposes dangers inherent in what looks like a virtue, her prudence: her calculation on the one hand,

and, on the other, the damaging suspiciousness which blinds her to the complexity of other people.

Then in the second movement she is imprisoned. Her letters give way to a journal, action almost disappears, and its place is taken by prolonged analysis. The ethical deepens into the religious; for, pointedly, forty days. Richardson makes use of her isolation to diagnose the basic source of her faults: the stubborn pride and self-reliance which are the obverse of the individualism that makes her a heroine. She takes pride in her prudence—suspicious, calculating, contriving—but her attempts to play Mr. B. at his own strategic game are disastrous, and from priding herself on her self-reliance she is thrown into despair until she contemplates suicide. The two carefully related scenes by the pond are the novel's turning-points, and what they reveal is Richardson's concern with faith. It appears that to rely on oneself is to court despair, when inevitably one's human fallibility is exposed; and it is by regaining faith, first in God, and then in man, that one redeems oneself and makes happiness and human relationship possible. In the first pond scene Pamela reaches a new self-knowledge and humility and realizes how guilty she has been of pride and presumption.[11] Then the second pond scene adds faith in man: for the first time, and against the dictates of prudence, Pamela opens her heart to Mr. B. and he to her; for the first time they can commincate in sincerity.

She fails, however, to live up to these new values. She gives way again to chronic suspiciousness in rejecting Mr. B.'s proposal. This time she is sent away, home to her parents as she has always wanted; but on the way a message from Mr. B. gives her another chance. One of the finest passages in the novel reveals her true feelings to her for the first time (though not so to us, if we have been paying attention). She is asked to have faith enough to put herself back in his power of her own free will, and in giving him the whole of her journal, to allow him to know her as we do. Prudence is clear on what she should do: she knows how mixed-up he is, what dangers she will run. Yet she also knows how much he has changed, she has converted her image of him from a cardboard villain into a confused and complex human being. She ignores prudence for trust, reinforcing humility and faith in God with humility and faith in man—and that is what is really 'rewarded' with happiness.

The last part of the novel is by far the least interesting and the most objectionable, though the spinning-out at least shows again that Richardson was not primarily interested in pursuit and capture. The imaginative drive, such as it is, is a kind of missionary wish-fulfilment. The series of debates and visitings provide a sort of 'whole duty of woman' (a companion piece to the *Whole Duty of Man* which Pamela sends Farmer Jones). Moreover the way the happy pair win over the society in which Mr. B. moves is a kind of wish-fulfilment of everything Richardson hoped for from the moral education of his story—and an early prefiguring of the idea of moral community in his last novel *Sir Charles Grandison* (1753–4). Everyone who meets them is 'improved', and in joining the concord of praise, all find their true selves and a true sense of community with their neighbours.

Few modern readers will make this response, indeed Richardson the didactic moralist is tiresome. His value lies in the exploratory power of his dramatic imagination and this, apart from one fine scene with Mr. B.'s haughty sister, is almost wholly in abeyance in the last section, as it is in the continuation of the novel he later forced himself to write.[12] There was always a tension in him between the didactic moralist and the imaginative explorer, and the former was always liable to fall back into attitudes the latter had transcended. The imaginative centre of *Pamela* is concerned precisely with her growth beyond calculating prudence, but the subtitle and concluding moral summary may well suggest that virtue is politic. In some directions, moreover, the novelist failed to transcend inadequate positions. His imagination is morally egalitarian at best, but it lapses sometimes into snobbery. His treatment of sex is very unsatisfactory, not because it is prurient as is sometimes suggested, but because he imagines sex as an aspect of pride, far too narrowly in its brutally egotistic and violating aspects; and he often, though by no means always, allows Pamela to confuse virtue with resistance to rape. (Her real testing times are not the seduction scenes at all, but those in which her unacknowledged love and Mr. B.'s gentleness make 'resistance' difficult.) The key failure of the novel, however, is its hero—and this makes an interesting illustration of how apparent moral inadequacy in fiction may be the product of formal defects. If we read closely enough, we can trace the growth of conflict and change in Mr. B.; but because the novel is told through Pamela, we never experience his transformation with anything like the depth and conviction that are needed to set off her simplified vision of him. So doubts can arise about his reformation, and consequently about Pamela's forgiveness and adulation of him, which could have been prevented if we had experienced him through his own eyes, as we experience her. Again, unwanted moral inference can arise from narrative necessity: the treatment of Pamela's vanity and purity is bedevilled by the fact that only she can tell us of the sexual attempts and the lavish praises. The multiplication of correspondences in *Clarissa* solved many problems; the huge difference between the novels is not the result of a moral transformation in Richardson, but springs from a technical advance which required far deeper exploration. The dramatic novel comes of age.

The original first instalment of *Clarissa*,[13] up to the 'elopement', confronts us with three worlds of value in dramatic conflict. With the Harlowe family we are back in Defoe territory, with people essentially governed by economic and acquisitive motives, though at a higher social level. For, having become rich, the Harlowes are bent on concentrating the various family estates on Clarissa's brother James, so as to break into the peerage.[14] The uncles renounce marriage so that their estates will pass to their nephew and the whole family becomes a centralized economic unit, with absolute authority vested in the patriarch, Clarissa's father. Moral ideas about filial obedience are called on, but in the cause of economic policy. The whole family combines to force Clarissa to marry a rich man she despises morally and finds physically repulsive, because his estates will contribute to the master-plan. Yet to understand what happens, as Clarissa never does until long afterwards, we have to understand James Harlowe. He shows the havoc wrought in a human being when he is made the centre of an entire family's acquisitive instincts. He is out to ruin his sister's prospects whether she marries Solmes or not, for he sees her as a threat to his whole position. Her grandfather has already left her part of his estate, and there is the danger that if she marries the rich young Lovelace, who is already in line for two titles, she may prove a better vehicle for the family ambition than James. So, with the help of the jealous Arabella, he contrives so to trap their sister that she must either marry Solmes, or ruin herself with the family. He continually inflames both sides, inexplicably if his real aim was simply the Solmes marriage. What he really wants is to destroy her as a threat to himself, whatever she does.

As the persecution mounts, as Clarissa is imprisoned, insulted, humiliated, we are made aware of how the Harlowes' greedy materialism excludes reason, conscience, honesty and human feeling. They are totally unscrupulous, they appeal to her morality for their own immoral ends, and they so attach dishonest implications to words and actions that she is made to seem to choose defiance and isolation. We see not only how many human values are excluded by economic motivation, but also how it opens the floodgates to ugly passions : envy, rage, hatred, cruelty, the enjoyment of inflicting pain. It creates a world of brutal egotism, whose only divinity is self and whose only reality is power. 'Radix malorum est cupiditas', as Clarissa tells her uncle Antony. Richardson explores what Defoe only allows us to see, not merely the gap between the economic and the moral that the new City was opening, but its ugliness; and this is not preached merely, but scene by scene, in action, gesture, expression, and the tone of the human voice, it is made a powerful dramatic experience.

The more sensitively we respond, the higher the emotional temperature, the more desirable Lovelace must seem to Clarissa and to us. His gaiety, his apparent candour, his wit, even his rakehell insouciance and energy, are like suddenly coming across a portrait of Charles II in a gallery of Breughels. Yet we must be careful, for in these opening volumes we see him mainly through the eyes of Clarissa and her friend Anna—eyes innocent and subject to emotional clouding. Only in three crucial letters to his friend Belford can we see him for ourselves, and what these reveal beneath their gay surface is a view of life and relationships remarkably love-less (as his own name was pronounced at the time). He is indeed a 'Restoration' figure, who finds in the romantic passions and posturings of Restoration tragedy, its ideas of 'love' and 'honour', an image of his own needs and a language to express them in. But his realities are also egotism and power, and he is as unscrupulous as the Harlowes. We discover that he is tightening their trap from his side, dancing them like puppets on his wires, using their persecution of Clarissa to get her into his own power, with the strongest of indications that he will marry her only if he has to. He is, however, a man in conflict. He cannot help but recognize in Clarissa a moral stature, and a kind of personality, to which he is drawn in tenderness and admiration despite himself. We discover how the better side of him can be liberated when his pride is soothed and his power acknowledged, but the seeds of tragedy are already present in our knowledge of how unlikely it is that Clarissa will fulfil these conditions.

Again, however, it is our dramatic experience of Lovelace that matters—and here his style reveals a crucial dimension of his being. If we respond to the three letters to Belford we understand a fourth, which he writes Clarissa from the copse, as she cannot. Lovelace is an incurable play-actor who can never be wholly sincere. He writes in a deeply emotional state, but even at his most passionate moments he cannot help making what he feels into a role, watching himself playing it, and improving the performance as he goes along. His style becomes a mask he makes himself, and we have to guess the real expression on the face behind. This shows a new and subtle understanding in the dramatic novelist, not only of character, but of 'acting'.

Against these superficially different but basically similar worlds of selfishness, power and deceit, we measure Clarissa's values, the other side of the middle-class inheritance; not self-centred individualism, but what puritan ethics at their noblest demanded, an absolute rectitude and purity, and relationships founded on genuine feeling. Clarissa is individualist in one sense, in that she demands to be self-determining, not treated as property, or the plaything of outside forces; but freedom for her is essentially freedom of conscience. She asks for no independence unsanctioned by the moral code that is on her family's lips, but which she tries to live by, and it is because she places duty at the heart of behaviour that she must demand freedom of conscience. Yet once again Richardson's art is exploratory. He may have meant to use Clarissa simply as an ideal, but if he did, his dramatic imagination uncovered some uncomfortable truths. It is precisely her moral absolutism that makes her so helpless and so passive; someone like Anna, willing to act less than perfectly for a moral end, could not have been trapped as Clarissa is. She cannot understand even what she knows of Lovelace, for she shares the ignorance of eighteenth-century middle-class girls in respectable families, cut off from male society before marriage. She assumes far too easily that morality controls not only what one does but what one feels, and so for all her meticulous self-examination she fails to be honest about the state of her own heart, believing that her feeling for Lovelace is 'conditional' on being satisfied about his character. She shares something of Anna's pride (though not the concept of relations with men as a sex-war, which makes Anna a female Lovelace); and like Pamela she has a dangerous self-reliance. Her tragedy is not that of a sacrificial lamb. The trap could not close without Clarissa herself. Finally, Lovelace is able to contrive the 'elopement' because, like her family in their otherwise incredible plan for a forced marriage, he understands the liability to nervous and emotional hysteria behind her moral courage. Her will is untouched, she screams 'no' all the way to the coach, but she has no command of her limbs. Charmingly 'feminine' characteristics—gentleness, a highly strung and delicate physique with great sensitivity and imagination—can look very different and less desirable in a crisis.

In the second instalment Clarissa is involved in a new trap, as Lovelace cleverly uses the promises she has insisted on, and her desire to be reconciled with her family, as excuses for not urging a speedy marriage. When he does speak it is in hints and hesitations, and when Clarissa's notions of propriety prevent her seizing on these, he quickly drops them. Meanwhile he plots to close all avenues of escape, to make the Harlowes believe she has gone by her own will, and to play on her suspiciousness so that she does what he wants her to do, because he urges the contrary. The aim is to entice her into a high-class private brothel in London, under the impression that it is a genteel lodging, and it succeeds.

The danger for a moden reader is to fall too simply into Lovelace's view that her behaviour is prudish. Marriage for Clarissa is a sacrament, and deeply serious. She will promise at God's altar the same kind of obedience she was prepared to give her father, so she must be convinced of the love and the probity of the man or the marriage would be as intolerable as all the Harlowe marriages can be seen to be. Isolated as she is, with no father as intermediary, and tricked into the power of a man with an immoral reputation, she can only judge him by the way he treats her; and the implications of behaviour and speech are important guides to the state of his heart and his mind, hence her 'delicacy' and 'punctilio', her sensitivity to details. It is no mere formality when she expects him to approach her according to the normal civilized code at the time. But Lovelace understands nothing of this; if the acknowledgment of his power and the soothing of his pride are the only ways to liberate the best side of him, what he sees as female affectation and female pride are a continual challenge to the worst.

Prudery will not do to explain Clarissa's behaviour, but Richardson is making further critical discoveries. We become even more aware of her dangerous inflexibility. She is quite incapable of adapting herself to circumstances as she believes them to be, let alone as they are; and she cannot meet a confused and imperfect human being on any ground but her own rigid perfectionism. This prevents the development of the side of Lovelace which does respond to her with the beginnings of genuine love. We may notice how often he casts himself in roles that represent this facet of him, and how he enjoys playing them. The blackest irony works of course against Lovelace, especially when he passes off on her a crooked agent of his own called Tomlinson as an emissary from her family, behaving with great tenderness himself, and a suddenly radiant and loving Clarissa shows a tragic might-have-been. Yet there are also three crucial occasions when the strength of Lovelace's feelings does surprise him into real and urgent proposals of marriage; and while there are reasons for her failure to respond to the first two, the third is significantly a pure failure of nerve. She cannot come to meet him. The book fills with tragic ironies. She not only helps to close another trap on herself, but her inflexibility allows him to be caught in his own machinations. The great strength of his earlier plots was that they could be dropped without her knowledge, but under the tauntings of the prostitutes he begins steadily to overreach himself. He begins to tamper with her letters and make mild attempts on her person, but it is the Tomlinson plot that is his rubicon, for this she must eventually unmask, and she will never forgive his cynical playing on her deepest feelings. They become two continents of thought and feeling drifting further apart, and Lovelace becomes ever more obsessive. The instalment ends with an attempt at rape and Clarissa's temporary escape; so that the close of the second phase echoes that of the first. But the tragedy is already determined.

In order to understand why it takes the form it does, however, and see what is at issue for Lovelace (and his author), we have to understand the theory about the nature of women, which is actually an expression of Lovelace's whole vision of himself and of his deepest psychological needs. He takes Pope seriously: 'Every woman is at heart a rake'. This means that woman's nature is essentially sexual; and it follows that moral resistance to seduction is not in human nature at all, but is a product merely of custom, and education, reinforced by female pride. Since it is equally man's nature to demand sexual submission, whereas society conditions woman to unnatural resistance, love in society becomes sexual war. To overcome a proud woman is the greatest triumph for the male ego, and it is domination not sexual pleasure that makes it so. Lovelace's male urge to dominate is the foundation of his being and the one reality he believes in. 'Importunity and opportunity no woman is proof against' follows logically; if woman's nature is essentially sexual the male only has to find the right strategy—in Clarissa's case the promise of reformation on the one hand, and the attempt to humble her pride on the other, which explains his oscillation between tenderness and bullying. The most important rake's maxim, however, is the last one: 'Once overcome, always overcome'. If the real nature of woman is sexual, if the only barriers are custom and pride, then the seduction which overthrows pride, puts a woman at one stroke outside the pale of custom, and reveals her true nature to her, must involve a decisive and irreversible change. Lovelace cannot be satisfied with knowing that she loves him, or with marriage on her terms, while he believes she can be overcome. His ideas give him an inside story more real than the living woman in the same room. He is committed (against all the evidence of his experience of Clarissa) to a total disbelief in the existence of a moral nature in her; because his ideology is a rationalization of his own deepest needs, and he cannot give up his idea of himself. He must go on with increasing desperation to prove that he is right; simply assuming that marriage afterwards will always be in his power because she is. So, as the last instalment plunges the tragedy into its darkest phase, Lovelace's letters become a world of blind obsession. But the mask of debonnaire levity and angry pride keeps slipping to reveal a twisted face beneath, more and more afraid of what failure would mean. He finally risks everything on a last desperate throw in one of the most extraordinary climaxes in any novel. He drugs Clarissa, and rapes her in front of the prostitutes. For, if his theory is right, it does not matter whether she consents. If he can only reveal to her what she really is, the rest will follow as of course—and the rape is an attempt, in the presence of experts, at public proof.

There is, moreover, a sense in which it is this for Richardson too. He is asking the most basic of questions, what is the human being essentially? To answer it he has to disintegrate Clarissa to the last possible point before she disappears, and this means cracking open her conscious mind to get at her unconscious— the first honest attempt since Shakespeare to do this, and the last until our own century. Clarissa goes mad as Ophelia and Lear do, to reveal their essential selves. It is an astonishing achievement for the middle of the eighteenth century. When her derangement is at its worst we find that Lovelace was within a hairsbreadth of being absolutely right. She does feel that she is changed for ever, that her previous self has vanished so that she has no identity, no name; and that Lovelace has touched her innermost being indelibly. She searches desperately for help outside herself, but the lifelines to her family and Anna have been cut. Slowly, however, groping within herself for her identity, she rediscovers it with increasing confidence in her moral being, and its criticism not only of Lovelace but of herself. Richard-

son's inward search has moved behind precept, behind character, behind sex; he sensed that what was really at stake was the
sacredness of the innermost self. What is really unforgiveable
about the rape is not the plundered virginity, the ruined reputation, the turpitude; it is that Lovelace has no concept of, and
no respect for, the inner being that makes Clarissa Clarissa. He
succeeds in revealing her to herself, but she is not as he supposed, and the result can only be her famous rejection, 'The
man who has been the villain to me you have been, shall never
make him his wife'.

She escapes again, only to be trapped in a debtors' prison by
the contrivance of the prostitutes. She is rescued by Belford,
under whose protection she remains, but her will to live has
been broken, and she dies. The curiously drawn-out ending cannot, however, be adequately explained in physical, psychological
or social terms, and *Clarissa* turns out to be a religious novel in
a far deeper sense than *Pamela*. In one sense Clarissa has moved
from one prison to another throughout; but the literal prison
begins to set her free. Our last real glimpse of her shows her
struggling to liberate herself from the remaining vestiges of
her pride, her vengefulness, and her own will. After this we see
her no longer, all our information comes from Belford, and we
can only infer what is happening within her being. Her protracted death is not so much a physical decline as a spiritual
progress, of which we see the effects but cannot measure the
process. For the action is now one that Richardson's art is
powerless to reach, and the actor is not Clarissa, but her God.
Her very last prison is her own body, from which she is re-
leased by a divine grace and mercy, given her death. Lovelace is
killed in a duel by her cousin. The Harlowes are left to their
baffled remorse.

The difference from *Pamela* in depth of exploration and
tragic resonance requires no underlining, though the cost is a
bulk and slowness of movement that make the novel something
of a dinosaur.[15] But if we now look back at Defoe, it becomes
clear that for all their common social background, the novelists
of the City imagine the interplay between man and his environment in antithetical ways. Defoe's Everywoman rides circumstance to survive and prosper, but as she does so we see more
and more clearly how her various situations determine the ways
she can behave. It turns out that the episodic form is also the
novelist's meaning, for Defoe is implicitly denying integrity of

character, and his art coheres not by relating scene to scene, but by showing the same pattern of determinism of situation in all the episodic variety. Richardson is concerned to show the opposite. He pits Clarissa against terrible onslaughts of circumstance and situation, but vindicates the integrity of her character against the worst her world can do to her. His novel acquires a sombre inevitability, where what happens scene by scene seems fatally determined by the characters of the protagonists.

Yet this discrimination, though it reinforces the point that 'reality' in fiction is determined by the angle of the author's imaginative vision, allows no evaluative judgement in itself. We cannot make literary criticism depend on a 'reality principle' that turns out to be an ethical or metaphysical assumption. Nevertheless, a discrimination is possible, on imaginative grounds. Both novelists expose the widening gap between individualism and morality in the new City; both help us to become more sharply aware of questions about man's basic nature which are posed by contradictory modes of behaviour. But where Defoe merely exposes, Richardson explores and counts the cost. Few novelists have submitted their instinctive way of looking at the human being to more rigorous and agonized testing, or contemplated the price of asserting it more seriously. One may not in the least share Richardson's belief in a moral nature, or in a grace and mercy which finally validate that nature supernaturally, but one must, I think, respect his power to imagine its implications to the end.

We may notice, in conclusion, how both novelists not only evoked the City but also provoked the Town to new imaginative life. What began in parody became creative in a new dimension. We should not see only the mockery of Defoe by Swift, and of Richardson by Fielding; for the novelists of the City turn out to have stimulated the Town to take stock of itself, in turn, more imaginatively than ever before and in new forms.

1. Defoe: *Robinson Crusoe, The Farther Adventures of Robinson Crusoe* (1719); *Memoirs of a Cavalier, Captain Singleton* (1720); *Moll Flanders, A Journal of the Plague Year, Colonel Jack* (1722); *Roxana* (1724).

Richardson: *Pamela* (1740); *Pamela in her Exalted Condition* (1742); *Clarissa* (1747–48); *Sir Charles Grandison* (1753–54).

2. Diana Spearman, *The Novel and Society*, London, 1966, ch. 1, warns against the possible distortions of using nineteenth-century social terminology.

3. E.M. Forster, *Aspects of the Novel*, London, 1927, reprinted 1961, p. 9.

4. This suspicion of fiction, inherited from puritanism and still widely held, was the reason why Defoe presented his fictions as true cases of rogue-biography or travel tale (the 'traditions' which, with puritan spiritual autobiography, lie behind his novels); and why Richardson posed as the editor of genuine correspondence.

5. *The Shortest-Way with the Dissenters*, the one work of Defoe's which we can be sure was intended ironically, misfired because its highly successful impersonation of High-Church bigotry was insufficiently controlled to point up its ironic purpose, so that it was misread by both High-Churchmen and Dissenters.

6. John Carroll (ed.), *Selected Letters of Samuel Richardson*, Oxford, 1964, p. 229. This letter to Johannes Stinstra is the primary source for our sketchy knowledge of Richardson's early life.

7. Edward Cave: see A. D. McKillop, *Samuel Richardson*, Chapel Hill, N.C., 1936 (reprinted 1960), p. 13.

8. In *Joseph Andrews* the point is no longer hypocrisy. We are made to laugh at Richardson, Joseph, and Parson Adams for the same reason: their idea that books and fairy-tale romances make one virtuous and teach one how to live (hence 'In the manner of Don Quixote').

9. Quoted by Ian Watt: *The Rise of the Novel*, London, 1957, p. 170.

10. John Carroll (ed.), *Selected Letters*, p. 64.

11. 'And how do I know but that God, who sees all the lurking vileness of my heart, may have permitted these sufferings on that very score, and to make me rely solely on his grace and assistance, who, perhaps, have too much prided myself in a vain dependence on my own foolish contrivances?' (Everyman edition, i. 151).

12. This continuation was no part of the original plan; it was undertaken to meet the challenge of an unscrupulous hack who advertised a sequel.

13. Two volumes were published in December 1747, two volumes in April 1748, and the last three volumes in December 1748. See Mark Kinkead-Weekes, 'Clarissa Restored?', *Review of English Studies*, x (1959), 156–71, for an argument that Richardson made

alterations in later editions, frequently for the worse, to meet misreadings he had become aware of in responses to the novel as it was coming out.

14. Christopher Hill, 'Clarissa Harlowe and her Times,' *Essays in Criticism*, v (1955), 315–40, (reprinted in his *Puritanism and Revolution*, London, 1958), shows how historical research has confirmed the practicability of the Harlowe plan, owing to the effects of changes in the law of inheritance, and of the increasing dependence of political power on the possession of land.

15. The enormous length comes partly from Richardson's fascination with exploring the day-to-day fluctuations of feeling, attitude, and behaviour, and his concern with prolonged self-analysis by his protagonists; and partly from the multiplication of correspondences, which means that many situations are gone over several times from the different points of view. Yet the method which produces the bulk and slowness, and sometimes tedium, that cause the novel to be neglected, is also the source of its strength. Abridgement destroys.

BIBLIOGRAPHY

A *Defoe*

I *Editions*

Novels and Selected Writings, 14 vols., Oxford, 1927–28 (Shakespeare Head edition).

Robinson Crusoe, Captain Singleton, Moll Flanders, and *A Journal of the Plague Year* are available in the Everyman Library. *Roxana*, ed. Jane Jack, London, 1964, *Colonel Jack*, ed. S. H. Monk, London, 1965, *A Journal of the Plague Year*, ed. L. Landa, London, 1969, and *Captain Singleton*, ed. S. K. Kumar, London, 1969, are in the Oxford English Novels.

Letters, ed. G. H. Healey, Oxford, 1955.

II *Biographical Studies*

Moore, J. R., *Daniel Defoe: Citizen of the Modern World*, Chicago, 1958.

Sutherland, James, *Defoe*, London, 1937.

III *Critical Studies*

(a) General :

McKillop, A. D., *The Early Masters of English Fiction*, Lawrence, Kansas, 1956; London, 1962.

Spearman, Diana, *The Novel and Society*, London, 1966. Partly a rejoinder to Watt below.

Watt, Ian, *The Rise of the Novel*, London, 1957. Still the most important work on the eighteenth-century novel.

Novak, Maximilian, *Defoe and the Nature of Man*, London, 1963.

Novak, Maximilian, *Economics and the Fiction of Daniel Defoe*, Berkeley, 1962.

Shinagel, M., *Daniel Defoe and Middle-Class Gentility*, Cambridge, Mass., 1968.

Starr, G. A., *Defoe and Spiritual Biography*, Princeton, 1965.

(b) On *Robinson Crusoe* and *Moll Flanders*:

Columbus, R. R., 'Conscious Artistry in *Moll Flanders*,' *Studies in English Literature*, iii (1963), 415–32.

Donoghue, D., 'The Values of *Moll Flanders*,' *Sewannee Review*, lxxii (1963), 287–303.

Hunter, J. P., *The Reluctant Pilgrim*, Baltimore, 1966.

Kettle, Arnold, 'In Defence of *Moll Flanders*,' in *Of Books and Humankind*, ed. J. Butt, London, 1964, pp. 55–67.

Koonce, Howard L., 'Moll's Muddle : Defoe's Use of Irony,' *ELH*, xxx (1963), 377–94.

Watt, Ian, 'The Recent Critical Fortunes of *Moll Flanders*,'
Eighteenth Century Studies, i (1967), 109–26.

B *Richardson*

I *Editions*

The Novels, 18 vols., Oxford, 1929–31 (Shakespeare Head edition).
Pamela (2 vols.) and *Clarissa* (4 vols.) are separately available in the
Everyman Library.
Familiar Letters on Important Occasions, ed. B. W. Downs, London, 1928.
Correspondence, ed. Mrs. A. L. Barbauld, 6 vols., London, 1804.
Selected Letters, ed. J. Carroll, Oxford, 1964.

II *Biographical Studies*

McKillop, A. D., *Samuel Richardson*, Chapel Hill, N.C., 1936 (repr. 1960).
Sale, W. M., *Samuel Richardson: Master Printer*, Ithaca, N.Y., 1950.

III *Critical Studies*

For general studies containing sections on Richardson, see the works
by McKillop, Spearman and Watt listed under Defoe above.
Golden, M., *Richardson's Characters*, Ann Arbor, 1963. A 'psychological' approach.
Kearney, A. M., '*Clarissa* and the Epistolary Form,' *Essays in Criticism*, xvi (1966), 44–56.
Kinkead-Weekes, M., 'Clarissa Restored?,' *Review of English Studies*, x (1959), 156–71.
Konigsberg, I., *Samuel Richardson and the Dramatic Novel*, Lexington, 1969.
Kreissman, B., *Pamela-Shamela*, Lincoln, Nebraska, 1960 (reprinted 1964). The debate among Richardson's contemporaries.
Sherburn, G., 'Samuel Richardson's Novels and the Theatre,' *Philological Quarterly*, xli (1962), 325–9.
Twentieth Century Interpretations of Pamela, ed. R. Cowler, Englewood Cliffs, N.J., 1969.
Twentieth Century Views of Samuel Richardson, ed. John Carroll, Englewood Cliffs, N.J., 1969. (Articles reprinted in full in this and the preceding item have not been separately listed).

8

FIELDING AND SMOLLETT [1]

C. J. Rawson, University of Warwick

Although Fielding * began his writing career as a dramatist, his
novels do not owe to this experience the sort of 'dramatic' narration in which characters and situations are left to speak entirely for themselves, and where the author's visible role in the
telling of the tale is eliminated or minimized. Playwriting
taught Fielding many skills: a keen and lively control of his
plots, a mastery of the well-shaped individual scene which rises

* Henry Fielding was born in Somerset in 1707, of a family with
aristocratic connections. He was educated at Eton and the University
of Leyden. His active career as a playwright ran from 1728 to 1737,
when the Stage Licensing Act, partly brought about by his own
anti-government plays, was passed. Among the best-known of his
twenty-odd plays are *The Author's Farce* (1730), *The Temple Beau*
(1730), *The Tragedy of Tragedies; or the Life and Death of Tom
Thumb the Great* (1731), *Don Quixote in England* (1734), *Pasquin,
A Dramatic Satire on the Times* (1736), *The Historical Register for
the Year 1736* (1737).

In 1737 Fielding became a law student at the Middle Temple, and
was called to the bar in 1740. He practised as a barrister for some
years. During 1739–41, he edited *The Champion*, a paper in opposition to Walpole's government, but also containing some essays by
Fielding of a more general, non-political kind. In 1741, Fielding broke
with the Opposition, and for a time sided with Walpole (who fell
the following year). In 1741 he brought out *An Apology for the Life
of Mrs. Shamela Andrews*, a parody of Richardson's very successful
novel *Pamela* (1740), with side-glances at other works, including
Colley Cibber's *Apology for the Life of Mr. Colley Cibber* (1740). In
1742, he published his first novel, *The History of the Adventures of
Joseph Andrews, And of his Friend Mr. Abraham Adams. Written in
Imitation of the Manner of Cervantes*, a work also partly concerned
to mock *Pamela*. In 1743 appeared three volumes of *Miscellanies*,
which contained some plays, poems, essays (including the 'Essay on
Conversation' and the 'Essay on the Knowledge of the Characters
of Men'), a Lucianic fiction (*A Journey from this World to the Next*),
and *The Life of Mr. Jonathan Wild the Great* (whose main, anti-

to a climax or surprising reversal, a gallery of comic character-types, some brilliant set-pieces of character-revealing dialogue. But authorial self-effacement was not one of these skills, and it seems significant in this connection that all of Fielding's plays belong to stylized genres: a 'polite' comedy derived from the Restoration masters, farces, burlesques, *Rehearsal* plays (which combine burlesque purpose with a play-within-a-play), genres, that is, in which an element of signposted 'artifice' is openly and actively at work. These various kinds of play have some connection with (though they are not the only sources of), respectively, an urbane 'pointedness' in some of the prose-style of the novels; a tendency to stylized play with farce-effects of 'lowness' and comic automatism; a strongly developed habit of parody (anti-Richardsonian, mock-heroic, etc.); and an authorial presence, somewhat external to the action, yet clearly visible, and controlling or commenting upon it. These stylistic tendencies or structural patterns combine two paradoxical features. They work against authorial self-effacement, in that they present themselves as artifice, as willed and strongly signposted transformations of *naked* reality which make us very conscious of the narrator's directing intelligence; and at the same time they guarantee a certain distance between the author and both the action and the reader.

This sense of authorial presence without intimacy, which vitalizes Fielding's best writing in the novels, is something which the plays themselves largely lack, as distinct from making available to the novelist some of the technical means to-

Walpole part was probably begun much earlier, in 1740). In 1745–46 he edited *The True Patriot*, supporting the Hanoverian cause against the Young Pretender, Charles Edward Stuart, and in 1747–48 he edited another periodical in the Hanoverian cause, *The Jacobite's Journal*. In 1749, *The History of Tom Jones, a Foundling* (whose main action is set in the period of the Jacobite Rebellion of 1745) was published, and in 1751, his last novel, *Amelia* (though dated 1752). In 1752, he edited the last of his periodicals, *The Covent-Garden Journal*.

Meanwhile, in 1748 he became Justice of the Peace for Westminster, and later for the whole of Middlesex. His experience as a magistrate gave rise to a series of important legal-sociological works, of which the best and most considerable are *An Enquiry into the Causes of the Late Increase of Robbers* (1751) and *A Proposal for Making an Effectual Provision for the Poor* (1753). In 1754 he resigned his office as magistrate, and left, in ill-health, on a voyage to Lisbon. He died near Lisbon in October, and his *Journal of a Voyage to Lisbon* was published posthumously in 1755.

wards it. Plays do not normally accommodate the open presence of a narrator or author. Those modelled on Buckingham's *Rehearsal* (e.g. *The Author's Farce, Pasquin, The Historical Register, Eurydice*, all written between 1730 and 1737) are partly an exception, since they contain 'authors'-within-the-play who stand outside their own play (the play-within-the-play), planning its production or commenting upon the text, and to this extent creating a skeletal model for that more plastic interplay between the teller and the tale which we find in the novels. But these 'authors' have very limited scope. In one sense, they are mere characters of the larger play we are watching, reduced to equal status with other characters. Often, moreover, they are rather foolish figures, whose power to transmit any impulse of self-expression from Fielding is very limited. Thus when Trapwit (*Pasquin*, II. i) announces at one point during the performance of his comedy, 'Now, sir, you shall see some scenes of politeness and fine conversation among the ladies', the remark has the somewhat limited energy of a well-tried satiric routine, common to *Rehearsal* plays and mocking incompetent writers without seriously transcending the (perfectly legitimate) element of parody. But when Fielding footnotes an unpleasant dialogue in *Joseph Andrews* (1742; IV. ix) with the words: 'Lest this should appear unnatural to some readers, we think proper to acquaint them, that it is taken *verbatim* from very polite conversation', the effect is to re-emphasize Fielding's knowledgeable, morally reliable and controlling presence at a moment when the rawness of the scene threatens to acquire an unbalancing vitality. A vividly specific incident becomes framed inside the author's knowing grasp of the world's ways, its uncouth factuality (while remaining undiminished and alive) brought under the ordering influence of comedy's firm and steady values. The note generalizes the situation, thus satisfying both neo-classic predilection, and a certain gentlemanly refusal to get embroiled in the *merely* specific. These effects depend on the words being Fielding's own, rather than those of a character in a play. The comment acquires not only a greater moral fervour, but a more central satiric pertinence: the silly Trapwit's comment does reflect on social usage, but its burlesque context makes it primarily a literary joke on the way plays are written.

Now consider the scene from *Joseph Andrews* to which the note refers. Lady Booby and others, including the effeminate Beau Didapper, who had recently tried to rape Fanny, are visiting Parson Adams's house. Fanny and Joseph are also there:

The parson and his company retreated from the chimney-side, where they had been seated, to give room to the lady and hers. Instead of returning any of the curtsies or extra-ordinary civility of Mrs. Adams, the lady, turning to Mr. Booby, cried out, '*Quelle Bête! Quel Animal!*' And presently after discovering Fanny (for she did not need the circumstance of her standing by Joseph to assure the identity of her person), she asked the beau, 'Whether he did not think her a pretty girl?'—'Begad, madam,' answered he, ''tis the very same I met.' 'I did not imagine,' replied the lady, 'you had so good a taste.' 'Because I never liked you, I warrant,' cries the beau. 'Ridiculous!' said she, 'you know you was always my aversion.' 'I would never mention aversion,' answered the beau, 'with that face; dear Lady Booby, wash your face before you mention aversion, I beseech you.' He then laughed, and turned about to coquet it with Fanny.

The dialogue, though placed within a continuous action, has that semi-autonomous quality of a set-piece which resembles certain individual scenes in stage-comedy. Moreover, whilst vividly true to colloquial speech, it maintains a self-contained and faintly fantasticated absurdity, almost balletic in its quality of routine interchange and shapely self-completion. It may be compared with a scene from an early play, *The Temple Beau* (1730; I. i), which likewise presents the vacuously uppish acidities of a 'polite' quarrel, and likewise (though too long to quote in full) has a distinct and self-completing internal rhythm :

LADY GRAVELY. . . . sister, since we are in private, I'll tell you what the world says of you.—In the first place, then, it says that you are both younger and handsomer than you seem.

LADY LUCY PEDANT. Nay, this is flattery, my dear !

LADY GRAVELY. No, indeed, my dear ! for that folly and affectation have disguised you all over with an air of dotage and deformity.

LADY LUCY PEDANT. This carries an air of sincerity—thank you, my dear. . . .

LADY GRAVELY. . . . In every circle you engross the whole conversation, where you say a thousand silly things, and laugh at them all; by both which the world is always convinced, that you have very fine teeth and very bad sense. . . . That you are not restrained from unlawful pleasures by the love of virtue, but variety; and that your husband is not safe from having no rival, but from having a great many; for your heart is like a coffee-house, where the beaus frisk in and out, one after another; and you are as little the worse for them, as the other is the better; for one lover, like one poison, is your antidote against another.

LADY LUCY PEDANT. Ha, ha, ha! I like your comparison of love and poison, for I hate them both alike.

LADY GRAVELY. . . . In short, to end my character, the world gives you the honour of being the most finished coquette in town.

The striking thing about this dialogue is its lifelessness. Lady Gravely's stiff, ponderously barbed harangues and Lady Lucy's flaccid sarcasms lack all edge and conviction, as they answer one another in a kind of elephantine ballet of pique (the dialogue, incidentally, 'neatly' balances some immediately preceding exchanges in which Lady Lucy makes the speeches and Lady Gravely is at the receiving end). Any sudden freshness ('your heart is like a coffee-house, where the beaus frisk in and out, one after another') is embedded almost beyond recovery in the stale epigrammatic routine. A glance at Congreve makes clear the extent to which Fielding fails to catch fire in a conventional mode of Restoration comedy. All suggestion of shapely interchange, both in the style of speech and in the larger organization of the scene, solidifies into a heavy dulness, instead of lifting the dialogue into that pointed world of satiric fantasy where the foolish and nasty speakers become (as in the novels) fantasticated into a disreputable 'unreality'.

For one of the uses of patterned artifice, and of a related tendency of individual scenes to seem self-enclosed, is, in Fielding, precisely to set vice and folly in the mad world of their own self-absorption, where they seem disconnected from all humane and rational purposes. In the dialogue from *Joseph Andrews*, Lady Booby and Beau Didapper perform a ritual of social nastiness, staged with clockwork precision, sign-posted by the author as typical or exemplary, and standing out slightly, in its clean and pointed outlines, from the (somewhat bustling) scene in which it is set. The dialogue is undoubtedly more 'realistic' than that of *The Temple Beau*, though one of its liveliest idiomatic exactitudes ('I would never mention aversion ... with that face; dear Lady Booby, wash your face before you mention aversion') happens to echo stage-comedy as well as real life (see Wesleyan Edition, p. 314n.); and the 'realism' exists in piquant relationship with the suggestion of autonomous artifice, rather than subverting it. This interplay the plays seldom achieve, despite comparable efforts to set certain things into relief through 'self-conscious' announcements of artifice, as when Trapwit advertises his scene of 'fine conversation' or Lady Gravely coyly speaks of her 'character' (i.e. character-sketch) of Lady Lucy. This is partly because the plays belong to genres in themselves highly stylized, where there is no strongly competing note of realism, and where the stylization (including these slightly externalized reminders) is of a sort that takes itself for granted, not easily permitting the author to use the sheer act of stylization as a form of self-expression and of commentary.

Some of the liveliest scenes in the novels occur in contexts where the novel imports elements of some other genre, whether plays, epic poems, or history, or even opera. Halfway through *Tom Jones*, VII. iii, we discover that the dialogue about marriage between Sophia and her aunt is being heard by Squire Western, and in a way which almost invites us to imagine him as skulking, with increasing impatience, in a half-hidden corner of the stage. He then explodes onto the scene, the greatest of all stage-squires (his very language, at times in the novel, seems drawn as much from stage Zummerzet as from the real-life region), and enters into a preposterous argument with his sister. The heaving absurdity of their dialogue becomes, almost *literally*, operatic, as, in reply to her taunt of 'boor', he cries:

Boar, . . . I am no boar; no, nor ass; no, nor rat neither, madam. Remember that—I am no rat.

The rhythms of mounting pique are, in an odd sense, 'realistically' captured: but they are bloated to a comic-opera extravagance, and evoke the rising trills of a deep comic baritone. Shortly after these cadences have subsided, the argument ends on a precisely timed note of farce, the squire announcing that he despises his sister's politics

'. . . as much as I do a f—t'. Which last word he accompanied and graced with the very action, which, of all others, was the most proper to it.

Farting (the blank is Fielding's, or his printer's, but Fielding's archness is visibly there to be enjoyed) is no extraordinary thing, but Western's timing is one which clowns might spend a long time in perfecting.

This wholly eclectic extravaganza of theatrical reminder may or may not be fully deliberate, but it occurs naturally and continually in the novels, creating bold and delightful effects of abundance (urbanity cheek by jowl with 'low' jests) under buoyant authorial control. It also, however, helps to bring out the nasty exfoliating fatuity of the Squire and his sister as they try to force Sophia to marry against her wishes, and the comic world of their mad self-centredness is made simultaneously 'unreal' and terribly threatening. Sophia, who is the main topic of conversation, speaks little, but remains in her very silence a lifeline to reality. When she does speak, compare the directness and centrality of her remarks, with her aunt's insane moral pedantry :

> . . . 'If I was not as great a philosopher as Socrates himself,' returned Mrs. Western, 'you would overcome my patience. What objection can you have to the young gentleman?'
>
> 'A very solid objection, in my opinion,' says Sophia,—'I hate him'.
>
> 'Will you never learn a proper use of words?' answered the aunt. 'Indeed, child, you should consult Bailey's *Dictionary*. It is impossible you should hate a man from whom you have received no injury. By hatred, therefore, you mean no more than dislike, which is no sufficient objection against your marrying of him . . .'

Not only the liveliness of Sophia's reply, but its vivid moral force and pertinence, depends on the fact that it wells up in this context of extravagant absurdity. (It may be contrasted with the relative deadness of a similar retort by the heroine of the play, *The Wedding-Day*, 1743, II. viii, in an unfantasticating context.) The staging of this exchange becomes a kind of vivid intervention from the author. The fantastication of Mrs. Western and her brother has a quality of sheer performance which contributes massively to our sense of the author's high-spirited presence, but the feeling of creative abundance is held in check by the small hard note of rueful distaste. The exchanges between Sophia and her aunt suggest not so much a confrontation between alternative points of view, nor merely between good and evil persons, as between a humane decency rooted in the real world, and a zany disconnected nastiness that lives in a world of its own yet would (and could) turn the real world into its own fetid image.

The scene from *Joseph Andrews* lacks those spectacular marks of authorial participation, the feats of exuberant stylization streaked with moral concern, of the scene from *Tom Jones*. But something of the same interplay exists between reality and artifice, and there is no less vitality. It is almost as though the mere fact of narration were enough to energize Fielding into all the ease, confidence and securely carried moral passion which the scene from *The Temple Beau* lacks. The preliminary narrative, for a start, crisply sketches the tense and unpleasant social mood in which the dialogue takes place: the grandee boorishness of the visitors, the flustered servility of Mrs. Adams, the sexual situation somewhat charged by Didapper's recent attempt on Fanny and by Lady Booby's desire (disclosed before) that Didapper should win Fanny so that she may have Joseph for herself. On the stage, much of the establishing of such social atmosphere would be done by actors and producer. But the vivid conciseness of this passage (narrative and dialogue together) contrasts with the verbose obviousness of much of Fielding's dramatic dialogue, as though he felt compelled to be sole master even in the plays and to leave as little as possible for anyone else to do. Moreover, even his most ordinary narrative links ('replied the lady', 'answered the beau') tend to become a purposeful part of the scene's overall rhythm, not merely identifying speakers, but modifying or heightening an emphasis. The particular placing of 'answered the beau' inside Didapper's last statement creates a pause which exquisitely intensifies the ensuing insult.

It is characteristic of Fielding that such almost neutral signs of authorial manipulation should become flecked with a purposeful vitality. This happens even when Fielding is not himself the official narrator. Even in *Shamela* (1741), Fielding's first parody of Richardson, where the narration is in letters written largely by the heroine, Shamela's use of such link-phrases as 'says I', 'says he', 'pert again', announces itself, in a way, as the author's:

Pamela, says he, what book is that? I warrant you Rochester's poems.—No, forsooth, says I, as pertly as I could; why how now saucy chops, boldface, says he—Mighty pretty words, says I, pert again.—Yes (says he) you are a d—d, impudent, stinking, cursed, confounded jade, and I have a great mind to kick your a—. You, kiss—says I. A-gad, says he, and so I will; with that he caught me in his arms, and kissed me till he made my face all over fire . . . I flung myself from him in a mighty rage, and pretended as how I would go out at the door; but when I came to the end of the room, I stood still, and my master cried out, hussy, slut, saucebox, boldface, come hither—Yes, to be sure, says I; why don't you come, says he; what should I come for, says I; if you don't come to me, I'll come to you, says he; I shan't come to you, I assure you, says I. Upon which he run up, caught me in his arms, and flung me upon a chair, and began to offer to touch my under-petticoat. Sir, says I, you had better not offer to be rude; well, says he, no more I won't then; and away he went out of the room. I was so mad to be sure I could have cried.

(Letter VI)

'Says I' and 'says he' have here a clockwork alternation which is accelerated and mechanized just sufficiently to hint at the zany tempos of farce. The farce element competes powerfully with the parodic purpose. Booby's invective, 'hussy, slut, saucebox, boldface', uses only words which occur in the relevant scenes of *Pamela* (Letters XI and XV), but the headlong juxtaposition turns them into a clownish routine; and the exchange 'kick your a—. You, kiss —' is one of the oldest farce rituals in the business. The point of all this is to mock Richardson, but it already has, in a rudimentary form, that interplay between realism and stylization which is a guarantee of Fielding's active self-projection in the writing, and its vigour goes beyond satiric piquancy into an independent comic world. Squire Booby, the impetuous lover easily cooled ('began to offer to touch my under-petticoat' is at four removes from doing anything to the girl) becomes at times less a parody of Mr. B. than a Fielding character in his own right, looking back to the spindle-shanked beaux of the plays, and forward to Didapper. Above all, the passage shows not only the comic novelist's energies over-whelming mere parodic objectives, but vitality of a kind which a purely dramatic medium would have made impossible. The action is brilliantly stage-managed by, among other things, the zany pointing of the narrative links. Stage-management is pre-cisely what the narrative mode permits Fielding to do in the novels and not in the theatre (where it is left to stage-managers), and Shamela's 'says I' and 'says he' become one of Fielding's most vivid means of control over the action. Unlike the mere submission, in *The Temple Beau* and other plays, to artificial modes which happen to belong conventionally to those plays and whose use therefore leaves no scope for obvious authorial intrusion, the exploitation of farce overtones in this epistolary fiction is a wilfully vitalizing intervention, gaily an-nouncing Fielding's full and buoyant mastery.

Shamela, however, remains primarily a parody in its purpose and structure, though bulging with energies that assert their independent comic life. Fielding never abandoned parody and burlesque, but his real beginning as a comic novelist occurs in *Jonathan Wild* (1743, published after but probably written before *Joseph Andrews*), where parody occurs on a large-scale but serves non-parodic purposes, and where it is systematically transcended and overwhelmed by the comic action. Some of the political plays had already used dramatic burlesque as a means to political satire, and the use of mock-heroic or other burlesque formulas to mock not merely heroic poems or other literary works but some moral or political evils was common in Augustan satire. *Jonathan Wild* is partly an example of this, setting up a mock-heroic idiom (eclectically drawn from heroic poems, plays, and especially perhaps histories and biographies of great men and the lives of famous rogues) as a pointed mock-aggrandizement of common criminals, and implying simultaneously a parallel between the criminal underworld and England's political masters. In this scheme, 'great men' and 'heroes' (gangsters, prime ministers, etc.) are ironically praised, while decent and unassuming persons are scorned as weak or silly. The success of this is limited. There are plenty of *local* mock-heroic effects, both bitter and playful, but the work as a whole differs from great Augustan mock-heroics like the *Dunciad* in resting not mainly on any fully-fledged epic fiction so much as on a framework of heroic *words* ('great', 'hero', 'admirable' etc.). This tends to the merely verbal in an abstract sense, turning the work into a 'moral allegory' coexisting with a vaguely novelistic plot, rather than a fable vitally coherent in all its parts. Nor is it helped by the reader's occasional temptation to rebel against the implied instruction to translate all terms into their moral opposites, especially when the virtuous Heartfree is called 'silly', 'mean-spirited' and so on. Heartfree's gullibility to Wild is outrageous enough to merit such language straight, and the trouble lies, in my view, in the stiffness of the formula rather than (as some critics hold) in Fielding's intention to expose the insufficiency of Heartfree, as having goodness without a certain legitimate seasoning of self-interested 'greatness'.[2] The trouble with the Heartfrees is not that active reservations about them are pressed upon us, but that Fielding celebrates them with all the overemphasis of an incomplete creative engagement. The accounts (see for example II. i) of Heartfree's 'cheerful entertainment[s] at home' and of Mrs. Heartfree's happiness in her family, the heavy detailing of the occasional 'moderate glass of wine' and the occasional theatrical outing, the virtuous or 'pathetic' exclamatoriness of their language at times of stress, the heart-rending tableaux of their family griefs and joys, amount to a singularly coarse-grained form of sentimentality on Fielding's part, to which the harsh topsy-turvy of the verbal irony merely *adds*. It seems fair to say that Heartfree's insufficiency may reside in the fact that, as a merely (though almost perfectly) virtuous person, and as a mere tradesman, he combines two types whom Fielding found it easier to sentimentalize than to respect.

The opposite irony, over Wild's evil 'greatness', is often just as crude, but it has a certain brash dynamism and answers to a well-captured quality of oafish energy in the character himself. And when the upside-down scheme yields to an impulse to take the heroic terms literally, the result creates a sense not (as with the Heartfrees) of deadening contradiction, but of a vitalizing comic complication. Wild's impetuosity, in anger or in love, involves a kind of grotesque courage. His plan to seduce Mrs. Heartfree is brought to a crisis because the ship in which he has carried her off seems about to sink in a storm. His reaction is to force the issue before death overtakes them both (II. x). Fielding sees to it that Mrs. Heartfree is rescued in the next paragraph, so that nothing irretrievably nasty is allowed to weigh things down. And we are left with a glimpse of absurd (but real) 'heroism' in Wild, and with a momentary comedy of situation, grotesque yet oddly engaging. A similar combination of preposterous grandeur and affectionate comedy occurs at the proud moment of death on the gallows:

> We must not, however, omit one circumstance, as it serves to show the most admirable conservation of character in our hero to the last moment, which was, that, whilst the ordinary [i.e. chaplain] was busy in his ejaculations, Wild, in the midst of the shower of stones, &c., which played upon him, applied his hands to the parson's pocket, and emptied it of his bottle-screw, which he carried out of the world in his hand.
>
> (IV. xiv)

In both passages, real oafish stature paradoxically combines with a sense of Wild's helpless automatism, his comically compulsive enslavement to habits of thieving, or of vicious lechery, even at the most overwhelmingly inappropriate moments. Time and again in the novel, Wild impresses more by his comic self-imprisonment in viciousness and (the point is hardly sufficiently recognized) his almost invariable failure in crime and in love, outwitted by his partners and robbed, betrayed or cuckolded by his women. His ability to maintain a grave unemotional demeanour as his trickeries reach crisis or become unexpectedly complicated evokes not so much a Machiavellian self-control as the dead-pan expression of the stage-comic.

The starkness of the mock-heroic formula has often led critics to stress Wild's implacable diabolism, and the book's unrelieved asperity. One of its charms, however, is that it fails to take Wild's wickedness anything like as seriously as the formula suggests. The effect may partly be unintentional (a fortunate accident as its counterpart with the Heartfrees is unfortunate), as though the comic novelist of the next few years were beginning to burst through the official formulaic purposes of the political satirist. However that may be, we already find many examples of the kind of comic distancing, the stylized reminders of plays (I. iii; II. xii; III. iii; IV. xiv) and the feats of farcical reduction (II. iii), which show the student of the human comedy consciously focusing his vision. Nothing, at any rate, could be more clearly deliberate than Fielding's indication at the start (I. iii), that Wild is not simply to be identified with the sour reverse of the heroic medal. The account of his literary interests as a boy notes not only his delight in the scabrous exploits of epic heroes ('an undeniable testimony of the great antiquity of priggism'), but also the fact that 'the Spanish Rogue was his favourite book, and the Cheats of Scapin his favourite play'. As mock-heroic grandiloquence turns genial along these lines, we are entering the world of *Joseph Andrews* and *Tom Jones*.

*   *   *   *

Mock-heroic does not, however, mean comic epic, and the Preface to *Joseph Andrews* (1742) stresses the difference: 'comic' means an action 'light and ridiculous' instead of 'grave and solemn', characters less exalted in rank and virtue than those of heroic poems or romances, 'sentiments and diction' which preserve 'the ludicrous instead of the sublime', and realism or truth to life ('exactest copying') in some sense. Comic epic does not imply burlesque or mock-heroic, which Fielding says he has sometimes admitted into his 'diction' for the amusement of 'the classical reader', but never into

> our sentiments and characters; for there it is never properly introduced, unless in writings of the burlesque kind, which this is not intended to be. Indeed, no two species of writing can differ more widely than the comic and the burlesque; for as the latter is ever the exhibition of what is monstrous and

unnatural, and where our delight, if we examine it, arises from the surprising absurdity, as in appropriating the manners of the highest to the lowest, or *è converso*; so in the former, we should ever confine ourselves strictly to nature, from the just imitation of which will flow all the pleasure we can this way convey to a sensible reader.

Fielding is clearly anxious to convey the notion that though *Joseph Andrews* (as later *Tom Jones*, 1749) contains many mock-heroic interludes (high-flown rhetoric, Homeric similes, mock-battles), these remain an incidental element of verbal or stylistic fun rather than the main essence of the novel. The distinction between burlesque of diction, and that of sentiments and characters, partly follows from this, possibly with some intention of distinguishing his mock-heroic flights from the more radical burlesque of some of the plays (or even of *Jonathan Wild*) and from the primary parodic purpose of *Shamela*. The distinction also suggests that the burlesque leaves the substance of the narrative unsubverted, so that the grandiloquent introduction of Sophia in *Tom Jones*, IV. ii, for example, entails no mockery of her, nor any serious diminution of Fielding's praise of her beauties and virtues, nor, for that manner, any dispraise of epic grandeur (though the epic pretensions of heroic romances *are* sometimes mocked).

In view of its frequency in *Joseph Andrews* and *Tom Jones*, we may feel that Fielding's suggestion that it is incidental is merely defensive. There is no doubt that Fielding is conscious of the conflicting claims of 'exactest copying' and of his own temperamental need to colour, point and frame a merely raw reality; and that his later writings (both his last novel *Amelia*, dated 1752 but actually published in December 1751, and his *Journal of a Voyage to Lisbon*, written in 1754 and posthumously published in 1755) mark a progressive emancipation from, though not a jettisoning of, habits of allusive stylization. The language in which he refers to his burlesque of diction suggests detachable ornament (for the 'entertainment' of the 'classical reader'), and he points out that since diction 'is the dress of poetry' rather than its substance, it would be as unfair to call his novel burlesque as to infer a man's character from his clothes. Fielding's application of the Renaissance commonplace that expression is the dress of thought is interesting in that (unlike, for example, Pope's famous lines in *An Essay on Criticism*, 318ff.) it does not advocate a decorous congruence between subject and style but proclaims a certain lack of it in his work. I suspect that Fielding may be using a burlesque dress not merely as extra fun, but as a means of clothing reality out of its nakedness, as a stylistic distancing from the raw untidiness of sheer fact or feeling. It certainly provides a guard where urbanity and poise are at risk, and also where the subject carries a danger of lapsing into the style of disreputable genres like the romances. Such risks tend to occur, and need to be neutralized, when, for example, a heroine is warmly celebrated, as in *Tom Jones*, IV. ii. And the burlesque additionally contributes to that ritual of abundance, already mentioned, in which an easy gentlemanliness, playful pedantries and some 'low' elements (the allusion to Rochester in *Tom Jones*, IV. ii, conceals a scurrilous joke)[3] miraculously cohere, creating an amalgam of exuberant stylization from which reality, when it comes, emerges startlingly fresh and delightful : 'Sophia, then, the only daughter of Mr. Western, was a middle-sized woman, but rather inclining to tall . . .' If the parody distances fact in a sense, it also liberates it in another, not only by making possible such vivifying contrasts, but also by freeing the author from the vulnerabilities of undue intimacy, thus releasing, not subduing, his most creative energies.

Joseph Andrews contains not only epic-burlesque, but also parody of Richardson's *Pamela*. Unlike *Shamela*, it transcends the parody almost entirely, inviting itself to be read as a fully-fledged comic novel in its own right. The element of anti-Pamelaic satire is sometimes underrated these days, and the example of it which follows shows the parody not only creating a local literary joke or some piquant interplay between style and fact, but helping with brilliant economy to define a moral nuance. One of the novel's best-known scenes tells of Joseph, robbed and beaten, lying naked by the roadside as a stagecoach passes by (I. xii). The passengers all debate whether to let him in, a prudish lady refusing to ride in the coach with a naked man, and all concerned refusing to lend their coats, so that Joseph 'must have perished, unless the postilion (a lad who hath been since transported for robbing a hen-roost) had voluntarily stript off his greatcoat, his only garment . . .' The passage is justly famous, and the parenthesis a memorable blend of moral fervour and of a righteously off-hand hauteur. But the full glory of the postilion is not merely that he is the one unselfish man in a crowd of egoists, but also, since Joseph himself is too shy to enter the coach naked, 'such mighty effects had the spotless example of the amiable Pamela, and the excellent sermons of Mr. Adams, wrought upon him', the only free spirit, capable of taking the entire situation, including Joseph's Pamelaic fatuity, in hand.

Joseph is here stiff and awkward, not mean and nastily selfish like the other passengers, but amiably locked in a Richardsonian moral pedantry for which Fielding has less than total respect. Fielding is affectionate towards Joseph, but this is edged with a note of uppish superiority to which Tom Jones, for example, is not subjected. In the descriptive set-piece (comically open to comparison in several respects with the later portrait of Sophia in *Tom Jones*, IV. ii, and aptly so, since Joseph, chastely resisting Lady Booby, is placed in a feminine role) early in the novel, we read of his 'air which, to those who have not seen many noblemen, would give an idea of nobility' (I. viii). The remark alludes to a common assumption in romances that the true nobility of a hero, however disguised, will always show (anti-romance and the anti-Richardsonian parody of Joseph's status as a male Pamela momentarily converging). One suggestion of the words, however, is that real-life noblemen are a degenerate lot, hardly handsome and healthy like Joseph. But another implication is that only 'those who have not seen many noblemen' could possibly take this blushing footman for one.

Tom is never so treated. He too has 'a natural gentility' which resides in a good heart and basically virtuous principles, but he is not undercut by suggestions of ungentlemanly stiffness, and even his social solecisms (e.g. XIII. iv) are made to seem signs of moral grace. As the illegitimate son of a gentleman, he has technical gentility as well, and is often taken as a gentleman in disguise. The old formula, guyed in the description of Joseph, according to which a hero's rank showed itself not only through disguises but even through his own ignorance of the facts of his birth, is part of the comedy of *Tom Jones*. Strictly, Joseph too has technical gentility, since he turns out at the end to be the son not of Gaffar Andrews but of Mr. Wilson. But his status, throughout most of the novel, as a mere footman, his extreme and somewhat comic chastity, and the residual tang of the anti-Richardsonian parody, conspire to dissipate any impression of inborn gentlemanly grace. If Tom too is only revealed a 'gentleman' at the end, he grows up not as a servant but as an accepted member of Allworthy's household, and at no point did Fielding need to visualize him, as he needed to visualize Joseph throughout, in a role which Fielding would instinctively regard as demeaning and slightly ridiculous. Viewed thus, Joseph's Pamelaic chastity becomes in some degree a kind of low-bred self-confinement, and Tom's ease with women a kind of gentlemanly grace.

The description must, however, be disentangled from any suggestion of shallow libertinism or crude snobbery on Fielding's part. In the scene with the postilion, Fielding's tone, witty and impassioned, belongs to a mental world where patrician hauteur and moral generosity are congruent. Fielding knew well that such congruences were not a fact of everyday life, and we may say that the tone of voice posits an ideal actively clung to, in which true nobility was felt to be a moral thing. He said in a note to *Tom Jones*, I. ix, that whenever he uses the word *mob*, 'it intends persons without virtue, or sense, in all stations, and many of the highest rank are often meant by it'. The claim is not entirely justified, in the sense that there are some moments of uppishness which are not easy to dignify in this way. But it is largely true both of his most serious social thinking, and of his best imaginative writing. His discussion in essays, early and late, about the relation of good-breeding (as the art of pleasing, of being considerate, of preventing distress to others) to good-nature or benevolence (the highest virtue in Fielding's moral world) is an example. So is his vivid habit of exposing vice, including snobbery, as a moral pedantry or self-enclosed meanness. Snobbery becomes a matter of fatuously systematized fine distinctions (see, for example, the 'dissertation', advisedly so called, on high and low people in *Joseph Andrews*, II. xiii, with its careful discriminations among 'those bordering nearly on each other, to wit, the lowest of the high, and the highest of the low') which rise at times to comic sublimities of bookish fervour :

> Mrs. Western's maid claimed great superiority over Mrs. Honour, on several accounts. First, her birth was higher : for her great grandmother by the mother's side was a cousin, not far removed, to an Irish peer . . .
>
> (*Tom Jones*, VII. viii)

Some of the piquancy of this depends on the fact that these snobberies come from servants, but Fielding is capable of the most blistering indignation against the snobberies of their 'betters', who have the technical 'claim to superiority' of high birth :

> I have myself seen a little female thing which they have called My Lady, of no greater dignity in the order of beings than a cat, and of no more use in society than a butterfly;

whose mien would not give even the idea of a gentle-woman, and whose face would cool the loosest libertine; with a mind as empty of ideas as an opera, and a body fuller of diseases than a hospital—I have seen this thing express contempt to a woman who was an honour to her sex, and an ornament to the creation.

(Essay on Conversation, 1743)

Such passionate hauteurs, like the preceding witty ones, glow with an uncanting righteousness: not only are snobs attacked on their own ground, snobbery thus becoming more than any other vice 'lowbred', but the gentlemanly ideal is raised, vividly, to the highest moral responsibility.

The enemy, for Fielding, is always that small-minded self-enclosure which inhibits generosity and mechanizes attitudes and behaviour. Bergsonian ideas of laughter would not have seemed strange to Fielding, but restrictions on the expansiveness and vital plasticity of human persons were for him no simple laughing matter. The most warmly endorsed characters in Fielding's novels are those whose humanity is free enough to over-flow any narrow conditioning, not only of bad or ill-applied ideologies (such as imprison Square and Thwackum) or profess-ional habit, or narrow moral outlooks, but even of the best and most sincerely endorsed moral standards. Parson Adams's impetuous inability to observe his own good principles (or even common decorum) when overwhelming calls are made upon his feelings (as in *Joseph Andrews*, IV. viii), or Tom Jones's unchaste lapses, become valued as Joseph's rigid chastity can never be, and it is this which gives so much status to the posti-lion's entirely spontaneous sense (against the nasty prejudices of the passengers and the chaste scruples of Joseph alike) of the one overriding, humanly important, need.

The treatment of the rigid chastity in that episode, then, has an undoubted uppish tang, both at Joseph's and at Richard-son's expense, but one which is profoundly charged with a humane liberality which transcends mere uppish overtones. Similarly, no crude identification may be made between Field-ing's mild mockery of Joseph or his warm endorsement of Tom, and the sort of shallow libertinism which claims for itself a gentlemanly largeness of view, although there may exist a dim and distant trace of such relationship. Love, even unchaste love, is, in Fielding, valued to the extent that it carries an outgoing warmth and mutuality of feeling. The grossest appetites of Jonathan Wild are, somehow, preferable to the coldness of Blifil. And if the preference seems a narrow one, there is no doubt about Fielding's celebration of another animal 'appetite', like Wild's compared with mere lust for food. Mrs. Waters, sensing that Tom loves another,

> could feast heartily at the table of love, without reflecting that some other already had been, or hereafter might be, feasted with the same repast. A sentiment which, if it deals but little in refinement, deals however much in substance; and is less capricious, and perhaps less ill-natured and selfish than the desires of those females who can be contented enough to abstain from the possession of their lovers, provided they are sufficiently satisfied that no one else possesses them.
>
> *(Tom Jones*, IX. vi)

By those cold and selfish women, Fielding may mean the *beau monde*, where, as Mrs. Western often reminds us, love is out of fashion. In any event, Fielding hardly conceives the upper ranks of society as a hotbed of carefree lechery, and he rebukes those satirists who 'have affixed the character of lewdness to these times', since 'there never was less of love intrigue carried among persons of condition, than now':

> Our present women have been taught by their mothers to fix their thoughts only on ambition and vanity, and to despise the pleasures of love as unworthy their regard . . . In my humble opinion, the true characteristick of the present *Beau Monde*, is rather folly than vice, and the only epithet which it deserves is that of *frivolous*.
>
> *(Tom Jones*, XIV. i)

These examples remain, however, on the foothills of Fielding's sexual ethic. Its *heights* are the pinnacle of Fielding's entire moral outlook, an outlook whose key-words are, in a manner, the key-words of *Tom Jones* : Good Nature and Benevolence. Fielding's use of these two terms is virtually synonymous, and is based on a traditional moral psychology (often directed against Hobbes and his followers, the 'philosophers' of the famous chapter 'Of Love', *Tom Jones*, VI. i), which claimed that man, far from being by nature purely a selfish animal, was capable of natural and spontaneous emotions of tenderness, pity, and benevolence towards others; and that these social emotions, when gratified through good actions, gave pleasure to the doer because, as a psychological fact, his natural instincts were thus being fulfilled. Versions of this psychology differed in various ways, and notably as to whether *all* men had such social feelings, or only *some*. Fielding held the latter view, thus (for example) distinguishing between Blifil and Tom:

> As there are some minds whose affections, like Master Blifil's, are solely placed in one single person, whose interest and indulgence alone they consider on every occasion; regarding the good and ill of all others as merely indifferent, any farther than as they contribute to the pleasure or advantage of that person: so there is a different temper of mind which borrows a degree of virtue even from self-love; such can never receive any kind of satisfaction from another, without loving the creature to whom that satisfaction is owing, and without making its well-being in some sort necessary to their own ease.
>
> Of this latter species was our hero.
>
> (Tom Jones, IV. vi)

A striking thing about this passage is that it has a specifically sexual emphasis, commenting on Tom's feelings for Molly Seagrim. It extends, quite unmistakably and with a certain boldness, the normal patterns of benevolist psychology into the field of sexual relations. Genuine erotic affection, even if largely carnal and, as 'love' (in the sense of *Tom Jones*, VI. i), incomplete, is seen as a form of benevolence, and this gives value to Tom's minor sexual adventures with Molly Seagrim and others, to his easy-going unchastities and his chivalrous inability to decline the advances of female admirers. The nicest touch is that because he loves to give pleasure and hates to give pain, Tom is shown in these affairs as satisfying his 'self-love', not merely or primarily for the obvious carnal reason, but for the larger reason made clear in the passage quoted from IV. vi. Booth's liaison with Miss Matthews in *Amelia* (1751: III. xii) is similarly interpreted, in a way different only in its higher degree from the words used about Mrs. Waters in *Tom Jones* (IX. vi) and quoted earlier: Booth 'was a man of consummate good nature, and had formerly had much affection for this young lady; indeed, more than the generality of people are capable of entertaining for any person whatsoever.'

It is thus no accident that the great chapter 'Of Love' should deal comprehensively with a benevolence larger than the merely sexual, and which may, but need not, include sexual feelings. 'Appetite alone', the kind of lust which lacks all outgoingness or mutuality, is the one form of sexual love for which Fielding does not 'here contend' (although, as I have suggested, Wild's lechery seems preferred to Blifil's coldness). But while this distinction needs to be conceded for the completeness of Fielding's statement, it is irrelevant to Tom's feelings in any of his affairs, since in none of them is there any suggestion of 'appetite alone' on his part. As critics are always reminding us, Fielding cared for what Empson called 'the Christian command of chastity'.[4] Both the unfolding of the chapter 'Of Love', and the entire moral atmosphere of the novels, leave us in no doubt that Fielding took for granted the superiority of Tom's chaste love for Sophia, and Booth's for Amelia, to these heroes' more transient passions. Novelistic convention would demand this, but few readers would dispute that far more is implied than a formal and perfunctory compliance with convention. Fielding values the restraints of a chaste love, just as he advocates certain restraints of prudence, caution and good sense, upon the spontaneous exercise of more general forms of benevolence. But the moral generosity which overspills prudence or violates chastity is also a matter of 'Christian command', and is larger than any code.

In this, *Tom Jones*, like *Joseph Andrews*, is a deeply anti-Richardsonian book, not merely or mainly in a limited sense of parody (and indeed Fielding was by the time of *Tom Jones* a devoted admirer of *Clarissa*), but in the whole fabric of its moral world. Fielding took seriously and eloquently his insistence on the importance of restraint and prudence as necessary controls to even the best human impulses. But there is always a sense (especially in the novels, where his moral outlook is presented with the urgency and completeness of a high imaginative involvement) in which prudence, even at its best, is seen as a secondary virtue, necessary for our self-interest (and even at times for the well-being of others), rather than as a creative and positive virtue in its own right. It is a quality which the best characters (Adams, Tom, Allworthy, Booth) tend to lack, though the novels insist that they need to acquire it. But in *Tom Jones* at least (for *Amelia* is a less expansive book), when the hero finally 'acquired a discretion and prudence very uncommon in one of his lively parts' (XVIII. xiii), we note the fact with satisfaction as an appropriate guarantee of the stability of the happy ending (a guarantee, that is, that he and Sophia will live happily forever after), and no doubt as a good thing in itself; but the point is, in all conscience, perfunctorily made, and we do not get any urgent sense that a major moral deficiency has been put right. As to the bad kinds of prudence, so much more frequent in *Tom Jones* than the good, they are always extremely distasteful, absurd as in Mrs. Western, coldly nasty as in Blifil.

And these anti-prudential overtones are, in a large sense, anti-Richardsonian, whether consciously or not. They go back to *Shamela*'s exposure of the 'virtue rewarded' theme, fanning out from there into the wider, more complex, increasingly sensitive and generous morality of *Joseph Andrews* and *Tom Jones*. The initial stereotype of Richardson was doubtless unfair, but it crystallized in Fielding's mind an image of awkward, reward-conscious, middle-class caution, and his counter-assertion of a freer, less constrained, 'aristocratic' temperament is the last and perhaps subtlest (for he admired Richardson's great gifts) in a tradition of Augustan hauteurs. What the cit was to the hero of Restoration comedy, and the dunces were to Swift and Pope, Richardson was to Fielding: an increasing (and increasingly talented) encroachment from the vulgarian merchant world upon a declining humane and gentlemanly culture. The attitude survived to the end, and in almost the last words he ever wrote Fielding gibed at Richardson's claim that entertainment in novels should be a *vehicle* for moral instruction (Fielding would hardly reject the sentiment, as distinct from what he considered to be Richardson's canting expression of it) by calling it

> an undertaking . . . of reforming a whole people by making use of a vehicular story, to wheel in among them worse manners than their own.
>
> (*Voyage to Lisbon*, 1754, Preface)

The gentlemanly recoil involved from the start not only morality but literary style. Here too there are reverberations of an older war between gentlemen-authors and Grub Street hacks, between wits and cits. When Shamela says 'You see I write in the present tense' (Letter VI), Fielding is guying that 'to the Moment' style (*Sir Charles Grandison*, 1753–4, Preface) which was rightly Richardson's pride, but the sentence looks back over four decades to the hack of Swift's *Tale of a Tub* (1704, Preface), who boasted 'that what I am going to say is literally true this Minute I am writing'. Swift's emphasis is perhaps more on the trivial ephemerality of his 'moderns', while Fielding complains of an immediacy too formulaically pressing. But both repudiate similar tendencies to a close confessional writing and to a tedious and 'impolite' proliferation of insignificant detail. These faults offended gentlemanly reticence and the decorum of conversation (the notion that literature should have the qualities of good conversation, correctness, wit, taste, considerateness to the reader, and so on, was a com-

279

monplace to traditionalist Augustans like Swift, Pope and Fielding) and there is much contemporary testimony, not only from Fielding, that Richardson's novels, for all their vivid readability and their great emotional power, seemed to many distressingly low-bred. Horace Walpole, in a letter to Sir Horace Mann, 20 December 1764, called them 'pictures of high life as conceived by a bookseller'. Lady Mary Wortley Montagu grudgingly admitted the unbecoming emotional involvement into which his novels drew her ('I heartily despise him and eagerly read him, nay, sob over his works in a most scandalous manner', letter to Lady Bute, 22 September, 1755), and made a famous remark about Clarissa's habit

> of declaring all she thinks to all the people she sees, without reflecting that in this Mortal state of Imperfection Fig leaves are as necessary for our Minds as our Bodies, and tis as indecent to shew all we think as all we have.
>   He has no Idea of the manners of high Life . . .
>   (to Lady Bute, 20 October 1755)[5]

The offence exceeds mere garrulous intimacies, which are probably all that Lady Mary meant. Fielding, whom Richardson thought of as a scurrilous libertine, was able long before Lady Mary's letter to expose the graphic lubricity of Richardson's erotic scenes. Parson Oliver made the point to Parson Tickletext in *Shamela*; and when, in *Tom Jones*, XIII. ix, Fielding avoids 'mentioning particulars' of what Tom did with Lady Bellaston, for the gratification of those 'whose devotion to the fair sex . . . wants to be raised by the help of pictures', what he mentions are 'certain French novels', but it is hard to believe that Richardson was not also in his mind.

The main effect, here, is to assure us of the narrator's worldly wisdom, that knows how to take sex for granted without either squeamishness or prurience. But Fielding's reminders that he is a gentleman readily couple with suggestions that Richardson is not. The fact invites no celebration, even though Richardson gave as good as he got. What should, however, be emphasised is that, behind some of the anti-Richardsonian hauteurs of Fielding and others, as in earlier hauteurs of Swift and Pope, a whole 'polite' civilization was felt to be at stake. The urgencies of *A Tale of a Tub* and the *Dunciad* make this clear, and if *Shamela* rejects the morality and style (together) of *Pamela*, Fielding offers noble alternatives in *Joseph Andrews* and *Tom Jones*.

The style of writing, in *Tom Jones* especially, presents itself

as a style of life. It proclaims civilized achievement above intro-
spective spontaneity. Pope's famous couplet,

> True Ease in Writing, comes from Art, not Chance,
> As those move easiest who have learn'd to dance,
>
> (*Essay on Criticism*, 362–3)

expresses two assumptions which were Fielding's also. Ease in
writing, as in social intercourse, is an inner grace that comes not
by itself, but from mastery over a skill. Secondly, writing is a
decorous social activity, like the dance, its forms, the well
shaped couplet, for example, or the rounded period, celebrating
values of grace, control and social cohesion, as well as of wit.
There is nothing mechanical or crudely ornamentalising about
this : the vitality of Pope's verse and Fielding's prose comes
from the fact that their styles are the natural literary expression
of proprieties and restraints inherent in a living civilization.
These proprieties and restraints may be felt, perhaps, to reflect
less an actual 'order' than a 'rage for order', and it may be
because the civilization seemed under threat that the 'ease' of
Pope's or Fielding's writing is charged with a glow of urgency.
Style becomes a weapon against the subversions (boorish or
worse) both of the man within, and of the mob outside. The
Horatian postures of urbane, rational and sensitive rectitude,
the rhetorical display of trustworthiness and the formalizing of
the Poet or Narrator away from the vulnerabilities of the man
who suffers, are things which Pope's 'imitations' of Horace carry
very far, and which Fielding adapts to the novel.

Authorial intrusions, and so-called 'self-conscious narration',
are nothing new in prose fiction. But the particular relation
which Fielding establishes with his reader through his narrator's
actes de presence (references to himself, direct addresses to the
reader, and above all, in *Joseph Andrews* and especially *Tom
Jones*, the framework of introductory discourses) is special to
Fielding. It is a relationship, active, adult, and fairly free of the
fussier postures to which authorial interventions are notoriously
prone; something on which the whole atmosphere of the novels
strongly depends, and which grows cumulatively as the novels
progress, without, as we saw, developing an unbalancing or
highly charged intimacy. It emphasises a firm and decorous
distance, a sense of the narrator's aloofness (tinged sometimes
with a slight superiority) and of his authority. Things are not
allowed to get unduly emotional, although we often know that
Fielding feels very strongly indeed. The wit, the urbanity, the
confident direct handling of the reader, suggest that the narrator

has things under control, and that his wise and companionable personality may be relied on not only for trustworthy narration, but for a humane understanding of the moral issues involved. The style implies no diminution of real seriousness, of the moral passion with which the doctrine of benevolence and the sexual ethic are expressed, or the hatred of humbug, or the delight in the splendid humanity of Adams and Tom. But it does express a temperamental, and a cultural, need to harness facts in order to preserve personal poise and certain cherished public decencies. It is ungentlemanly to submit the reader to the mere factuality of fact. A naked unselective representation shows not only a tendency to undue and indecorous intimacy, but an undeveloped sense of priorities and an insecure sense of the significance of events. Fielding's claim of 'exactest copying' in the Preface to *Joseph Andrews* indicates not a Richardsonian realism, but a realism of strongly sketched types, general rather than particular, and painted in bold comic strokes. Fielding's ironic inflections, his mock-heroic stylizations, the reductions to clockwork farce (we recall how brilliantly these heterogeneous effects are held together), combine triumphantly with the rhetorical assertions of control, and the buoyant symmetries and finalities of the prose syntax, to suggest not evasion, but organization, of brute fact.

*　　*　　*　　*

In Fielding's last novel, *Amelia* (1751), the tone changes. The urbanity has become strenuous, and relations with the reader have suffered a deadening. When in *Tom Jones*, VI. i ('Of Love'), Fielding tells the reader that if he does not believe in love he should put down the book, since 'you have . . already read more than you have understood', he is doing so with an aggressive buoyancy which is supremely confident. The challenge is total, and if taken up, puts the reader badly in the wrong; but it is not unfriendly, and one senses that while Fielding stands by every word of his statement on love, he does not expect any reader to stop. In *Amelia*, III. i, Booth wants to omit describing to Miss Matthews a 'tender scene' which passed between him and his wife. Miss Matthews presses to hear it, because 'nothing delights me more than scenes of tenderness'. Fielding means us to dislike her shallowness, but there is an odd nastiness which he does not intend in the fact that she is an ex-mistress preparing to enjoy the account of a loving and painful scene between her former lover and his wife. For Fielding, the scene, as subsequently described, stands as a 'pathetic' set-piece, claiming its full straightforward emotional value. Booth, he tells his readers,

> then proceeded as Miss Matthews desired; but, lest all our readers should not be of her opinion, we will, according to our usual custom, endeavour to accommodate ourselves to every taste, and shall, therefore, place this scene in a chapter by itself, which we desire all our readers who do not love, or who, perhaps, do not know the pleasure of tenderness, to pass over; since they may do this without any prejudice to the thread of the narrative.

Here, the accommodating 'ourselves to every taste' and the 'chapter by itself' are somehow strained in their harshness. The note is quite different from the easy defiance with which, in *Tom Jones*, he tells unsuitable readers to stop reading altogether. It is not just that, by merely asking him to skip the chapter, he foregoes a grand gesture, resignedly and somewhat naggingly accepting that the reader will go on, and yet not change into a better man. The irony throbs and wavers, as if between a strident, aggressive shoulder-shrugging, and something like an exasperated sob. The scene itself duly follows in the next chapter, at the end of which Fielding makes Booth weakly conclude:

> This I am convinced of, that no one is capable of tasting such a scene who hath not a heart full of tenderness, and perhaps not even then, unless he hath been in the same situation.

This has, among other things, the accidental effect of sentimentalizing Fielding's own earlier statement out of much of its bite. The reader is partly let off by Booth's last remark, so that the earlier intensity now hangs in the air, even more undirected. We are meant to take Booth's remark feelingly. And the language, here as in the chapter as a whole, though perhaps too crudely overstated by our standards, is fairly natural novelistic rhetoric in an age when the self-conscious relishing of the emotions was more normal and more open than it is today. Even so, for Booth to talk of 'tasting such a scene' is unwittingly to put the whole thing on Miss Matthews's level.

Much of the old characteristic blend of urbanity and moral passion gives way to a new dogged literalism about details of feeling and emotion, and a new readiness to give full (sometimes exclamatory) expression to emotional moments, without undercutting them with ironic defences. He learnt some of the style from Richardson, whose *Clarissa* he warmly admired, and three years later he was to say, in what seems in part to be a defence of unstylized literalness, that he now wished his beloved Homer had written, instead of his great poems, 'a true history of his own times in humble prose' (*Voyage to Lisbon*, Preface). In *Amelia*, much of the earlier protective urbanity, the mock-heroic high-spirits, and the rest, have been dropped. A new mock-heroic element exists, as a part of Fielding's conscious and declared use of the *Aeneid* as his model (*Covent-Garden Journal*, no. 8, 28 January 1752), but where this is really active, deflation or self-deflation by way of parody is no longer the main point. The irony is sombre rather than playful, and uses the heroic in a new way, at times closer to Eliot and Joyce than to Pope, not to suggest, satirically, a modern lapse from ancient grandeurs, so much as a wry, universalizing sense of continuity. It has been well said that the parallel between the amour of Booth and Miss Matthews in prison, and that of Dido and Aeneas, has a Joycean quality.[6]

The abandonment of stylistic high-spirits goes also with a more cautious moral tone, less confident of the sheer power of expansive goodness to triumph in a wicked world. It is both more insecure, and somewhat more prudential, although Booth remains a sort of older Tom Jones, chastened and subdued by hard and nagging troubles, yet still an aristocrat of the good heart whose sexual sins, though they *are* sins, clearly reflect a generosity of temperament on which Fielding uncompromisingly insisted.

The new insecurity, strangely, leads to no necessary slackening of those ordered stylistic patterns which, in the earlier work, helped to convey a strong sense of confidence and of urbane high spirits. In *Amelia*, these patterns are notably and paradoxically in evidence in the great, grim prison-scenes of the opening chapters. Here a new, absurdist note is struck, in which all faith in the fitnesses of an ordered and predictable world seems to have been torn away. Instances of legal injustice monstrously compounded by excruciating cruelties of circumstance, expectations violently wrenched when, for example, a beautiful and innocent-looking woman suddenly bursts into obscene abuse, surround the extraordinary set-piece which follows here:

The first person who accosted him was called Blear-eyed Moll, a woman of no very comely appearance. Her eye (for she had but one), whence she derived her nickname, was such

284

as that nickname bespoke; besides which it had two remarkable qualities; for first, as if Nature had been careful to provide for her own defect, it constantly looked towards her blind side; and secondly, the ball consisted almost entirely of white, or rather yellow, with a little grey spot in the corner, so small that it was scarce discernible. Nose she had none; for Venus, envious perhaps at her former charms, had carried off the gristly part; and some earthly damsel, perhaps, from the same envy, had levelled the bone with the rest of her face: indeed it was far beneath the bones of her cheeks, which rose proportionally higher than is usual. About half a dozen ebony teeth fortified that large and long canal which nature had cut from ear to ear, at the bottom of which was a chin preposterously short, nature having turned up the bottom, instead of suffering it to grow to its due length.

Her body was well adapted to her face; she measured full as much round the middle as from head to foot; for, besides the extreme breadth of her back, her vast breasts had long since forsaken their native home, and had settled themselves a little below the girdle.

I wish certain actresses on the stage, when they are to perform characters of no amiable cast, would study to dress themselves with the propriety with which Blear-eyed Moll was now arrayed. For the sake of our squeamish reader, we shall not descend to particulars; let it suffice to say, nothing more ragged or more dirty was ever emptied out of the round-house at St. Giles's.

We have taken the more pains to describe this person, for two remarkable reasons; the one is, that this unlovely creature was taken in the fact with a very pretty young fellow; the other, which is more productive of moral lesson, is, that however wretched her fortune may appear to the reader, she was one of the merriest persons in the whole prison.

(*Amelia*, I. iii)

The language suggests a grotesquely ironic obsession with fitness and propriety : the nickname matching the appearance, the body 'well adapted' to the face, the 'propriety' with which Moll is arrayed, the balancing operations of Nature, Venus and the rest. The formal completeness of the 'character' goes hand in hand with the self-completing balances and patternings of the prose rhythms, and a great firmness of notation. 'True Ease in Writing', and notions of a harmonious universe, are not so much losing their step, as performing a dance of death.

The final paragraph is notable both for the hard unflinching style, and the almost desperate bewilderment which it conveys. Fielding's earlier style was full of barbed mock-bewilderments. Bewilderment is not his normal state, and where it occurred, it was usually an ironic device over which he had full command, rather than a primary experience which he must come to terms with: one thinks of his puzzlement over Jenny Jones's 'bitterness' at a reflection on her beauty, after she has patiently borne all 'affronts to her chastity'; or over Mrs. Western's litigious fury against Mrs. Honour for merely calling her ugly, whereas she had refused to prosecute a highwayman who had stolen her money and ear-rings, 'at the same time d—ning her, and saying "such handsome b—s as you, don't want jewels to set them off"' (*Tom Jones*, I. vi; VII. ix). Such bewilderments are the ironic instruments of sharp certainty. But in the last paragraph of Moll's 'character' no certainty remains despite the style's hard finish. The 'two remarkable reasons' are almost more shocking because they are not, like the conclusions of some of the other vignettes in these early chapters, in themselves painful. The other examples (the victims of cruel injustice and their appalling suffering, the obscenities of the innocent-looking girl), for all their gratuitous surprises, are still part of a graspable moral theme, concerned with injustice and the topsy-turviness of prison-life: because the surprises are painful, we at least know why we are shocked. The conclusion of Moll's 'character' has, instead, a startling inconsequence whose very element of gaiety contains a touch of the hysterical. Nor are we able to set much store by the suggestion that the second 're-markable reason' is 'productive of moral lesson', although the paradoxical gaiety of prison-life had already been noted just before (it is noted in other prison novels of the time, notably *Moll Flanders*), and certain pieties *might* suggest themselves from this. For no such pieties are in fact entered into, and this 'merriest person' is next seen, immediately after, abusing Booth with 'dreadful oaths', and, in the following chapter, taking part in the gruesome baiting of a homosexual inmate.

The facts can no longer, as the earlier style claimed, be brought under control. They have become too untidy for anything but a kind of desperate shrug. This is not, however, a desperation which merely eschews explanations, so much as one which pointedly refuses them. If fact defies explanation, it is noted in such a way that its outrageousness is starkly highlighted, and the violated expectation still remains as a helpless norm. The style's outward pretences to certainty are if anything stepped up. Despite an occasional faltering of cadence, there is a hardening of witty incisiveness and of the old syntactical symmetries. The irony of this portrait, as of the other exemplary episodes in the prison chapters, is stiffened by a grim patness, as if the unexplainable could only be harnessed by a laconic, but *pointed* factuality. But the characteristic thing is Fielding's feeling, even here, that fact needs to be harnessed, instead of being left to tell its tale in a barer, unmannered (say Defoe-like) narration. And so, organized into pointedly inclusive parables, the brutal forces of an absurd universe meet the Augustan rage for order face to face. The collision produces some of the greatest moments in Augustan literature outside Swift, and if sustained might have altered the history of the novel. Unfortunately, its biographical causes, illness, the cares of magistracy and the painfully direct view of crime which these provided, seem to have produced a demoralization which led, equally logically, to the slackening of the largest part of the novel; and within three years prevented the writing of any more by killing the author off.

*　　*　　*　　*

II

Grotesque portraiture, painful or startling in the strange vitality of its ugliness, splenetically or despondently exuberant in recording weird physicalities of detail, is more Smollett's* province than Fielding's. At least, it is an element which, in the portraits of Moll or of Mrs. Francis (*Voyage to Lisbon*, '19'

* Tobias Smollett was born in 1721 in Dunbartonshire. He attended Dumbarton Grammar School and Glasgow University. He was apprenticed to surgery at Glasgow in 1736, became a surgeon's second mate in the Navy in 1740 and saw service in the Carthagena expedition that year. He subsequently practised as a surgeon in London. Both his medical and his naval experiences are reflected in his novels. In the 1740s he wrote a number of poems, and published a play, *The Regicide*, in 1749, after trying for years to have it produced on the stage. (Another play, *The Reprisal*, was produced and published in 1757.) His first novel, *The Adventures of Roderick Random*, had appeared in 1748; it was followed by *The Adventures of Peregrine Pickle* (1751), *The Adventures of Ferdinand Count Fathom* (1753), *The Adventures of Sir Launcelot Greaves* (serialized in Smollett's new *British Magazine*, 1760–61), and *The Expedition of Humphry Clinker* (1771).

[really 14] July 1754), enters for the most part late in Fielding's writings, and is put to special uses. It is normal in Smollett from the start, almost his usual descriptive idiom, as in these examples, taken virtually at random, from his first (1748) and his fourth (1760–1) novels:

> The apothecary, who was a little old withered man, with a forehead about an inch high, a nose turned up at the end, large cheek-bones that helped to form a pit for his little grey eyes, a great bag of loose skin hanging down on each side in wrinkles like the alforjas of a baboon; and a mouth so accustomed to that contraction which produces grinning, that he could not pronounce a syllable without discovering the remains of his teeth, which consisted of four yellow fangs, not improperly, by anatomists, called *canine* . . .
>
> (*Roderick Random*, ch. XVIII)

> [Crabshaw's] stature was below the middle size; he was thick, squat, and brawny, with a small protuberance on one shoulder, and a prominent belly, which, in consequence of the water he had swallowed, now strutted beyond its usual dimensions. His forehead was remarkably convex, and so very low, that his black bushy hair descended within an inch of his nose; but this did not conceal the wrinkles of his front, which were manifold. His small glimmering eyes resembled those of the Hampshire porker, that turns up the soil with his projecting snout. His cheeks were shrivelled and puckered at the corners, like the seams of a regimental coat as it comes from the hands of the contractor. His nose bore a strong analogy in shape to a tennis-ball, and in colour to a mulberry; for all the water of the river had not been able to quench the natural fire of that feature. His upper

---

During the years of his novel-writing career, he repeatedly visited the Continent, publishing his *Travels through France and Italy* in 1766, and settling in Italy (near Leghorn) from 1768 to his death in 1771.

In 1748 he completed his translation of *Gil Blas*, and in 1755 of *Don Quixote*. In the latter year he began to write *A Complete History of England* (published from 1757 onwards). He worked for the *Critical Review* as editor and reviewer from its foundation in 1756 until 1763, completed *The Present State of all Nations*, 8 vols., in 1768, and was probably the author of the satirical *History and Adventures of an Atom* (1769). He also wrote on medical and political subjects, and engaged in various other journalistic and editorial activities in the 1750s and 1760s.

jaw was furnished with two long white sharp-pointed teeth or fangs, such as the reader may have observed in the chaps of a wolf, or full-grown mastiff, and an anatomist would describe as a preternatural elongation of the *dentes canini*. His chin was so long, so peaked, and incurvated, as to form in profile, with his impending forehead, the exact resemblance of a moon in the first quarter . . .

(*Sir Launcelot Greaves*, ch. II)

There is in these passages none of the emphatic play with notions of natural order and harmony, nor with stylistic forms of neat balance and antithesis, which, in Fielding, reflect not (of course) any simple-minded belief that the universe was a great 'cosmic dance', but a strong aspiration to order, comically or grimly disappointed. Wry allusions to Nature's ordering role, both explicit and implied by pointedly described symmetries and strong syntactical patternings, exist not only in late bitter works like *Amelia* and the *Voyage*, but also in portraits of earlier characters, e.g. Didapper in *Joseph Andrews*, IV. ix, or Mrs. Western in *Tom Jones*, VI. ii (compare the latter with Jerry Melford's description of Tabitha Bramble in *Humphry Clinker*, letter of 6 May, Oxford English Novels, pp. 60–1). Details which Fielding presents as an ironic challenge to a sense of fitness, Smollett presents for their own, abundant, chaotic yet oddly hard and metallic sakes. Occasional suggestions of pictorial symmetry, like the apothecary's 'great bag of loose skin hanging down on each side in wrinkles', exist, like all the other details, only in a world of grotesquely whimsical factu-ality. They readily end on a pattern-subverting note of delighted, explosive concreteness, as here : 'like the alforjas of a baboon'. The effect is simply to annihilate any live suggestion of pattern, rather than, as in Fielding, to emphasise betrayal of expectation by elaborate descriptions of mock-fitness, and a pointed stylistic mimicry of the sense of order.

The types Smollett portrays in such language are sometimes disreputable, and the dehumanizing of the victim in images of animals or things is in some ways a ritual punishment of a kind long familiar in moral satire. But the style's real energies operate less on a level of moral critique than in the cantankerous self-delight of the vision itself. Crabshaw's nose, with its 'strong analogy in shape to a tennis-ball, and in colour to a mulberry', carries little or no moral hostility, but a sense of the huge sheer fun of fantastic ugliness. A similar concreteness of uglifying simile in Fielding's portrait of Mrs. Francis (her complexion 'seemed to be able to turn milk to curds' and 'not a little resembled in colour such milk as had already undergone that operation') is, on the other hand, almost entirely at the service of a moral definition of her unpleasant character. Even Fielding's bare arithmetical details of Didapper's size ('about four foot five inches in height') contribute towards the moral picture of malicious, spindle-shanked effeminacy; whereas Smollett, at his most geometrically abstract ('His forehead was remarkably convex', 'His chin was . . . incurvated . . .') is always close to hard fact as such, the geometric jargon suggesting merely a concreteness re-arranged or re-focused to a fresh precision, momentarily in a rather new-novelish way (but the device is old in comic narrative). And while, in Fielding's writing, there is often a suggestion of leisured commentary, the rhythms not slow but reflective, the descriptions measured and thoughtful, Smollett's, even at its more periphrastic (as at the end of both the apothecary's and Crabshaw's portraits), manages to suggest a brisk efficiency, enjoying the present detail but anxious to pass on to the next, because round the corner of every observation lies the possibility of sudden coruscating enrichments, noses like tennis-balls, chins like the 'moon in the first quarter'.

What we may call, by comparison with Fielding, the pure and unpointed 'factuality' of this style is not, of course, a matter of simple or sober representational realism. It is part of a long tradition of grotesque caricature, of men reduced to things and to animals (and acquiring by that fact a curious blend of automatism and animal vitality, the mechanical, so to speak, turned organic), looking back to before Ben Jonson and forward to Dickens, and particularly strong in Scottish moral and satiric literature 'from Dunbar to Carlyle'; and, as a 'factuality', is correspondingly remote from what A. D. McKillop, in an excellent discussion, has called 'the business-like inventories of Defoe and Richardson'.[7]

Nevertheless, a good deal of Smollett's writing, especially his town scenes and some of the naval ones, are excellent reportage, often edged with a note of anger. To emphasise the harshness of Smollett's writing is probably a mistake, since the anger is one which, when transmuted into such a style, so manifestly enjoys itself. And it seems also wrong to assimilate Smollett too closely to a tradition of moral satire, or to take him at his word when he professes, in the Preface to *Roderick Random*, to aim at arousing 'that generous indignation which ought to animate the reader against the sordid and vicious disposition of the world.' 'Generous indignation' is not his kind of thing, and his writing lacks Juvenalian urgency or any Jonsonian sense of the menace of grotesque mushroomings of folly and vice. Smollett's satire is both too external and too self-enjoying, cantankerous to a degree of fantasticating brilliance, but ultimately shallow, diffuse, and lacking in generous purposes. For this reason, it easily lapses into a form of coy or self-righteous sentimentality, so that he can describe a crisply metallic fiction like *Roderick Random* as attempting 'to represent modest merit struggling with every difficulty to which a friendless orphan is exposed.' The rather unattractive shallowness of his early heroes, Roderick and especially Peregrine Pickle, is sometimes explained by the fact that the tradition of picaresque fiction, to which these early novels partly belong, conventionally focuses attention on rogue escapades rather than on character. This explanation only works up to a point, since (as the Preface to *Roderick* indicates) he aimed, for the purposes of 'generous indignation', to charge the picaresque formula with a human warmth which he found lacking in his admired *Gil Blas*, and seems, in *Peregrine Pickle* (1751), to be making some efforts to achieve a fictional world somewhat like that of *Tom Jones*, more tender and larger-hearted. There is at least, in *Peregrine*, an oscillation between, on the one hand, a high-spirited uncanting presentation of his hero as frankly and callously self-interested, and on the other, a hankering to show him as full of spontaneous benevolence, integrity and even a certain moral delicacy. In a sense, this novel, Smollett's longest and in many ways liveliest, is one half the best of all *Lucky Jim* books, lightly carried, inventive, verbally brilliant, and one half *Tom Jones* manqué.

In such a context, many of the novel's effects are not surprisingly split in two. Pickle's adventures hover between a skeleton of moral action and a relentless extravagance of pure practical joke, the whole oddly unreal and tending to a certain nastiness. There is no Jonesian generosity about his amours, which are either purely perfunctory, or machines for incidents of bedroom farce. His treatment of Emilia Gauntlet is, of course, avowedly unworthy, but when Smollett intrudes to tell us so, the result has a mealy-mouthed and get-it-over-with air :

> Sorry am I, that the task I have undertaken, lays me under the necessity of divulging this degeneracy in the sentiments of our imperious youth, who was now in the heyday of his blood, flushed with the consciousness of his own qualifica-

tions, vain of his fortune, and elated on the wings of imaginary expectation. Tho' he was deeply enamoured of miss
Gauntlet, he was far from proposing her heart as the ultimate
aim of his gallantry, which (he did not doubt) would triumph
o'er the most illustrious females of the land, and at once
regale his appetite and ambition.

(Peregrine Pickle, ch. LXXI)

The authorial intrusion is rare, as it is perfunctory. Smollett
gibed (ch. CV) at Fielding's intrusions as 'paultry shifts, in order
to eke out the volume', but the lack of a steadily established
authorial presence makes his own appearance on this occasion
fussy and distasteful. Instead of the sensitively pondered sexual
ethic established by Fielding through all the resonances of his
style, plot and commentary, there is here an unresolved ambiguity between censorious disapproval, and a winking readiness to sentimentalize wild oats ('imperious youth', 'heyday of
his blood' etc.). When Smollett takes a real plunge in the latter
direction, the link between libertine passions and good nature is
asserted not, as in *Tom Jones*, by a fully established sense of
the value of outgoingness and mutuality, and a tender as well as
hardheaded insistence on the responsibilities which attend even
passing amours, but by facile avuncular commonplaces which
the chuckling humour does not improve :

[Tom Clarke] was so replete with human kindness, that as
often as an affecting story or circumstance was told in his
hearing, it overflowed at his eyes. Being of a warm complexion, he was very susceptible of passion, and somewhat
libertine in his amours.

(Sir Launcelot Greaves, ch. I)

Smollett's third novel, *Ferdinand Count Fathom* (1753), also
invites (and has often received) comparison with Fielding. It is
his only novel with a purely vicious hero, and critics often
treat it as a counterpart to *Jonathan Wild*. Sir Walter Scott
noted in his Life of Smollett that Smollett's hero is realistically
presented as 'a living and existing miscreant', while Fielding's
is 'a cold personification of the abstract principle of evil' who
at times is more tiresome than terrible.[8] I have argued earlier
that Wild emerges as less than terrible, not because he is tire-
somely simplified or 'cold', but because he is almost genially
fantasticated. Scott's comment (unusual among critics in his
preference for Smollett's novel, not in his view of Wild's character) seems a good example of the way critics form their view of

Wild not on the character in action, nor on the genially oafish grandiloquence which surrounds him, but on the abstract verbal harping of the author on the official satiric scheme.

But it is certainly true that Fathom is more realistically treated. His criminal ingenuities are sober, controlled and plausible, not, like Wild's, frenetic, compulsive and bordering on absurdity. Like Wild, Fathom has his share of tribulations and is sometimes 'gulled by the party he intended to gull',[9] but these seem the normal scrapes of an adventurer, and have nothing resembling the relentless clockwork routine of Wild's continuous failures (as though a clown were being knocked down again every time he tried to rise). When Fathom absconds from his Tyrolese accomplice with a booty of jewels, and finds that the Tyrolese has outwitted him by substituting a 'a parcel of rusty nails' (ch. XX), we recall Wild's discomfiture at La Ruse's similar substitution of counterfeit jewels (*Jonathan Wild*, II. iii). But where Smollett speaks factually of the nails, of Fathom's anger, of his coming to terms with the situation, Fielding reminds us of the jewels worn in drollic plays, adds some comic mock-mythology, and closes with a blowsily high-flown humiliation of the hero at the hands of the indignant (and faithless) Laetitia. Laetitia, indeed, is always reducing Wild to the level of a chastened schoolboy, whereas Fathom is reasonably successful with women, a fairly attractive and efficient wooer. Moreover, though Fathom's sexual appetites are strong, they are restrained both by expediency and by sheer normality, whereas Wild's appetites have an extravagant and absurd excessiveness. Both Wild and Fathom are caught out in the end, but Wild, in keeping with the novel's whole style, is given a mock-apotheosis by hanging, whereas Fathom crudely, sentimentally repents. Those critics who, unlike Scott, prefer Fielding's novel, sometimes do *Fathom* less than justice. It has a genuine directness of movement, something like Smollett's usual vitality of notation, and rather more indignation of a convincing kind than the earlier work. But the note of hard realism is in the end too strident. It is Smollett's insistence on this, and not Fielding's comic modulations, that become tiresome. As in other places, the anger easily becomes sentimental. Not only the soft ending, but the general devolution of the novel's second half into a 'romantic tale' are, as Robert Alter says, 'as disastrous a failure of imagination as any novelist of stature has ever been guilty of'.[10]

And so, with a tendency to simplify his morality into declaratory or formulaic patterns, making it seem super-added and faintly trifling, rather than, as in Fielding, passionately, wittily fused into every sentence of the writing, it is not surprising to find Smollett mellowing into the overstated postures of the cult of sensibility. *Sir Launcelot Greaves* (1760–61) is a novel of real liveliness and buoyancy, offering a formula of delightfully fantastic possibilities (a Quixote of the eighteenth century, *mutandis non mutatis*, since, to the unnecessary discomfiture of some readers, he actually wears armour) and containing a good deal of the kind of energetic writing described earlier, but drenched in preposterous excesses of insane tenderheartedness and flowing tears.

The cult of sensibility had entered fiction several decades earlier. An interest in the analysis, indulgence and display of the emotional life, was a matter of fashionable posture throughout the middle and late years of the century. It gave rise to many absurdities, in life and in literature, as well as to a real flowering of humanitarian ideals and philanthropic action. None of the major eighteenth-century novelists can be thought of as reflecting the cult of sensibility in any simple or crude sense, but equally none after Defoe escaped a real and important involvement with it. Richardson's close detailing of feelings, his (and at times Fielding's) dwelling on emotionally 'interesting' situations, the immediacy ('to the moment') of Richardson's epistolary narrative, Fielding's conception of virtue as a spontaneous and warm-hearted benevolence, and his peculiar blend of parody, humour and moral passion, may not have made their novels 'sentimental' in the strict sense, but certainly exercised a powerful influence on the 'sentimental' novels of the 1760s and 1770s. This is true not only of minor fiction, but of respectable and still readable achievements like Goldsmith's *The Vicar of Wakefield* (1766) and Mackenzie's *The Man of Feeling* (1771), and of the great experiments of Sterne and Rousseau's *Nouvelle Héloïse* (1761). Smollett did not escape these influences (and in some ways he added his own). Nor, though he was of all these novelists the one with the hardest surface, did he escape, as we saw, a progressive encroachment of 'sensibility' upon his novels. (In some ways, he had dabbled, several years before Walpole's *Castle of Otranto*, 1764, with that more extreme form of 'sentimental' expressionism, Gothic horror. Elements of this exist as early as *Roderick Random*, 1748, and very notably in *Ferdinand Count Fathom*, 1753.) What he failed to do was to assimilate 'sensibility' fully into his creative personality, so that it often seems, in the novels, a matter of somewhat external gesturing.

His last novel, *Humphry Clinker* (1771), where its presence is strongest and where a real attempt is made to express a mellowed and more or less thorough-going benevolism, still suffers from a kind of emotional facility; and despite its real if superficial charm, seems to me often over-rated. It is a 'sentimental' travelogue (frequently readable and informative as reportage of eighteenth-century life in several parts of Britain, including Smollett's own Scotland) with a thin romantic plot, written in the form of letters by an affectionately portrayed group of characters, some of whom take to its utmost limits that coy eighteenth-century genre, the misspelt, malapropist letter, so that a significant part of the novel is merely an extension of the same trivial joke. The epistolary technique is used without much real point. It explores only superficially a limited range of (not very searching) points of view, and lacks any vital relationship to character or action. The interplay of the several letter-writers' outlooks serves less to deepen understanding than to indulge or variegate Smollett's play with the small collection of whimsical postures which they stand for. The principal character, Matthew Bramble, is simultaneously 'misanthrope' ('my misanthropy increases every day—The longer I live, I find the folly and the fraud of mankind grow more and more intolerable', p. 47) and Man of Feeling (his 'peevishness' itself arising 'partly from a natural excess of mental sensibility', p. 17), thus bringing into a coy and explicit combination two forms of shallowness which are never, really, far below the surface of Smollett's other writings.

1. Parts of this essay belong to work in progress, to be published later in a different form. A number of passages also draw on previously published material: 'Professor Empson's *Tom Jones*,' *Notes and Queries*, cciv (1959), 400–4; three essays in *Eighteenth-Century Studies*, i (1967) and iii (1970); and *Henry Fielding*, Profiles in Literature, London, Routledge, 1968. Acknowledgments are due to Messrs. Routledge, and to the editors and publishers (Oxford University Press, University of California Press) of the two journals. © C. J. Rawson throughout.

2. See especially Allan Wendt, 'The Moral Allegory of *Jonathan Wild*,' *ELH*, xxiv (1957), 306–20. In the Preface to the *Miscellanies* (where the novel first appeared), Fielding speaks of the 'great and good' as the 'true sublime in human nature . . . the Iliad of Nature.' He describes it as a rare gift, and one readily admits that there is nothing 'sublime' about Heartfree, especially when compared with Socrates or Brutus, Fielding's two named examples of the great and good conjoined (*Works*, ed. Henley, xii. 245). The argument of the Preface is anyway at best an *ex post facto* rationalization of the novel. The starkness of the contrast within the novel between Wild's vicious 'greatness' and Heartfree's long-suffering, victimized 'goodness' leaves little room for any deliberate exploration of Heartfree's deficiencies to assert itself, and the irritations with Heartfree which the reader feels seem to me not under Fielding's control. The novel is not sufficiently subtly organized to permit deliberate and systematic complications of its formulaic pattern, and gives no 'great and good' character who might act as a point of reference, nor any strong explicit hint that Heartfree's deficiencies are a serious concern within the tale. I suspect that the critics' argument that the novel is concerned to expose such deficiencies is a wishful abstraction, just as Fielding's mention in the Preface (*Works*, xii. 246) of Heartfree's 'too little of parts or courage to have any pretensions to greatness' is mere common-sense after the event and in a context of general moralizing.

3. 'If you have seen all this, then kiss mine A[rs]e,' the last line of a poem, 'To all Curious Criticks and Admirers of Metre,' published in Rochester's *Poems*, 1680, but probably not by him.

4. 'Tom Jones,' *Kenyon Review*, xx (1958), rep. in *Fielding: A Collection of Critical Essays*, ed. R. Paulson, Englewood Cliffs, N.J., 1962, p. 124.

5. *Correspondence of Horace Walpole*, ed. W. S. Lewis and others, xxii (New Haven, 1960), 271; *Complete Letters of Lady Mary Wortley Montagu*, ed. R. Halsband, 3 vols., Oxford, 1965–67, iii. 90, 97.

6. George Sherburn, 'Fielding's *Amelia*: An interpretation,' *ELH*, iii (1936), 1–14, rep. in Paulson, ed. cit., see p. 148.

7. *The Early Masters of English Fiction*, Lawrence, Kansas, 1956, pp. 152–3, 157–8.

8. *Sir Walter Scott on Novelists and Fiction*, ed. Ioan Williams, London, 1968, p. 67.

9. Ronald Paulson, *Satire and the Novel in Eighteenth-Century England*, New Haven and London, 1967, p. 188.

10. *Rogue's Progress. Studies in the Picaresque Novel*, Cambridge, Mass., 1964, p. 76.

BIBLIOGRAPHY

A *Fielding*

1 *Editions* (for plays see bibliography to chapter 6).

Complete Works, ed. W. E. Henley, London, 1903, 16 vols. Not complete nor very accurate, but best now available. The 'Wesleyan Edition' of Fielding's works, now in progress, will supersede Henley. One volume, *Joseph Andrews*, ed. Martin C. Battestin, Oxford, 1967, has been published, and is excellently annotated.

Joseph Andrews (1742), ed. Martin C. Battestin, Riverside Editions, Boston, 1961, and London, 1965. Available in England with, and in the U.S.A. with or without, *Shamela* (1741). Excellent notes, and easily the best edition for undergraduate or general reader; for definitive scholarly edition, see 'Wesleyan Edition' above.

Jonathan Wild (1743; revised 1754). Many modern editions, none outstandingly good.

The True Patriot: and The History of Our Own Times (periodical, 1745–46), ed. Miriam A. Locke, London, 1965.

Tom Jones (1749), ed. R. P. C. Mutter, Penguin English Library, London, 1966. Useful annotation. Many other editions.

Amelia (1751), Everyman's Library, London and New York, 1930 and reprints. Original introduction by George Saintsbury; in current reprints, by A. R. Humphreys.

Covent-Garden Journal (periodical, 1752), ed. G. E. Jensen, New Haven, 1915. Full annotation.

Journal of a Voyage to Lisbon (1755), ed. Harold E. Pagliaro, New York, 1963. Annotation.

The Criticism of Henry Fielding, ed. Ioan Williams, London, 1970.

II *Biographical Studies*

Cross, Wilbur L., *The History of Henry Fielding*, New Haven, 1918, 3 vols. Standard biography.

Dudden, F. Holmes, *Henry Fielding, His Life, Works and Times*, 2 vols, Oxford, 1952.

III *Critical Studies*

Alter, Robert, *Rogue's Progress. Studies in the Picaresque Novel*, Cambridge, Mass., 1964. Chapter on *Tom Jones* (and another on *Roderick Random*).

—— *Fielding and the Nature of the Novel*, Cambridge, Mass., 1968.

Battestin, Martin C., *The Moral Basis of Fielding's Art. A Study of Joseph Andrews*, Middletown, 1959.

Battestin, Martin C., ed. *Twentieth Century Interpretations of Tom Jones. A Collection of Critical Essays*, Englewood Cliffs, 1968. Reprints essays and extracts from books by F. R. Leavis, Ian Watt, William Empson, Andrew Wright, R. S. Crane, Wayne C. Booth, Robert Alter.

Blanchard, F. T., *Fielding the Novelist. A Study in Historical*

Criticism, New Haven and London, 1926. Surveys critical reactions to the novels, from the 1740s onwards.

Butt, John, *Fielding*, Writers and their Work, No. 59, London and New York, revised edition, 1959. Best brief guide.

Digeon, A., *Les Romans de Fielding*, Paris, 1923; trs. *The Novels of Fielding*, London, 1925. Still useful as a general study.

Ehrenpreis, Irvin, *Fielding: Tom Jones*, London, 1964. A good brief study, with excellent comments on authorial 'presence', tone, etc.

Ford, Ford Madox, *The March of Literature*, New York, 1938, and London, 1939. Lively hostile comments, fuller than in Ford's *The English Novel*, Philadelphia, 1929, and London, 1930 (also deals with Smollett).

Goldberg, H., 'Comic Prose Epic or Comic Romance : The Argument of the Preface to *Joseph Andrews*,' *Philological Quarterly*, xliii (1964), 193–215. Valuable controversial discussion.

Golden, Morris, *Fielding's Moral Psychology*, Amherst, 1966.

Hatfield, Glenn W., *Henry Fielding and the Language of Irony*, Chicago and London, 1968. Useful recent book, one of several on Fielding's irony. Chapter V contains one of the best expressions of a view of 'prudence' in *Tom Jones* opposite to that argued here.

Irwin, W. R., *The Making of Jonathan Wild*, New York, 1941. Informative background to the novel.

McKillop, A. D., *The Early Masters of English Fiction*, Lawrence, 1956; London, 1962. Best introduction to the subject known to me, with good chapters on both Fielding and Smollett.

Miller, Henry Knight, *Essays on Fielding's Miscellanies. A Commentary on Volume One*, Princeton, 1961. Far more important and central than title indicates. Excellent index worth looking up on almost any topic of interest to students of Fielding.

Paulson, Ronald, ed., *Fielding: A Collection of Critical Essays*, Englewood Cliffs, 1962. Reprints essays and extracts from books by A. R. Humphreys, Winfield H. Rogers, Ian Watt (on *Shamela* and on *Tom Jones*), Maynard Mack, Mark Spilka, A. Digeon, André Gide, Arnold Kettle, J. Middleton Murry, William Empson, George Sherburn, and John S. Coolidge.

—— *Satire and the Novel in Eighteenth-Century England*, New Haven and London, 1967. Lively and wide-ranging.

—— and T. Lockwood, *Henry Fielding: The Critical Heritage*, London and New York, 1969.

Scott, Walter, *Sir Walter Scott on Novelists and Fiction*, ed. Ioan Williams, London, 1968. Contains extracts from lives of Fielding and Smollett, and other useful material.

Sherburn, George, 'Fielding's Social Outlook,' *Philological Quarterly*, xxxv (1956), 1–23. Reprinted in *Eighteenth-Century English Literature. Modern Essays in Criticism*, ed. James L. Clifford, New York, 1959.

Spector, R. D., ed., *Essays on the Eighteenth-Century Novel*, Bloom-
ington and London, 1965. Reprints essays on Fielding by Frank
Kermode, Mark Spilka and R. S. Crane (and on Smollett by
Robert Alter and Sheridan Baker).

Thackeray, W. M., 'Hogarth, Smollett, and Fielding,' *English
Humourists of the Eighteenth Century*, 1853. An interesting
and lively mid-Victorian view. Of several briefer comments by
Thackeray, the best-known is in the Preface to *Pendennis*, 1850.

Watt, Ian, *The Rise of the Novel*, Berkeley, Los Angeles and London, 1957. Very important and controversial book.

West, Rebecca, 'The Great Optimist,' *The Court and the Castle*,
New Haven, 1957, and London, 1958. A vivid and individual
essay, concentrating on *Amelia*.

Williams, Ioan, ed., *Novel and Romance 1700–1800: A Documentary
Record*, London, 1970.

Zirker, Malvin R., Jr., *Fielding's Social Pamphlets*, Berkeley and Los
Angeles, 1966. A study of the legal-sociological writings of
Fielding's last years, and an important account of his social
outlook.

B *Smollett*

I *Editions*

There is no authoritative modern edition of Smollett's works. Those
by George Saintsbury, London, 1895, W. E. Henley, London and
New York, 1899–1901, and G. H. Maynadier, New York, 1902
(all three in 12 vols.), and the Shakespeare Head Edition of the
Novels, Oxford, 1925–26, 11 vols., may be used until superseded. Good modern texts exist for two novels (see below).

Roderick Random (1748). Many modern editions, none scholarly.

Peregrine Pickle (1751), ed. James L. Clifford, Oxford English Novels,
London, New York and Toronto, 1964. Important edition textually, and useful introduction and notes.

Ferdinand Count Fathom (1753).

Sir Launcelot Greaves (published serially in *British Magazine*,
1760–61).

Travels through France and Italy (1766), ed. T. Seccombe, World's
Classics, London, New York and Toronto, 1907; Chiltern
Library, London, 1949, introduction by Osbert Sitwell.

History and Adventures of an Atom (1769). Political satire, probably
by Smollett.

Humphry Clinker (1771), ed. Lewis M. Knapp, Oxford English
Novels, London, New York and Toronto, 1966. Authoritative
scholarly edition. Another usefully annotated (paperback) edition, by André Parreaux, Riverside Editions, Boston, 1968. There
is a Penguin edition by Angus Ross, 1967. Many modern reprints.

Letters of Tobias Smollett, M.D., ed. Edward S. Noyes, Cambridge,
Mass., 1926.

II Biography

Knapp, Lewis M., *Tobias Smollett: Doctor of Men and Manners*, Princeton, 1949.

III Critical Studies

(see also Fielding section, under Alter's *Rogue's Progress*, Ford, McKillop, Paulson on *Satire and the Novel*, Scott, Spector, Thackeray).

Boege, Fred W., *Smollett's Reputation as a Novelist*, Princeton, 1947.

Giddings, Robert, *The Tradition of Smollett*, London, 1967. Inaccurate. Some insights. Partly studies Smollett in the light of later novels, notably John Barth's *Sot-Weed Factor*, 1960.

Kahrl, George M., *Tobias Smollett, Traveller-Novelist*, Chicago, 1945.

Martz, Louis L., *The Later Career of Tobias Smollett*, New Haven, 1942. Analysis of later works, chiefly the *Travels*, *History and Adventures of an Atom*, and *Humphry Clinker*.

9

LAURENCE STERNE

Ian Jack, Pembroke College, Cambridge

The history of prose fiction is a history of statement and counter-statement, of stimulus and reaction, of challenge and response. But for the chivalric romances, Cervantes would not have written *Don Quixote*. But for *Pamela*, Fielding would not have written *Joseph Andrews*. But for Mrs. Radcliffe and her followers, Jane Austen would not have written *Northanger Abbey*. Laurence Sterne was the last of the major novelists of the eighteenth century to turn his attention to fiction, and *Tristram Shandy* could never have been written but for the preceding work of Richardson, Fielding and Smollett. Sterne's famous book stands as a sort of large and irreverent question-mark at the end of the first confident chapter in the history of the English Novel.

If we wish to understand Sterne it is useful to recall one or two facts about his early life. He was born in Ireland in the year 1713, the son of an improvident soldier who came from a gifted and hard-headed family which had produced an Archbishop of York (a great-grandfather of the novelist). Sterne disliked his mother, who may have been partly of French descent; but he idolized his father, and his early memories of Ensign Sterne and of the military humours that came under his observation as he accompanied his mother in the wake of his father's regiment remained to stimulate his imagination when he became a novelist in the last decade of his life. At Cambridge, where we are told that he 'read a little, laugh'd a great deal, and sometimes took the diversion of puzzling his tutors', he became friendly with John Hall (later Hall-Stevenson), a wealthy young man of dissipated habits whose home at Skelton Castle (nicknamed 'Crazy Castle') he was often to visit. The great comic writers have almost all been men of wide reading, and to this rule Sterne is no exception. His favourite writers included

Horace, Rabelais, Erasmus, Cervantes and Swift, while he was a great reader of the *Essays* of Montaigne and of Burton's *Anatomy of Melancholy*. He knew the Bible intimately, as his *Sermons* bear witness,[1] and was an admirer of 'the sagacious Locke', whose theory of 'the association of ideas' lies behind *Tristram Shandy*.[2]

In view of his family background it was natural (if hardly a matter of vocation) that Sterne should have entered the church, as he did in 1738. Although his vicarage was at Sutton-on-the Forest he preferred to live in York, which was then a centre of church politics and of fashionable life. He often preached in York, and although he had a weak voice he enjoyed considerable success as a preacher: his writings bear witness to his careful study of the arts of declamation and gesture. It was an ecclesiastical controversy which led indirectly to his writing the most curious of novels. About the year 1758, as Sterne later told a friend, 'a squabble breaking out at York ... he sided with the Dean and his friends, and tried to throw the laugh on the other party, by writing the History of an Old Watchcoat'. *A Political Romance*, in which he attacks an arrogant man who had drawn into his own hands most of the lucrative legal offices connected with the diocese of York, is a skilful burlesque by a man who was interested in the theory and technique of comic writing. 'The happiness of the Cervantic humour', Sterne told a correspondent in 1759, the year in which his work was printed, 'arises from ... describing silly and trifling Events, with the Circumstantial Pomp of great Ones'.[3] In his own satire he takes the opposite course, reducing the important diocese of York to an insignificant country parish, the powerful Archbishop to an ordinary parson, and the Dean to his parish clerk. His aim was to reduce the scale of the events he was describing without offending either of these potentates. Dr. Topham, on the other hand, who was a prominent and aggressive person, is rendered ridiculous by being described as the sexton and dog-whipper of the parish. 'Are you not Sexton and Dog-Whipper, worth Three Pounds a Year?', he is asked indignantly:

'—Then you begg'd the Church-Wardens to let your Wife have the Washing and Darning of the Surplice and Church-Linen, which brings you in Thirteen Shillings and Four Pence. —Then you have Six Shillings and Eight Pence for oiling and winding up the Clock ... The Pinder's Place, which is worth Forty Shillings a Year,—you have got that too ... Besides all this, you have Six Pounds a Year . . for being Mole-Catcher to the Parish . . .' (p. 208)

A Political Romance is obviously the work of an admirer of the great satiric writers. The allegory on which the story is based owes something to *A Tale of a Tub* (and we note that a relation of Sterne's had been a close friend of Swift and his Stella); while in the satirical *Key*, in which Sterne introduces a number of friends arguing about the meaning of the pamphlet, we are told that

as great a Variety of Personages, Opinions, Transactions, and Truths, [were] found to lay hid under the dark Veil of its Allegory, as ever were discovered in the thrice-renowned History of the Acts of *Gargantua* and *Pantagruel*. (pp. 221–2)

The introduction of another cause of quarrel between the Archbishop and the Dean—a dispute over the appointment of preachers in the Cathedral, in which Dr. Topham once again makes his appearance—leads Sterne into a clear reminiscence of Boileau's satirical poem, *Le Lutrin*. But most interesting of all is the anticipation of *Tristram Shandy* in the discussion among the members of the club about the meaning of the allegory : each disputant rides his own hobby-horse, and none shows the slightest interest in the views advanced by his fellows.

Unfortunately for Sterne the quarrel was made up before *A Political Romance* could be published, and to avoid further mischief almost every copy was 'committed to the flames'. This explains a passage in a letter from Sterne to a lady who wrote to ask him, one day in 1759, for news of 'an extraordinary book' that he was rumoured to be writing :

Now for your desire of knowing the reason of my turning author? why truly I am tired of employing my brains for other people's advantage.—'Tis a foolish sacrifice I have made for some years to an ungrateful person.[4]

At the age of 45, accordingly, Sterne sat down to write a book for his own advantage, a book which retains (indeed) traces of his earlier preoccupation with parish-pump ecclesiastical politics (the egregious Dr. Topham reappears in *Tristram Shandy* as Didius, 'the great church lawyer'), but which greatly transcends the issues which form the subject-matter of *A Political Romance*.

As soon as we open *Tristram Shandy* we are reminded of *A Tale of a Tub*, with its satire on pedantry, its satire on book-making, its misplaced preface, its rows of asterisks, and its ubiquitous digressions. As it happens, however, the fact that Sterne drew strength from the same satiric tradition as the great Dean of St. Patrick's is best illustrated by the debt of his strange novel to one of the *parerga* of the Scriblerus circle, *Memoirs of the Extraordinary Life, Works, and Discoveries of Martinus Scriblerus*. Here are the headings of the first few chapters:

> Chap. 1. Of the Parentage and Family of *Scriblerus*, how he was begot, what Care was taken of him before he was born, and what Prodigies attended his Birth.
>
> Chap. 2. The Speech of *Cornelius* over his Son, at the Hour of his Birth.
>
> Chap. 3. Shewing what befel the Doctor's Son and his Shield, on the Day of the Christ'ning.
>
> Chap. 4. Of the Suction and Nutrition of the Great *Scriblerus* in his Infancy, and of the first Rudiments of his Learning.[5]

Doctor Cornelius, who traces his ancestry back to Albertus Magnus, Paracelsus Bombastus and the Scaligers, is as interested in the theory of generation as Walter Shandy himself:

> For he never had cohabitation with his spouse, but he ponder'd on the Rules of the Ancients, for the generation of Children of Wit. He ordered his diet according to the prescription of Galen, confining himself and his wife for almost the whole first year to Goat's Milk and Honey.

Later,

> Having discovered that Galen's prescription could not determine the sex [of a child], he forthwith betook himself to Aristotle. Accordingly he withheld the nuptial embrace when the wind was in any point of the South; this Author asserting that the grossness and moisture of the southerly winds occasion the procreation of females, and not of males. But he redoubled his diligence when the wind was at West . . . For our learned man was clearly of opinion, that the Semina out of which Animals are produced, are Animalcula ready formed, and received in with the Air.[6]

Tristram Shandy begins to appear a trifle less unaccountable when it is seen as the culmination of a tradition of learned fooling that stretches back beyond Swift through Erasmus and other writers of the Renaissance and the later Middle Ages.

But the best guide to the nature of Sterne's book is that provided by its title: *The Life and Opinions of Tristram Shandy, Gentleman*. By 1760, when the first two volumes appeared,[7] the reading public had at its disposal a shelf-full of books entitled 'The Life and Adventures' of a varied collection of heroes. Defoe had written *The Life and Strange Surprizing Adventures of Robinson Crusoe*, *The Farther Adventures of Robinson Crusoe*, *The History of the Life and Adventures of Mr. Duncan Campbell*, *The Life, Adventures, and Pyracies of the famous Captain Singleton*, as well as other books with similar titles, while Fielding and Smollett had followed in his wake, as had a number of lesser men. What Sterne is offering us is *The Life and OPINIONS of Tristram Shandy*, and the motto of the first two volumes bears out our initial impression that we are now being presented with a book of a very different sort: 'It is not actions that throw men into confusion, but opinions about actions'.

Tristram Shandy is among other things a critique or comical satire on the English Novel up to its time. In the hands of Sterne's immediate predecessors prose fiction had developed far beyond the point it had reached in the previous century. Yet although the work of Richardson, Fielding and Smollett is splendidly varied, certain common features may be noticed in many of the novels of the mid-century, some of them inherited from the picaresque tradition, some from the earlier prose romance, others again from the ancient conventions of comic writing. Anyone taking up a new novel in the year 1760 would have been likely to expect a description of the fortunes of a young man or woman in the years or months preceding marriage and settling-down: a period of travel, adventure and of cheerful wild oats (in the case of a man) or of virginity heroically defended (in the case of a woman). If the novel was the work of Fielding or Smollett (at least) the reader could rely on plenty of action: pursuits, robberies, fisticuffs, seductions accomplished or averted—a true taste of the violence and crudity of English life in the age of Hogarth. The principal characters were likely to be young and vigorous, and the book might be expected to end in the marriage of the hero and heroine, with whom the reader has been encouraged to identify himself.

None of this is to be found in *Tristram Shandy*, in which Sterne is determined to deny every shred of comfort to the cliché-loving reader. His shock-tactics begin with the opening paragraph of the book:

> I wish either my father or my mother, or indeed both of
> them, as they were in duty both equally bound to it, had
> minded what they were about when they begot me . . . Had
> they duly weighed and considered [the matter], and pro-
> ceeded accordingly,—I am verily persuaded I should have
> made a quite different figure in the world, from that, in which
> the reader is likely to see me. (I. i)

The initial conception (it may be noted in passing) is almost the
only unambiguous evidence of sexual potency in the whole
book, in which practically every male character is accompanied
by an unmistakable suggestion of impotence. In Sterne's book
the middle-aged and elderly characters who had most often
been confined to 'supporting roles' in earlier novels are at last
beckoned to the centre of the stage. This is no story of youthful
love and adventure. So far from being the great object of mascu-
line pursuit, the women are uninteresting, undesirable, and
characterless (like Mrs. Shandy), or a source of frustrated incomprehension (like the Widow Wadman). The most important love-affair in the book is the innocent fraternal affection
between Mr. Shandy and his brother, My Uncle Toby.

The narrator is as fascinated by Mr. Shandy as Boswell was
to be by Samuel Johnson, and 'the progress and establishment
of my father's many odd opinions' is much more truly the
subject of the novel than the opinions of Tristram Shandy.
'An excellent natural philosopher . . . much given to
close reasoning upon the smallest matters' (I. iii), Mr. Shandy
is 'a philosopher in grain,—speculative,—systematical' (I. xxi):

> There was not a stage in the life of man, from the very first
> act of his begetting,—down to the lean and slipper'd panta-
> loon in his second childishness, but he had some favourite
> notion to himself, springing out of it, as sceptical, and as far
> out of the high-way of thinking, as these two which have
> been explained.
>
> (II. xix)

'Like all systematick reasoners, he would move heaven and
earth, and twist and torture every thing in nature to support
his hypothesis' (I. xix). Mr. Shandy's greatest hobby-horse is
Education. Once a child has been rightly begotten, Mr. Shandy
believes that it should be born in the country (not in London),
preferably by Caesarean section (a mode of giving birth to
which his wife has an inexplicable objection)—and in any event
by some form of 'pressureless delivery'. A further matter of

great importance, to which accordingly he has devoted a great deal of consideration, is the proper choice of a name.

As often happens with people who have strong views on Education, Mr. Shandy finds that nothing turns out as he has planned. Whereas he is thrown into dismay (however) by the initial frustration of his intentions, and particularly by the accident by which his son is not christened Trismegistus but Tristram (a name so inauspicious that he has written a pamphlet against it)—there is always another aspect of his character to be reckoned with, his unpredictability :

> As many pictures as have been given of my father, how like him so ever in different airs and attitudes—not one, or all of them, can ever help the reader to any kind of pre-conception of how my father would think, speak, or act, upon any untried occasion or occurrence of life.—There was that infinitude of oddities in him, and of chances along with it, by which handle he would take a thing,—it baffled, Sir, all calculations.—The truth was, his road lay so very far on one side, from that wherein most men travelled,—that every object before him presented a face and section of itself to his eye, altogether different from the plan and elevation of it seen by the rest of mankind.
>
> (V. xxiv)

One remarkable manifestation of this unpredictability is Mr. Shandy's reception of the news that his little son has been circumcised by the fall of a window-sash. It is a scene of magnificent comedy when Yorick and Uncle Toby, with Corporal Trim 'a few paces behind' and Susannah in the rear, form a procession and march to tell Mr. Shandy of the accident that has befallen his son—only to find that the man who has been so deeply distressed by the trivial misfortunes that have so far occurred regards this untoward event as a matter of little importance.[8] The practice of circumcision is of such antiquity that he asks rhetorically : 'Who am I, that I should fret and fume one moment about the matter?' (V. xxvii). Ignoring the accident, therefore, as something beneath the notice of a true philosopher, he proceeds to read aloud the chapter on Health from his own Treatise on Education, the *Tristrapædia*.

It is Mr. Shandy's fortune to have a brother of a very different character—an 'original' (like all his family), but an original of a different cast. When we are presented with a pair of comic characters we often find that the one is clever and dominant (Sir Toby in *Twelfth Night*, for example), the other innocent and 'put-upon' (Sir Andrew), but the relationship between My Father and My Uncle Toby is by no means as simple as that. Although Uncle Toby entirely lacks the eloquence of his brother—as a substitute for argument, indeed, he is in the habit of whistling a tune—and has to admit that he has no more ideas in his head than has his horse, he emerges less as a satiric butt than as a kind of innocent hero. He is not overshadowed by Mr. Shandy, but allowed space and sunshine in which to develop and display his own 'most whimsical character'. At the end of the first volume we are told that he was wounded fighting at the siege of Namur, and in the second volume (of which he is the hero) we hear how the frequent necessity of explaining how he got his wound leads to the development of his great hobby-horse. He becomes an expert on military affairs, and buys 'almost as many . . . books on military architecture, as *Don Quixote* was found to have of chivalry, when the curate and barber invaded his library' (II. iii). Uncle Toby's Sancho Panza, the worthy and resourceful Corporal Trim, suggests that if only they had at their disposal 'a rood, or a rood and a half of ground to do what we pleased with' (II. v) they could lay out a large-scale model of the environs and fortifications of Namur on which Uncle Toby could illustrate his discourse while Trim (as it were) moved the pieces on the board. Trim's suggestion is a momentous one :

> When a man gives himself up to the government of a ruling passion,—or in other words, when his HOBBY-HORSE grows head-strong,—farewell cool reason and fair discretion !
>
> (II. v)

As Uncle Toby's hobby-horse is quite unrelated to his brother's, their attempts at conversation are apt to founder, as invariably occurs when Mr. Shandy tries to explain one of his philosophical concepts :

> Now, whether we observe it or no, continued my father, in every sound man's head, there is a regular succession of ideas of one sort or other, which follow each other in train just like—A train of artillery? said my uncle *Toby*.—A train of a fiddle stick !—quoth my father,—which follow and succeed one another in our minds at certain distances, just like

the images in the inside of a lanthorn turned round by the heat of a candle.

(III. xviii)

'By the mother who bore us!—brother Toby',—as Mr. Shandy breaks out on another occasion—'you would provoke a saint; —here have you got us, I know not how, . . . souse into the middle of the old subject again . . . I wish the whole science of fortification, with all its inventors, at the devil;—it has been the death of thousands,—and it will be mine, in the end' (II. xii).

'If you were to read Richardson for the story', Samuel Johnson once remarked, 'your impatience would be so much fretted that you would hang yourself. But you must read him for the sentiment, and consider the story as only giving occasion to the sentiment'.[9] In the obvious sense of the word *Tristram Shandy* has even less 'story' than *Clarissa* or *Sir Charles Grandison*. At one point Sterne goes so far as to claim that he has written the book

> to rebuke a vicious taste which has crept into thousands. . .— of reading straight forwards, more in quest of the adventures, than of the deep erudition and knowledge which a book of this cast, if read over as it should be, would infallibly impart with them.

(I. xx)

No one has praised digressions more eloquently than Sterne himself :

> Digressions, incontestably, are the sunshine;—they are the life, the soul of reading;—take them out of this book for instance,—you might as well take the book along with them; —one cold eternal winter would reign in every page of it; restore them to the writer;—he steps forth like a bridegroom, —bids All hail; brings in variety, and forbids the appetite to fail.

(I. xxii)

Yet if a digression is defined as a passage in which an author steps aside from the main subject of his book, it is questionable how far the digressions in *Tristram Shandy* are digressions at all : a point which Sterne himself is careful to make immediately after the chapter in which he favours his reader with the words and musical score of his uncle's favourite song, 'Lilliburlero' :

> In this long digression which I was accidentally led into, as

in all my digressions (one only excepted) there is a master-stroke of digressive skill, the merit of which has all along, I fear, been overlooked by my reader . . . and it is this: That tho' my digressions are all fair, as you observe,—and that I fly off from what I am about, as far and as often too as any writer in *Great-Britain*; yet I constantly take care to order affairs so, that my main business does not stand still in my absence . . .

By this contrivance the machinery of my work is of a species by itself; two contrary motions are introduced into it, and reconciled, which were thought to be at variance with each other. In other words, my work is digressive, and it is progressive too,—and at the same time.

(I. xxii)

What Sterne is concerned with is not what happens in the external world of actions and things, but what happens in the minds of his characters (the world of opinions and ideas)—as he makes clear in a famous reference to Locke:

Pray, Sir, in all the reading which you have ever read, did you ever read such a book as *Locke*'s Essay upon the Human Understanding?—Don't answer me rashly,—because many, I know, quote the book, who have not read it,—and many have read it who understand it not:—If either of these is your case, as I write to instruct, I will tell you in three words what the book is.—It is a history.—A history! of who? what? where? when? Don't hurry yourself.—It is a history-book, Sir, (which may possibly recommend it to the world) of what passes in a man's own mind.

(II. ii)

The 'history of what passes in a man's own mind' is not to be written in the prose style of Samuel Johnson—or (for that matter) in that of Henry Fielding: therein lies the justification of Sterne's own prose style, a subtle and flexible medium of expression which enables him to anticipate many of the effects which have more recently been achieved by writers in the 'stream of consciousness' tradition. Here again Sterne may be seen as criticizing the very postulates of his predecessors in the English Novel, and suggesting that the swift and often disconcerting processes of the human mind and heart are unlikely to be captured in a series of balanced, Addisonian sentences. With the difference in style comes a difference of tone. Whereas the tone of Fielding's prose is that of a sensible man—a gentleman with a sound classical education, tolerant yet responsible, the master of a telling irony based on a long tradition of what might be termed public writing—Sterne's tone is much more intimate, confidential and at times button-holing : he addresses himself to a more private part of our consciousness, and his voice is lowered accordingly.

Although he is one of the most original of writers, Sterne is also one of the most derivative. He is derivative not only in the sense that he plagiarises passages from the *Essays* of Montaigne, Burton's *Anatomy of Melancholy*, and many other sources, but also in the deeper sense that he is stimulated by earlier writers to go and do otherwise. Just as *Tristram Shandy* could never have been the first novel—since it implies earlier 'straight' novels which it criticizes and makes fun of—so *A Sentimental Journey* could never have been the first travel book. In volume vii of *Tristram Shandy* Sterne had included 'as odd a tour through France as ever was projected or executed by traveller or travel-writer, since the world began'. The nature of this 'laughing good tempered Satyr against Traveling (as puppies travel)' may be seen from the following passage :

> 'Now before I quit *Calais*,' a travel-writer would say, 'it would not be amiss to give some account of it.'—Now I think it very much amiss—that a man cannot go quietly through a town, and let it alone, when it does not meddle with him ...
>
> For my own part, as heaven is my judge, . . . I know no more of *Calais*, (except the little my barber told me of it, as he was whetting his razor) than I do this moment of *Grand Cairo*; for it was dusky in the evening when I landed, and dark as pitch in the morning when I set out. . . .
>
> (VII. iv)

Sterne's predecessors in the novel had been prominent among the travel-writers of the century. In 1724–7 Defoe had published *A Tour Thro' the Whole Island of Great Britain*, while Fielding's *Journal of a Voyage to Lisbon* had appeared (posthumously) in 1755 and Smollett's *Travels through France and Italy* eleven years later.

One has only to compare the opening of Sterne's Travels with the Travels of his predecessors to see that he brought to his last work the same verve and the same audacity that he had displayed when the first volumes of *Tristram Shandy* had burst on a disconcerted world. Smollett's book begins straightforwardly :

Dear Sir,

   You laid your commands upon me at parting, to communicate from time to time the observations I should make
in the course of my travels, and it was an injunction I received with pleasure.

Fielding's *Journal* opens a little more strikingly:

Wednesday, June 26, 1754. On this day, the most melancholy
sun I had ever beheld arose, and found me awake at my
house at Fordhook.

In marked contrast to these two openings—the pedestrian and
the sombre—is the insouciant abruptness of Sterne's:

   —They order, said I, this matter better in France—
   —You have been in France? said my gentleman turning quick
upon me with the most civil triumph in the world.

After the *andante* and the *largo*, the *scherzo*. The reader might
be forgiven for supposing that Sterne's situation, as he wrote
his book, must have been more cheerful than that of his predecessors. In fact he wrote as a dying man. *A Sentimental
Journey* is a sort of comic *danse macabre*, a minuet danced with
various partners by an amorous *picaro* who knew pretty well
that Death was waiting for him at the end of the dance.

   While it is possible that Sterne made some jottings for his
Journey before he returned to England in 1766, it is certain
that a book published in the spring of that year helped to determine the form taken by his own notably oblique contribution
to the literature of travel. *Travels through France and Italy*,
'Containing Observations on Character, Customs, Religion,
Government, Police, Commerce, Arts, and Antiquities. With a
particular Description of the Town, Territory, and Climate of
Nice. To which is added A Register of the Weather, kept during
a Residence of Eighteen Months in that City'—such is the
pompous title of Smollett's *Travels*, to which he added (for
good measure) the letters 'M. D.' after his name, and a Latin
motto from Ennius. Sterne clearly determined not to imitate
the pomposity of Smollett—and to avoid at all costs the
querulous tone so common in travel books written by ailing
Englishmen:

   I pity the man who can travel from *Dan* to *Beersheba*, and
cry, 'Tis all barren—and so it is; and so is all the world to
him who will not cultivate the fruits it offers.

                                                        (p. 28)

Sterne would not be a Splenetic Traveller (like Smollett), but a Sentimental Traveller.

The word was of recent origin. 'What, in your opinion, is the meaning of the word *sentimental*, so much in vogue among the polite?', Lady Bradshaigh had asked Richardson: '... Every thing clever and agreeable is comprehended in that word ... I am frequently astonished to hear such a one is a *sentimental* man; we were a *sentimental* party; I have been taking a *sentimental* walk.' More than twenty years later the word could still be unacceptable to a purist, as we know from a comment on the title of Sterne's book in the *Journal* of John Wesley: '*Sentimental*! what is that? It is not English; he might as well say, *Continental*. It is not sense. It conveys no determinate idea ...'[10] Whether or not the word conveyed any 'determinate idea' before the appearance of Sterne's *Journey*, it certainly bore a fairly precise meaning thereafter, and it is evident that the conception it embodied had been particularly important to him in the early stages of the composition of the book.

The chorus of disapproval which had greeted the later volumes of *Tristram Shandy* had disconcerted its author. One reviewer gave it as his opinion that the true excellence of the book 'lay in the PATHETIC' episodes, while another summed the matter up in the following way:

> In my opinion, the little story of Le Fevre has done you more honour than every thing else you have wrote, except your Sermons. Suppose you were to strike out a new plan? Give us none but amiable or worthy, or exemplary characters; or, if you will, to enliven the drama, throw in the *innocently humorous* ... Paint Nature in her loveliest dress— her native simplicity ... In fine, Mr. Shandy ... excite our passions to *laudable* purposes ... Let morality, let the cultivation of virtue be your aim—let wit, humour, elegance and pathos be the means.[11]

It is interesting to notice that the first person to comment on *A Sentimental Journey* while it was being written, a certain Richard Griffith, wrote as follows:

> It has all the Humour and Address of the best Parts of Tristram, and is quite free from the Grossness of the worst. There is but about Half a Volume of it wrote yet. He promises to spin the Idea through several Volumes in the same chaste way, and calls it his *Work of Redemption.* ...[12]

The most celebrated ingredient of the book is the series of Pathetic Vignettes—the highly-wrought yet apparently simple passages describing The Monk (Calais), The Dead Ass (Nampont), The Dwarf (with the description of the kindly French officer), The Starling, Le Patisser (the aristocratic beggar), The Sword, Maria (Moulines), and—perhaps the most delightful of all—The Supper, where Yorick is the guest of a family of simple French peasants, and sees 'Religion mixing in the dance'. These are precisely the sort of scenes that the reviewers had called for, and their popularity is proved by the existence of numerous volumes of *Beauties of Sterne*, as well as imitations and translations in many of the languages of the world.

Besides these Pathetic incidents, however—or rather, interspersed between them—we come on episodes of a different nature. In such passages as the description of Yorick's setting out, his first meeting with La Fleur, his buying a wig in Paris, his journey to Versailles in search of a passport—in such passages there is little or nothing of the Pathetic, and Yorick appears simply as a quizzical and observant traveller, jotting down amusing or illuminating incidents that befell him on his journey:

> I think I can see the precise and distinguishing marks of national characters more in these nonsensical *minutiæ*, than in the most important matters of state; where great men of all nations talk and stalk so much alike, that I would not give ninepence to chuse amongst them.

(p. 50)

In these passages, and in such more overtly satirical passages as those in which Yorick describes the beggar who approaches only women, and his meeting with the sexually ambiguous Count de Faineant, we see a different side of Sterne's character, and sense that we may be dealing with material that has a closer relationship with biographical fact than in the Pathetic episodes.

There is also a third ingredient in this simple-seeming book, an ingredient which Sterne no doubt proscribed as he sat down to write but which found its way back to his pages in spite of his good resolutions. It is interesting that he alludes to this ingredient only when the book is almost completed. 'If it is not thought a chaste book', he commented to one correspondent in November 1767, only a few weeks before *A Sentimental Journey* reached publication, 'mercy on them that read it, for they must have warm imaginations indeed!' A few days later he promises Sir George Macartney 'a *couple of as clean brats* as ever chaste brain conceiv'd', adding (however) 'they are frolicksome too, *mais cela n'empeche pas*'.[13] This third ingredient is of course Yorick's descriptions of his encounters with women. Yorick tells us that it 'had ever . . . been one of the singular blessings of my life, to be almost every hour of it miserably in love with some one' (p. 43), and the account of his travels abundantly bears this out. Near the beginning of the book he observes, with all the emphasis of italic type, that '*an English man does not travel to see English men*' (p. 13), and almost immediately afterwards—when he encounters the charming young Frenchwoman at Calais, as he negotiates to hire a coach—there enters the first of the women and girls who make their way, charmingly, tantalisingly, elusively, provocatively, through the pages of this most unusual 'Work of Redemption'. Without the coquettish young woman from whom Yorick buys a pair of gloves, taking care to feel her pulse as he does so, and the fille de chambre whom he encounters in the bookshop and who later accompanies him to his hotel, and the enigmatic heroine of 'A Case of Delicacy' at the end—without these, *A Sentimental Journey* would lack some of its most characteristic episodes, and a good deal of its flavour. The danger of The Pathetic is that it so easily subsides into The Insipid—as Sterne's imitators so often inadvertently demonstrated. He himself avoids this danger by insisting on the connection between Sentiment and sexual feeling,[14] and so giving admission to a group of desirable young women who add an element of mischievous eroticism to a book that ends as brilliantly and as audaciously as his other famous novel had begun. Sterne is the great English master of the filibuster, yet it can never be said of him that he did not know when to leave off.

1. The often-quoted phrase, 'God tempers the wind to the shorn lamb,' occurs for the first time in *A Sentimental Journey*. See *A Sentimental Journey through France and Italy by Mr. Yorick to which are added The Journal to Eliza and A Political Romance*, ed. Ian Jack, London, 1968, Oxford English Novels, p. 115. This is the edition cited hereafter.

2. It should be mentioned that some experts on Sterne now consider that the influence of Locke on his work has been greatly exaggerated. 'If it lies behind *Tristram Shandy*'—they would comment—'it lies a long way behind it.'

3. *Letters*, ed. L. P. Curtis, Oxford, 1935, p. 77.

4. *Ibid.*, p. 84.

5. *Memoirs of Martinus Scriblerus*, ed. C. Kerby-Miller, New Haven, 1950, p. 89.

6. Ibid., pp. 96–7.

7. Later volumes were published as follows: III–IV (Jan. 1761); V–VI (Dec. 1761, dated '1762'); VII–VIII (Jan. 1765); IX (Jan. 1767). See Wayne Booth, 'Did Sterne complete *Tristram Shandy*?', *Modern Philology*, xlviii (1950–51), 172–83, for a discussion of the ending.

8. It is just possible that more happens to Tristram than circumcision, but Sterne characteristically leaves the matter uncertain.

9. James Boswell, *Life of Johnson*, ed. G. B. Hill, revised L. F. Powell, Oxford, 1934–50, ii. 175.

10. *Correspondence of Samuel Richardson*, ed. Mrs. A. L. Barbauld, 6 vols., London, 1804, iv. 282; John Wesley, *Journal*, 4 vols., London, 1864, iii. 429 (11 Feb. 1772).

11. *Monthly Review*, xxxii (1765), 138–9.

12. Elizabeth and Richard Griffith, *A Series of Genuine Letters, between Henry and Frances*, 6 vols., London, 1786, v. 83.

13. *Letters*, pp. 403, 405.

14. 'If ever I do a mean action, it must be in some interval betwixt one passion and another: whilst this interregnum lasts, I always perceive my heart locked up—I can scarcely find in it, to give Misery a sixpence; and therefore I always get out of it as fast as I can, and the moment I am re-kindled, I am all generosity and good will again' (p. 34).

BIBLIOGRAPHY

I *Editions*

The Works, ed. W. L. Cross, 12 vols., New York, 1904.

The Works ('Shakespeare Head Edition'), 7 vols., Oxford, 1926–7.

Tristram Shandy, ed. James A. Work, New York, 1940. A most useful edition, with helpful introduction and notes; also available in paperback. Other paperback editions by Ian Watt, Boston, 1965; and G. Petrie, with introduction by C. Ricks, Penguin English Library, London, 1967.

A Sentimental Journey, ed. Gardner D. Stout, Berkeley, California, 1967. The standard edition.

A Sentimental Journey, with *The Journal to Eliza and A Political Romance*, ed. Ian Jack, London, 1968, 'Oxford Standard Novels'. Useful because it includes Sterne's scarce first satire.

Letters, ed. L. P. Curtis, Oxford, 1935. Indispensable : also includes *The Journal to Eliza* and full annotation.

II *Biographical and Critical Studies*

Cash, Arthur Hill, *Sterne's Comedy of Moral Sentiments: The Ethical Dimension of the 'Journey'*, Pittsburgh, 1966.

Cross, Wilbur L., *The Life and Times of Laurence Sterne*, 3rd edn., New Haven, 1929. Still the best book on Sterne, as biography and general criticsm, though out-of-date here and there.

Curtis, L. P., *The Politicks of Laurence Sterne*, Oxford, 1929.

Dilworth, E. N., *The Unsentimental Journey of Laurence Sterne*, New York, 1948.

Ferriar, John, *Illustrations of Sterne*, London, 1798; 2nd edn., 2 vols., 1812. Interesting as the first source-study of an English novelist.

Fluchère, Henri, *Laurence Sterne: de l'homme à l'œuvre*, Paris, 1961; translated and abridged by Barbara Bray, London, 1965.

Fredman, Alice G., *Diderot and Sterne*, New York, 1955.

Hammond, L. Van der H., *Laurence Sterne's 'Sermons of Mr. Yorick,'* New Haven, 1948.

Hartley, L., *Laurence Sterne in the Twentieth Century: An Essay and a Bibliography*, Chapel Hill, North Carolina, 1966.

Howes, A. B., *Yorick and the Critics: Sterne's Reputation in England, 1760–1868*, New Haven, 1958.

Stedmond, John M., *The Comic Art of Laurence Sterne*, Toronto, 1967.

Traugott, John, *Tristram Shandy's World: Sterne's Philosophical Rhetoric*, Berkeley, California, 1954.

Laurence Sterne: A Collection of Critical Essays, ed. John Traugott, Twentieth Century Views; Englewood Cliffs, New Jersey, 1968.

There are also noteworthy discussions of Sterne in the following general books :

Booth, Wayne C., *The Rhetoric of Fiction*, Chicago, 1961.

McKillop, A. D., *The Early Masters of English Fiction*, Lawrence, Kansas, 1956.

Mendilow, A. A., *Time and the Novel*, London, 1952.

Stephen, Sir Leslie, *Hours in a Library*, vol. iii, London, 1879.

Van Ghent, Dorothy, *The English Novel: Form and Function*, New York, 1953.

Watkins, W. B. C., *Perilous Balance: The Tragic Genius of Swift, Johnson, and Sterne*, Princeton, 1939.

10

SAMUEL JOHNSON

John Hardy, University of New England, Armidale, N.S.W.

That Dr. Samuel Johnson has lived so vividly in the popular imagination is due, of course, to his younger friend James Boswell, whose *Life of Johnson* (1791) brilliantly captures both the living person and the epic conversationalist. My present purpose is, however, to focus almost exclusively on Johnson's own writings in order to highlight not only their intrinsic interest and historical importance, but also the image they reflect of his personality, his social and intellectual milieu, and his gradual emergence as the foremost man of letters of his age. It has therefore seemed best to proceed more or less chronologically within a largely biographical framework. In this way it is possible to distinguish Johnson's early involvement in various forms of political writing, his later reputation as both the great English lexicographer and the great eighteenth-century moralist, and his active engagement in criticism during those last twenty years or so, when he produced a body of work that represents the culmination of a lifelong concern with literature and still remains challenging today. It will, however, become clear (witness the *Life of Savage* among his early works, or his later political tracts of the 1770s) that no arbitrary division of his life into separate periods can ever do justice to the eager curiosity and intellectual vigour with which he constantly approached the world around him.

I

Born in 1709, Johnson was the son of a provincial bookseller. His father Michael Johnson was sheriff of Lichfield at the time of his birth; his mother, formerly Sarah Ford, of substantial yeoman stock, was openly proud of her own more prosperous relations. Though they began life together in a new, four-storied house, Michael's improvidence in business matters was increasingly to lead to straitened circumstances. It was lack of funds which forced the young Johnson, after only thirteen months' residence at Pembroke College, to go down from Oxford without a degree in 1729; and during the following years, when he was struggling to establish himself in some profession, this want of a degree several times prevented him from securing a position as a schoolmaster.

From his relatively humble beginnings Johnson derived, however, certain advantages. His 'great ambition to excel', noticeable even during his adolescent years at Lichfield Grammar School,[1] was doubtless strengthened by his having to fight his way in the world. Possessing an outstanding intellect, he was able by reading in his father's bookshop to lay the foundations of a learning that was both wide and deep. Nor did he ever forget his origins; indeed, his genuine concern for common humanity contributes to the greatness of his works and conversation.

In 1732 Johnson went to Birmingham at the invitation of his former school-fellow Edmund Hector. There he translated, from the French version of Joachim Le Grand, an account of Abyssinia by Father Jeronymo Lobo, a Portuguese Jesuit. Published in 1735, this was Johnson's first book, and is of interest in that it made him familiar with a body of material he was later to draw on in writing his greatest creative work, *Rasselas*. In Birmingham he also met his future wife Elizabeth Porter, twenty years his senior. Her daughter Lucy was later to provide Boswell with a graphic portrait of the figure Johnson cut on being first introduced to her mother :

He was then lean and lank, so that his immense structure of bones was hideously striking to the eye, and the scars of the scrophula were deeply visible. He also wore his hair, which was straight and stiff, and separated behind; and he often had, seemingly, convulsive starts and odd gesticulations, which tended to excite at once surprize and ridicule.

Mrs. Porter did not, however, assess Johnson on his unprepossessing appearance. His conversation so impressed her that she said to her daughter : 'This is the most sensible man that I ever saw in my life'. Their wedding took place in July 1735, after she had been ten months a widow; and in Johnson's own words, 'it was a love marriage upon both sides'.[2] With such financial assistance as his 'Tetty' could provide he opened a private school at Edial, near Lichfield. But this venture was not a success. Doubtless he was temperamentally unsuited to the vocation of schoolmaster. Certainly he found it impossible to attract enough students. As an episode in his life Edial remains chiefly memorable because David Garrick, afterwards the most famous actor of the day, was one of his pupils.

The failure of his school forced Johnson to explore other means of earning a living. In an attempt to make a fresh start he set out for London in March 1737, in company with the young Garrick; and then, later the same year, returned to accompany his wife to the capital. On the day of his first setting-out Gilbert Walmesley, that kindly supporter of Lichfield youth, wrote of him to a friend : 'Johnson is a very good scholar and poet, and I have great hopes will turn out a fine tragedy-writer'.[3] Clearly Johnson himself was meditating a literary career of some sort. Not only did he carry with him an unfinished tragedy, but several years previously had written to Edward Cave, the editor of the *Gentleman's Magazine*, offering 'sometimes to fill a column'.[4] Establishing himself as an author in London proved, however, to be a slow and arduous undertaking.

It was the phlegmatic, hard-working Cave rather than the carefully nurtured tragedy that gave him his start during those difficult, poverty-stricken, early years. The two probably met after Johnson had proposed a new English translation of Father Paul Sarpi's *History of the Council of Trent*,[5] a project which came to nothing. It did, however, lead to his writing for the *Gentleman's Magazine* a short Life of Sarpi, which was followed during the next four years by Lives of Boerhaave, Admiral Blake, Drake, Baratier ('Barretier'), Dr. Louis Morin (translated from an *éloge* by Fontenelle), Peter Burman, and Dr. Thomas Sydenham. These are important as Johnson's first attempts at biography, which with the growth of the reading public was to become widely popular during the century. Almost immediately he returned to this form in his incomparable *Life of Savage* (1744); then between 1748 and 1763 he published Lives of Roscommon, Francis Cheynel, Cave, Frederick III of Prussia, Sir Thomas Browne, Ascham and Collins; while his last major work was the famous *Lives of the Poets* (1779–81). Doubtless Johnson's own fondness for biography in part prompted these works. His contribution to this genre was not, however, in the field of original research since for the most part he merely reworked and compressed available material (though always with a shrewd sense of the factually credible). What distinguishes his from many other eighteenth-century Lives is that kind of excellence in biography which he was later to signalize in *Rambler* no. 60: the ability to select for inclusion and emphasis such details as clearly bring out the individual character. Of all his early subjects it was the famous Dutch physician Dr. Herman Boerhaave, who had by his 'genius and industry' so resolutely overcome his initial poverty, that touched the author most nearly, and from this Life, as has rightly been suggested, 'one might almost piece together a picture of Johnson as he saw himself, or as he hoped to be'.[6]

Up till the end of April 1738, Johnson's poetic pieces had been limited to schoolboy translations and undergraduate exercises, and several occasional verses. Then in May his more ambitious *London*, an imitation in the Augustan manner of Juvenal's famous satire on Rome, gained the notice of the literary world. Pope himself endeavoured to find out the name of its anonymous author, declaring he would 'soon be *déterré*'.[7] Many modern critics, however, consider this poem unimpressive, regarding it either as 'a skilfully executed exercise' in slavish imitation of Juvenal, or as structurally defective, 'a masterpiece of the higgledy-piggledy'.[8] On the contrary, not only is its satire both vivacious and biting, but Johnson here combines with his *saeva indignatio* an imagination so active that the poem's diverse material is skilfully organized within a coherent framework. The central, controlling image is the city-country antithesis, which Juvenal had treated ironically,[9] but which Johnson uses without irony to express his own independent theme. Blending two traditions, the sturdy independence associated with the *beatus ille* theme, and the heroic virtue associated with Britain's legendary and historical past, he identifies the country with the native seats of the true Briton. The city, on the other hand, is identified with the corrupt present, with a state of moral and even physical degeneracy that is represented as the direct result of the reign of George II, the policy of appeasement towards France and Spain, and the political turpitude of Sir Robert Walpole's administration. Throughout the poem Johnson continually juxtaposes these conflicting sets of values; and in the extended portrait of Orgilio, which is a veiled treatment of Walpole as a second Verres, the moral and political satire is brought to a sharp focus.[10] Because of this, we must regard the poem's other political allusions as not merely incidental, but integral to the main design.

In one sense, then, *London* looks forward to Johnson's political pamphlets of the following year, *Marmor Norfolciense* and *A Compleat Vindication of the Licensers of the Stage*, the former of which (except for the original *Idler* no. 22) represents his closest approach to the manner of Swift. First there is his skilful use of the persona of pedantic commentator when, having imagined the discovery (in Walpole's home county) of a large stone bearing an ancient inscription in Latin verse, he proceeds to puzzle over its supposedly obscure allusions. These refer unambiguously to the evils that the opposition party was currently laying at the door of the Court and administration— the maintenance of standing armies, the dangerous and un-challenged ascendancy of France, and the subordination of British to Hanoverian interests. Thus a horse (so the prophecy runs) shall suck the blood of a cowardly passive lion—though the pedantic commentator expressly hopes that an interpreta-tion involving Hanover and England (whose respective arms featured a horse and a lion) 'can enter into the Mind of none but a virulent Republican, or bloody Jacobite'. Then follows a sentence in which the ambiguities are so skilfully couched that the satire rivals Swift's at his most subtle :

> There is not one honest Man in the Nation unconvinced how weak an Attempt it would be to endeavour to confute this Insinuation. An Insinuation which no Party will dare to abet, and of so fatal and destructive a Tendency, that it may prove equally dangerous to the Author whether true or false.[11]

Marmor Norfolciense was sufficiently explosive to have given rise to a rumour (reported by Sir John Hawkins in his biography of Johnson) that the government had sought to arrest its anony-mous author. Yet this seems unlikely given the almost im-mediate publication of Johnson's other, though more pedestrian, anti-Walpole tract. Again making use of sustained irony, he attacks the Stage Licensing Act of 1737 on the occasion of the Lord Chamberlain's refusal (in March 1739) to grant a licence to Henry Brooke's political allegory *Gustavus Vasa*, the first play since the Act to be banned in the theatre.

Johnson was also currently employed by Cave on a very different kind of political writing. Before 1738, when the House resolved that the publication of parliamentary debates was a notorious breach of its privilege, the *Gentleman's Magazine* and the rival *London Magazine* had supplied readers with unofficial versions of proceedings in Parliament. In order to continue this popular feature the *Gentleman's Magazine* adopted the in-genious device of reporting parliamentary proceedings in a Swiftian disguise. 'Debates in the Senate of Magna Lilliputia', which opened the issue of June 1738, recounted the voyage of Gulliver's grandson to Lilliput, thus providing the means of introducing readers to the further 'historical and political novelties' of that kingdom. Perhaps this idea originated with Johnson. Certainly the style of the introductory piece is unmistakably his. At first he was employed in revising speeches supplied by William Guthrie. Later he was to take the whole task upon himself, becoming the 'sole composer' [12] of those debates appearing between July 1741 and March 1744, and dealing with events in Parliament between November 1740 and February 1743. Johnson sometimes 'had nothing more communicated to him than the names of the several speakers, and the part which they had taken in the debate'.[13] Yet partly because his authorship was such a well-kept secret, these speeches were widely regarded as authentic. Arthur Murphy describes a dinner-party at which Dr. Philip Francis, the translator of Demosthenes, remarked that one of Pitt's speeches was 'the best he had ever read'. After Johnson had owned himself the author, Francis said: 'Then, Sir, you have exceeded Demosthenes himself'. Another of those present went on to praise his 'impartiality', adding that 'he dealt out reason and eloquence with an equal hand to both parties'. To this Johnson replied: 'I saved appearances tolerably well; but I took care that the WHIG DOGS should not have the best of it'.[14]

The widely accepted authenticity of these speeches was, perhaps, one reason why Johnson discontinued writing them, for he told Boswell that 'he would not be accessary to the propagation of falsehood'.[15] To the modern reader, however, the belief that they were genuine occasions some surprise. Their style is uniformly Johnsonian—balanced, measured and formal; and particular questions are invariably argued in terms of general and abstract principles.[16] Moreover, despite Johnson's later, humorous, and not very accurate, reference to the 'Whigs' (since Walpole was opposed by a rival group within his own party), these speeches, in giving comparable weight to opposing points of view, illustrate their author's well-known ability to argue forcefully on either side of a question. In another way, too, they may be taken as representing what proved to be a formative experience, for from this date Johnson began to moderate his enthusiasm for opposition and be more critical of 'patriots' and the rancour of parties.

Two other, very different, literary ventures occupied him during his middle thirties. First the bookseller Thomas Osborne, who hoped to realize a substantial profit from the sale of the Harleian Library, engaged him to help in cataloguing this famous collection. Despite the uncongenial character of his employer, Johnson's insatiable thirst for knowledge must have welcomed this opportunity of turning over thousands of rare books, and of examining some in detail. Indeed it is possible that, besides contributing to the *Catalogus Bibliothecæ Harleianæ* (1743–45), he himself suggested the publication of *The Harleian Miscellany* (1744–46), a series of rare pamphlets from this collection for which he wrote the proposals and introduction.

But the early work for which Johnson is now remembered is his *Account of the Life of Richard Savage* (1744). In it he wrote of one he had known intimately, with whom he had enjoyed lively conversation and literary gossip during those nocturnal rambles around London when the two friends had been too poor to provide themselves with a bed or even refreshment. Perhaps nowhere else—except in parts of his later *Journey to the Western Islands of Scotland*—did Johnson write so freshly and engagingly, while revealing his capacity for eloquent generalized reflection on human life. He accepted unquestioningly Savage's claim to be the illegitimate son of the Countess of Macclesfield, who spurned him and opposed his fortunes in the world; and such apparently cruel neglect of one possessed of acknowledged (if erratic) brilliance ensured a sympathetic treatment from his younger biographer. The traits that endeared Savage to him were ingenuousness, courage, generosity, compassion. Yet in remaining alive to his many faults—intemperance, imprudence, ingratitude, petulance—Johnson allowed his sympathy to be qualified by a characteristically discriminating intelligence that penetrated to the very heart of Savage's character :

> . . . having accustomed himself to impute all deviations from the right to foreign causes, it is certain that he was upon every occasion too easily reconciled to himself; and that he appeared very little to regret those practices which had impaired his reputation. The reigning error of his life was, that he mistook the love for the practice of virtue, and was indeed not so much a good man, as the friend of goodness.[17]

II

Despite *London*, the political reporting for Cave, and the *Life of Savage* (all anonymous works), Johnson had his fame and fortune still to seek. Doubtless it was with an eye to both that he now contemplated an edition of Shakespeare's plays, presenting to the public his *Miscellaneous Observations on the*

Tragedy of Macbeth (1745) as a sample of his abilities as editor and critic. But the bookseller Jacob Tonson intervened to point out that he and his associates alone controlled Shakespeare's copyright [18]—thereby thwarting for what was effectively another twenty years the publication of Johnson's own edition. An even more ambitious undertaking was, however, soon to present itself. Another bookseller, Robert Dodsley, proposed the compilation of an English dictionary to Johnson, who despite some initial hesitation in accepting the task must have found it too challenging an enterprise, and too promising financially, to resist. He began by publishing his *Plan of a Dictionary of the English Language* (1747), addressed to Lord Chesterfield, in which he set out the intended scope and nature of the work. To it he devoted much of the next seven years.

The future dictionary did not, however, absorb all Johnson's energy during that time. Indeed, it was at this period that he emerged as the foremost moralist of his day. One work which he himself valued highly, but which carries for the modern reader only occasional conviction, is his allegory on human life entitled 'The Vision of Theodore, the Hermit of Teneriffe' written for the second volume of Dodsley's *Preceptor*.[19] Nevertheless, Johnson's next published work, the first of any importance to bear his name on the titlepage, was his famous *Vanity of Human Wishes* (1749), an imitation of Juvenal's tenth satire. Introduced and sustained with greater moral seriousness than in his Latin original, Johnson's various examples do not so much provide a bitter comment on human fate as demonstrate the unhappiness that results from man's inability to circumscribe his hopes and desires. Conspicuous throughout is the imagery of warfare,[20] which reminds us that 'life is combat to Johnson, and the combat is moral'.[21] The following semi-autobiographical lines, for example, depict the dangers that lie in wait for the young scholar :

> Yet should thy soul indulge the gen'rous heat,
> Till captive Science yields her last retreat;
> Should Reason guide thee with her brightest ray,
> And pour on misty Doubt resistless day;
> Should no false Kindness lure to loose delight,
> Nor Praise relax, nor Difficulty fright;
> Should tempting Novelty thy cell refrain,
> And Sloth effuse her opiate fumes in vain;
> Should Beauty blunt on fops her fatal dart,
> Nor claim the triumph of a letter'd heart;

Should no Disease thy torpid veins invade,
Nor Melancholy's phantoms haunt thy shade;
Yet hope not life from grief or danger free,
Nor think the doom of man revers'd for thee:
Deign on the passing world to turn thine eyes,
And pause awhile from letters, to be wise;
There mark what ills the scholar's life assail,
Toil, envy, want, the patron, and the jail.

(143–60)

In other passages, too, whether Johnson is enumerating the
more frequent occurrences of everyday life, or citing an awful
warning from the pages of history, he preserves the image of
man beset by the vicissitudes of life, and especially by dangers
that arise from his own irrationality and pride.

The recent suggestion that this poem is 'close in mood to
comedy'[22] has no relevance except intermittently in the first
hundred lines. Beginning with the portrait of Wolsey, the insight is not so much satirically as tragically ironic. For example,
in the justly acclaimed description of 'Swedish Charles', the
haughty hope of military conquest and glory is treated with a
moving sense of the wilful waste and uncertain fortunes of
war:

The vanquish'd hero leaves his broken bands,
And shews his miseries in distant lands;
Condemn'd a needy supplicant to wait,
While ladies interpose, and slaves debate.
But did not Chance at length her error mend?
Did no subverted empire mark his end?
Did rival monarchs give the fatal wound?
Or hostile millions press him to the ground?
His fall was destin'd to a barren strand,
A petty fortress, and a dubious hand;
He left the name, at which the world grew pale,
To point a moral, or adorn a tale.

(211–22)

As one critic has remarked, 'the awe and pity with which
Johnson contemplates the spectacle of human unfulfilment
makes of *The Vanity of Human Wishes* a great tragic poem'.[23]
The ending, if it mitigates the sense of tragedy, preserves the
seriousness and emphasises the difference from Johnson's
original. Conscious of a greater goal to which human hope can

aspire, he characteristically substitutes for Juvenal's mock-reverence an exhortation that is deeply Christian.

Whereas Juvenal had been imitated by other English poets, really only Johnson can be said to have captured the 'state-liness' and 'declamatory grandeur' that he recognized as inseparable from the Roman poet's style.[24] Though his individual handling of the Augustan couplet is not as varied, flexible or subtle as Pope's, he nevertheless imparts to it a characteristic resonance that makes it 'sing in the mind'.[25] His brand of wit unites imaginative vigour with weighty finality of statement. Hence the extraordinary concision and impressiveness of single lines and couplets. Yet longer passages also show his disciplined sense of the musical, syntactic and rhetorical possibilities of his verse-form; and sometimes, as in the lines on Charles or Xerxes (ll. 225–240), he achieves an unquestionable sublimity.

When in 1747 Garrick became manager of Drury Lane, Johnson had composed the most famous of all his prologues for the opening performance of the new season. In it he offers a trenchant survey of English drama from Shakespeare to his own day, characteristically exhorting the audience to exercise moral judgement in preferring 'useful mirth, and salutary woe' to empty sound and show. Garrick's arrival at Drury Lane also meant that Johnson was at last assured of seeing his own tragedy *Irene* appear on the stage. Produced on 6 February 1749, it ran for nine nights, and was at least a financial success in that the author netted almost £300 from his three benefit nights and its publication. It was, however, never revived. To it may be applied Johnson's later criticism of Addison's *Cato* as 'rather a poem in dialogue than a drama'.[26] Its formal and stilted language robs the characters of any individuality of speech or emotional immediacy. Much of the original audience's pleasure seems to have been derived from the costumes and setting, but as a printed text *Irene* serves merely to illustrate the undramatic cast of Johnson's creative imagination.[27] His moralistic bent was soon to receive its most convincing expression in other literary forms. In *Irene* the heavy weight of moral argument issues too obviously and insistently from the author's own mouth.

From this date or a little earlier, having previously occupied obscure lodgings in different houses in the city, Johnson resided in the handsome dwelling in Gough Square which is today known by his name. According to Hawkins, he took it to be near the printers engaged in his *Dictionary*. In its spacious garret his six amanuenses were kept busy transcribing selected passages to be appended to the etymologies and definitions. Johnson was to live there until 1 March 1759, meantime producing not only the *Dictionary* but those other two works of the 1750s that were to bring him widespread fame, *The Rambler* and *Rasselas*. Another event of some significance was his formation, in 1749, of the Ivy Lane Club, of which his fellow-members included John Hawkins, his future biographer, and Dr. John Hawkesworth, who several years later edited *The Adventurer*.

The Rambler, appearing twice weekly from 20 March 1750 to 14 March 1752, brought Johnson widespread fame as moralist and philosophic sage. Since he wrote all but some half-dozen numbers himself, producing copy by the required time involved him in a continual struggle with his 'constitutional indolence', and he told Boswell that many of the papers 'were written in haste as the moment pressed, without even being read over by him before they were printed'.[28] This in itself provides ample testimony of his extraordinary capaciousness of mind, for *The Rambler*, in ranging freely over a variety of literary and moral topics, gives constant evidence of wide reading. What especially distinguishes it from earlier periodical essays like *The Tatler* and *The Spectator* is the tone of almost unrelieved seriousness in which it deals with morals rather than manners. Boswell aptly described its author as 'a majestick teacher of moral and religious wisdom';[29] and the kind of tribute here paid to his didacticism reminds us that, on undertaking the work, Johnson had prayed that he might promote God's glory 'and the Salvation both of myself and others'.[30]

To Johnson, moral and religious wisdom were one. A fervent Christian, with a vivid sense of traditional eschatology, he set out to impress on his readers the importance of 'a life usefully and virtuously employed' (no. 41), seeking to bring home to them the full implications and importance of self-knowledge, which he considered in its widest sense as compromising 'all the speculation requisite to a moral agent' (no. 24), and as diametrically opposed to the vagaries of hope, a wayward imagination, or misdirected curiosity. In a number of papers he satirizes virtuosi and other such 'curious' men as isolate themselves from that general converse with mankind which he considered necessary to an intellectual and moral being. He also continually scrutinizes motives and traits of character with a view to exposing those 'numerous stratagems, by which pride endeavours to recommend folly to regard' (no. 20). Above all, he endeavours to persuade his readers to review their hopes for happiness in this world in the light of their experience of human limitations—or, in Ruskin's words, 'carefully to measure life, and distrust fortune'.[31]

The moral content of *The Rambler* is conveyed in a variety of ways: in allegories and dream-visions, tales with an eastern setting, fictitious 'histories' or accounts of or by those whose names are indicative of character or circumstances, and disquisitions on particular vices and virtues, or on the effect on conduct of changing fortunes. Another large and significant group of papers deals with a variety of literary topics and it is interesting to compare Johnson's later criticism with the attitudes and judgements embodied in these papers. One important question they raise is the extent of his commitment at this date to traditional 'rules'. Already one notices the kind of independence of mind that was to characterize the future critic of Shakespeare and the English poets. Johnson readily acknowledges those 'nameless and inexplicable elegancies which appeal wholly to the fancy, from which we feel delight, but know not how they produce it' (no. 92), and describes 'imagination' as 'a licentious and vagrant faculty, unsusceptible of limitations, and impatient of restraint' (no. 125). He is also prepared to defend Shakespearean tragi-comedy against accepted neo-classical strictures. Yet this defence of Shakespeare is arguably different in its emphasis from that to be found in the famous *Preface* of 1765. In *Rambler* no. 156 he acclaims Shakespeare's 'transcendent and undoubted genius' without allowing him to have set a precedent which other writers ought to follow. And still firmly uppermost in Johnson's mind is the concept that, though the occasional dictates of individual critics may constitute but a spurious authority, certain 'principles' are nevertheless 'essential' or fundamental to works written in a particular genre.

The style of *The Rambler* has been criticized as too ponderous and Latinate. Indeed Johnson himself, on being later asked by a friend how he liked a particular paper, is said to have 'shook his head and answered, "too wordy" '.[32] Certainly in no other work did he use longer sentences or as many 'hard' words. Yet there are a number of possible explanations for this. At the time he wrote *The Rambler* Johnson was collecting material for the *Dictionary*, a fact which doubtless encouraged him to use some words of philosophic or scientific import.[33] Again, it may be suggested that the subject-matter of *The Rambler* was usually such as to invite those qualities of abstraction, balance and cumulative emphasis which are generally features of his prose.

The circumstances of composition could also have affected the style since the necessity of supplying, every few days, enough words for each number doubtless encouraged Johnson to use some forms of amplification. Dr. Hugh Blair, for example, attempted an imitation intended to highlight the author's frequent use of genitival constructions in this paper.[34] Yet in fairness to Johnson it must also be said that such parodists have rarely succeeded in approaching his verbal precision and imagistic accuracy of phrase.[35] It is this which, in large measure, gives solidity and distinction to his prose, making him one of the most memorable stylists in the whole history of English literature.

In 1753 Johnson began writing for Hawkesworth's *Adventurer*, a periodical paper also published twice weekly. About his own part in it he always remained reticent. According to the blind Anna Williams (one of those who gained a shelter under Johnson's roof and thus benefited from his compassion towards others less fortunate than himself), he would never own that he was the author since he had 'given' those essays to his close friend Dr. Richard Bathurst, 'who sold them at two guineas each'.[36] What is certain is that Johnson became one of the regular contributors to the periodical, supplying twenty-nine papers in all. These, which range over a variety of subjects, are mainly devoted, like *The Rambler*, to moral and literary topics. The style of *The Adventurer*, in its amplitude and measured balance, resembles that of the earlier periodical. Yet it is free of *The Rambler*'s occasional heaviness—perhaps because Johnson here took his turn with other contributors and the demand for copy was thus less onerous.

Two descriptions of Johnson during the early 1750s help to fill out our impression of him during this period. Hawkins tells us that, when his friend Mrs. Charlotte Lennox's first novel appeared in 1750, a party attended by members of the Ivy Lane Club was held in her honour:

> Our supper was elegant, and Johnson had directed that a magnificent hot apple-pye should make a part of it, and this he would have stuck with bay-leaves, because, forsooth, Mrs. Lenox was an authoress, and had written verses; and further, he had prepared for her a crown of laurel, with which, but not till he had invoked the muses by some ceremonies of his own invention, he encircled her brows . . . About five, Johnson's face shone with meridian splendour, though his drink had been only lemonade.[37]

The other account includes details of that aspect of Johnson which popular tradition has come too readily to accept as exclusively authentic. Bennet Langton of Lincolnshire had been so impressed by *The Rambler* that he had, as a young man, come to London chiefly in the hope of meeting its author. Through the good offices of Robert Levett, the poor, self-styled physician who was for many years to live with Johnson, Langton was introduced, and their meeting is recorded thus by Boswell:

> From perusing his writings, he fancied he should see a decent, well-drest, in short, a remarkably decorous philosopher. Instead of which, down from the bed-chamber, about noon, came, as newly risen, a huge uncouth figure, with a little dark wig which scarcely covered his head, and his clothes hanging loose about him. But his conversation was so rich, so animated, and so forcible, and his religious and political notions so congenial with those in which Mr. Langton had been educated, that he conceived for him that veneration and attachment which he ever preserved.[38]

Johnson's next major work, published in two large folio volumes in April 1755, earned for him the soubriquet 'Dictionary' Johnson. That it appeared so soon stamped him as something of a prodigy, the forty members of the French Academy having produced their dictionary only after as many years. During the period since 1747 he had received from the urbane Chesterfield, to whom he had addressed his *Plan*, nothing except a gift of ten pounds, and then, at the end of 1754, flattering notice in one of the weekly periodicals, *The World*. Doubtless Dodsley, with an eye to profits, had encouraged this puffing of the work by such an acknowledged exponent of polite letters; but Johnson, in order to set the record straight, sent Chesterfield his famous letter setting out the difficulties he had overcome in bringing his task to completion, and dissociating himself from such spurious and unwelcome patronage.[39] An infinitely greater cause for congratulation was the degree of M.A. which the University of Oxford conferred on the author, and which appeared after his name on the titlepage.

For almost a hundred years before the *Dictionary* appeared, English scientists and men of letters had consistently advocated that, in the interests of both intelligibility and permanence, language and usage should be standardized or 'fixed'. In his *Plan* Johnson had begun by acknowledging it as his 'chief intent' to 'preserve the purity, and ascertain the meaning of our

English idiom'—though he also realized the infeasibility of such an ideal given both the need for comprehensiveness and the obvious vagaries of current usage (whether these resulted from anomalies long established or individual capriciousness). It was with an awareness of these conflicting claims that he there presented his views on vocabulary, spelling, pronunciation, etymology, syntax, definition, lexical annotation, and illustrative quotation. He posited, unlike the modern lexicographer, a 'golden age of our language', which he dated from the time of Elizabeth;[40] and though foreseeing the limitations of judicial or prescriptive lexicography, he clearly intended to try to further, whenever possible, the cause of regularity. Yet the actual task of compilation must soon have convinced him that the standardization of language was utterly impracticable, and in the Preface to the completed work he represents it as an aim that can be justified by 'neither reason nor experience'.[41]

The most important consequence of the reigning linguistic and literary ideal was, however, that it encouraged Johnson to make language itself the focal point of his work, to concern himself with such features as were proper to dictionaries. Previously, the title of 'Dictionary' had conveyed (as he himself states in the *Plan*) 'a very miscellaneous idea'[42] since earlier lexicographers had tended not only to copy word-lists and definitions from one another, but to produce compendious amalgams of diverse kinds of knowledge more reminiscent of an encyclopedia than a dictionary. Johnson omitted this rather esoteric material, setting himself instead to read at firsthand the works of English authors. As a result he was able to collect and introduce into his *Dictionary* illustrative quotations which not merely lend substance to the definitions of meaning but also provide some record of the language (from about 1580 to 1750) as a changing, complex, developing system.

The excellence of Johnson's definitions has perhaps never been adequately recognized. Too often he is remembered for those few which are consciously whimsical, reflecting personal or political prejudices he was prepared to acknowledge openly. Some others that are unwarrantably verbose or laboured provoked the scorn of contemporary parodists. In general, however, the modern reader will find that, besides providing a valuable storehouse of eighteenth-century meaning and usage, Johnson's definitions are notable for their accuracy and concision, for the kind of lucidity that results from a disciplined use of language. Indeed, the sense of relevance they so often display is one of the hallmarks of their author's genius as both conversationalist and writer.

Though the *Dictionary* brought Johnson lasting fame, it did not bring him financial independence, and in 1756, a year in which he was even arrested for debt, his writings included a perceptive criticism of Pope's epitaphs in *The Universal Visiter*, numerous articles and reviews in *The Literary Magazine* (in which he seems during its first year of publication to have taken a leading part), and *Proposals* for a new edition of Shakespeare (a work that he completed relatively slowly). The most interesting of his contributions to the *Literary Magazine* are the 'Memoirs' of Frederick III of Prussia, several substantial political essays dealing with the Anglo-French situation at the outset of the Seven Years' War and reviews of Joseph Warton's *Essay on Pope* and Soame Jenyns's *Free Inquiry into the Nature and Origin of Evil*. In this last work Johnson, with relentless logic, demolishes the currently popular analogy of the 'chain of being', and commands our respect as a moralist by denouncing that complacent optimism and pretentious moralizing by which Jenyns sought to justify his apparent unconcern for the poor and wretched.

During the years he worked on Shakespeare, Johnson engaged in other literary ventures both because he needed money and doubtless also because he welcomed some diversion from the task of editing. In 1758, a year in which he was again arrested for debt, he began to contribute his *Idler* essays to a new weekly newspaper (*The Universal Chronicle*). As one would expect from the title, many of these are shorter and lighter in tone than his earlier periodical essays, being more topical in their references and containing portraits that stop well short of human wretchedness or extreme moral folly. Yet *The Idler* also contains a few papers thoroughly characteristic of Johnson's more serious vein. At one point he delivers a warning against the 'habitual subjection of reason to fancy' (no. 32); while the final number (published during Holy Week) stresses not only the shortness and uncertainty of human life, but the inevitability of that final day 'in which every work of the hand, and imagination of the heart shall be brought to judgement, and an everlasting futurity shall be determined by the past'.

The Idler ran from 15 April 1758 to 5 April 1760. Meantime Johnson had published his famous *History of Rasselas, Prince of Abissinia*, which in his own day won the kind of praise accorded to *The Rambler*. On hearing that Boswell had met its author Sir David Dalrymple wrote to him :

It gives me great pleasure to think that you have obtained the friendship of Mr. Samuel Johnson. He is one of the best moral writers which England has produced . . . May I beg you to present my best respects to him, and to assure him of the veneration which I entertain for the author of the Rambler and of Rasselas? [43]

Written in January 1759, in about a week, to raise money for his dying mother, *Rasselas* has often been called its author's *Vanity of Human Wishes* in prose. From the opening sentence it sets out to dispel the 'phantoms of hope', for Rasselas and his companions fail to find perfect happiness either in the so-called 'Happy Valley', or in that outside world into which they escape in order to experience life at first hand. The nominally exotic, eastern setting, as well as that whole literary tradition which had placed the Earthly Paradise in Abyssinia, is put by Johnson to ironic use in a searching and deliberately un-optimistic analysis of the human condition. For this reason *Rasselas* is an eastern tale only in name. Instead of dismissing his characters to the happiness-ever-after of romance, he forces upon them and his reader the realization that no such happiness exists in this world.

Nor is the book's episodic quality reminiscent of the eastern tale, where episodes exist solely for the story, and usually occur within a larger plot. Critics inclined to complain of its being an 'ill-contrived' and 'uninstructive' tale [44] fail to appreciate the expressiveness of its form. No artifice of plot could have made us so aware of the tentative, experimental, unpredictable nature of life itself, or of its constant and basic ironies. In their search for happiness, the youthful travellers traverse both country and city, mix with shepherds and philosophers, enter the homes of the lowly as well as the courts of the great, and encounter youthful roisterers as well as men of venerable age, piety and learning. Yet all their searches only prove the truth of the tutor Imlac's earlier remark to Rasselas in the 'Happy Valley': 'Human life is every where a state in which much is to be endured, and little to be enjoyed' (chap. XI).

Johnson presents as the main cause of human unhappiness the perennial conflict between hope and reality, or the essentially quixotic tendencies of the mind itself. Continually restless in a way that is destructive of present happiness, man possesses the inveterate habit of building pyramids in the air, and only slowly learns—if he learns at all— that his circumstantial involvement in the finite, temporal world inevitably limits the choices open to him. The travellers' search for such an ideal 'choice of life' as would enable them to enjoy every conceivable advantage open to man is thus bound to end in disappointment.

Yet Johnson, characteristically, does not leave either them or his reader without some sense of hope. When they visit the catacombs, Rasselas, in full consciousness of the irony of their search, ponders on the scene : 'Those that lie here stretched before us, the wise and the powerful of antient times . . . were, perhaps, snatched away while they were busy, like us, in the choice of life'. And his sister Nekayah, in the book's last piece of direct speech, utters what is surely, in one sense, Johnson's conclusion : 'To me, said the princess, the choice of life is become less important; I hope hereafter to think only on the choice of eternity' (chap. XLVIII). Since the theme of the 'choice of life' is here finally set within the larger context of eternity, *Rasselas* cannot adequately be described, along with Voltaire's sardonically mocking *Candide* (published almost simultaneously), as a pessimistic work.

The last chapter, 'The conclusion, in which nothing is concluded', which follows the book itself like a 'trailing coda',[45] arguably ends on a more positive note than has often been supposed. Admittedly the youthful travellers are here prompted to outline 'the various schemes of happiness which each of them had formed'. But they are no longer deluded : as the text makes clear, they are now merely talking for their diversion. Having seen the unhappiness of the world, they now know where unreal hopes must end. Yet, though their initial optimism has been tempered by experience, they do not altogether abandon their hopes. Still young, with life still before them, they refuse to be forced into adopting the resignation of age. And so they remain far from that unenviable state (described in *The Rambler*, and more nearly approached by Imlac himself and the astronomer) in which man openly 'abandons himself to chance and to the wind, and glides careless and idle down the current of life, without resolution to make another effort' to reach a particular port.[46] Some of the eager enthusiasm which had prompted Rasselas to escape from the dispiriting 'imprisonment' of the 'Happy Valley' inspires him to the end, and for this reason it is the young prince, and not his world-weary tutor, who is, first and last, Johnson's hero.

III

James Boswell first met Johnson in May 1763, in the back-parlour of Tom Davies's bookshop. Thoroughly characteristic of both men and their future relationship was the exchange of wit and conversation that followed. Introduced as a Scot, the twenty-two-year-old Boswell said: 'Mr. Johnson, I do indeed come from Scotland, but I cannot help it'. To this came the deft reply: 'That, Sir, I find, is what a very great many of your countrymen cannot help'. When Johnson went on to complain that Garrick had denied him a small favour, the perky and irrepressible Boswell, 'eager to take any opening to get into conversation with him', demurred: 'O, Sir, I cannot think Mr. Garrick would grudge such a trifle to you'. This time Johnson's answer was measured and reproving, for Boswell, given the greater formality of eighteenth-century manners, would seem to have come close to incivility: 'Sir, (said he, with a stern look,) I have known David Garrick longer than you have done: and I know no right you have to talk to me on the subject'.[47] Yet despite this unpromising start the two men soon became firm friends. Having quarrelled with his own father, Boswell was still young enough to revere the older man; with distinct literary ambitions of his own, he was quick to admire the greatness of Johnson's achievement; and his own ready sympathy found in Johnson a capacity for friendship and a degree of human warmth possessed by few other men. Johnson, in turn, must have responded to the youthful and talented Boswell's gaiety, eagerness, curiosity and open friendliness. More than ten years later, after they had travelled together through the Scottish Highlands, he began his *Journey* by recalling his willingness to undertake the trip on 'finding in Mr. Boswell a companion, whose acuteness would help my inquiry, and whose gaiety of conversation and civility of manners are sufficient to counteract the inconveniences of travel, in countries less hospitable than we have passed'.

About this time three other events occurred to brighten Johnson's life. First, in 1762, he was given by the government an annual pension of £300 as a reward for his services to literature. Such an income, though it did not make him rich, at least provided him with enough money to avoid the distressing embarrassments of poverty. Then, early in 1764, was formed the club later known as the Literary Club, which numbered among its original members the distinguished contemporaries Sir Joshua Reynolds, Edmund Burke and Oliver Goldsmith. Johnson eagerly supported Reynolds's suggestion that this club should be formed, and its congenial society was to provide him both with the means of keeping his own melancholy at bay, and with the kind of intellectual stimulation that allowed him to shine so brilliantly as the foremost conversationalist of his day.

An even happier association began the following year when Johnson accepted an invitation to dine at the home of the wealthy brewer Henry Thrale and his vivacious and cultivated young wife. Their friendship only ended with Thrale's death in 1781, and Mrs. Thrale's second marriage to the Italian singer Gabriel Piozzi in the year of Johnson's own death. For Thrale, who was elected M.P. for Southwark later in 1765, Johnson wrote a number of electioneering notices and addresses over the next fifteen years.[48] With Mrs. Thrale, who shared his own literary interests, he began a long-continued and intimate correspondence. So much a member of their family did he become that he went with them to Brighton, Bath, North Wales and France, and would have accompanied them to Italy had not this journey been put off on the death of their only son. The times of happy domesticity he spent at their home can be gleaned both from Mrs. Thrale's account of these years,[49] and from passages in the *Diary and Letters of Madame D'Arblay*, who as the young and precocious Fanny Burney, the author of *Evelina*, was a welcome visitor to Streatham from 1778, enjoying in its informal and congenial atmosphere Johnson's conversation and esteem.[50]

The edition of Shakespeare's plays, which had been planned for so many years, was finally published in October 1765. In his earlier *Proposals* Johnson had stated his intention of producing a good text, explaining obscure passages, and procuring Shakespeare 'more rational approbation'.[51] He showed sound sense in disregarding all Folios after the First, but his edition is defective in its concept of textual authority largely because he failed to take the texts of the various Quartos into consideration. Nor did prevailing attitudes to poetic language and dramatic speech encourage him to produce, by modern standards, a good text. Most eighteenth-century editors had felt justified in suggesting emendations wherever a text seemed to them corrupt. In this respect, however, Johnson is far less culpable than many of his predecessors. His extraordinarily wide knowledge of the language not only prompted some discerning explanations of particular passages, but (especially by comparison with the host of fanciful conjectures suggested by Shakespeare's previous editor, William Warburton) combined with his innate scepticism to limit the number of proposed changes within reasonable bounds.

Johnson's edition is remarkable for the famous *Preface* and distinctive notes that it contains. These, which gain from being considered together (since many of the notes illuminate more general remarks in the *Preface*), add up to a body of criticism very different from the disconcertingly naïve approach of most other contemporary critics. Like his predecessors, he sets out in a traditional way to examine 'beauties' and 'defects', to apportion 'praise' and 'blame'. But unlike them, he also succeeds in conveying his own individual response to the plays. For this reason his assessment is not only more complex and sophisticated, but more interesting and immediate as well.

'Shakespeare', he writes 'is above all writers, at least above all modern writers, the poet of nature; the poet that holds up to his readers a faithful mirrour of manners and of life'.[52] The phrase 'poet of nature' carries, in fact, favourable aesthetic and moral overtones. Yet this praise as first looks paradoxical both because Johnson apparently goes on to deny individuality to Shakespeare's characters, and because he states, later in the *Preface*, that Shakespeare 'seems to write without any moral purpose'.[53] When Johnson says that 'in the writings of other poets a character is too often an individual; in those of Shakespeare it is commonly a species', he is not, however, maintaining that the Shakespearian character is left unindividualized. In the *Preface* itself he adds that 'perhaps no poet ever kept his personages more distinct from each other'[54]; while in the notes (of which the most famous are probably those on Falstaff and Polonius),[55] he shows that he read the plays with a well-defined conception of individual characters. Pope had said that 'every single character in *Shakespeare* is as much an Individual as those in Life itself'[56]—and Johnson praised Pope highly as a critic of Shakespeare. The sense in which he was himself using 'individual' can be illustrated from his observations to Boswell on the broad mimicry of the notorious caricaturist Samuel Foote. On one occasion he maintained that Foote indulged not in comedy but 'farce, which exhibits individuals', adding on another:

He goes out of himself, without going into other people. He cannot take off any person unless he is very strongly marked. . . . He is like a painter, who can draw the portrait of a man who has a wen on his face, and who, therefore, is easily known.[57]

In using 'species' in antithesis to 'individual', Johnson clearly intended to suggest the rounded or three-dimensional—it being the measure of lifelike authenticity reflected in Shakespeare's characterization that prompted Johnson's praise of him as 'the poet of nature'. It is, moreover, in terms of such verisimilitude that the moral implications of this phrase need to be explained. Johnson complained of his seeming lack of moral purpose. Yet, though Shakespeare lived before 'speculation had . . . attempted to analyse the mind, to trace the passions to their sources, to unfold the seminal principles of vice and virtue, or sound the depths of the heart for the motives of action',[58] Johnson implies that by holding up to his readers 'a faithful mirrour of manners and of life' he at least invites them to look more deeply into human nature, including their own. That Shakespearian drama conveyed a salutary portrait of human nature was attested by such different eighteenth-century writers as Shaftesbury and William Richardson; and as an insistent moralist, and habitual scrutineer of human motive, Johnson would not therefore have ignored this aspect of the moral relevance of Shakespeare's art.[59] Arguably many of his notes on individual characters, like the famous note on *Othello*,[60] were intended to highlight aspects of human behaviour which a discerning audience could glean from the plays. At least it is certain that the definition in the *Preface* of 'the end of the poetry' ('to instruct by pleasing')[61] far from keeping 'instruction' distinct from 'delight', indicates Johnson's wholehearted engagement in the work before him.

Objection was made to Shakespeare's seeming lack of moral purpose primarily because of the kind of moral indifference that Johnson readily detected in the ending of some of the plays. His own view of human nature was sufficiently pessimistic for him to believe that the fear of punishment was a necessary spur to virtue, and that, unless justice were seen to be administered, man would no longer be deterred from evil. And as a markedly moralistic critic, he expected a work of art to preserve the same kind of strict and unambiguous justice as he looked for in life itself. For this reason he was particularly offended that Shakespeare had suffered 'the virtue of Cordelia to perish in a just cause'; and from his note on *King Lear* it is obvious that the ending of no other play disturbed him so deeply.[62] Furthermore, this note is interesting because, in alluding to the disagree-

341

ment between Addison and Dennis concerning 'poetical justice', it allows us to interpret Johnson's response in the light of the extra-literary, eschatological argument adduced by Dennis. This critic, following Rymer, had maintained that the justice a dramatist meted out to his 'creatures' ought to be a type of God's final Judgement.[63] To the Johnson who was so painfully apprehensive of his own ultimate fate in the next world, the death of the apparently innocent Cordelia must therefore have been too terrifying a reminder of the Judgement awaiting imperfect man. Perhaps the seemingly senseless fortuitousness of her death even aroused in the depths of his being a fear of annihilation, of which, as Boswell tells us, he always found the apprehension 'dreadful'.[64]

Many of the remarks in *Preface* and notes are to be related to that set of literary and dramatic conventions which for Johnson and his age constituted 'the only right method of making plays'.[65] The eighteenth-century critic regarded a play as a credible imitation of real events and real people realistically contained within its own world. Hence the importance of having soliloquies properly motivated, and not just addressed to the audience. Hence also the infelicity of highly-wrought imagery or word-play in the mouth of a character supposedly suffering the stress of strong emotion. It is this view—common in earlier criticism—of the dramatic impropriety of certain modes of expression which goes a long way towards explaining Johnson's surprising stricture on Shakespearian tragedy :

> In tragedy he often writes with great appearance of toil and study, what is written at last with little felicity; but in his comick scenes, he seems to produce without labour, what no labour can improve. In tragedy he is always struggling after some occasion to be comick, but in comedy he seems to repose, or to luxuriate, as in a mode of thinking congenial to his nature . . . His comedy pleases by the thoughts and the language, and his tragedy for the greater part by incident and action. His tragedy seems to be skill, his comedy to be instinct.[66]

In some respects Johnson's *incredulus odi* was very marked,[67] and his acceptance of certain arbitrary conventions no less literal-minded than that of his age. Yet so outspoken was his defence of Shakespearean drama on two important counts that he has been hailed as 'an outright dissenter against the neoclassic rules and proprieties'.[68] In defending the distinctive inclusiveness of Shakespearian tragi-comedy against more rigid definitions of form, Johnson emphatically pointed out that 'there is always an appeal open from criticism to nature'.[69] Less original, but no less forcible, was his defence of Shakespeare against the spurious unities of time and place on the grounds that those who subscribed to them failed to distinguish between the real world and the imaginary world of the play. As an editor, he confined himself to commonsense adjustments designed to accommodate lapses of time and changes of place to a more convenient distribution of acts and scenes.

Johnson read Shakespeare's plays as dramatic narratives, not as thematic poems, and displayed a lively and discriminating, if not decidedly poetic, intelligence in grappling with plot and character. His reasoned estimate of Shakespeare is in no sense grudging; indeed, his cool and dispassionate objectivity is ultimately compelling and persuasive. Moreover, the observation that Johnson on Shakespeare tells us as much about Johnson as Shakespeare [70] is a testimony not so much to his literary preconceptions or prejudices as to the overall coherence and personally realized quality of his critical dialectic.

For the next four years Johnson read more than he wrote. When during an informal meeting with George III in February 1767 the King enquired 'if he was then writing any thing', Johnson replied 'he was not, for he had pretty well told the world what he knew, and must now read to acquire more knowledge'.[71] Early in the following decade events at home and abroad did, however, prompt Johnson to write his four famous political tracts. In *The False Alarm* (1770) he defended the House's action in excluding the already imprisoned John Wilkes (who had easily topped the poll in the Middlesex election) and declaring elected a rival candidate. When many people, fearing that constitutional liberty was being threatened, expressed their alarm, Johnson denounced this as false, on the one hand upholding the autonomy of the House of Commons, and maintaining on the other that Wilkes was unworthy of a voice in the affairs of Parliament. From this it is clear that he was neither egalitarian nor a political ancestor of those who agitated for the Reform Bill of 1832. In his own words he was 'a friend to subordination, as most conducive to the happiness of society'.[72] With this as his settled conviction he had no qualms about opposing what seemed to him mere rabble-rousing. Nor would he have agreed that such an attitude, however paternalistic, called his humanity into question.

His next pamphlet, *Thoughts on the Late Transactions respecting Falkland's Islands* (1771), is noteworthy for its humane and impassioned denunciation of the evils of war. Having previously evicted a small British garrison from Saunders Island, Spain agreed, after lengthy negotiations, to make restitution for this injury without in any way prejudicing the question of prior sovereignty. Taking the enlightened view that it would be foolish to risk reprisals by further demands, Johnson dismissed with contempt the war-mongering of extremists among the opposition, and used all his powers of rhetoric to discredit the more formidable Junius:

Junius is an unusual phænomenon, on which some have gazed with wonder and some with terrour, but wonder and terrour are transitory passions. He will soon be more closely viewed or more attentively examined, and what folly has taken for a comet that from its flaming hair shook pestilence and war, inquiry will find to be only a meteor formed by the vapours of putrefying democracy, and kindled into flame by the effervescence of interest struggling with conviction; which after having plunged its followers in a bog, will leave us inquiring why we regarded it.[73]

Johnson's last two political pamphlets were more nearly concerned with events just prior to the American War of Independence. *The Patriot* was an attempt to lay down guide-lines for voters in the election of 1774 (called early in order that a new Parliament could be elected before events in America reached a fresh crisis). In this pamphlet Johnson cleverly distinguishes between what he takes to be the misguided clamour and counterfeit zeal of the professed 'patriots' and the genuine virtue of the true lover of his country. *Taxation No Tyranny* (March 1775) was explicitly an answer to the published proceedings of the American Continental Congress. In opposing the colonists' cry of 'no taxation without representation', Johnson argued that as subjects of the British Crown they were bound to pay any tax laid upon them by the home government. That there was no member of it to represent them directly made them no different from many other subjects living within the realm. By emigrating to America they had, in Johnson's view, voluntarily forfeited any right of representation they might otherwise have possessed. And since Britain assumed responsibility for their defence, it seemed reasonable for them to contribute to the expense involved. What today is interpreted as the view of a Tory diehard was at the time shared by many Englishmen, and was prompted by the author's deep conviction that the colonies should willingly submit to both the authority and national interests of the mother-country.

Taxation No Tyranny, which today seems repellent in its paternalistic authoritarianism, can, ironically enough, in one way be linked with Johnson's engaging *Journey to the Western Islands of Scotland*, published in the same year. The kind of thinking (involving a recognition of the reciprocal obligations of governor and governed) which led Johnson to oppose so resolutely the demands of the American colonists, made him feel deeply sympathetic towards the poor crofters of Scotland, many of whom were being forced to turn unwilling backs on their own country and seek a new home in America. When Johnson set out with Boswell on his tour of Scotland in the late summer of 1773, one of his motives for undertaking the trip was the opportunity to view the social life and economic conditions of the Highlanders at first hand. An observant traveller, eager for detailed information about everything presented to his view, he was prepared to savour to the full this mixture of real hospitality and rugged hardship. Always more interested in men and manners than scenery, he pondered the evils that resulted from absentee ownership and the disinclination of some chieftains to assume a proper responsibility towards the members of their clan. But the cause of the trouble, as Johnson realized, was really more deep-seated than any lack of personal responsibility for individual tenants. Various pressures, social, economic and political, were eroding clan-life; and it was impossible to turn the clock back and preserve the old allegiances. In his published *Journey*, which has been aptly described as 'a singular compound of narrative and argument',[74] it is Johnson's sympathetic realization of the plight of a whole people that so often gives point to his narrative and depth to his argument.

During 1776 Johnson mentioned in a letter to Boswell what was to be his last major work : 'I am engaged to write little Lives, and little Prefaces, to a little edition of the English Poets. I think I have persuaded the booksellers to insert something of Thomson'.[75] Four other poets, Pomfret, Blackmore, Yalden and Watts, were included at Johnson's suggestion, the total number of Lives being eventually fifty-two. Much of the Life of Edmund Smith was taken from a memoir by William Oldisworth; while the biographical part of Young's was written by Sir Herbert Croft. In his letters Johnson occasionally solicited information about individual poets; he waited on Lord Marchmont to learn details of Pope; he asked the printer John Nichols for books; and the Duke of Newcastle permitted the use of his manuscript of Spence's *Anecdotes*. But the great bulk of the task he accomplished himself, without looking for assistance from others. It occupied him for almost four years, the first four volumes of *Prefaces, Biographical and Critical* (containing twenty-two Lives) being published in 1779, and the last six volumes (containing the remaining thirty) in 1781.

The finished work went far beyond the scope that Johnson had earlier envisaged in his letter to Boswell.[76] *The Lives of the Poets* (as it came to be called) is a comprehensive, critical account of the lives and works of poets spanning the period from Cowley (as a representative of the Metaphysical school) to Gray and his contemporaries. In writing it Johnson was able to indulge both his great fondness for biography and a lifelong interest in the criticism of literature, especially poetry. The result is an early and important example of the now established genre of literary biography.

The combination of percipience and reasoned argument which these Lives display entitles Johnson to a high place among English critics. It has been suggested that he was most at ease in dealing with poets who wrote within the Augustan tradition, and that his best Lives are those of Dryden and Pope.[77] Certainly he realized a lifelong ambition in writing Dryden's life, where the critical insights are frequently penetrating and, together with remarks in the Lives of Cowley, Denham and Waller, give the reader a clear impression of an important chapter in the history of seventeenth-century poetry. Yet the Life of Pope, for all its excellence as biography, is relatively perfunctory as criticism in that Johnson makes little attempt to grapple with those objections to the poet's reputation which by this time were already being advanced. It must, however, be said that he fully acknowledges the witty elegance and imaginative power that sets Pope so far above his near-contemporaries like Addison and Prior, whose more ambitious verse, though 'correct', remains basically dull and lifeless. No one, in fact, has discerned more clearly than Johnson the kind of inbuilt, lacklustre tautology that so often characterizes the second-rate poetry of this period.

Johnson considered Cowley's his best Life because of its discussion of 'Metaphysical' poetry,[78] and such a view naturally prompts us to ask how successful is his criticism of other than Augustan poetic modes. In general it must be said that, however discerning his critical intelligence, he could not always free himself from neo-classical assumptions about language and poetic form. He condemned most of Gray's poetry—the *Elegy* excepted—for a use of language which seemed to him artificial and affected; and in passages recalling his strictures on certain types of dramatic speech, he argued that the presence of Metaphysical wit in avowedly elegiac poetry was enough to declare the professed emotion counterfeit. The same naïve (though thoroughly neo-classical) criterion of sincerity was responsible for his greatest howler in dismissing 'Lycidas'. Yet it is also true that he was generally disposed to acknowledge poetic originality in whatever form. To the Metaphysicals' vigorous wit he could respond quite positively :

If they frequently threw away their wit upon false conceits, they likewise sometimes struck out unexpected truth : if their conceits were far-fetched, they were often worth the carriage. To write on their plan it was at least necessary to read and think. No man could be born a metaphysical poet, nor assume the dignity of a writer by descriptions copied from descriptions, by imitations borrowed from imitations, by traditional imagery and hereditary similes, by readiness of rhyme and volubility of syllables.[79]

And Johnson responded no less readily to the kind of sensibility and quality of perception reflected in the very different poetic mode of Thomson's *Seasons* :

As a writer he is entitled to one praise of the highest kind : his mode of thinking and of expressing his thoughts is original ... He looks round on Nature and on Life with the eye which Nature bestows only on a poet, the eye that distinguishes in every thing presented to its view whatever there is on which imagination can delight to be detained, and with a mind that at once comprehends the vast, and attends to the minute. The reader of *The Seasons* wonders that he never saw before what Thomson shews him, and that he never yet has felt what Thomson impresses.[80]

Johnson's criticism is, indeed, something more than the product of an age, and its student cannot therefore leave either the tradition or the man out of account. Even where he most obviously employs the analytic method of the neo-classical period, as in discussing *Paradise Lost* under the conventional Aristotelian headings of fable, characters, sentiments and diction, Johnson makes us feel the force of his own individual response. What finally differentiates his criticism of Milton's epic from Addison's (in *The Spectator*) is the conflict it sets up within his own breast. Though imaginatively committed for moral and religious reasons to the excellence of its grand design, another side of his nature is compelled to acknowledge the poem's 'want of human interest'.[81] And this is but the central paradox in an argument fraught with fascinating contradictions. These can only be explained by seeing the man as the author of the criticism. They cannot be explained away by any description of his critical method as that of a 'moderator considering both sides of the argument to reach his judgement'.[82] Indeed, such a description, though it underlines Johnson's attempt at objectivity, only denatures the quality and immediacy of his complex and divided response to the work.

Apart from the *Lives*, Johnson composed nothing of note during the last years of his life except two of his best occasional poems, 'A Short Song of Congratulation' (1780) and 'On the Death of Dr. Robert Levet' (1782). The playful seriousness of the former poem, with its bantering tone and skilfully directed satire, illustrates one side of Johnson's personality as surely as the melancholy seriousness of the lines on Levett illustrates another. In its controlled language and heartfelt grief, Johnson's elegy is a paradigm of what the neo-classical age expected from this genre. It stamps itself, however, as peculiarly Johnsonian in its apprehension of the illusory nature of hope, the travail of human life, and the importance of an active and virtuous life in ensuring man's happiness in a future state.

IV

The foregoing account has left many of Johnson's works unmentioned. Throughout a long literary life he wrote so many pieces of a miscellaneous nature that only from some firsthand knowledge of them can one form an adequate idea of the extent of his learning and range of intellectual interests. Often he wrote to help friends. For his former school-fellow Dr. John Taylor of Ashbourne, he composed a number of sermons (including the one Taylor preached at the funeral of Johnson's wife in 1752);[83] and among his numerous dedications were those written for Dr. Robert James, Charlotte Lennox, Giuseppe Baretti, Bishop Percy, Sir Joshua Reynolds and Dr. Charles Burney. Of the many introductions and prefaces for works other than his own perhaps the most notable is that to the *Proceedings of the Committee for Cloathing French Prisoners of War* (1760), where Johnson's characteristic humanity finds ready expression.

During his closing years, Johnson was racked by increasing ill-health. In 1783 he not only suffered a stroke that for a time deprived him of speech, but was troubled by a sarcocele. Chronic asthma made breathing difficult, and in the winter of 1783–84 illness confined him to his house for three months on end. Though in the summer he was well enough to pay an extended visit to Oxford, Lichfield and Ashbourne, which had long been almost an annual event, soon after his return to London in November the spasms in his chest grew more violent. His friends and doctors did what they could, but he died on 13 December, having shown till the last a characteristic resignation and fortitude. He was buried in Poets' Corner, Westminster Abbey, where Dr. Taylor read the burial service.

So impressive and many-sided were Johnson's personality and achievement that he attracted the attention of a number of contemporary biographers, most notably Mrs. Thrale-Piozzi (1786), Sir John Hawkins (1787), and Boswell (1791). Of these Hawkins is the least interesting and informative in that his own rather stern aloofness casts his subject in something of the same mould. Boswell's pages, on the other hand, come to life because of his eye for detail, his incomparable, firsthand reporting of Johnson's witty and vigorous conversation with a host of distinguished contemporaries, and his own contrasting personality, which so often acts as a foil to Johnson's. But whereas Boswell saw his subject mainly in the world, arguing with his intellectual peers and talking them down, Mrs. Thrale and Fanny Burney had known him at his ease in the relatively relaxed circle at Streatham. Their pages therefore capture an important further side to his personality. Moreover, despite the element of pique that has often been read into the account of the recently estranged Mrs. Piozzi, as she had become, she is in some ways a better guide to Johnson's literary opinions and preferences than Boswell himself.

As a person, Johnson possessed his share of those 'contradictory qualities' that Boswell declared to be so characteristic of him.[84] No one had a rougher exterior, or a kinder heart. Though untidy and shambling in appearance, he valued true politeness. Though he rarely showed forbearance towards an opponent in conversation, he was sincere in making charity one of the guiding principles of his life. Though an obvious authoritarian, he prized human liberty. A man of strong passions and appetites, he set a high value on chastity and moderation. Inclined to ridicule those who complained of low spirits, he suffered from acute melancholia. Though a devout Christian, he feared that he might not be saved.

Such contradictory qualities reflected in Johnson's personality impart to his writings their peculiar depth and resonance. As a good Augustan, he used his powerful intellect in an attempt to impose order on the world around him. But his honesty to his own vivid sensations forced him to recognize the multifarious, fragmented, chaotic nature of life itself. His philosophic work was, significantly, not the *Essay on Man* but *Rasselas*. He responded to Augustanism, to its exaltation of order and reason; but he saw that these were virtues that could not be easily won. Indeed, though firmly placed by temperament and circumstance within the neo-classical period, Johnson holds our interest as both man and writer because he was at once less complacent and more committed to the complexities of human experience than most of his contemporaries.

1. *Boswell's Life of Johnson* (hereafter cited as *Life*), ed. G. B. Hill, rev. L. F. Powell, 6 vols., Oxford, 1934–50, 1964, i. 48.

2. *Ibid.*, i. 94–5, 96.

3. Quoted, *ibid.*, i. 102.

4. *The Letters of Samuel Johnson* (hereafter cited as *Letters*), ed. R. W. Chapman, Oxford, 1952, i. 3. (Reference is given to this work for all letters, even those for which the source is Boswell's *Life*.)

5. J. L. Clifford, *Young Samuel Johnson*, London, 1955, p. 176.

6. *Ibid.*, p. 244.

7. *Life*, i. 129.

8. See J. W. Krutch, *Samuel Johnson*, New York, 1944, p. 64; S. C. Roberts, *Samuel Johnson*, London, 1954, p. 8; D. J. Greene, ' "Logical Structure" in Eighteenth-Century Poetry', *Philological Quarterly*, xxxi (1952), 332.

9. Mary Lascelles, 'Johnson and Juvenal', in *New Light on Dr. Johnson*, ed. F. W. Hilles, New Haven, 1959, pp. 41–2.

10. John Hardy, 'Johnson's *London*: The Country Versus the City', in *Studies in the Eighteenth Century*, ed. R. F. Brissenden, Canberra, 1968, pp. 251–268.

11. *Marmor Norfolciense*, London, 1739, p. 41.

12. *Life*, i. 150.

13. *Ibid.*, i. 118, 509.

14. *An Essay on the Life and Genius of Samuel Johnson, LL.D.*, in *The Works of Samuel Johnson, LL.D.*, London, 1792, i. 43–5.

15. *Life*, i. 152, 505.

16. B. B. Hoover, *Samuel Johnson's Parliamentary Reporting: Debates in the Senate of Lilliput*, Berkeley and Los Angeles, 1953 (University of California Publications, English Studies, no. 7), p. 150.

17. *Lives of the Poets* (hereafter cited as *Lives*), ed. G. B. Hill, Oxford, 1905, ii. 380.

18. Clifford, *Young Samuel Johnson*, p. 272.

19. *Life*, i. 192, 537.

20. E. A. Bloom, '*The Vanity of Human Wishes*: Reason's Images', *Essays in Criticism*, xv (1965), 185 ff.

21. Paul Fussell, *The Rhetorical World of Augustan Humanism*, Oxford, 1965, p. 147.

22. F. W. Hilles, 'Johnson's Poetic Fire', in *From Sensibility to Romanticism: Essays Presented to Frederick A. Pottle*, ed. F. W. Hilles and Harold Bloom, New York, 1965, p. 69.

23. Mary Lascelles, 'Johnson and Juvenal', in *New Light on Dr. Johnson*, p. 55.

24. *Lives*, i. 447.

25. Cited by Hilles (op. cit. p. 77) as Benét's phrase (C. A. Fenton, *Stephen Vincent Benét*, New Haven, 1958, p. 304).

26. *Lives*, ii. 132.

27. Cf. B. H. Bronson, 'Johnson's *Irene*', in *Johnson Agonistes and Other Essays*, Cambridge, 1946, esp. pp. 123 ff.

28. *Life*, i. 203.

29. *Ibid.*, i. 201.

30. *Diaries, Prayers, and Annals*, ed. E. L. McAdam, Jr., with Donald and Mary Hyde, New Haven, 1958, The Yale Edition of the Works of Samuel Johnson (hereafter cited as *Works: Yale*), gen. ed. A. T. Hazen, i. 43.

31. *Præterita*, I. xii. 252.

32. *Life*, iv. 5.

33. Cf. W. K. Wimsatt, Jr., *Philosophic Words: A Study of Style and Meaning in the 'Rambler' and 'Dictionary' of Samuel Johnson*, New Haven, 1948, passim.

34. *Life*, iii. 172.

35. Cf. J. P. Hardy, *'Dictionary' Johnson*, Armidale, 1967, pp. 9–11.

36. *Life*, i. 254.

37. *The Life of Samuel Johnson, LL.D.*, London, 1787, 2nd edn., p. 286.

38. *Life*, i. 247–8.

39. *Letters*, i. 64–5.

40. *Works*, 1792 edn., ii. 6, 25.

41. *Ibid.*, ii. 60.

42. *Ibid.*, ii. 6.

43. *Life*, i. 432–3.

44. Cf. Hester Chapone, *The Posthumous Works*, London, 1807, i. 108 ff.

45. Emrys Jones, 'The Artistic Form of *Rasselas*', *Review of English Studies*, new series, xviii (1967), 400.

46. *Rambler*, no. 127.

47. *Life*, i. 392.

48. J. D. Fleeman, 'Dr. Johnson and Henry Thrale, M.P.', in *Johnson, Boswell and their Circle: Essays Presented to Lawrence Fitzroy Powell*, ed. M. M. Lascelles *et al.*, Oxford, 1965, pp. 170–89.

49. H. L. Piozzi, *Anecdotes of the late Samuel Johnson, LL.D.*, London, 1786; *Thraliana*, ed. K. C. Balderston, Oxford, 1942, 1951, esp. vol. i.

50. The Johnsonian portions are reproduced in *Dr. Johnson and Fanny Burney*, ed. C. B. Tinker, New York, 1911.

51. *Works: Yale*, vii. 58.

52. *Ibid.*, vii. 62.

53. *Ibid.*, vii. 71.

54. *Ibid.*, vii. 64.

55. *Ibid.*, vii. 523, viii. 973–4.

56. *The Works of Shakespear*, London, 1723–25, i. p. iii.

57. *Life*, ii. 95, 154.

58. *Works: Yale*, vii. 88.

59. Cf. John Hardy, ' "The Poet of Nature" and Self-Knowledge:

One Aspect of Johnson's Moral Reading of Shakespeare', *University of Toronto Quarterly*, xxxvi (1966–67), 141–60.

60. *Works: Yale*, viii. 1047–8.

61. *Ibid.*, vii. 67.

62. *Ibid.*, viii. 704.

63. *The Critical Works of John Dennis*, ed. E. N. Hooker, Baltimore, 1939–43, ii. 20–1; cf. *The Critical Works of Thomas Rymer*, ed. C. A. Zimansky, New Haven, 1956, pp. 22–3, 27–8.

64. *Life*, iii. 296; cf. *ibid.*, v. 180.

65. M. C. Bradbrook, *Themes and Conventions of Elizabethan Tragedy*, Cambridge, 1935, p. 4.

66. *Works: Yale*, vii. 69.

67. Cf. *Life*, iii. 229.

68. *Samuel Johnson on Shakespeare*, ed. W. K. Wimsatt, New York, 1960, p. xx.

69. *Works: Yale*, vii. 67.

70. Cf. Lytton Strachey's review of Raleigh's *Johnson on Shakespeare* in *The Spectator*, ci (1 August 1908), 164–5.

71. *Life*, ii. 35.

72. *Ibid.*, i. 408; cf. *ibid.*, i. 442, ii. 219, 329, iii. 26, v. 353.

73. *The Political Writings of Dr. Johnson: A Selection*, ed. J. P. Hardy, London, 1968, p. 83.

74. Mary Lascelles, 'Notions and Facts: Johnson and Boswell on their Travels', in *Johnson, Boswell and their Circle*, p. 229.

75. *Letters*, ii. 170.

76. Cf. *Life*, iv. 35 and n.

77. George Watson, *The Literary Critics: A Study of English Descriptive Criticism*, London, 1964, p. 94.

78. *Life*, iv. 38.

79. *Lives*, i. 21.

80. *Ibid.*, iii. 298–9.

81. *Ibid.*, i. 170, 183.

82. D. M. Hill, 'Johnson as Moderator', *Notes and Queries*, cci (1956), 522.

83. Cf. M. J. Quinlan, *Samuel Johnson: A Layman's Religion*, Madison, 1964, p. 85.

84. *Life*, iv. 426.

BIBLIOGRAPHY

I *Collected Works*

Of the early editions the first two are most reliable textually :

*The Works of Samuel Johnson, LL.D. Together with his Life . . .
by Sir John Hawkins*, 11 vols., London, 1787;

*The Works of Samuel Johnson, LL.D. A New Edition . . . with An
Essay on his Life and Genius, by Arthur Murphy*, 12 vols., London, 1792.

The standard modern edition (still in preparation) is the Yale Edition
of the Works of Samuel Johnson (gen. ed. formerly A. T. Hazen,
presently J. H. Middendorf) of which the following volumes have
so far appeared :

i. *Diaries, Prayers, and Annals*, ed. E. L. McAdam, Jr., with Donald
and Mary Hyde, 1958;

ii. *The Idler and the Adventurer*, ed. W. J. Bate, J. M. Bullitt, and
L. F. Powell, 1963;

iii–iv. *The Rambler*, ed. W. J. Bate and A. B. Strauss, 1969;

vi. *Poems*, ed. E. L. McAdam, Jr., with George Milne, 1964;

vii–viii. *Johnson on Shakespeare*, ed. Arthur Sherbo, with an introduction by B. H. Bronson, 1968.

II. *Individual Works and Selections*

The Critical Opinions of Samuel Johnson, ed. J. E. Brown, Princeton,
1926 (reissued New York, 1961).

Johnson's Dictionary: A Modern Selection, ed. E. L. McAdam, Jr.
and George Milne, New York, 1963.

*Johnson's Journey to the Western Islands of Scotland, and Boswell's
Journal of a Tour to the Hebrides with Samuel Johnson, LL.D.*,
ed. R. W. Chapman, London, 1924, 1930; paperback edn, 1970.

The Letters of Samuel Johnson, ed. R. W. Chapman, 3 vols., Oxford, 1952.

The Lives of the Poets, ed. G. B. Hill, 3 vols., Oxford, 1905 (reprinted,
New York, 1967).

The Poems of Samuel Johnson, ed. D. Nichol Smith and E. L. McAdam, Jr., Oxford, 1941 (reissued, 1951).

The Political Writings of Dr. Johnson: A Selection, ed. J. P. Hardy,
London, 1968.

Samuel Johnson's Prefaces and Dedications, ed. A. T. Hazen, New
Haven, 1937.

Selected Prose and Poetry, ed. B. H. Bronson (Rinehart), New York,
1952; *Rasselas, Poems, and Selected Prose*, enlarged edn., New
York, 1958.

Prose and Poetry, ed. Mona Wilson (Reynard Library), London, 1950
(reissued, 1957).

The History of Rasselas, Prince of Abissinia, ed. J. P. Hardy, Oxford, 1968.

'Rasselas' and Essays, ed. Charles Peake (Routledge English Texts), London, 1967.

Johnson on Shakespeare, ed. Walter Raleigh, London, 1908 (frequently reprinted).

Samuel Johnson on Shakespeare, ed. W. K. Wimsatt, Jr., New York, 1960; London, 1969 (Penguin Shakespeare Library).

III Critical and Biographical Studies

Bate, W. J., The Achievement of Samuel Johnson, New York, 1955. An illuminating treatment of Johnson's psychological make-up as reflected in the themes and character of his writings.

Bloom, E. A., Samuel Johnson in Grub Street, Providence, 1957. A comprehensive account of Johnson's work as journalist.

Bronson, B. H., Johnson and Boswell: Three Essays, Berkeley and Los Angeles, 1944; Johnson Agonistes and Other Essays, Cambridge, 1946. The first essay offers a discerning portrait of Johnson's personality and character.

Clifford, J. L., Young Sam Johnson, New York, 1955; Young Samuel Johnson, London, 1955. A freshly written and informative biography up to 1749.

Greene, D. J., The Politics of Samuel Johnson, New Haven, 1960. Generally informative but some misplaced emphases.

—— (ed.), Samuel Johnson: A Collection of Critical Essays (Twentieth Century Views), Englewood Cliffs, 1965.

Hagstrum, J. H., Samuel Johnson's Literary Criticism, Minneapolis, 1952; rev. edn. Chicago, 1967. Rather schematic in its enunciation of principles governing Johnson's critical practice, but containing, even so, its share of helpful insights.

Hardy, J. P., 'Dictionary' Johnson, Armidale, 1967. An historical reappraisal of the Dictionary and Johnson's linguistic preconceptions.

Hilles, F. W. (ed.), New Light on Dr. Johnson, New Haven, 1959.

Hoover, B. B., Samuel Johnson's Parliamentary Reporting: Debates in the Senate of Lilliput, Berkeley and Los Angeles, 1953. Comprehensive account of Johnson's 'Debates'.

Krutch, J. W., Samuel Johnson, New York, 1944; London, 1948. A perceptive study of the man and his work.

Lascelles, M. M. (ed. et al.), Johnson, Boswell and their Circle: Essays Presented to Lawrence Fitzroy Powell, Oxford, 1965.

Quinlan, M. J., Samuel Johnson: A Layman's Religion, Wisconsin, 1964. A discerning treatment of Johnson's religious position.

Raleigh, Walter, Six Essays on Johnson, Oxford, 1910. Often perceptive and informative.

Sachs, Arieh, Passionate Intelligence: Imagination and Reason in the Work of Samuel Johnson, Baltimore, 1967. A generally discriminating, synthesizing treatment of the polarities of Johnson's thought.

Sledd, J. H. and Kolb, G. J., Dr. Johnson's Dictionary: Essays in the

Biography of a Book, Chicago, 1955. A detailed account of the *Dictionary's* composition, with two chapters on earlier and later lexicographical tradition.

Voitle, Robert, *Samuel Johnson the Moralist*, Cambridge, Mass., 1961. A useful study of Johnson's rationalism as the basis of his concept of morality.

Wahba, Magdi (ed.), *Johnsonian Studies*, Cairo, 1962.

Wimsatt, W. K., Jr., *The Prose Style of Samuel Johnson*, New Haven, 1941. A general treatment of Johnson's prose style.

—— *Philosophic Words: A Study of Style and Meaning in the 'Rambler' and 'Dictionary' of Samuel Johnson*, New Haven, 1948. A persuasive explanation and perceptive analysis of Johnson's *Rambler* style.

IV *Bibliographies* (*in order of appearance*)

W. P. Courtney, *Bibliography of Johnson*, rev. D. Nichol Smith (*Oxford Historical and Literary Studies*, vol. IV), Oxford, 1915 (reprinted with facsimiles, 1925, 1968).

R. W. Chapman and A. T. Hazen, 'Johnsonian Bibliography: A Supplement to Courtney,' *Proceedings of the Oxford Bibliographical Society*, v (1939), 119–66.

J. L. Clifford, *Johnsonian Studies 1887–1950: A Survey and Bibliography*, Minneapolis, 1951 (in this and the following item important editions, books and articles are marked with an asterisk).

J. L. Clifford and D. J. Greene, 'A Bibliography of Johnsonian Studies, 1950–1960,' *Johnsonian Studies*, ed. Magdi Wahba, Cairo, 1962, pp. 293–350.

11

POETRY AND CRITICISM AFTER 1740

Arthur Johnston, University College of Aberystwyth

Dryden, writing in 1668 of the dramatists of the previous age, Jonson, Fletcher and Shakespeare, declared, 'they are honoured, and almost adored by us, as they deserve . . . we shall never equal them'. But, he went on, we shall never equal them *because* 'they have ruined their estates themselves before they came to their children's hands. There is scarce an humour, a character, or any kind of plot, which they have not blown upon [i.e. used]: all comes sullied or wasted to us'. Dryden is the first English poet to express the feeling that, after such a flowering of poetic and dramatic genius, it is not going to be easy to find subject-matter and a manner of treating it that will be new. Either he must not write at all, or 'attempt some other way'. 'There is no bays to be expected in their walks'.[1] Dryden had the confidence to see that there was one way among many in which his own age excelled the Elizabethans, the use of the rhymed heroic couplet. He comforted himself with the thought that 'the genius of every age is different' and worked hard in his critical prefaces to mould the taste of his readers for his own plays and poems.

The great poet of the next generation, Pope, had that self-confidence which is 'the first requisite to great undertakings'. At the outset of his career 'he tried all styles and many subjects'. But he valued the advice of William Walsh, who told him to cultivate in his verse 'correctness', which 'the English poets had hitherto neglected, and which therefore was left to him as a basis of fame'. Pope was able to do new things. But as early as 1726 James Thomson, in the preface to *Winter* (a poem in blank verse, a metre Pope very rarely used, and based on Virgil's *Georgics*, a genre Pope did not attempt on this scale), announced the discovery—or recovery—of a new-old subject-matter for the poet. Thomson considered the poetry then being written as having only a 'dry, barren theme', full of 'forced unaffecting fancies, little glittering prettinesses, mixed turns of wit and expression'. 'Let poetry once more be restored to her ancient truth and purity; let her be inspired from heaven, . . . let her . . . please, instruct, surprise and astonish.' The subject he discovered was 'the Works of Nature', sung in the book of Job, in the *Georgics* of Virgil, and by the best ancient and modern poets.[2] Thomson was able to do new things in *The Seasons* by concentrating on natural description as a major part of a kind of poem which owed much to the *Georgics* and to the physico-theological tradition which in prose and verse declared the wisdom and providence of God as manifested in the creation.

It is always necessary for a young poet to feel that he has something new to say and a new way of saying it. So we are not surprised to find Joseph Warton, twenty years after Thomson's declaration, announcing that he too was bringing poetry back into its proper channel.

> The Public has been so much accustom'd of late to didactic Poetry alone, and Essays on moral Subjects, that any work where the imagination is much indulged will perhaps not be relished or regarded . . . the fashion of moralizing in verse has been carried too far, and as [the author] looks upon Invention and Imagination to be the chief faculties of a Poet, so he will be happy if the following Odes may be look'd upon as an attempt to bring back Poetry into its right channel.[3]

No poet, least of all Pope, would have disagreed with the statement that 'Invention and Imagination [are] the chief faculties of a Poet'. Pope, using the principles of Longinus, had made this the basis for his praise of Homer, in the preface to his translation of the *Iliad* in 1715.[4] But Warton clearly feels that he must lay claim to some poetic ground unoccupied by Pope, who had 'moralized his song'. Mark Akenside (1721–1770), writing in 1744 in the introduction to a poem that he must have started to write before he was twenty, is equally clear that 'there is no bays' to be expected in Pope's walks. He admits that public taste was 'in a great measure formed' by 'the most perfect of modern poets' to the 'familiar epistolary way of Horace', and that this manner allows a poet great variety of style, and close and concise expression, and attracts a wide range of readers. But he was eager to find a new subject for a long poem, and the one he found, an account of the Pleasures of the Imagination, demanded a different manner—blank verse—and a different model—'that antient and simple' model 'of the first Greeks as it is refined by Virgil in the *Georgics*'. That is, Akenside is about to try to make poetry, as Virgil had done in the *Georgics*, out of 'unpoetic' material, in this case the psychological-cum-literary-critical ideas of Addison and Shaftesbury. He needs, therefore, a model in diction and prosody that will hide the unpoetical nature of his material and give him an excuse to be consistently serious-minded, that is, to be sublime. When reading the best work of Dryden, Pope, Swift, Prior or Gay, we are often made to laugh. After 1740 poets want us to weep or sigh, to gasp with awe or shudder with fear, but they do not ask us to laugh. One of the main characteristics of the poets writing between 1740 and 1780 is their desire to restore poetry 'to her antient truth and purity'. And to do this they sought new models—genres, styles, dictions, prosodic devices that had been used by writers they admired—as an aid to being different, new and serious.

The reader accustomed to twentieth-century poetry will be astonished at the range of poetic forms available to the poet in the eighteenth century. The Georgic-descriptive poem, in blank-verse or the heroic couplet, epic and mock-epic, verse tragedy and satire were used for longer flights. Poetical 'Essays' and 'Epistles', 'Imitations' of Spenser, or Juvenal, and verse translations or paraphrases from the Bible or the classical poets provided an intermediate length. Short forms included Pastoral, Fable, Prospect poem, Elegy or Monody, Hymn, Song, Ballad (humorous or serious), Ode (Horatian or Pindaric), Inscription, Epigram, Epitaph and 'occasional' poem. But while all the forms were used, the poets of this period that are now read are re-membered for poems in the lyric mode—elegy, ode, song or hymn. The forms that all the critics of the period continued to regard as the supreme poetic forms, epic and tragedy, were never used with any success. If we think of tragedy in this period, it is not of any of the actual tragedies written, but of Collins's ambition to write tragedy. When we think of epic, it is of Macpherson's forgery of Gaelic epics supposedly written in the middle ages. It is symptomatic of this period that when Robert Lowth succeeded Joseph Spence as Professor of Poetry in Oxford in 1741 he chose to lecture for the next ten years not on Classical poetry, nor on English poetry—too little was then known of the history of English poetry and the subject was re-garded as lacking dignity for a public lecture in a University; instead he chose Hebrew poetry. Thereby he could hope to be 'new' as a critic by applying Longinian principles in an un-familiar field, he was not hampered by the weight of existing criticism, he could ignore epic and tragedy, plot and character, and concentrate on the ode and the hymn, on sublimity, language, style, allegory, personification, imagery and unusual metrical forms.[5] When Joseph Warton (who, with Collins, was probably a member of Lowth's original audience) attempted to 'bring back poetry into its right channel', he was aware that the 'right channel' was the 'original' channel. And Lowth had shown in detail what earlier critics had generally maintained, that poetry in its origin was lyrical, an almost involuntary overflow from an enraptured mind, its language the language of passion, remote from that of prose.[6] We find, therefore, that poets, unable or unwilling to compete in the well-worked forms of satire and Georgic-descriptive poems begin to turn to models earlier than Horace, Juvenal and Virgil. One such source was Greek poetry. Joseph Warton, for example recommended his father's translation of three Greek epigrams 'as a Pattern of the Simplicity so much admir'd in the Grecian writings, so foreign to the present prevailing Taste, to the Love of Modern Witticism, and Italian conceit.'[7] Akenside, in his odes, hoped to write such verse 'as when Greece to her immortal shell/ Rejoicing listened',

> And English fancy's eager flame
> To Grecian purity chastize.[8]

In his 'Ode on Lyric Poetry' (I. xiii) he mentions only Greek poets; his 'Hymn to the Naiads' is in the manner of Callimachus, and the notes to the poem are crammed with Greek mythological lore; and in his nine short blank-verse Inscriptions he succeeded in creating in English a particularly Greek form of poem.[9] Shenstone also wrote Inscriptions modelled on the Greek. Collins, whose odes refer frequently to Greek tragedy, longed to 'Revive the just Designs of Greece'. William Mason (1725–1797) revived the Greek chorus for his closet-plays, and was mocked by Goldsmith and Robert Lloyd for his folly.[10] But it was Pindar who inspired most poets, and in particular Collins and Gray.

Pindar was classed with Homer, Shakespeare and the poets of the Old Testament as an 'original' genius, in contrast to Virgil and Milton, great poets who had submitted their genius to the rules of 'art'. The 'original' poet was seen as one who, by the accident of history, had had no great predecessor to 'imitate'. His work therefore was an example of what 'pure poetry' was. The conscious problem for many of the poets writing in this period was how to become an 'original' poet. Edward Young in particular was 'willing to make an attempt where [he] had fewest rivals' (Preface to *Imperium Pelagi. A Naval Lyric*, 1729) in the sublime mode of Pindar, and claimed that though in one sense his poem was an 'imitation', what he had imitated was Pindar's energy and spirit, not his subject and design, and so had written an 'original' poem. Even at the age of 76 he was still optimistic; modern poets must 'emulate' the great 'originals', by drinking 'at the breast of Nature', not slavishly 'imitate' or copy other works. These may 'nourish' the modern poet, but should not intimidate him. The writer's harvest is *not* over.[11]

The Pindaric form of the ode involved a complicated stanza, with lines of varying length. Because Pindar was always celebrating the victor at some games, he was forced to vary his subject-matter by boldly digressing to other topics. Boldness of transition from topic to topic and from mood to mood, 'Wild as the lightning, various as the moon', and the apparent dominance of imagination over judgement, were regarded as the characteristics of this form of poem. Gray and Collins, Akenside and Mason, and a host of lesser poets, followed Cowley, Congreve, Dryden, Pope, Pomfret, Watts and Young in using the form; the difference between the earlier and the later poets is that after 1740 poets tended to do some of their best work in Pindarics.

Besides the Greeks as the exemplars of what true poetry should be, it became common after 1740 to place Milton and Spenser. Akenside, for example, says that Milton is 'the only modern poet (unless perhaps it be necessary to except Spenser) who . . . had a heart to feel, and words to express the simple and solitary genius of antiquity'.[12] For Gray in 'The Progress of Poesy' Milton is

> He that rode sublime
> Upon the seraph-wings of Extasy.

(95–96)

For Collins in a despairing mood in the 'Ode on the Poetical Character' (1746) Milton is the last poet who could hear the native strains of Heaven. Collins, like his friends Joseph and Thomas Warton, is in retreat from 'Waller's Myrtle Shades', that is, from the tradition of poetry descended from Waller, which included Dryden and Pope. Milton, in *Paradise Lost*, appealed to the new poets as an exemplar of sublime narrative. It was his handling of blank verse, not Shakespeare's, that was influential, in spite of the fact that Shakespeare was more generally admired as a great 'original'. Milton was capable of sustained sublimity in style, and it was sublimity that was most eagerly sought. For an enthusiast such as Edward Young 'blank verse is verse unfallen, uncurst; verse reclaimed, reinthroned in the true language of the gods'. Rhymed verse was a 'Gothic' invention.[13] To Johnson and Goldsmith blank verse was 'pedantic', 'in description exuberant, in argument loquacious, and in narration tiresome'. Even those poets who continued to use the couplet or the rhymed lyric stanza forms borrowed and echoed phrases and rhythms from *Paradise Lost*, as Gray and Collins did. The blank-verse poets, Thomson, Akenside, Young, Armstrong, Dyer and Grainger, not only borrow and echo, but imitate Milton in their love of Latinate diction, of the extended and involved sentence, of the soundingness of a word-order remote from that of prose.[14]

It was, however, what one might call the 'discovery' of Milton's minor poems, 'Lycidas', 'Il Penseroso', 'L Allegro', and 'Comus' that, in the eyes of some critics, bedevilled much of the poetry of the mid-eighteenth century. One reason for Johnson's attack on 'Lycidas' in his life of Milton was that its pastoral form and its irregular verse had become a pattern for the elegies of poetasters. But for Joseph Warton delight in 'Lycidas' was a sure test of a man's 'true taste for Poetry';[15] his brother agreed that it was not expressive of deep and immediate grief, 'but let us read it for its Poetry'. 'L'Allegro' and 'Il Penseroso', according to Warton, 'by a strange fatality lay in a sort of obscurity, the private enjoyment of a few curious readers, till they were set to admirable music by Mr. Handel'.[16] It was in fact 'Il Penseroso' that held most attraction; but the existence of two complementary poems, on cheerfulness and melancholy, with the poet apparently committed to neither, seems to have suggested to the Wartons—and much of the critical writing of the period would have supported them in this—that poetry involved commitment to an emotion, not to an idea. They further suggested, since Milton was trying on roles, and was concerned to describe, by a selection of generalized images from nature, the moods of a sensitive and solitary poet, that this was a satisfying technique to follow. In their early poetry Joseph and Thomas Warton indulged in sensations of melancholy, horror and isolation, collecting all the images in earlier poetry that evoked such feelings—such images as Gray more gently uses in the opening stanzas of the *Elegy*. They cultivated a special kind of sensibility, to be experienced in solitude, in wilder and more grotesque scenery. It required gross stimulants and was self-indulgent, it contemplated ruins and death with more 'transport' and 'rapture' than ever could be found in the real world. It was poetry made out of a response to carefully selected pieces of earlier poetry, their main source of imaginative nourishment.

William Collins (1721–59) went to Milton's minor poems for verse-forms; the blank-verse stanza of his 'Ode to Evening' is taken from Milton's version of Horace's ode 'To Pyrrha', the ode 'To Simplicity' uses the first six lines of Milton's stanza in the *Nativity Ode*. He borrows or adapts characteristic words and phrases—'votarist', 'the meeting soul', the 'folding star', the beetle 'winds/His small but sullen horn' (Milton has 'sultry'). He borrows and adapts popular superstitions. Milton's

> Tells how the drudging Goblin sweat
> To earn his cream-bowl duly set
>
> ('L'Allegro', 105–6)

becomes

> There each trim lass that skims the milky store
> To the swart tribes their creamy bowl allots.
> ('Ode on Popular Superstitions', 22–3)

But more important for Collins is the pattern of 'L'Allegro' and 'Il Penseroso' in the shaping of his own odes. He likes to use the forms of prayer—invocation, vow and obsecration, as well as the fervent tone and the mood of imploring adoration—in poems addressed to literary abstractions, Pity, Fear, Simplicity, the Manners and the Passions. Robert Lowth's conjecture that the earliest verse would be praise of the creator flowing almost involuntarily from an enraptured mind, may or may not have been known to Collins. But some of Collins's odes are secular versions of what Lowth was describing.[17] And for his purpose 'Il Penseroso' helped him to a useful formula. Milton's 'But hail thou Goddess sage and holy' introduces a train of images—studious cloisters, dim religious light, the mossy cell, Jove's altar, the cherub Contemplation—that would not be out of place in one of Collins's poems. The ending—

> These pleasures, Melancholy, give
> And I with thee will choose to live—

is adapted and varied for the ending of Collins's 'Ode to Fear' and 'The Manners'. In the latter poem Milton's formula 'Hence . . . But come thou' is copied as 'Farewell . . . Thy walks . . . more invite, O thou. . . .' Collins remains original, in the mood, tone and structure of ideas but he clearly learned his general formula from 'Il Penseroso'.

Thomas Gray (1716–1771) borrowed diction widely from

earlier poets, delighting to revive words that had been lost to the language, as well as to enrich his meaning by deliberate quotation or allusion. From Milton's minor poems he takes such phrases as 'rosy-bosom'd Hours', 'margent green', 'echoing horn', 'solemn-breathing', 'desert cave', 'starry fronts', 'Right against the eastern gate', 'build the lofty verse'. It is important to remember that Gray was aware of his borrowings and stressed that in order to appreciate his poetry the reader required not only imagination and sensibility but also learning 'and a long acquaintance with the good Writers ancient and modern'.[18]

One modern writer with whom Gray was intimately acquainted, though his indebtedness to his work was always indirect, was Spenser. Gray read Spenser whenever he was preparing himself to write verse, partly to induce the right mood, partly to attune his ear to a rich rhythmic language, and partly to remind himself of the achievement of one of the great poets whom he was about to emulate.[19] Spenser was no new discovery to poets and critics after 1740 but he was in some ways a special possession. He was clearly a learned and difficult poet, but his learning had not led him to write *The Faerie Queene* on the model of Homer or Virgil. He could therefore be regarded as 'Gothick', as an example of a mode of procedure other than the Roman. Since this was the period which above all others was seeking for new literary models, Spenser was particularly attractive. His work was naturally valued in terms acceptable to the time. He was seen as a poet of infinite 'Fancy' and rich description, a poet of allegory and vivid personification. His language was antiquated, but varied, his versification was odd, but a model of assonance and alliteration. Above all he was the poet of 'fine fabling', the last poet to use medieval romances which, with their magic and enchantment, 'rouse and invigorate all the powers of imagination' and 'store the fancy with those sublime and alarming images, which true poetry best delights to display'.[20]

James Thomson (1700–48), always an innovator in poetry, was one of the first eighteenth-century poets to attempt an elaborate poem 'in the manner of Spenser'. *The Castle of Indolence* was begun about 1733 as 'a few detached stanzas in the way of raillery on himself, and on some of his friends, who would reproach him with indolence, while he thought them at least as indolent as himself'.[21] But by the time it was published in 1748 it contained 158 stanzas in Spenser's manner, in praise of industry. The poem as originally motivated required a verse form suitable for light-hearted narrative, and for this an octosyllabic couplet measure would have been suitable. Spenser's stanza was, however, the inevitable choice for an allegorical poem, and with the allegory, says Thomson, came Spenser's 'simplicity of diction . . .which borders on the ludicrous'. Clearly Spenser's manner provided him with a model for a narrative poem of some length; it gave him a means of putting allegorical figures, the wizard Indolence and the Knight Industry, in an extended action, with elaborate description of scene and person; it allowed him to vary his style and his matter and to say serious things about life and society in a fresh and interesting way. The stanza and the allegory impose their own decorum, which is more embracing than the decorum of epistle, essay or georgic, so that the poem can contain the delicacy of the land of Innocence :

> A pleasing land of drowsyhed it was :
> Of dreams that wave before the half-shut eye;
> And of gay castles in the clouds that pass,
> For ever flushing round a summer sky

(I. vi)

as well as the vitality of the land of idealized experience :

> Then towns he quickened by mechanic arts,
> And bade the fervent city glow with toil;
> Bade social commerce raise renowned marts,
> Join land to land, and marry soil to soil.

(II. xx)

Before Thomson's poem was published, William Shenstone (1714–63) printed an imitation of Spenser, *The Schoolmistress* (1737); this grew from 12 stanzas to 28 and finally, in 1748, to 35. Shenstone indicates that it was Pope's youthful imitation of Spenser in 'The Alley' that made him notice the 'ludicrous' side of Spenser, so that it was difficult not to 'trifle and laugh' at him. But both Shenstone and Thomson found that, though they began by choosing subjects for their imitations that fitted their initial response to Spenser—Shenstone's subject, his schoolmistress, was one that it was not possible for the poet to treat seriously in verse—their subjects grew in seriousness as their poems developed. What Shenstone called Spenser's 'tenderness of sentiment' is applied in a condescending but sympathetic manner to one 'hardly known to Fame', dwelling 'in lowly shed, and mean attire'. Only in a poem avowedly written in

365

imitation of Spenser could Shenstone have given a long account of the beating of a small boy, and the response of his sister and schoolfellows to the incident. He felt he was protected from the ridicule 'which might fall on so *low* a subject . . . by pretending to *simper* all the time [he] was writing'.[22] He is ashamed of his dissatisfaction with the polite and refined, of his feeling that 'modest worth neglected lies' and that 'simplicity' has retreated from 'thane and lordling' to 'this humble cell'; he needs Spenser's manner, because he has to grope back to the Elizabethan age to find a form that will hold simple sentiment and simple subject-matter.

Gilbert West's imitations of Spenser, *On the Abuse of Travelling* (1739), and *Education* (1751), deal with subjects that do not require or benefit from the disguise of archaism. So also does William Julius Mickle's *Sir Martyn* (1777, the original title in 1767 was *The Concubine*), though Mickle thought that Spenser's 'fullness and wantonness of description', quaint simplicity and above all ludicrousness, made his manner the only possible one for an account of the progress of dissipation. All these poets, and others such as William Thompson, provide glossaries of the archaic diction they use—words such as 'whilom', 'wonne', 'sooth', and, surprisingly, words such as 'to carol', 'lea', 'fay', 'fray', 'glen', 'ken', 'wend', 'welkin'. Spenserian imitation brought such words back into the language of poetry. But this deliberate adoption of an archaic style also offered a particular kind of pleasure. Dr. Johnson in his Life of Shenstone described it as being entertained 'with two imitations, of nature in the sentiments, of the original author in the style, and between them the mind is kept in perpetual employment'. But he was careful to add, in his Life of West, that such works appealed more to memory than to reason or passion, and 'presuppose an accidental or artificial state of mind'. 'An imitation of Spenser, is nothing to a reader, however acute, by whom Spenser has never been perused.'

With James Beattie's *The Minstrel, or the Progress of Genius* (1771–4) we need not, as readers, be aware that the poem is an imitation of Spenser. The stanza form has become one of the many forms available to the poet. Beattie, a Scottish poet (as were Thomson and Mickle), uses none of the deliberate archaisms of his predecessors, and defended his inclusion of such words as 'ween', 'shene', 'eschew', 'aye', 'meed' and 'wight' by reference to Milton, Dryden and Pope. He felt that he had completely renounced Spenser's oddities. He retains the stanza, because it gives him the excuse for description, and because 'a poor villager inspires [his] strain'. His poem is fictionalized autobiography. His shepherd, Edwin, 'takes pleasure in the scenes in which I took pleasure . . . the scenery of mountain country, the ocean, the sky, thoughtfulness and retirement, and sometimes melancholy objects and ideas'.[23] He did not expect that his private and personal experiences would be interesting to many readers, since they were unusual, the experiences of a gifted, sensitive, melancholy, solitary boy. He cast his story in the form suggested by Thomas Percy's account of the minstrel in *The Reliques of Ancient English Poetry* (1765). Edwin, who has a wild and romantic imagination, is instructed by a hermit in history, philosophy and music, and prepares to follow the profession of wandering minstrel. The poem, however, breaks off and is unfinished. It was enthusiastically received because it 'touched the heart', it excited strong sympathy and made a deep impression by interesting the reader in a particular individual, Beattie would not have dared to write about himself in this way except in the stanza of Spenser. Its use in the previous thirty years had been such that it set up in the reader a certain kind of expectation, which Beattie must have felt supplied a distancing effect for his personal subject-matter.

Spenser's influence was general in the period. Akenside revised the first book of his *Pleasures of Imagination* in a way that 'reflected a growing sympathy with Spenser and an interest in "the fairy way of writing".'[24] Thomas Warton, in his *Observations on the Faerie Queene* (1754, revised 1762) and Richard Hurd in his *Letters on Chivalry and Romance* (1762) examined *The Faerie Queene* in order to encourage readers to respond more sympathetically to 'Gothic manners . . . as adapted to the uses of the greater poetry'.[25] Spenser was the gateway to the 'romantic' middle ages, seen as an age of chivalry and 'fine fabling', an age when imagination could flourish because it was not stifled by polite society. Scholars and critics developed an historical approach, maintaining, like Lowth, that Hebrew poetry should be read in the context of the society that produced it, or, like Hurd and Warton, that Milton, Spenser and the medieval poets were interesting in themselves and as a means of investigating earlier forms of culture. The growth of this interest is seen in the editorial work on Shakespeare, the accumulation of information about the Elizabethan theatre, the beliefs and customs of the Elizabethans, and the sources of Shakespeare's plots, as material for elucidating the plays. Spenser, Milton, Chaucer, and many lesser poets were lovingly annotated and edited.[26] So much work of this kind was done after 1750 that it has become possible to talk of a medieval and renaissance revival. By the early nineteenth century it was an axiom of historical criticism that there had been 'a strange and ungrateful forgetfulness of our elder poets, which began with the Restoration, and continued almost unbroken' until about 1750.[27] Such statements were based on the evidence of the scholarly editions of our earlier poets that were published, and on Thomas Warton's *History of English Poetry* (1774–81) which, for the first time and in great detail, charted the poetic ancestry of Spenser. Warton himself felt that it was necessary to read and understand the poetry of the ages before Milton, in order to restore poetry to its proper channel of 'fiction and fancy, picturesque description and romantic imagery', after a period dominated by 'wit and rhyme, sentiment and satire, polished numbers, sparkling couplets, and pointed periods'.[28] In one respect the period 1740–1780 is engaged on a quest for a lost literary culture, which was found in the Elizabethan age, when 'national credulity, chastened by reason, had produced a sort of civilized superstition, and left a set of traditions fanciful enough for poetic decoration, and yet not too violent and chimerical for common sense'.[29] Hence the importance of Spenser.

Spenser was 'Fancy's pleasing son' who 'pour'd his song/O'er all the mazes of enchanted ground'. Hurd and Warton both argued that Milton and Spenser had minds 'deeply tinctured with romance-reading' and that it was this that had inspired their sublime imaginative poetry. The basis of such criticism was Addison's essay (*Spectator*, no. 419) on 'the fairy way of writing'. Addison characterized the middle ages as a period of superstition, when men looked on nature with 'more reverence and horror', and 'loved to astonish themselves with the apprehensions of witchcraft, prodigies, charms, and enchantments'. The Englishman felt at home with such tales because he belonged to the Northern races that had originally elaborated them; he was naturally 'fanciful' and superior to other Europeans and to the writers of Greece and Rome in creating worlds outside nature, peopled by fairies, demons, spirits, etc. This fancifulness also led to allegory and to personification, the representation of passions, virtues, and vices, such as Milton's Sin and Death, 'under a visible shape'.[30] The pictorial quality of the personified abstractions who inhabited Spenser's allegory was attractive to Collins and the Wartons. Joseph Warton believed that 'the use, the force and the excellence of language, certainly consists in raising *clear*, *complete* and *circumstantial* images, and in turning *readers* into *spectators*'.[31] Such a 'spectator' would be presented by some poets (Thomson for example) with an imitation of the ordinary world in which he lived, but, by a superior poet, with an imitation of a consistent world created by the imagination. Such a poet—and Spenser was commonly the example chosen—'has a world of his own', said Hurd; and his 'air-form'd visions' could be based on 'a legend, a tale, a tradition, a rumour, a superstition'.

William Collins represents such ideas about the nature of poetry in his 'Ode on the Poetical Character',[32] which draws on Spenser for its initial image. Florimel's girdle of chastity (*Faerie Queene*, IV, v. 1–20) had been made by Vulcan for Venus and is now owned by Florimel. At the 'solemn Turney'

> One, only One, unrival'd Fair
> Might hope the magic Girdle wear
>
> (5–6)

and this is Amoret.[33] But it is given to the false Florimel, from whose 'loath'd dishonour'd Side' it falls away. This piece of Spenserian fiction is exactly paralleled, says Collins, by the girdle of Imagination, which also is given to few to wear,

> To gird their blest prophetic Loins,
> And gaze her Visions wild, and feel unmix'd her Flame!
>
> (21–2)

Collins's main subject-matter for poetry is poetry. In this ode he makes a poem out of his response to Spenser and Milton. Like their poems its subject is not the ordinary world, but a world known only to the imagination. In that world of 'Fairy Legends' known only to the poet, the girdle of imagination is woven on that day of Creation

> When He, who call'd with Thought to Birth
> Yon tented Sky, this laughing Earth . . .
> Long by the lov'd *Enthusiast* woo'd
> Himself in some Diviner Mood,
> Retiring, sate with her alone.
>
> (25–6, 29–31)

As part of the act of divine goodness, God created the world of nature and the 'rich-hair'd Youth of Morn', that is the Sun/Apollo, god of prophecy, music and song. Collins is writing a Spenserian allegory of the origin of poetry or the imaginative gift, and exhibiting his own creative gift in vividly describing —making the reader *see*—an event outside the knowledge of ordinary men.

The dangerous Passions kept aloof,
Far from the sainted growing Woof:
But near it sate Ecstatic *Wonder*,
List'ning the deep applauding Thunder:
And *Truth* in sunny Vest array'd,
By whose the Tarsel's Eyes were made;
All the shad'wy Tribes of *Mind*,
In braided Dance their Murmurs join'd,
And all the bright uncounted *Pow'rs*,
Who feed on Heav'n's ambrosial Flow'rs.

(41–50)

For this section of the poem he uses Milton's octosyllabic couplet; he uses Spenserian and Miltonic archaisms—'woof', 'sate', 'array'd', 'Tarsel', 'braided', 'ambrosial'. In terms of his allegory he is saying that the gift of poetry is holy, that it creates a response of awe and surprise, that the poet must have penetrating and far-seeing eyes, that his creations have the validity of truth, that the creative imagination is seen at work in 'the shad'wy Tribes of Mind', the allegorical personifications the creation of which was seen by Joseph Warton as being analogous to the creation of living creatures by God.[34] It was Spenser, even more than Milton, whose poems encouraged the writing of this kind of creative allegory, which gives life and body to an imaginative idea.

Tasso and Spenser, Shakespeare and Milton, as Addison, Warton and Hurd showed, exemplified also the belief that 'true' poetry could only be written in an age that believed in what the critics called 'popular superstitions'. Dr. Johnson criticized Collins because 'he loved fairies, genii, giants, and monsters' and 'was eminently delighted with those flights of imagination which pass the bounds of nature, and to which the mind is reconciled only by a passive acquiescence in popular traditions'. Johnson is a generous and alert critic who, even when he cannot approve, is always able to describe accurately the work in front of him. Here he carefully qualifies his statement by adding that this 'was the character rather of his inclination than his genius'. Collins, in his 'Ode on the Popular Superstitions of the Highlands of Scotland, considered as the Subject of Poetry' (written c. 1749), shows how much he envies the Scottish dramatist, John Home, who lives in an environment where it *is* possible to have 'a passive acquiescence in popular traditions'. He constructs his poem in the form of an epistle to Home, in effect congratulating him on living in a society that still believes in the sort of marvellous material that Tasso, Shakespeare, Spenser and Milton used. By describing that material he is able, as an emancipated southern English poet, to incorporate it in his poem. But there is no actual 'passive acquiescence' in it. These are

> the tales which, simply told,
> Could *once* so well *my* answ'ring bosom pierce.
>> (183–4, my italics)

They are available for the Scottish poet, but not (except in a poem such as this, which uses an old rhetorical figure in order to incorporate them) for the English poet. Collins was fascinated by what he had heard and read of Scotland, where ordinary life was shot through with imagination. The milk-maid skimming 'the milky store' puts out a bowl for the brownies; the cattle are attacked by fairy-bolts; the spade turns up pigmy bones; travellers, who as ordinary men have wives and children, are lured to their deaths by Kelpies. ''Tis Fancy's land'. None of it is 'true', Collins admits, but Shakespeare used such things in *Macbeth*, and Tasso, *because* he

> Believ'd the magic wonders which he sung,
> Hence at each sound imagination glows;
> Hence his warm lay with softest sweetness flows.
>> (199–201)

It was the loss of such material that Thomas Warton lamented when he said that 'ignorance and superstition, so opposite to the real interests of society, are the parents of imagination,' and went on : 'we have parted with extravagancies that are above propriety, with incredibilities that are more acceptable than truth, and with fictions that are more valuable than reality'.[35] The difficulties of being a 'true' poet were thought to be almost insuperable in an enlightened age, and this explains the quest for new models and new material. Collins's 'Ode on the Popular Superstitions' has a sad air; it is a lament for, as well as a celebration of, a 'world of fine fabling' that is lost to the modern poet.

> These are the themes of simple, sure effect,
> That add new conquests to her [the Muse's] boundless reign,
> And fill, with double force, her heart-commanding strain.
>> (33–5)

The quest for 'Poetry endued with new manners, and new

images', for what Shenstone called 'the more striking efforts of wild, original, enthusiastic genius', was met by Gray in his second Pindaric ode, 'The Bard' (written 1754-7), and in his translations from Old Norse and early Welsh poetry (written 1761). Nothing in the period better indicates the difficulty for a poet of finding something to write *about*, if observed facts of the natural and social world were not sufficient inspiration. Nothing in the period better indicates the need of the poet to examine the nature of poetry and its function, to be aware of his own sensibility and to probe it and portray it, to adopt poetic styles and startling roles in order to find out what he might be, and so discover what he is.[36] In 'The Bard' Gray is writing a Pindaric ode; his 'model' is therefore Greek. Doubtless Gray chose it because this was the form accepted for the sublime poem in the lyric mode. But it fitted his subject-matter too. The poem freezes a moment in 1283 when the army of Edward I is on the slopes of Snowdon and the last of the Welsh bards (who has survived Edward's massacre) looks down and curses the conqueror. The bulk of the poem is made up of the Bard's lament, a chorus of ghosts of the slaughtered bards prophesying the distresses of the English ruling house to 1485, and a vision of the house of Tudor with the accompanying revival of poetry at the hands of Spenser, Shakespeare and Milton. The central strophe, antistrophe and epode, which describe the reigns from Edward II to Richard III, are three great allegorical paintings, each with its cluster of personified abstractions carefully arranged:

> What Terrors round him wait!
> Amazement in his van, with Flight combined,
> And Sorrow's faded form, and Solitude behind.

and (60-62)

> Close by the regal chair
> Fell Thirst and Famine scowl
> A baleful smile upon their baffled Guest.

(80-82)

The need, stressed by critics, to create rich allegorical descriptions makes the poem static, so that the action in the final lines of the poem, the Bard's suicide, is a surprise. Within the descriptions everything is energetic and active:

> Long Years of havock urge their destined course,
> And thro' the kindred squadrons mow their way.

(85-6)

But the energy and action of the detail is not paralleled in the poem's structure.

What Gray is doing in this poem is astonishing. As Collins managed to use popular superstitions in a poem by describing what Home had access to, Gray uses ghosts and prophecy in the setting of a poem set back five hundred years.

He writes what we may call an 'historical poem', using 'historical' in the sense in which we use it in 'historical novel'. Instead of putting on Spenser's stanza and diction, he transports himself back into the middle ages, not formally or linguistically, as Chatterton pretends he is doing, but, he hopes, mentally. 'I felt myself the Bard', was his comment. By becoming the Bard he can say things that as Gray he cannot say, just as Beattie wearing Spenser's mantle felt that he could talk about his own experiences. Gray in his own persona writes of himself :

> Too poor for a bribe, and too proud to importune,
> He had not the method of making a fortune :
> Could love and could hate, so was thought somewhat odd;
> No very great wit, he believed in a God :
> A place or a pension he did not desire,
> But left church and state to Charles Townshend and Squire.
> ('Sketch of his own Character'.)

The ineffectualness of a good man, poor, proud, without ambition, but with a power of emotional attachment and a faith superior to those about him, is clear. Such a man may be above corruption, but he is powerless to save state and church from corruption. As the Bard, however, in place of quiet, sad, irony, Gray offers anguished defiance. The good, within the poem, is not ineffectual. The natural world, 'each giant oak and desert cave', breathes revenge on Edward; the supernatural world of ghosts 'weave the winding-sheet of Edward's race'. The poet is not alone and helpless, but the mouthpiece of an order natural and supernatural that will ensure, in time, the destruction of the corrupt and the restoration of good government and poetry, the recipient of a vision that authenticates and justifies his feeling of moral and spiritual superiority. This is what Gray can say when he puts on Pindar's form and projects himself back into the past. It indicates the importance for the period of the concept of sublimity. Contemporary events and manners, what, in Johnson's words, was 'co-extended with rational nature, or at least with the whole circle of polished life', were inadequate material for the poet. It restricted what he could say and the effects he could produce in a reader. To read 'The Bard' was to be 'plunged into sudden fearful perplexity' and 'overpowered'. Its very obscurity, that perplexed some readers, for others was a source of excitement.[37] They recognized that prophecy must be obscure, must work by sketching out 'a few striking circumstances' and excite the reader to fill in the rest. The 'rude scenes of nature, rocks and torrents and whirlwinds and battles' which were the source of the sublime, were all present. The hyperbole, personification and imagery, the heroic, savage, noble, wild, spiritually superior figure of the Bard, the prophetic ghosts, the dark and difficult style, were all sublime. And in that context Gray, in the role of a thirteenth-century Welsh bard, can say things in terms of his historical myth that he can say in no other poetic genre.

The whole poem tries to create the effect of the spontaneous out-pouring of a bard in a more than ordinary state of emotion. But its highly sophisticated prosody and its ornate language give it a contrived air. Johnson did not believe that a modern poet could revive the fiction of prophecy and ghosts: 'we are affected only as we believe'. There was, he thought, 'too little appearance of ease and nature', qualities not in fact being aimed at by Gray in his representation of an unusual state of mind. Johnson even disliked the alliteration of 'ruin' and 'ruthless', which Gray felt was a necessary piece of historical colouring.[38] The Old Norse and Welsh poetry that Gray had read used a prosody that was based on alliteration; Gray is being deliberately archaic, just as he is when he uses a metre that he thinks 'bears some affinity to a peculiar measure in the Welsh Prosody, called Gorchest-Beirdh, i.e. the *Excellent of the Bards*' :

> No more I weep. They do not sleep.
> On yonder cliffs, a griesly band,
> I see them sit, they linger yet,
> Avengers of their native land.[39]

(ll. 43–46)

If we see this period as one in which many of the poets were seeking new models for poetry, Gray is interesting because, as a literary historian, he is able to go farther back than Spenser and Milton, and discover the usefulness of Norse mythology and Welsh prosody.

The translations of fragments of the *Gododdin* and Gwalchmai's ode to Owen Gwynedd, of 'The Fatal Sisters' from Njal's Saga and 'The Descent of Odin' from the Poetic Edda, were all that Gray published of his work on the history of poetry in Britain. But these few pieces fit into a pattern of growing interest in specimens of primitive poetry and the societies that produced them. Paul-Henri Mallet's account of the religion, laws, customs and manners of the Norse people, with a translation of the Edda (1755–6) opened a new field of study, the origins of the nations of Northern Europe. Thomas Percy translated Mallet's work as *Northern Antiquities* (1770). He planned to introduce specimens of the ancient poetry of different nations to modern readers—Erse, Runic, Chinese, Arabic, Hebrew, East-Indian, Peruvian, Lapland, Greenland, Welsh and Saxon,[40] as well as late-medieval English ballads. Percy's interest was in examples of the primitive sublime, the 'forcible Images . . . strong paintings . . . curious displays of manners' of the ancient poets.[41] But he was aware also that readers of poetry were tiring of Greek and Roman mythology, manners, genres, styles and attitudes. He felt that by going back to new and exciting material, poetry might be rejuvenated. Antiquarian studies could be a valuable stimulus for the modern poet as they had been for Gray. The 'fictions of classical antiquity', said Warton, are no longer adequate 'to answer the purposes of pure poetry'; in fact, they never were so successful as the manners and beliefs of the middle ages.[42] What was needed was 'some new Spenser'[43] who could use the multifarious lore that Percy's labours in primitive poetry provided. Gray had partly shown the way, by adapting the Norse myth of the weaving of the fates of men by 'the fatal sisters' for his Celtic poem about the Bard.

The new interest in the primitive poetry and lore of Northern Europe, Celtic and Norse, was stimulated by the growth of local and national patriotism. The period of English poetry between 1660 and 1740 was seen as an interpolation of 'French' influence, the effect of which, it was thought, had been to deflect English poetry from its true tradition, which went back from Milton, through Spenser, to Chaucer and the 'romantic' middle ages. One aim of critics and poets was to restore this tradition; another was to counteract the tendency to feel 'that original poetic genius will in general be displayed in its ultimate vigour in the early . . . periods of society . . . and that it will seldom appear in a very great degree in cultivated life'.[44] The hold that an idealized Roman civilization had exercised over the imagination, and which, in conjunction with the improvements in society and manners, had produced 'much good sense', was waning, its function being achieved. To continue to go forward demanded new models. 'Shall we feel the fire of heroic poetry in translations from Greece and Rome, and never search for it in the native products of our own country?' asked John Aikin in 1773.[45] The Englishman was the descendant of the Northern races that had produced the wild poems that Gray translated. By translating them he had produced, in effect, modern poems that dealt with magic and prophecy, horror and superstition, in an incantatory verse and a language which Johnson said was 'unlike the language of other poets'.

Gray's 'translations' did in fact have authentic Norse and Welsh originals, though his handling of these was quite free. But James Macpherson (1736–96), who offered prose translations of very early Gaelic poems, had very little in the way of authentic texts from which to 'translate'. A modern poet borrowing the style, metre and diction of Milton or Spenser in an avowed 'imitation' is one thing; Gray imagining himself a medieval Welsh bard while he constructs a Pindaric ode is another; the next step is the one Macpherson took. He imagined himself as Ossian, the son and bard of Fingal, a Caledonian chieftain at some very early period of Scottish history. With some fragments of Gaelic poetry to help him, he produced, and offered as authentic, 'translations' into measured prose of two epic poems, *Fingal* (1762) and *Temora* (1763) and a large number of shorter elegiac poems. He steadily maintained their genuineness, despite growing scepticism; his reply to the unbelievers was, 'those who have doubted my veracity have paid a compliment to my genius'. 'This Man', wrote Gray (to Wharton, in June, 1760), 'is the very Demon of Poetry, or he has lighted on a treasure hid for ages'. For the original reader in the 1760s, the appeal lay partly in the excitement of discovering new records of 'the history of human imagination and passion'. This is the only period in the history of English poetry when the printing of fragments of early verse aroused intense interest in the general world of letters, not only in Edinburgh, but throughout Europe. It is also the only period when a poet would go to the lengths of fabricating poetic antiquities. What Macpherson did was, however, inevitable at a time when most writers believed that the only genuine poetry was that written in primitive societies. The taste for an Ossian was there already; Macpherson merely supplied poems to satisfy it, and in a form that was more attractive than the genuinely antique. Percy's authentic *Five Pieces of Runic Poetry* (1763) and Evan Evans's *Specimens of the Poetry of the Ancient Welsh Bards* (1764) fell still-born from the press. Macpherson wrote primitive poetry with the sort of sublimity that his contemporaries *thought* such poetry should have, and added what no genuine primitive poetry could offer, 'an exquisite sensibility of heart . . . that tender melancholy which is so often an attendant on great genius', and 'an amazing degree of regularity and art'.[46] The arguments used by Blair to prove the authenticity of Ossian indicate Macpherson's success in projecting himself into the habits of mind of a primitive bard. The society portrayed in the poems depends on hunting and some pasturage, but there is no mention of agriculture; there are no cities and the only arts are those of navigation and working in iron; there is no mention of Christianity, or indeed of any religion; there are no indications that clans existed; the warriors prepare their own food and eat it in halls through which the wind whistles; they admire valour and bodily strength, they have no drums, trumpets or bagpipes, nor any military discipline. The words used are all particular, there are no abstract concepts, even a hill is 'the hill of Cromla'; there are no personifications of abstracts such as Virtue, but only of winds, trees and flowers, there are no 'allegorical personages'. The scenery is consistently one of 'a country wholly uncultivated, thinly inhabited, and recently peopled'; the imagery is drawn from a narrow circle of natural objects, sun, moon, stars, clouds, meteors, lightning, thunder, seas, rivers, torrents, winds, ice, rain, snow, grass and flowers, spirits and ghosts. It is the imagery of a northern mountainous region. In the technique, there are 'no artful transitions, nor full and extended connexion of parts'; the style is 'rapid and vehement', and 'crowded with imagery', the narration 'concise and abrupt, leaving several circumstances to be supplied by the reader's imagination'. Any passage of Ossian will vindicate Macpherson's comment that it was very different from 'modern, connected, polished poetry'.

A Tale of the times of old!
Why, thou wanderer unseen! thou bender of the thistle of Lora; why, thou breeze of the valley, hast thou left mine ear? I hear no distant roar of streams! No sound of the harp from the rock! Come, thou huntress of Lutha, Malvina, call back his soul to the bard. I look forward to Lochlin of lakes, to the dark billowy bay of U-thorno, where Fingal descends from ocean, from the roar of winds. Few are the heroes of Morven in a land unknown!

('Cath-Loda', Duan I.)

Here is such poetry 'restored to her ancient truth and purity' as Macpherson's fellow-Scot, James Thomson, had longed for, poetry that would 'please, instruct, surprise and astonish'; it continued to interest men of letters for half a century. It has all the 'invention and imagination' that Joseph Warton required; all the vivid description—'he makes us imagine that we see it before our eyes', said Blair; 'a painter could copy after him'. But its success depended equally on its having what William Shenstone called 'the true Chemical Spirit or Essence of Poetry', 'the voice of Sentiment rather than the Language of Reflection, and adapted peculiarly to strike the Passions'.[47]

Macpherson's, or rather Ossian's world, is, compared with the normal eighteenth-century literary scene, a desert. Not only is it scenically bare, but it lacks culture, it lacks society. Human activities are limited to fighting and dying and lamenting; human relationships are restricted to the minimum of father, son, daughter, lover, friend. Blair noted with approval that Ossian had 'assembled almost all the tender images that can touch the heart of man; friendship, love, the afflictions of parents, sons, brothers, the distress of the aged, and the unavailing bravery of the young'.[48] It is 'the poetry of the heart', 'tenderness and delicacy of sentiment' predominate; 'in point of humanity, magnanimity, virtuous feeling of every kind' Ossian's heroes leave those of Homer and Virgil far behind. Blair, and the admirers of Ossian, were in no danger of ceasing to admire Homer and Virgil, or indeed Dryden and Pope. Yet the discovery of poems that could vie with those of the classical world, but actually written in Britain, was exciting. Macpherson would probably have agreed with Thomas Percy that 'it is nearly as much merit to retrieve' such poems 'from that oblivion which they are falling into, as to compose them at first'.

What was remarkable was that Ossian was 'the only poet that never relaxes, or lets himself down into the light and amusing strain'; all was solemnity and seriousness, the tone elegiac, the mood 'the joy of grief'. The debt to Gray's 'Bard' is clear; the old, blind warrior-poet, sole survivor of his generation, strikes 'the deep sorrows of *his* lyre' and laments *his* 'dear lost companions' amid equally bleak mountain scenery. Macpherson looked back to the distant past in which to set his bard, and then made him a poet who looks back into the past, to an age that is gone. It may be that this is his response to the crushing of the 1745 rebellion, which he witnessed as a boy of nine. His own family and clan were heavily involved on the Jacobite side. The poems are uniformly sad, the melancholy of a young man put into the mouth of an old one. Their theme is the transience of life, the inevitability of loss, decay and death: 'they went forth to war, but they always fell'. The sadness is like that of the young Gray,

> I fruitless mourn, to him that cannot hear,
> And weep the more, because I weep in vain.
>
>   ('Sonnet on the Death of West', 13–14)

but it is more self-indulgent, without Gray's saving virtues of stoical acceptance and sad, humorous self-awareness.

The abrupt, rhythmic prose that Macpherson used was regarded by Shenstone as a welcome relief from the polished perfection of English verse.[49] Even in prosody something new was desired. Macpherson not only made his 'translations' sound like literal translations of primitive poetry, but he made them sound like the most familiar of all literal translations, the Authorized version of the Bible. Robert Lowth, in his Oxford lectures on the Hebrew poetry of the Old Testament, had shown that the prosodic principle was one of parallelism, synonymous, antithetic and synthetic.[50] The important elements in a line of Hebrew verse were not syllables, accents or stresses, but *things*, e.g.

> My-doctrine | shall-drop | as-the-rain;
> My-word | shall-distill | as-the-dew
>
>   Deuteronomy, xxxii, 2.

Macpherson writes on this principle.

> It-is-night, | I-am-alone, | forlorn | on-the-hill-of-storms.
> The-wind | is-heard | on-the-mountain.
> The-torrent | pours-down | the rock.
> No-hut | receives | me-from-the-rain;
> Forlorn | on-the-hill-of-winds!
>
>   ('Songs of Selma')

His diction is simple, 'his practice was to use a large number of concrete monosyllabic words of Anglo-Saxon origin to describe objects and forces common to rural life'.[51] This, combined with his profusion of images and biblical rhythms, contributed largely to his serious and solemn grandeur, his sublimity of pathos. His experiment in 'irregular poetry' or 'measured prose' was not the least of his original contributions to the quest for some newer way to write.

Finally, before leaving Macpherson, there is one aspect of his complicated experiment that indicates a profound change in sensibility. A poet trying on strange roles at this time sometimes suggests not that he is a man writing to men, but that he is a being through whom some mysterious power speaks. Gray's Bard is 'taken over' by such powers:

> Visions of glory, spare my aching sight;
> Ye unborn ages, crowd not on my soul
>
> ('The Bard', 107–8)

Ossian, as Blair realized, gives the appearance not of a poet writing to please readers and critics, but of one who writes from love of poetry and song. He works himself into a sort of trance by thinking of the 'heroes among whom he has flourished', he recalls 'the affecting incidents of his life', he 'dwells upon his past wars, and loves, and friendships' until

> there comes a voice to Ossian, and awakes his soul. It is the voice of years that are gone; they roll before me with all their deeds.

It is at this point that the writing begins, and the effect on the reader is that of an incantation, sustaining a single emotion by means of the minimum variation in rhythm, image, scene and subject.[52]

Macpherson's Ossian poems are clearly not great literature; they are the astonishing product of an age devoted to the quest for 'pure poetry'. Equally astonishing are Thomas Chatterton's Rowley poems. Between 1768 and 1770, when he committed suicide at the age of 17, Chatterton created a world of poets and patrons set in fifteenth-century Bristol. The central figure, a monk called Thomas Rowley, was a priest of St. John's, Bristol; his friend and patron was William Canynge, mayor of Bristol and restorer of St. Mary Redcliffe. The circle of friends exists in the poems and prose fragments that Chatterton wrote for them, in a language that in orthography and diction looked sufficiently archaic; it was invented by Chatterton from a study of glossaries and dictionaries. Rowley, Canynge, John Iscam, Syr Thybbot Gorges and others feast together, act in plays, write poems, even borrow lines and phrases from each other; they are interested in local church matters and politics, antiquities, heraldry, drawings and manuscripts. The forged poems and documents which body forth this world were known only to Chatterton's Bristol patrons until 1777, when the Chaucerian scholar Thomas Tyrrwhit collected and edited them, and the controversy about their authenticity began. What is interesting is that Chatterton, who wrote an even larger number of poems in his own name, was, like Macpherson, willing to allow the credit for much of what he wrote to go to a poet supposedly long since dead. He had a facility in writing verses, but preferred a subject-matter that his own age could not supply; a distant age which he had experienced in books was a greater spur to his imagination.

The image of the young poet committing suicide, the proud and unappreciated genius, profoundly affected the public image of the poet. In the controversy after his death, Chatterton was cast in the role of Gray's Bard, with Horace Walpole as Edward I. But Chatterton's assumed role in his short life was that of a medieval priest and poet living in a bustling and interesting world of church and chivalry, plays and patrons. He created a distanced, impersonal, objective, artistic world, not without anachronisms in detail, not without borrowing material from Spenser and Pope's translation of the *Iliad*, and phrases from Shakespeare, Dryden, Pope, Rowe, Gray and the ballads. But that world is cut off from Chatterton's own sordid world.

Chatterton knew that 'the Sentiment, Description, and Versification' of his pseudo-medieval poems were 'highly deserving the attention of the literati'.[53] Writing in his invented language he was able to make metrical experiments that produced new sounds. Keats was interested in the interplay of vowels—and of consonants—in

> Comme, wythe acorme-coppe & thorne,
> Drayne mie hartys blodde awaie;
> Lyfe & all yttes goode I scorne,
> Daunce bie nete, or feaste by daie.
> > Mi love ys dedde,
> > Gone to hys death-bedde,
> > All under the wyllowe tree.[54]

Chatterton also 'invented' what Scott later called 'the Romantic stanza' when he used it for his *Lay of the Last Minstrel*. This is a form of the octosyllabic couplet in which the iambic movement is varied with anapaests. It is the metre Coleridge used in *Christabel*.[55] Chatterton, with Macpherson, showed that new subjects called for new metres.

Chatterton's brief life was devoted to poetry. Christopher Smart (1722–71) was only too well aware that he also was one who had 'made poetry, perhaps, too much the business of his life'.[56] He wrote odes, epigrams, epitaphs, hymns, fables, prologues, epilogues, oratorios, a georgic and a mock-heroic poem, he translated the psalms, and the poems of Horace; he was a learned and energetic poet who handled every form with originality. Like all the other poets of this period he is remembered now for only a small part of his work : for one poem, *A Song to David* (1763) which is remarkable for its 'combination of careful structure and rhapsodic tone',[57] and for another, *Jubilate Agno* (written 1759–63, printed 1939) which is remarkable for its new metre and its collapsing structure. In this period, though poets and critics were often interested in poetry that created the effect of an unpremeditated, passionate cry, they were also very conscious of structure.[58] One of the things wrong with Charles Churchill's satires (written 1761–4), vigorous as they are, is, as he admits, that he had not time 'to design/A plan, to methodize each thought, each line/Highly to finish'.[59] Joseph Warton approved what he thought was the practice of Racine and Pope in writing the first drafts of their work in prose. Gray certainly planned some of his poems in prose. Young was conscious of the rhapsodic lack of structure in his *Night Thoughts*; 'the Method pursued in it', he wrote, 'was rather imposed, by what spontaneously arose in the Author's Mind, on that Occasion, than meditated or designed'.[60] Smart's main theme in his poetry was a rhapsodic one, the praise of the wisdom of God in the creation. The role he commonly assumes as a poet is that of David, the author of the psalms, singing a hymn of praise for all created things.[61] Creation is multifarious *and* ordered; Smart's *Song to David* in its structure and its detail embodies both these qualities. Stanzas are grouped in threes, fives and sevens, a mathematical and mystical ordering. Stanzas 30 to 38 for example, a group of nine (three by three) stanzas, have an introductory and concluding stanza, with seven central stanzas each beginning with a letter of the Greek alphabet. These describe the seven 'pillars of the Lord', the 'monuments of God's works in the first week'. The order of creation is built up also by numerous vivid images

> The spotted ounce and playsome cubs
> Run rustling 'mongst the flow'ring shrubs,
> And lizards feed the moss. . . .
>
> (Stanza 55)

They are drawn from the Bible, from science and travel books, to give the sense of plenitude. They are related in terms of contrast and comparison; all forms of activity and existence are forms of praise. The resulting poem is the finest of all the many poems written in this period; its critical justification for its own age is to be found in the writings of Lowth and Hugh Blair.

Lowth, who was one of Smart's friends, provided also the groundwork for Smart's *Jubilate Agno*, the poem which he wrote when confined to various asylums between 1756 and 1763. In his nineteenth lecture Lowth showed that Hebrew poetry, the psalms and prophetic books, took its structure from the liturgical practice of two choirs singing alternate verses of a hymn.[62] Smart was interested in liturgical reform, and wrote his version of the psalms and his hymns for the Christian year probably during his confinement. For the *Jubilate* he adapted the Hebrew antiphonal prosody; from what has survived of the poem it is clear that there were to be two parallel sets of verses, one in which each verse begins 'Let . . .', another beginning 'For . . .'

> Let Sarah rejoice with the Redwing, whose harvest is in the
> frost and snow.

has as its response

> For the hour of my felicity, like the womb of Sarah, shall
> come at the latter end.
>
> (Fragment B1, 16)

In the 'Let' verses individuals—from the Bible or from Smart's acquaintance—are exhorted to rejoice, i.e. to worship God, with some creature; in the 'For' verses, where the parallels have survived, Smart responds with some personal information or learned detail in some way suggested by each 'Let' verse. In the verses just quoted the relevance depends on our knowing that Sarah gave birth to Isaac in her old age, and that the Redwing is only seen in Britain in the winter. It is a strange fact that the poem was not discovered until there were readers prepared to accept its cross-word puzzle references as the stuff of poetry. Clearly Smart sees himself as the psalmist, offering praise to the Creator while in exile and distress. As he praises he embodies, by his wide range of natural and scientific references, a concept of a world united in harmonious praise by fulfilling its nature. The poem is full of strange erudition, but it is not learning derived from Homer, Pindar, Virgil, Horace, Juvenal, or Ovid; its learning is from the Bible, Pliny's *Natural History* and contemporary works on botany and gardening, works of physico-theology and hermetic philosophy or Free Masonry. These are, presumably, the works he read when composing his

Seatonian prize poems (1750–56); in his psychotic state their substance provided the details for this strange ruin of a poem.

To concentrate on *A Song to David* and *Jubilate Agno*, on the Ossian and Rowley poems and Gray's 'The Bard', is necessary if we are to see clearly how boldly experimental poets were in this period, how they tried to break out of their own restricted world and make new worlds. Verse was immensely popular as an activity of polite society; it was produced by young men as a means of attracting attention and securing a place, by aristocrats and clergymen, doctors and lawyers as a form of gracious entertainment, by poor hacks as a method of earning a guinea from the publisher of a magazine. The problem for any poet was how to gain distinction in such a crowd. Gray, for example, with his social pretentions, had no desire to be known as 'a fetcher and carrier of sing-song'. The concept of the poet as mere entertainer was anathema to most of the poets and poetasters.

To be new and different even in the verse epistle, the most social form of verse, John Gilbert Cooper imitated a French model, Gresset, whose poems Gray admired. The octosyllabic couplet was used as the basis of his metre, but it was interspersed with quatrains and with passages of varied rhyming.[63] Experiment was not, however, uniformly welcomed. Robert Lloyd and George Colman mocked it :

> The shallow fop in antic vest,
>   Tir'd of the beaten road,
> Proud to be singly drest,
> Changes with every changing mood, the mode.
> Say, shall not then the heav'n-born muses too
>   Variety pursue?
> Shall not applauding critics hail the vogue?
> Whether the muse the style of Cambria's sons,
>   Or the rude gabble of the Huns,
>   Or the broader dialect
>   Of Caledonia she affect,
> Or take, Hibernia, thy still broader brogue? [64]

Goldsmith, in the dedication of *The Traveller* (1764), complained that the threat to poetry came 'from the mistaken efforts of the learned to improve it. What criticism have we not heard of late', he went on, 'in favour of blank verse, and Pindaric odes, chorusses, anapests and iambics, alliterative care and happy negligence'. As one might expect, some of the best poetry of this period was written by men whose sympathies were conservative.

The two greatest of these, Goldsmith and Johnson, preferred the heroic couplet to all other verse forms, and looked to poetry 'to be told something new' about men. Johnson found little to praise in contemporary poetry; Collins 'did not sufficiently cultivate sentiment', that is, thoughts about the human condition; Gray had thoughts but too often they had 'nothing new', his 'Bard' promoted no truth, moral or political; Shenstone's mind could have been better stored with knowledge. Johnson looked to poetry for the sort of pregnant, moving wisdom that he himself wrote:

> How small, of all that human hearts endure,
> That part which laws or kings can cause or cure.

It was not descriptions of natural scenery or allegorical figures that moved him; poetical devotion, he thought, could not often please; but imaginative thinking about the human condition always excited him. The poems he picked out for praise were Goldsmith's *The Traveller* (1764), which he called the finest poem to appear since the death of Pope, and Gray's *Elegy* (1751), which unerringly evoked images and ideas in every man's mind and which said something new and true about the human attitude to death. The third great poem of this period is Johnson's own *Vanity of Human Wishes* (1749).

This was an imitation of Juvenal's tenth satire, and Johnson would have agreed that it was therefore not the highest form of poem. But the original is new-modelled so that it is completely Johnsonian. Both the *Vanity* and Goldsmith's *Traveller* 'survey mankind', seeing mankind as Western European civilized man. Johnson is interested in 'primitive' man, but his concept of such a figure is that of everyman in a fallen world, of whom it is possible to

> Remark each anxious toil, each eager strife,
> And watch the busy scenes of crowded life;
> Then say how hope and fear, desire and hate,
> O'er spread with snares the clouded maze of fate,
> Where wav'ring man, betray'd by vent'rous pride,
> To tread the dreary paths without a guide,
> As treach'rous phantoms in the mist delude,
> Shuns fancied ills, or chases airy good.

> (3–10)

This is the nature of the human condition in all places and at all times, stripped of adventitious details and urgently embodied in images. It asks the reader to assent to its complicated truth, and an honest reader would say of these lines what Johnson said of stanzas 20–23 of Gray's *Elegy* :

> I have never seen the notions in any other place; yet he that reads them here, persuades himself that he has always felt them.

Goldsmith thinks less powerfully, but then Johnson is the most powerful thinker in English literature. Goldsmith's 'primitive' man is the concept that emerges as he analyses the Italian, Swiss, French, Dutch and British cultures as they are determined by climatic and natural conditions. Each possesses some virtue which is the seed of its ultimate dissatisfaction :

> Hence every state, to one lov'd blessing prone,
> Conforms and models life to that alone.
> Each to the favourite happiness attends,
> And spurns the plan that aims at other ends;
> 'Till, carried to excess in each domain,
> This favourite good begets peculiar pain.
>
> (93–8)

Man in his essence is a being impelled 'to pursue some fleeting good' that constantly eludes him. With all that Nature and Art can give him,

> Yet oft a sigh prevails, and sorrows fall,
> To see the hoard of human bliss so small.
>
> (57–8)

Goldsmith presents himself as an exile, a lonely wanderer pursuing an ever elusive 'spot to real happiness consign'd', seeking, in fact, what he had left behind, the simple, poor, rural retreat, where alone is kindness, generosity and virtuous feeling. The nostalgic quest for a lost Eden is Goldsmith's strongest motif. In *The Deserted Village* (1770) he imagines such an Eden in vivid detail as a particular village :

> The sheltered cot, the cultivated farm,
> The never failing brook, the busy mill,
> The decent church that topp'd the neighbouring hill,
> The hawthorn bush, with seats beneath the shade,
> For talking age and whispering lovers made.
>
> (10–14)

It is pastoralized, idealized, set in the past, and its destruction angrily lamented. The growth of trade and wealth has led to its depopulation, it is now a desolate waste land, its simple, virtuous inhabitants are exiled to alien and unfriendly environments. Goldsmith feels for the village and its people, but they are the invented 'objective correlative' of his feeling that society in his day is inimical to poetry. Neither the village nor its destruction are historical 'facts'. As the Wartons had argued that 'true' poetry could only be written in more 'primitive' forms of society, so Goldsmith is here lamenting the destruction of just such a society. Poetry is 'neglected and decried' in 'these degenerate times of shame'. It will be found, if at all in the future, 'On Torno's cliffs, or Pambamarca's side' (i.e. in Sweden or Ecuador). Its function will be to tell men that they have embraced a wrong set of values, commercial values. The poet can no longer, as Thomson and Dyer did, celebrate England's growing prosperity; he is an exile in his community.

This feeling is shared by Thomas Gray. The basis for it in both poets is personal, since both achieved considerable contemporary fame for their utterance of it—society did not exile them, they exiled themselves. In the *Elegy* Gray sees the poet as having a choice between a corrupt world of power and social success, and a humble, lonely world of personal and poetic integrity. He can at the same time present the pathos of a situation in which society fails to develop latent abilities—'Some mute inglorious Milton here may rest'—and the distaste he feels at the probable use to which such talents would be put in his society:

> Or heap the shrine of Luxury and Pride
> With incense kindled at the Muse's flame.
>
> (71–2)

He can acknowledge the ideal potentialities of statesmen

> To scatter plenty o'er a smiling land,
> And read their hist'ry in a nation's eyes.
>
> (63–4)

But he sets against this what really happens to most people in society as it is governed—

> Chill Penury repress'd their noble rage,
> And froze the genial current of the soul.
>
> (51–2)

And yet, the poem says, it is somehow better in contemporary society to remain in ignorance, 'far from the madding crowd'.

The poem says many things about the condition of man, not least:

> For who to dumb Forgetfulness a prey,
> This pleasing anxious being e'er resign'd,
> Left the warm precincts of the chearful day,
> Nor cast one longing ling'ring look behind?
>
> (85–8)

But its main statement is a justification for Gray himself, for his own withdrawal from active life. The fiction he chooses for his exculpation involves his assuming the role of the melancholy man, and to create this figure he pillages much contemporary and earlier poetry. The melancholy man loves church-yards and night, moping owls and rugged elms; at dawn he is alone 'upon the upland lawn', at noon alone poring upon the brook; his cult of melancholy is shared with one friend, and produces in him the kind of simple moral elevation that it was supposed to produce. It is the assumption of this role that makes the poem strange for the reader today. But without the assumption of some role, developed by casting a 'longing ling'ring look behind' to the psalmist, Pindar, Juvenal, medieval bards, Spenser or Milton, poets in this period found it difficult to write.

William Cowper (1731–1800), however, normally adopts as his persona in verse a role that is as close as possible to that of the 'real' Cowper. The intense consciousness of himself that precipitated his bouts of insanity militated against such imaginative projections as attracted Gray, Macpherson and Chatterton. He has no nostalgia for past ages, no idealization of earlier societies. He avoided reading English poetry and avowed that he 'hated and despised' imitation.[65] The 'I' of his poems *is* Cowper, who uses verse for his personal confession.

> For I have lov'd the rural walk through lanes
> Of grassy swarth, close cropt by nibbling sheep,
> And skirted thick with intertexture firm
> Of thorny boughs; have lov'd the rural walk
> O'er hills, through valleys, and by rivers' brink,
> E'er since a truant boy I pass'd my bounds
> T'enjoy a ramble on the banks of Thames.
>
> (*The Task*, i. 109–115)

Living in rural seclusion at Olney, he is not ashamed to write about his own simple pleasures, activities and experiences, and to confine himself to these. He does not build his poems out of a sensibility nourished only on other poems, and, unlike Beattie, he does not feel the need for the disguise of archaism when talking about himself.

Like other poets of the period he is aware of the heavy weight of the giants of the past. After Addison, Pope and Swift, 'the world in vain/Must hope to look upon their like again' ('Table-Talk', 660–61):

> And 'tis the sad complaint, and almost true,
> What'er we write, we bring forth nothing new.
>
> (732–3)

What he admires in poetry is what the group of young poets at Westminster School—Robert Lloyd, Charles Churchill and George Colman—admired in the late 1740s, 'Butler's wit, Pope's numbers, Prior's ease' (ibid., 764), the 'line that plows its stately course/Like a proud swan, conq'ring the stream by force' (522–3),

> Fervency, freedom, fluency of thought,
> Harmony, strength, words exquisitely sought.
>
> (700–701)

Coleridge praised Cowper's blank-verse poem, The Task (1785) as an example of the 'more sustained and elevated style' in which 'natural thoughts' were combined with 'natural diction', the heart reconciled with the head (Biographia Literaria, Ch. 1). Cowper, at his best, writes with a simple dignity, he notices detail unobtrusively, as when he is describing 'rural sounds':

> Nor less composure waits upon the roar
> Of distant floods, or on the softer voice
> Of neighbouring fountain, or of rills that slip
> Through the cleft rock, and, chiming as they fall
> Upon loose pebbles, loose themselves at length
> In matted grass, that with a livelier green
> Betrays the secret of their silent course.
>
> (The Task, i. 190–196)

But Cowper cannot fill a long, desultory poem such as The Task with description alone, though the aesthetic contemplation of rural scenery is what he has most strongly to recommend, as being the only safe road to piety and virtue. His aim is also to argue against the attractions of life in towns. He is a relaxed, confident and rhetorical thinker on such subjects, as he can well afford to be when he assumes general agreement with his premise 'God made the country, and man made the town' (l. 749). As a Calvinist, a patriotic Whig of the age of Chatham, an opponent of the slave-trade and of boarding-schools, and a hypersensitive middle-class gentleman, he had a sufficient number of positions from which to argue the inferiority of the bustle and evil of town life, both in *The Task* and in his didactic and satirical poems. Since he aims not at sublimity but at natural ease and writes only from his own experiences, he extends the range of both couplet and blank-verse as verse forms. He can deal with the growing suburbia—

> Suburban villas, highway-side retreats,
> That dread th' encroachment of our growing streets,
> Tight boxes, neatly sash'd, and in a blaze
> With all a July sun's collected rays,
> Delight the citizen, who, gasping there,
> Breathes clouds of dust, and calls it country air—
>
> ('Retirement', 481–86)

and, in the same poem, with the ultimate end of life:

> Is there, as reason, conscience, Scripture, say,
> Cause to provide for a great future day,
> When, earth's assign'd duration at an end,
> Man shall be summon'd and the dead attend?
>
> (651–54)

He likes to describe and reflect in a leisurely manner; his writing of verse was a therapy for his despondent religious melancholia, but he hoped that what he wrote would bring him 'a monitor's, [if] not a poet's praise'.

Almost all Cowper's experiences, 'shut out from more important views', were sufficiently close to those of sensitive middle-class people living in rural and semi-rural England, for his natural expression of them to appeal instantly. Jane Austen and the Brontës, for example, knew the poems intimately. His hymns, which include 'O for a closer walk with God', 'Hark my soul it is the Lord', and 'God moves in a mysterious way/His wonders to perform', have expressed for many people something of the simple fervency that Cowper felt. His moral seriousness, the simplicity of his emotions and very often of his language, and the confident acceptance of the significance of whatever he did or saw or thought, sprang in part from the Christian tradition to which Bunyan belongs, and to which, though in a much weakened form, many of Cowper's readers still belonged. But there was one area of Cowper's experience which not all his readers shared, but to which he was able to give them imaginative entry. This was his bouts of religious depression, in which he felt intense alienation from all human society. When he first embodied the experience in verse in 1763 he differentiated the poem from all his other verses by using an unusual metre, attempting to reproduce in English the stanza of Sappho, which by its associations suggests passion :

> Hatred and vengeance, my eternal portion,
> Scarce can endure delay of execution,
> Wait, with impatient readiness, to seize my
> Soul in a moment.
> ('Lines written during a Period of Insanity')

In part he uses this metre because he is aware of Isaac Watts' poem in the same metre, 'The Day of Judgment', to which Cowper's poem is a terrible counterpart. But he is also conscious that the obscene horror of the experience demands a metre that rings strange and inflexible in English ears.

At other times, in order to express this area of his experience, he is forced into an identification of himself either with 'a stricken deer'—

> I was a stricken deer, that left the herd
> Long since; with many an arrow deep infixt
> My panting side was charged, when I withdrew
> To seek a tranquil death in distant shades—
> (*The Task*, iii. 108–111)

or with a sailor overwhelmed by a storm at sea :

> Always from port withheld, always distress'd—
> Me howling winds drive devious, tempest-toss'd.
> ('On the Receipt of My Mother's Picture', 101–102)

'The Castaway', written in 1799, is his most powerful poem, a poem that with a madman's lucidity expresses his conviction that he is damned. The sailor, washed overboard from Anson's ship, is left to drown; in his plight Cowper saw his own :

> No voice divine the storm allay'd,
>   No light propitious shone;
> When, snatch'd from all effectual aid,
>   We perish'd, each alone :
> But I beneath a rougher sea,
> And whelm'd in deeper gulphs than he.
> (61–66)

Such 'nakedness of sentiment', the intensity of despair, is rare in poetry. Cowper's success as a poet was in showing what most of the poets of the previous forty years had been unable to accept, that individual human experience in the present was still the best material for the poet and that out of it he could make something new.

1. Dryden, *Of Dramatic Poesy and Other Critical Essays*, ed. G. Watson, London, 1962, i. 85.

2. Cf. Addison, *Spectator*, no. 414, which Thomson clearly had in mind.

3. J. Warton, Preface to *Odes on Various Subjects*, dated 1747, but published Dec. 1746.

4. Joseph Warton later turns the statement of Pope's preface against Pope, in his *Essay on the Genius and Writings of Pope*, ed. 1805, ii. 402.

5. R. Lowth, *De Sacra Poesi Hebraeorum*, 1753, trs. G. Gregory, 2 vols., 1787. See S. H. Monk, *The Sublime*, New York, 1935, p. 80.

6. Lowth, ed. 1816, i. 38–9, ii. 199. See also M. H. Abrams, *The Mirror and the Lamp*, New York, 1953, pp. 84–8.

7. Thomas Warton, Senior, *Poems on Several Occasions*, 1748.

8. M. Akenside, *Odes*, I. xviii. 34–5; I. xvi. 43–4 (in *Poems*, 1772). Smart called him 'Athenian Akenside' in 1754.

9. See G. H. Hartman, 'Wordsworth, Inscriptions, and Romantic Nature Poetry,' in *From Sensibility to Romanticism*, ed. F. W. Hilles and H. Bloom, New York, 1965.

10. Goldsmith in the dedication to *The Traveller* (1764), Lloyd in his 'Prologue to Hecuba,' 1761.

11. Edward Young, *Conjectures on Original Composition*, 1759.

12. Akenside's note to his 'Hymn to the Naiads,' l. 29.

13. Isaac D'Israeli surveys theories of the origin of rhyme in *Amenities of Literature*, 1841.

14. See R. Havens, *The Influence of Milton on English Poetry*, Cambridge, Mass., 1922.

15. Thomas Warton's edn. of Milton's *Poems upon Several Occasions*, 1785, p. 34.

16. Joseph Warton, *Essay on Pope*, 1756, i. 38.

17. Lowth, ed. 1816, i. 38.

18. *Correspondence of Thomas Gray*, ed. P. Toynbee and L. Whibley, Oxford, 1935, ii. 478.

19. *Ibid.*, iii. 1290.

20. T. Warton, *Observations on the Faerie Queene*, 1762, ii. 268.

21. *Poetical Works of James Thomson*, ed. J. L. Robertson, Oxford, 1908, 1951, p. 306.

22. *Letters of William Shenstone*, ed. M. Williams, 1939, p. 145.

23. Gray, *Correspondence*, iii. 1084, 1168 f., and M. Forbes, *Beattie and his Friends*, London, 1904, p. 55.

24. J. Hart, 'Akenside's revision of *The Pleasures of Imagination*', *PMLA*, lxxiv (1959), 67 f.

25. R. Hurd, *Letters on Chivalry and Romance*, 1762, Letter 7, ad fin.

26. See R. Wellek, *The Rise of English Literary History*, Chapel

Hill, 1941, and *Cambridge Bibliography of English Literature*, ed. F. W. Bateson, Cambridge, 1940, ii. 892–931.

27. Francis Jeffrey, in *Edinburgh Review*, March, 1819, reviewing T. Campbell's *Specimens of the British Poets*; and Coleridge, *Biographia Literaria*, 1817, ch. 1.

28. T. Warton, Preface to Milton's *Poems upon Several Occasions*, 1785, p. iii.

29. T. Warton, *History of English Poetry*, 3 vols., 1774–81, iii. 497.

30. See M. H. Abrams, *The Mirror and the Lamp*, pp. 272–89; Addison, *Spectator*, nos. 419, 421; J. Warton, *The Adventurer*, no. 57, 22 May 1753.

31. J. Warton, *Essay on Pope*, ed. 1805, ii. 160.

32. See A. S. P. Woodhouse, 'The Poetry of Collins Reconsidered,' in *From Sensibility to Romanticism*, and P. M. Spacks, *The Poetry of Vision*, Cambridge, Mass., 1967, ch. 4.

33. Collins's note here says 'Florimel,' which is wrong.

34. Joseph Warton in *The Adventurer*, 1753, no. 57.

35. T. Warton, *History of English Poetry*, ii (1778), 462–63.

36. See M. Price, *To the Palace of Wisdom*, New York, 1964, ch. 13, 'The Theatre of Mind.'

37. Gray, *Correspondence*, ii. 540–41.

38. Gray thought Beattie affected too much alliteration, see Gray, *Correspondence*, iii. 1170.

39. See A. Johnston, 'Gray's use of the Gorchest y Beirdd in "The Bard"', *Modern Language Review*, lix (1964), 335–8.

40. *Correspondence of Thomas Percy and Evan Evans*, ed. A. Lewis, Baton Rouge, 1957, p. 31.

41. *Ibid.*, p. 17.

42. T. Warton, *History*, i (1774), 434.

43. *Percy–Warton Correspondence*, ed. M. G. Robinson and L. Dennis, Baton Rouge, 1951, pp. 44–5.

44. The title of the concluding chapter of William Duff's *Essay on Original Genius*, 1767.

45. J. and A. L. Aikin, *Miscellaneous Pieces in Prose*, 1773, p. 140.

46. Hugh Blair, *A Critical Dissertation on the Poems of Ossian*, 1763, in *The Poems of Ossian*, London, 1825, pp. 84, 81.

47. Shenstone to Percy, 10 November 1760.

48. Sterne's 'power of approaching and touching the finer feelings of the heart' (Scott) is relevant at this point.

49. Shenstone to MacGowan in 1760, quoted in J. Butt, *The Augustan Age*, London, 1950, p. 135.

50. Lowth, ed. 1816, ii. 24 f., 54–6.

51. J. Macpherson, *Fragments of Ancient Poetry*, Edinburgh, 1760, ed. J. J. Dunn, Augustan Reprint Society, Los Angeles, 1966, p. viii.

52. See Price, *To the Palace of Wisdom*, p. 374, and N. Frye, 'Towards defining an Age of Sensibility,' in *Fables of Identity*, New York, 1963, pp. 130 ff.

53. Chatterton letter of 4 July 1770 to the editor of *The Town and Country Magazine* with 'An Excelente Balade of Charitie.'

54. From the minstrel's song in 'Aella : A Tragycal Enterlude.'

55. See Chatterton's poem 'The Unknown Knight' and S. T. Coleridge, *Collected Letters*, Oxford, 1959, iii. 355–61.

56. He says this in the introduction to his prose translation of the works of Horace, 1756.

57. Spacks, *Poetry of Vision*, p. 124.

58. On Dr. Johnson's interest in literary structure see J. H. Hagstrum, *Samuel Johnson's Literary Criticism*, Chicago, 1967, pp. 122–8.

59. C. Churchill, *Gotham*, 1764, ii. 164.

60. E. Young, Preface to *The Complaint: Or Night Thoughts*, 'Night the Fourth', 1743.

61. Before reading Smart one should re-read the Benedicite, in the service for Morning Prayer in the Book of Common Prayer.

62. Psalm 136 shows this at its simplest, the second choir repeating the line 'For his mercy endureth for ever' after every verse. Usually the response is varied. Smart would have found many examples of the 'Let . . . For . . .' formula in the psalms.

63. J. G. Cooper, *Epistles to the Great*, 1758, and *The Call of Aristippus*, 1758.

64. Colman and Lloyd parodied Gray's 'Progress of Poesy' and 'The Bard' in an 'Ode to Obscurity' from which these lines come (ll. 12–23), in *Two Odes*, 1760.

65. T. Wright, ed., *Correspondence of William Cowper*, London, 1904, i. 386; ii. 127, 280; iii. 46. Cowper mocked the fashion for writing odes, and the cult of Milton's minor poems, in his 'Dissertation on the Modern Ode' (1763), reprinted in C. Ryskamp, *William Cowper*, Cambridge, 1959, pp. 200–11.

BIBLIOGRAPHY

I *Editions (in chronological order of poets)*

Gray, Thomas (1716–71) *Complete Poems*, ed. H. W. Starr and J. R. Hendrickson, Oxford, 1966 (with translations of Latin and Greek poems, and a few notes).

    Poetical Works (English poems only, with those of William Collins), ed. A. L. Poole, Oxford, 1917; revised by L. Whibley and F. Page, 1937.

    The Poems (with those of Collins and Goldsmith), ed. R. Lonsdale, London, 1969 (with translations of Latin and Greek poems, and heavy annotation).

    Selected Poems of Gray and Collins, ed. A. Johnston, London, 1967 (with critical introductions and annotations).

    Correspondence of Gray, ed. L. Whibley and P. Toynbee, Oxford, 3 vols., 1935. Selections of letters in World's Classics and, with poems and essays, in Everyman's Library.

    R. W. Ketton-Cremer, *Thomas Gray: A Biography*, Cambridge, 1955.

    W. P. Jones, *Thomas Gray, Scholar*, Cambridge, Mass., 1937 (a more specialized biographical study).

Collins, William (1721–59). See editions by Poole, Lonsdale and Johnston under Gray above. J. S. Cunningham, *William Collins: Drafts and Fragments of Verses*, Oxford, 1956, prints newly discovered fragments of poems, also included by Lonsdale.

Smart, Christopher (1722–71) *Collected Poems*, ed. N. Callan, 2 vols., London, 1949 (excludes translations, libretti, and Latin poems). Selections in *Poems*, ed. R. E. Brittain, Princeton, 1950 (includes some translations and has a good introduction). *Rejoice in the Lamb*, ed. W. F. Stead, London, 1939. This was later edited as *Jubilate Agno*, by W. H. Bond, Cambridge, Mass., 1954. For a study of the poetry see M. Dearnley, *The Poetry of Christopher Smart*, 1968.

Warton, Joseph (1722–1800).

Warton, Thomas (1728–90).

    E. Partridge, ed., *The Three Wartons. A Choice of their Verse*, London, 1927. Includes selections from Thomas Warton the elder.

Goldsmith, Oliver (1730?–74).

    Works, ed. A. Friedman, Oxford, 5 vols., 1966.

    Poems, ed. A. Dobson, Oxford, 1887, and (with Gray and Collins), ed. R. Lonsdale, 1969. Also in Everyman's Library and World's Classics. Selections (with Johnson), ed. A. Rudrum and P. Dixon, 1965.

Cowper, William (1731–1800) *Poetical Works*, ed. H. S. Milford, Oxford, 1934. Selections, ed. H. I'A Fausset, 1931, in Everyman's Library.

    Correspondence, ed. T. Wright, 5 vols., 1904–25. Selections in

World's Classics and Everyman's Library.

Macpherson, James (1736–96) *Poems of Ossian*, ed. M. Laing, 2 vols., Edinburgh, 1805; ed. W. Sharp, Edinburgh, 1896.

Chatterton, Thomas (1752–70) *Poetical Works*, ed. W. W. Skeat, 2 vols., London, 1871, etc. *Complete Works*, ed. H. D. Roberts, 2 vols., London, 1906. *Poems*, ed. S. Lee, 2 vols., London, 1905. *Rowley Poems*, ed. M. E. Hare, Oxford, 1911.

II *Selections from other poets*

The Oxford Book of Eighteenth Century Poetry, ed. D. Nichol Smith, Oxford, 1926 (for a good selection of shorter poems, and extracts from longer works); *The English Poets*, ed. T. H. Ward, London, 1880, vol. 3, 'Addison to Blake'; *The Late Augustans*, ed. D. Davie, London, 1958 (contains Shenstone's *School-Mistress*, Johnson's *Vanity of Human Wishes*, Gray's *Elegy*, Smart's *Song to David*, Goldsmith's *Deserted Village*, Cowper's *Yardley-Oak*, etc., together with introduction and notes); *English Satiric Poetry: Dryden to Byron*, ed. J. Kinsley and J. T. Boulton, London, 1966; *Poetry of Landscape and the Night: Two Eighteenth-Century Traditions*, ed. C. Peake, London, 1967 (the last two, in Arnold's English Texts Series, have good introductions and notes).

III *Critical and Historical Studies*

J. Arthos, *The Language of Natural Description in Eighteenth-Century Poetry*, Ann Arbor, 1949.

J. Butt, *The Augustan Age*, 1950. A good general survey of the period.

C. F. Chapin, *Personification in Eighteenth-Century English Poetry*, New York, 1955.

C. V. Deane, *Aspects of Eighteenth-Century Nature Poetry*, Oxford, 1935. A good work on 'stock' diction in the period.

R. D. Havens, *The Influence of Milton on English Poetry*, Cambridge, Mass., 1922.

E. N. Hooker, 'The Reviewers and the new trends in poetry, 1754–70', *Modern Language Notes*, li (1936), 207–14.

W. P. Jones, *The Rhetoric of Science. A Study of Scientific Ideas and Imagery in Eighteenth-Century English Poetry*, London, 1966. A thorough study of physico-theological poems.

J. Miles, *Eras and Modes in English Poetry*, Berkeley and Los Angeles, 1964, ch. 4, 'The Sublime Poem.' On the characteristic linguistic modes of the poetry of this period.

P. M. Spacks, *The Insistence of Horror. Aspects of the Supernatural in Eighteenth-Century Poetry*, Cambridge, Mass., 1962.

P. M. Spacks, *The Poetry of Vision: Five Eighteenth-Century Poets— Thomson, Collins, Gray, Smart, Cowper*, Cambridge, Mass., 1967. Interesting critical essays on these five poets.

G. Tillotson, *Augustan Studies*, London, 1961. Has discussions of poetic diction, Gray's 'Ode on the Spring' and 'Ode on the Death of a Favourite Cat'.

IV Criticism

The most important literary critic in this period is Samuel Johnson. The reader should also consult R. Lowth, *De Sacra Poesi Hebraeorum*, 1753, trans. G. Gregory, 2 vols., 1787; Edmund Burke, *Philosophical Enquiry into the origin of our Ideas of the Sublime and the Beautiful*, 1757, ed. J. T. Boulton, 1958; J. Warton, *An Essay on the Genius and Writings of Pope*, 2 vols., 1756–82; T. Warton, *Observations on the Fairy Queen of Spenser*, 1754, rev. 1762; R. Hurd, *Letters on Chivalry and Romance*, 1762, ed. E. Morley, 1911, and ed. H. Trowbridge, Los Angeles, 1963 (Augustan Reprint Society).

The criticism of the period is surveyed in:

A. Bosker, *Literary Criticism in the Age of Johnson*, Groningen, 1930, revised 1953.

S. H. Monk, *The Sublime: A Study of Critical Theories in Eighteenth-Century England*, New York, 1935.

W. J. Bate, *From Classic to Romantic. Premises of Taste in Eighteenth-Century England*, Cambridge, Mass., 1946, reprinted New York, 1961.

N. Maclean, 'From Action to Image: Theories of the Lyric in the Eighteenth Century,' in *Critics and Criticism*, ed. R. S. Crane, Chicago, 1952.

M. H. Abrams, *The Mirror and the Lamp. Romantic Theory and the Critical Tradition*, New York, 1953. A scholarly and stimulating account of eighteenth-century critical theories and of the genesis of romantic theories.

P. W. R. Stone, *The Art of Poetry, 1750–1820. Theories of Poetic Composition and Style in the late Neo-Classical and Early Romantic Periods*, London, 1967.

V General Studies

R. Wellek, *The Rise of English Literary History*, Chapel Hill, 1941. A thorough survey of the literary scholarship of the period, the growth of interest in earlier literature, in editorial procedure, etc.

A. Johnston, *Enchanted Ground: the study of Medieval Romance in the Eighteenth Century*, 1964. A study of the revival of interest in medieval narrative poems by Hurd, Percy, T. Warton, Scott, etc.

M. Roston, *Prophet and Poet: The Bible and the Growth of Romanticism*, 1965. On Lowth, Ossian, Smart, Cowper and Gray.

12

RELIGIOUS AND PHILOSOPHICAL THEMES

IN

RESTORATION AND EIGHTEENTH-CENTURY LITERATURE

William Frost, University of California, Santa Barbara

The great transcendental topics animating or adding variety to earlier English literature—God, the freedom of the will, redemption, and the like—do not simply quit the stage of imaginative literature after the ages of Chaucer and Langland, Marlowe and Donne, or Milton and Bunyan have passed. But a change takes place in the characteristic forms under which such matters are treated. If we think of religious experience as resembling in differing ways two other kinds of human experience that also often inspire literary creation—political experience and the experience of dreams—then it might be said that religious experience can have either personal (dreamlike) or public ('political') aspects. Though both these aspects interest each man, the shift from Donne to Dryden is partly a shift from the personal to the public; and the same thing might be said of the shift from *Lycidas* to *A Tale of a Tub*. Milton and Edward King are as much concerned by corruptions in Christian institutions as is Swift in the next century; but where their interest had been more personal, his has become more social, or even sociological. Doctrines and institutions, rather than the drama of the inner life (the hell or paradise within), now become a central concern in the era between the lifetimes of Bunyan and Blake.

RELIGIO LAICI. *Religio Laici* (1682),[1] the first of Dryden's two major poetic statements of faith, confronts directly the choice of faith in a world of irreconcilably conflicting creeds. Dryden begins with the dilemma in its most general form and narrows his discussion down till at the conclusion he and the reader come face to face over the debris of a series of rejected alternatives. The poem falls into three parts, proceeding from general to specific, like boxes inside one another : I) Religion contrasted with no religion at all (reliance simply on human reason). II) The Christian religion contrasted with a more generalized religious form, supposedly embracing all faiths, as proposed by deism. III) Dryden's inherited form of Christianity— 'my own Mother-Church,' the Church of England—contrasted first with Roman Catholicism and its claims to universality and second with the miscellaneous non-Anglican protestant sects (the Dissenters) and their claims to individually divine inspiration and authenticity. Since Dryden's strategy calls for an emphatic final rejection of both Catholicism and Dissent, the poem moves from panegyric to satire; it begins with an exalted image of the relation of reason and religion—an image in the tradition of devotional poetry like that of Dante or Greville—and concludes with two long, energetic passages of anti-religious (or anti-clerical) comedy, comedy not less spirited than the attack on friars in the opening of Chaucer's *Wife of Bath's Tale*.

Religio Laici is thus unified logically by its plan and emotionally by its gradual change of mood. A third source of unity comes from its occasion, the recent translation by Henry Dickinson of Father Simon's *Critical History of the Old Testament* (1682), an historic advance in the scientific study of the origins of European faith—historic, and highly controversial. Addressed to translator Dickinson (the 'friend' of lines 228 and 398), *Religio Laici* is poetry built around the importance to Dryden's religion of Christianity's perpetual involvement with a book : 'Scripture', 'the Scriptures', 'Both Testaments', 'the blest Original' [from which the various translations have been made], 'the Sacred Page', 'the Work', 'the Page', 'the Book', 'the welcome News' [gospel=good news], 'the Bible', 'God's Word', 'the Will', 'the written Word', 'the tender Page', 'the sacred viands', 'the fly-blown text', 'so rich a treasure'. The book makes its appearance early in the poem, during the attack on the Deists, who want to rely wholly on human reason, a faculty which according to Dryden only serves to illuminate our dilemmas :

> That [Reason] shews us *sick*; and sadly are we sure
> *Still* to be *Sick*, till *Heav'n* reveal the *Cure* :
> If then *Heav'ns Will* must needs be understood
> (Which must, if we want *Cure*, and *Heaven* be *Good*)
> Let all Records of *Will reveal'd* be shown;
> With *Scripture*, all in equal ballance thrown,
> And *our one Sacred Book* will be *That one*.

(119–25)

The true nature, and the proper or improper use, of this book thus becomes the central dramatic issue of the poem.

As for the book's nature, this is a compound of strengths and weaknesses. The strength of the book (Dryden believes) is the specific content that differentiates it both from the writings of ancient philosophers about the Supreme Good in life and from the abstract notions of modern Deists about God, guilt, repentance, worship, and immortality. The Bible's central specific content for Dryden is the power of Christ's death to dramatize God's forgiveness of man's wrong-doing:

> Look humbly upward, see his Will disclose:
> The *Forfeit* first, and then the *Fine* impose: ...
> His *Justice* makes the *Fine*, his *Mercy* quits the *Score*.
>
> (101–2, 106)

This is the revelation needed by faith, Dryden says, the crucial matter separating reason (man's intelligent pursuit of goodness) from religion (God's assistance to man in this pursuit).

The defects of Scripture, as the poem presents them, are two-fold. First, as the discovery of the western hemisphere in 1492 has made abundantly clear, the revelation contained in Scripture was not and could not have been a worldwide one, for at least the first millenium and a half of its existence. Second, as Father Simon's critical study of the Biblical text has recently demonstrated,

> ... *Scripture*, though derived from *heav'nly birth*,
> Has been but carelessly preserv'd on *Earth*,
>
> (258–59)

for despite human diligence and heavenly inspiration the possessors of Scripture have

> Let in gross *Errours* to corrupt the *Text*:
> Omitted *paragraphs*, embroyl'd the *Sense*;
>
> (265—66)

so that both the existing manuscripts and the various translations are to some extent imperfect—are demonstrably *not* true representations of what was first set down.

The first of these two defects Dryden deals with by asserting his own opinion[2] that salvation is possible to those who have never heard of Christianity. He buttresses this idea by citing St. Paul, who said that uninstructed heathen might successfully live according to their own lights (be a law unto themselves); and Dryden further dramatizes his opinion by rejecting as too polemical the early Church father Athanasius, who had held Catholicism necessary to salvation:

> Then let us either think he meant to say
> *This Faith*, where *publish'd*, was the onely way;
> Or else conclude that, [the anti-trinitarian] *Arius* to confute,
> The good old Man, too eager in dispute,
> Flew high; and as his *Christian* Fury rose
> Damn'd all for *Hereticks* who durst *oppose*.
>
> (218–223)

This satiric thrust concludes the first half of *Religio Laici*; the second takes up the consequences of Father Simon's new, scientific analysis of Scripture's internal imperfections. These imperfections do not affect Dryden's faith, for he holds the Anglican view that the Bible's central message (Christ's significance) is simple and clear enough, and that anything more elaborate is unnecessary to religion:

> More Safe, and much more modest 'tis, to say
> *God wou'd not leave Mankind without a way*:
> And that the *Scriptures*, though not *every where*
> Free from Corruption, or intire, or clear,
> Are uncorrupt, sufficient, clear, intire,
> In *all* things which our needfull *Faith* require.
>
> (295–300)

Scriptural imperfections do, however, throw doubt, Dryden argues, on Roman Catholicism's claim to exclusive authority, for if a text can fail at some points, why not an institution? By Father Simon's efforts we now

> ... may see what *Errours* have been made
> Both in the *Copiers* and *Translaters Trade*:
> How *Jewish*, *Popish*, Interests have prevail'd,
> And where *Infallibility* has *fail'd*.
>
> (248–51)

The implication is that, from Dryden's point of view, Roman Catholicism should abandon any claim to infallibility and exclusive truth and instead accept a place as one among several Biblically derived religions: Catholics should cease to 'assume, with wondrous Art,/*Themselves* to be the *whole*, who are but *part*/Of that vast Frame, the Church' (358–60), as Dryden puts it.

Returning to the Book in the poem's spirited conclusion, Dryden contrasts its lack of use in the authoritarian Middle Ages,

> When want of Learning kept the *Laymen* low
> And none but *Priests* were *Authoriz'd* to *know*
>
> (372–73)

with its overuse or misuse in the individualistic Reformation,
when printing, literacy, and vernacular translations had made
its text so widely available that too many 'men wou'd still be
itching to *expound*' (410). The upshot of this historical contrast
is a dilemma : we neither can live with the Book nor live without it, according to Dryden :

> So all we make of Heavens discover'd Will
> Is, not to have it [the middle ages], or to use it ill
> [the Reformation].
> The Danger's much the same : on several Shelves
> If *others* [the Catholic priesthood] wreck *us*, or we
> [as Protestant individualists] wreck our *selves*.
>
> (423–26)

The final formula comes as a response to this impasse : we
should accept most pre-medieval Church traditions; suspend
judgement about disputed points; exercise forethought but
avoid needless debate; follow Reason, but submit it to the test
of a generally accepted consensus.

The modesty of this ending illustrates the strength of the
poem. Dryden's stance is most persuasive in being least dogmatic. His doctrine is like his poetry—the very assertion of its
limitations reveals its sinewy power :

> Thus have I made my own Opinions clear :
> Yet neither Praise expect, nor Censure fear :
> And this unpolish'd, rugged Verse, I chose;
> As fittest for Discourse, and nearest Prose.
>
> (451–54)

THE HIND AND THE PANTHER (1687). Regarding religion
from the point of view of a concerned, politically aware English
citizen of the 1670s or 1680s, its more sinister aspects had in
the fairly recent past taken two chief forms. In the first place,
religious enthusiasm, embodied in a Roman Catholic plot, had
attempted to extirpate by assassination the government of the
nation in 1605; and, in the second place, religious enthusiasm
embodied in the dissenting sects' objections to the Church of
England had supplied much of the zeal behind Parliament's

successful overthrowing of Charles I in the Civil Wars of the 1640s.

Published in 1682 on the occasion of Father Simon's book's appearance in its English version, *Religio Laici* seems addressed to the questions, first, why have a religion at all? (for the age was in general sceptical, atheistic, and hostile to religion); and second, if one must have a religion, which religion is the least open to obvious objections? The first question can only be dealt with by a direct assertion of faith, such as the one with which the poem opens; the second is handled by satire of the rejected alternatives. The sects are satirized as chaotic; Catholicism is satirized as pretending to more authoritativeness than the circumstances—historic and religious—could possibly warrant. The poem shows a lively, if still rather detached, religious interest; its tone is forthright and outspoken, but tentative, as the concluding lines just quoted show.

Later in the decade Dryden is more deeply engaged, while the occasions calling for discussion are much more dramatic than the mere publication of a controversial scholarly study. Dryden has become a Catholic convert; James II, a Catholic king, has succeeded to the throne, and is about to be forcibly replaced by his Protestant son-in-law William of Orange; and the nation is in ferment. At this point, in 1687, Dryden publishes his longest single original poem and the last important English poem on a religious topic in the century of Donne's *Holy Sonnets*, *Lycidas*, and *Paradise Lost*, not to mention the works of Herbert, Crashaw, and Vaughan.

Though a religious poem, *The Hind and the Panther* [3] is at first sight a striking violation of the traditions of religious poetry preceding it in the seventeenth century or earlier. It is not on a Biblical theme; it does not dramatize an event of sacred history or the meaning of a sacrament; though containing autobiographical passages, it does not make a central issue of the speaker's own religious experience, his quarrel with God or his conviction of sin; and it does not record a triumph over evil, or a visionary experience. Though the second of its three parts is a debate, in this respect resembling the basic structure of that fine religious poem *Paradise Regained* (1671), the issue at stake, instead of being religious against secular values as in Milton, is Anglican vs. Roman Catholic theology, a much more technical topic productive of some wit but little drama. On many major points the two churches were, after all, not far apart.

For a poem which is, among other things, a statement of faith—and a more fervent one than its predecessor, *Religio Laici*—*The Hind and the Panther* also presents a seemingly incongruous spectacle in its choice of central imagery. To a confrontation of allegorical beasts among whom the Hind represents Catholicism, the Panther Anglicanism, the Lion James II, the Wolf the Presbyterians, the Boar the Independents or Baptists, the Ape the Atheists, and the Fox the Socinians or Unitarians, Dryden adds, in the third part, two fables, first the Martin and the Swallows and second the Buzzard and the Pigeons. Cataloguing the beasts occupies Part I, and telling the fables occupies a major portion of Part III. Quite apart from the fact that this method often involves the reader in the solution of elaborate ideological riddles in order to keep abreast of the poetry,[4] the type of metaphor derives from a tradition of folklore and literature (Aesop, Chaucer, Reynard the Fox, Uncle Remus) which is predominantly light and seldom more than obliquely political or religious. Yet *The Hind and the Panther*, though enlivened by a number of delicately comic touches rising from incongruities between its imagery and its argument, succeeds mainly as a serious poem, tapping deep reserves of feeling.

Its success could hardly be achieved if the imagery were not in some basic way appropriate to Dryden's purposes. It has often been noted that the three parts of the poem have a temporal relation, Part I (the catalogue of beasts) referring mainly to the past, Part II (the Catholic-Anglican debate) mainly to the present, and Part III (the fables of the swallows and pigeons) mainly to the future. Also important is the fact that the shift in metaphor from beasts to birds corresponds to a shift in feeling toward religion and religious groups as the poem progresses. When these groups are symbolized as beasts, they mostly arouse fear (the bloody boar) or disgust (the copulation of wolf and panther); but when metamorphosed into swallows or chickens they stimulate a spectator's protective instincts by their foolishness (inability to follow rational courses) and vulnerability. Thus Dryden can make the fable method work polemically by using beast imagery to suggest the origins of the English church in Henry VIII's frustrated sexuality, and later get good cautionary effects (fables were traditionally supposed to embody predictive wisdom) by using bird imagery to predict the future persecution of English Catholics (unless they take immediate conciliatory measures) after the friendly summer of

James II has been followed by the harder season of a Protestant regime :

> What shou'd they doe, beset with dangers round,
> No neighb'ring Dorp, no lodging to be found,
> But bleaky plains, and bare unhospitable ground.
> The latter brood, who just began to fly
> Sick-feather'd, and unpractis'd in the sky,
> For succour to their helpless mother call,
> She spread her wings; some few beneath 'em craul,
> She spread 'em wider yet, but cou'd not cover all.
> T' augment their woes, the winds began to move
> Debate in air, for empty fields above,
> Till *Boreas* got the skyes, and powr'd amain
> His ratling hail-stones mix'd with snow and rain.
>
> The joyless morning late arose, and found
> A dreadfull desolation reign a-round,
> Some buried in the Snow, some frozen to the ground :
> The rest were strugling still with death, and lay
> The *Crows* and *Ravens* rights, an undefended prey; ...
> [The *Hind*] then said, I take th' advice in friendly part,
> You clear your conscience, or at least your heart; ...
> But, through your parable I plainly see
> The bloudy laws, the crowds barbarity :
> The sun-shine that offends the purblind sight,
> Had some their wishes, it wou'd soon be night.

(iii. 610 ff.)

In the second bird-fable, told by the Hind with pigeons for Anglicans and chickens for Catholics, interfaith hostility is dramatized ludicrously by a hideous propaganda poster put up in the Anglican pigeon-house to convict the Roman Catholic chickens (especially the roosters) of idolatry :

> ... Great and Small
> To view the Monster crowded Pidgeon-hall.
> There Chanticleer was drawn upon his knees
> Adoring shrines, and Stocks of Sainted Trees. ...

(iii. 1050–54)

If we compare the imagery of the last two quotations with its most immediate predecessor in great English poetry of that century, Milton's

> Even them who kept thy truth so pure of old
> When all our fathers worshiped stocks and stones,
> Forget not : in thy book record their groans
> Who were thy sheep and in their ancient fold
> Slain by the bloody Piedmontese that rolled
> Mother with infant down the rocks.—
>
> (Sonnet xv, 3–8)

it would be entirely wrong to say that Dryden is trivializing issues Milton had treated as enormously important or even that he is transmuting into light satiric comedy aspects of existence which for Milton had had a life-and-death seriousness. Dryden's images of persecution ('the bloudy laws, the crowds barbarity', 'the *Crows* and *Ravens* rights, an undefended prey') are as serious and in their way as well realized as 'Mother with infant down the rocks'; and Dryden's shudder at idolatry ('Stocks') is no doubt as truly Hebraic as Milton's had been.

But the purpose of Dryden's religious poetry is as different from Milton's as are the circumstances out of which it arose. In 1687, for the first and only time between the Reformation and the nineteenth century, there seemed a brief possibility that all three major forms of Christianity, the sects, the state church, and the Catholics, might coexist in some sort of peaceable legal equilibrium within one political entity, England. This possibility *The Hind and the Panther*, though exalting Catholicism above the others, dramatically endorses. Without averting its eyes from any of the formidable difficulties involved in such a programme in that epoch (feeling ran high, unlicensed preachers like Bunyan were promptly jailed, disasters like the fire of London were at once attributed to subversive religious plotters), *The Hind and the Panther* imaginatively directs its bird and beast imagery toward reconciliation, both humorously (as when the Panther 'pacify'd her tail, and lick'd her frothy jaws') and with entire philosophic seriousness :

> From *Celtique* woods is chas'd the wolfish crew;
> But ah! some pity e'en to brutes is due :
> Their native walks, methinks, they might enjoy
> Curb'd of their native malice to destroy.
> Of all the tyrannies on humane kind
> The worst is that which persecutes the mind.
>
> (i. 235–40)

Though his commitment has evolved from one particular church to another, Dryden's faith in the process by which truth is to be sought remains that of Milton earlier and John Stuart Mill later on; his faith that (as he put it in *Religio Laici*) despite many a 'difference' in the telling of religion's 'oft-told Tale', nevertheless 'Truth by its own sinews will prevail' if free discussion is allowed and persecution prevented. Since this is not a faith always or invariably practised or believed, its dramatic embodiment in an eloquent, serious, and entertaining poem cannot yet be regarded as out of date or irrelevant to a common reader's concerns.

THE SHORTEST-WAY WITH THE DISSENTERS. The next English literary work of comparable power on a topic similar to *Religio Laici* or *The Hind and the Panther* is Defoe's *Shortest Way with the Dissenters* (1702),[5] a minor masterpiece of partisan pamphleteering. Defoe had scored a resounding public success the previous year with his satiric political poem *The True-Born Englishman*, in which he vigorously argued that William III's Dutch origins no more incapacitated him from being truly British than did William I's Norman birth, James I's Scotch antecedents, Charles I's French mistresses, or the generally mongrel nature of a populace descended from Britons, Romans, Saxons, French Huguenot immigrants, and other variegated species. Now, after William's death and the succession of the far more pro-Anglican Queen Anne, an opportunity arose to make further literary capital out of new proposals being advanced in high places to take a harder line against the Dissenters, to exclude them from public office, to suppress their academies (in one of which Defoe had been educated), and the like. Just as in *The True-Born Englishman* Defoe had ridiculed patriotic snobbery by satirically exaggerated national self-abasement—

> And lest by Length of Time it be pretended,
> The Climate may this Modern Breed ha' mended;
> Wise Providence to keep us where we are,
> Mixes us daily with exceeding Care :
> We have been *Europe's* Sink, *the Jakes* [privy] where she
> Voids all her Offal Out-cast Progeny—

so in *The Shortest-Way*, Defoe counters religious chauvinism by another technique of exaggeration :— he produces a fictional proposal supposedly written by a pro-Anglican propagandist, suggesting that the Dissenters simply be wiped out. The result, a classic paradigm of all such propositions, is made up of the following sterling ingredients :

A) *Doctored History* : in a rapid, highly partisan sketch of the last century all disasters are laid at the Dissenters' doors ('You have *Butcher'd* one King, *Depos'd* another King, and made a *mock King* of a Third,' etc., etc.).

B) *Stimulation of Paranoia* (under William III, the Dissenters 'crope into all Places of Trust and Profit').

C) *Invocation of Group Enthusiasm* ('the Time is come which all good Men ha' wish'd for. . . . If ever you will establish the best Christian Church in the World. . . . If [ever] you will leave your Posterity free from Faction and Rebellion, this is the time').

D) *Defense of Violence as Preventive Medicine* (' 'Tis Cruelty to kill a Snake or a Toad in cold Blood, but the Poyson of their Nature makes it a Charity to our Neighbours'. . . . 'Tho' at the first, Severity may seem hard, . . . the Contagion will be rooted out').

E) *Loaded Analogy* ('. . . the *French* King effectually cleared the Nation of Protestants at once [by revocation of the Edict of Nantes in 1687], and we don't find he misses them at home').

F) *Frank Appeal to Blood Lust* ('Some Beasts are for sport, . . . but some are knockt on the Head by all possible ways of Violence and Surprize').

G) *The Argument that Much Smaller Offences are Treated More Severely* ('We hang Men for Trifles, and Banish them for things not worth naming, but that an Offence against God and the Church, against the Welfare of the World, and the Dignity of Religion, shall be bought off for 5s. [a small fine sometimes imposed on Dissenters] this is such a shame to a Christian Government, that 'tis with regret I transmit it to Posterity').

H) *The Argument that what Separates us is so Small that it's no Cruelty to the Opposition to Force Them to Join Us* ('Now, if as by their own acknowledgement, the Church of *England* is a true Church, and the Difference between them is only in a few *Modes and Accidents*, Why shou'd we expect that they will suffer Gallows and Gallies, corporeal Punishment and Banishment for these trifles?').

I) *The Argument that What Separates us is So Great that it's Intolerable for us to Have to Endure their Dissent* ('What's the Difference betwixt this, and being subjected to the Power of the Church of *Rome*, from whence we have reform'd? . . . Both are Enemies of our Church. . . . Why shou'd the *Papist* with his Seven Sacraments be worse than the *Quaker* with no Sacraments at all? . . . *Alas the Church of England!* What with Popery on one Hand, and Schismaticks on the other; how has she been Crucify'd between two Thieves').

J) *The Call to Immediate Action* ('NOW, let us crucifie the Thieves. . . . Let all true Sons of so Holy an Oppressed Mother, exasperated by her Afflictions, harden their Hearts against those who have oppress'd her.')

The last four arguments are especially double-edged. The analogy to trivial offenses implies both the brutality of the existing criminal code and the criminality of imposing 5 shilling penalties in the name of windy generalities like (an especially good touch) 'the Welfare of the World.' The argument from smallness of separation implies the moral pettiness of objecting to such differences. And the final two appeals forcibly remind the reader that the barbarities urged by the pamphlet are being invoked in the very name of a religion whose founder died a symbol of protest against institutionalized barbarity: 'Let us crucify the thieves' means let us become crucifiers in the name of Jesus, while the phrase 'harden their hearts' would remind any Bible-reader of the hardening of Pharaoh's heart against the enslaved Israelites.

No doubt the reason for the brilliance of the pamphlet was the fact that Defoe had correctly diagnosed a latent malady in the public temper of 1702. The reception proved the keenness of his creative insight. At first taken seriously and apparently given a momentary welcome in some extremist Anglican circles, the anonymous pamphlet on a more careful reading was soon repudiated with dislike by churchmen and with horror by Dissenters, its art so powerful that no one could see it as art at all; and its author was promptly identified, hunted down, fined, pilloried and imprisoned. Later, however, the fine was remitted when the gifted pamphleteer's services were secretly enlisted by powerful politicians. In an age of journalism and the systematic persuasion of public opinion, talents so great as Defoe's could ill be spared.

A TALE OF A TUB. One of Defoe's fellow journalists in the benign task of preparing English public opinion during the next decade for the peaceful settlement of the War of the Spanish Succession in 1713 was Swift, whose first major work, *A Tale of a Tub* (1704)[6] can be read in part as a sort of reply to *The Hind and the Panther*. Like Dryden, Swift confronts systems of religious belief and practice under symbolic guise. Like Dryden, he contrives a major allegory (the brothers and the coats) into which he inserts two shorter subordinate fables (the clothes worshippers who symbolize religion's compromise with the world, and the Aeolists who symbolize 'All Pretenders to

410

Inspiration' including all leaders of dissenting sects). Like Dryden, he loads the narrative heavily in favour of the faith he himself espouses and against the other two, but at the same time argues at a crucial point for reconciliation among all three (the Anglican Martin tells the dissenting Jack that the Catholic Peter 'was still their Brother'; that their father had strictly prescribed 'Agreement, and Friendship, and Affection between them'; and that Jack should seek 'the Advance of Unity, rather than Increase of Contradiction'—p. 139).

The narrative differs, however, from Dryden's in that the standpoint and medium have shifted: Swift's standpoint is Church of England, and his medium prose fiction (interspersed with brilliant excursions into essays or bogus imitations of learned apparatus—footnotes, prefaces, Latin tags indicating gaps in the 'manuscript', etc.). The enterprise, in short, has the air of a game whose object is partly laughter at the expense of scholarship's solemn machinery, partly exuberant delight in riddle-solving, and partly the kind of suspense aroused by any lively account of unscrupulous roguery. For Swift, a man of deepest lifelong religious conviction and commitment, nevertheless plays with fire in *A Tale of a Tub*—whose authorship he never acknowledged—by allegorizing the sometimes spotted history of Christianity in the form of a picaresque novel. After an early period in which the three brothers (who will eventually become Catholicism, Anglicanism, and Dissent) 'carefully observed their Father's Will . . . travelled thro' several Countries, encountred a reasonable Quantity of Gyants, and slew certain Dragons [the growth of the early church],' 'they came up to Town and fell in love with the Ladies, but especially Three [avarice, ambition, and pride],' but 'met with a very bad Reception; and soon with great Sagacity guessing out the Reason, they quickly began to improve in the good Qualities of the Town: They Writ, and Raillyed, and Rhymed, and Sung, and Said, and said Nothing: They Drank, and Fought, and Whor'd, and Slept, and Swore, and took Snuff' (p. 74)—and much more, until we have a complete thumbnail sketch of contemporary London life, vivid, racy, and clearly only in a loose, general way allegorical at all.

In short, where Dryden's method looks back to the allegorical successes of Chaucer or of *The Faerie Queene*, whose verse texture the beautiful opening lines of *The Hind and the Panther* strikingly resemble, Swift's method looks forward to the constantly needling prose of novels, like *Tom Jones* or *Tristram Shandy*, whose objective might be said to be that no intelligent reader ever fall asleep over their pages. Though at first sight an incongruous vehicle for the kinds of meaning Swift wanted it to purvey, the scandalousness of his narrative turns out to have several definite advantages.

First, in a scandal-mongering, sceptical, secular-minded age, the reader is shocked into attention at such a treatment of matters often treated only with ponderous solemnity. Swift, for example, is well aware of 'the noblest Branch of *Modern* Wit or Invention . . . that highly celebrated Talent . . . of deducing Similitudes, Allusions, and Applications, very Surprizing, Agreeable, and Apposite, from the *Pudenda* of either Sex, together with *their proper Uses*' (pp. 146–7); and he is willing to meet such an age initially on its own terms, for the purpose of arousing healthy reflection and self-examination.

Second, the novelistic method brilliantly dramatizes Swift's sense that the intrinsically irreligious accretions on the fabric of existing religion have corrupted what should be one of civilization's beneficial possessions. In the following passage, for example, where the brothers are trying to justify from their father's will the addition of silver fringe (which the will forbids) to their coats, Swift vitalizes by incongruity traditional criticisms of religion for obscurantism, pomp, and other irrelevance :

[one brother] had found in a certain Author . . . that the same Word which in the Will is called *Fringe*, does also signifie a *Broom-stick*; . . . This, another of the Brothers disliked, because of that Epithet, *Silver*, which could not, he humbly conceived, in Propriety of Speech be reasonably applied to a *Broom-stick* : but it was replied upon him, that this Epithet was understood in a *Mythological*, and *Allegorical* Sense. However, he objected again, why their Father should forbid them to wear *Broom-stick* on their Coats, a Caution that seemed unnatural and impertinent; upon which he was taken up short, as one that spoke irreverently of a *Mystery*, which doubtless was very useful and significant, but ought not to be over-curiously pryed into, or nicely reasoned upon (p. 88).

Third, the geniality and broad comic value of some of the symbolism suggests Swift's warm appreciation of many lesser religious elaborations, at the same time that he ostensibly attacks them. Holy water, for example, is affectionately presented as brother Peter's famous Universal *Pickle*. For having remark'd how your Common *Pickle* in use among Huswives, was of no farther Benefit than to preserve dead Flesh, and certain kinds of Vegetables; *Peter*, with great Cost as well as Art had contrived a *Pickle* proper for Houses, Gardens, Towns, Men, Women, Children, and Cattle; wherein he could preserve them as Sound as Insects in Amber (p. 109).

Finally, and this was of course one of the *Tale*'s great immediate sources of appeal, Swift's method allows him to combine doctrinal polemics—in other hands a dull or embittering subject-matter—with symbolic criticism provoking meditation without being inflammatory. Two examples will illustrate his procedures.

The sacrament of communion, which Swift subtly works into the conclusion of *Gulliver's Travels* twenty years later as an obvious symbol of human brotherhood and good will, had become a bone of contention in the sixteenth and seventeenth centuries because of differing philosophies concerning its relation to the Biblical episode from which it derives. Dryden, for example, expounds the Catholic doctrine of transubstantiation in *The Hind and the Panther* and mocks the awkward Anglican compromise between Catholic and Calvinist views in the couplet

> The lit'ral sense is hard to flesh and blood,
> But nonsense never can be understood.
>
> (i. 428–29)

Swift, whose defense of Anglican muddle is of course a sharp attack on the Catholic doctrine of transubstantiation, transforms the whole issue in Section IV of the *Tale* into an hilariously dramatic piece of Gogolesque fiction capable of symbolizing many things, but among them certainly an attack on dogma and the suggestion of a non-polemic response to it.

Another suggestion Dryden had introduced into *The Hind and the Panther* was that the Church of England, by the very fact of being an established church, must be an organization of time-servers, in contrast to the occasionally persecuted (and always illegal) British papists. The Hind tells the Panther that

> Thus fear [of the King] and int'rest [in a safe salary] will
>   prevail with some,
> For all have not the gift of martyrdome.
>
> (ii. 58–59)

'Martyrdome' is taken up by Swift in a passage allegorizing the reputed tendency of the Dissenters 'to run into persecution, and count vast merit upon every little hardship they suffer' :

> He would stand in the Turning of a Street, and calling to those who passed by, would cry to One; *Worthy Sir, do me the honour of a good Slap in the Chaps* : To another, *Honest Friend, pray, favour me with a handsom Kick on the Arse: Madam, shall I entreat a small Box on the Ear, from your Ladyship's fair Hands? Noble Captain, Lend a reasonable Thwack, for the Love of God, with that Cane of yours, over these poor Shoulders.* And when he had by such earnest Sollicitations, made a shift to procure a Basting sufficient to swell up his Fancy and his Sides, He would return home extremely comforted, and full of terrible Accounts of what he had undergone for the *Publick Good. Observe this Stroak,* (said he, shewing his bare Shoulders) *a plaguy* Janisary *gave it me this very Morning at seven a Clock, as, with much ado, I was driving off the* Great Turk. *Neighbours mine, this broken Head deserves a Plaister; had poor* Jack *been tender of his Noddle, you would have seen the* Pope, *and the* French King, *long before this time of Day, among your Wives and your Warehouses. Dear* Christians, *the* Great Mogul *was come as far as* White-Chappel, *and you may thank these poor Sides that he hath not (God bless us) already swallowed up Man, Woman, and Child.*

(pp. 197–98)

While such language obviously has no relevance to cases of genuine oppression ('little hardships' like Bunyan's years in Bedford jail, Defoe's hours in the pillory, or Roger Williams' ousting from Massachusetts), the passage still makes valid use of the phenomenon of the martyr complex, the kind of indulgent revelling in thoughts of persecution no doubt experienced by at least some readers of Foxe's *Book of Martyrs* and similar bestsellers of the age. Always the thrust in Swift is positive : to retrieve the symbolic and moral imagination from too widely rambling a circuit and fix it instead on more pressing matters nearer home.

AN ARGUMENT AGAINST ABOLISHING CHRISTIANITY (1708).[7] With a wealth of coruscating dialectics, this pamphlet of Swift's extends and complicates the method of *The Shortest-Way with the Dissenters* six years earlier. Where Defoe had ostensibly presented the arguments of a rabidly ethno-centered Anglican in favour of abolishing Dissent, Swift outlines a proposal for wiping out Christianity altogether, and writes his pamphlet (reversing Defoe's technique) as an ostensibly pro-Christian defense—but a defense on grounds that are worse than the attack itself. Where Defoe's point had been the un-Christian inhumanity of persecution-minded pretenders to Christianity (the same point Shaw makes with De Stogumber in *St. Joan*), Swift's is now the questionableness of a chameleon Christianity so well-adjusted as to be wholly consistent 'with our present Schemes of Wealth and Power' (p. 28) (he thus anticipates Kierkegaard a century later). Thus a series of secularist 'objections' to Christianity are dexterously disposed of by even more secularist 'defenses' : abolishing Sunday won't gain time for business or pleasure, since Sunday is already simply a more convenient occasion for pursuing them; repealing anti-blasphemy legislation won't promote irreverence, since it is impossible to imagine *less* reverence than we take for granted at present. Eliminating church doctrine won't eliminate ideological quarrels; prohibiting preaching against immorality won't advance morality but will only remove one source of public pleasure ('a wonderful Incitement, by reflecting it was a Thing forbidden'); abolishing Christianity (i.e. Anglicanism) won't abolish Dissent, since Dissenters will go on dissenting out of a sheer spirit of opposition; and, finally, abolishing Christianity (again, Anglicanism) might actually cause some risk to the established church(!) not to mention perhaps opening the door to Presbyterianism or Popery. Here the pamphlet suggests that what Swift's spokesman values about the conventionally accepted religion is not anything intrinsic to it but simply its being different from religious forms against which he is prejudiced. The fact that the War of the Spanish Succession is still in progress in 1708 enables Swift to incorporate a final glance at the diversity of European religion and even at Mohammedanism, as follows :

Upon the whole; if it shall still be thought for the Benefit of Church and State, that Christianity be abolished; I conceive, however, it may be more convenient to defer the Execution to a Time of Peace; and not venture in this Conjuncture to disoblige our Allies; who, as it falls out, are all Christians; and many of them, by the Prejudices of their Education, so bigotted, as to place a Sort of Pride in the Appellation. If, upon being rejected by them, we are to trust to an Alliance with the *Turk*, we shall find our selves much deceived : For, as he is too remote, and generally engaged in War with the

Persian Emperor; so his People would be more scandalized at our Infidelity, than our Christian Neighbours. Because, the *Turks* are not only strict Observers of religious Worship; but, what is worse, believe a God; which is more than is required of us, even while we preserve the Name of Christians (p. 38).

Although hypocrisy is sometimes said to be the target of the satire in the *Argument Against Abolishing Christianity*, a more precise definition of what Swift attacks might well be emptiness: the failure to give any significant content whatever to an ostensibly accepted faith.

CHARACTERISTICKS OF MEN, MANNERS, OPINIONS, TIMES. In the same year with Swift's Argument appeared the Earl of Shaftesbury's *A Letter Concerning Enthusiasm*, followed by more essays in the next two years and Shaftesbury's *Characteristicks of Men, Manners, Opinions, Times* [8] in 1711. Shaftesbury treats some of the same sort of differences between religion and philosophy as Dryden does in the first part of *Religio Laici* but obliterates the sharp distinction between reason and revelation by positing a natural moral sense in man—akin to man's instinctive aesthetic sense and his quasi-mathematical (or quasi-musical) preference for order and harmony. This natural moral sense, Shaftesbury argues, can be affected, for good or ill, by the kind of religion, or irreligion, that an individual might adopt or inherit. In general Shaftesbury contrasts superstition, bigotry, or fanaticism with altruism, good humour, public spirit, and an almost fanatical (but quite undogmatic) enthusiasm for nature, by which he means the physical and biological universe around us.

His own religion Shaftesbury declares to be the orthodox Protestantism of the Church of England, and his conception of this faith is that it should be, above all, non-persecuting. A passage in the *Letter Concerning Enthusiasm* directly addressed to Lord Somers, a contemporary statesman Shaftesbury admired, conveys the unusual combination of political and metaphysical imagery—not without dry wit—by means of which Shaftesbury suggests that the best treatment of religious enemies is pity, raillery, or magnanimous unconcern:

> To love the public, to study universal good, and to promote the interest of the whole world, as far as lies within our power, is surely the height of goodness, and makes that temper which we call divine. In this temper, my lord (for surely you should know it well), 'tis natural for us to wish that others should partake with us, by being convinced of the

sincerity of our exemple. 'Tis natural for us to wish our merit should be known; particularly if it be our fortune to have served a nation as a good Minister; or as some prince, or father of a country, to have rendered happy a considerable part of mankind under our care. But if it happened that of this number there should be some so ignorantly bred, and of so remote a province, as to have lain out of the hearing of our name and actions; or hearing of them should be so puzzled with odd and contrary stories told up and down concerning us, that they knew not what to think, whether there were really in the world any such person as ourself; should we not, in good truth, be ridiculous to take offence at this? And should we not pass for extravagantly morose and ill-humoured if, instead of treating the matter in raillery, we should think in earnest of revenging ourselves on the offending parties, who, out of their rustic ignorance, ill-judgment, or incredulity, had detracted from our renown? (i. 27)

And he goes on, 'How comes it then, that what is so divine in us, should lose its character in the Divine Being?' Even the persecution of blasphemy or atheism—not to mention differing forms of faith—is deprecated by the implications of this politico-religious comparison.

Though well aware that the history of religion has included many polemical pages, Shaftesbury is inclined to test doctrinal validity against our best moral instincts. Reading the Old Testament, he says in his essay 'Advice to an Author,'

We can hardly endure to see heathen treated as heathen, and the faithful made the executioners of the divine wrath. There is a certain perverse humanity in us which inwardly resists the divine commission, though ever so plainly revealed. The wit of the best poet is not sufficient to reconcile us to the campaign of a Joshua, or the retreat of a Moses by the assistance of an Egyptian loan [which he never repaid] (i. 230).

But though according to Shaftesbury we would expect a modern poet or playwright to entertain and instruct his audience according to values more consistent with enlightened moral instincts, Shaftesbury is willing to allow an ancient religion (as by law established) what he calls 'the same privilege as Heraldry.'

[The herald's] lion or bear must be figured as the science appoints, and their supporters and crest must be such as their wise and gallant ancestors have procured for them. No mat-

417

ter whether the shapes of these animals hold just proportion with Nature (i. 233).

and no matter whether the sacred scriptures always conform to the natural moral sense as we experience it. But, Shaftesbury goes on, heraldry must nowadays recognize its limits:

> Having been reduced by law or settled practice from the power they once enjoyed, they will not, 'tis presumed, in defiance of the magistrate and civil power, erect anew their stages and lists, introduce the manner of civil combat, set us to tilt and tournament, and raise again those defiances and moral frays of which their Order were once the chief managers and promoters (i. 233).

In Shaftesbury's characteristic harmonizing of enthusiasm for nature, an educated taste in politics and morals, and inherited religious traditions, religion plays a coordinate but not predominant role. Violence inspired by religion would be as out of place in Shaftesbury's scheme as would a revival of the Round Table or the Crusades.

A MODEST PROPOSAL. Shaftesbury, Whig grandson of Charles II's opponent whom Dryden attacked in *Absalom and Achitophel*, radiates an optimistic view of the world he was born into, the age of relative political freedom and scientific progress ushered in by the Whig Revolution of 1688. Reading him, one feels that men of good will, if given free rein by the Neanderthal ignoramuses who too often infest public life, can readily move in the direction of a Utopian society. Swift, who on retiring from English politics after the death of Queen Anne sometimes occupied himself with pamphleteering on behalf of the welfare of Ireland, where he now lived, never promotes such assurance. His *Modest Proposal for preventing the Children of Poor People in Ireland from being a Burden to their Parents or Country*[9] (1729), the famous cannibalistic population control scheme by which one-year-olds would be butchered for fresh meat, shares with *Gulliver's Travels* (1726) an implied portrait of a society from which religious beliefs and practices have for all effective purposes simply evaporated, leaving behind them a great deal of vapid chatter about pity and humanity:

> There is likewise another great Advantage in my *Scheme* that it will prevent those *voluntary Abortions*, and that horrid Practise of *Women murdering their Bastard Children*; alas! too frequent among us; sacrificing the *poor innocent Babes*, I doubt, more to avoid the Expence than the Shame;

which would move Tears and Pity in the most Savage and inhuman Breast (p. 110).

PHILOSOPHICAL LETTERS. Though written in French in the form of epistles from a French traveller in England to a friend at home, Voltaire's *Philosophical Letters* [10] were first published in an English translation as *Letters Concerning the English Nation* (1733) and deserve assimilation into England's collective literary inheritance at least as much as Mrs Trollope's *Domestic Manners of the Americans* does into that of the western hemisphere later on. A supremely talented and blessedly succinct proto-anthropologist, Voltaire comments on the religious phenomena of the England he visited, treating the topic first among a series including parliamentary government, commerce, smallpox-inoculation (which England pioneered in Europe), the growth of science (Bacon, Descartes, Newton, Locke), gravitation, Shakespearean tragedy, and the current literary scene from Wycherley to Pope. At least nominally a representative of a Roman Catholic culture, Voltaire treats all varieties of English faith with impartial satire but differs from the Dryden-Swift tradition of hostility to the sects by presenting one of their more extreme varieties, Quakerism, with fascinated attention to several of its characteristic details:

> Our Lord [he causes a Quaker friend to explain], who has commanded us to love our enemies and to endure without complaint, certainly does not wish us to cross the sea and cut the throats of our brothers because some murderers dressed in red, and wearing hats two feet high, are enlisting citizens by making a noise with two little sticks on the tightly stretched skin of an ass (p. 7).

And Voltaire's last vignette of the doctrinal scene is more sympathetic than hostile:

> Go into the Exchange in London, that place more venerable than many a court, and you will see representatives of all the nations assembled there for the profit of mankind. There the Jew, the Mahometan, and the Christian deal with one another as if they were of the same religion, and reserve the name of infidel for those who go bankrupt. There the Presbyterian trusts the Anabaptist, and the Church of England man accepts the promise of the Quaker. On leaving these peaceable and free assemblies, some go to the synagogue, others in search of a drink; this man is to be baptized in a great tub in the name of the Father, by the Son, to the Holy Ghost; that man is

having the foreskin of his son cut off, and a Hebraic formula mumbled over the child that he himself can make nothing of; these others are going to their church to await the inspiration of God with their hats on; and all are satisfied.

If there were only one religion in England, there would be danger of tyranny; if there were two, they would cut each other's throats; but there are thirty, and they live happily together in peace.

AN ESSAY ON MAN. Published in the same two years, 1733 and 1734, when the *Philosophical Letters* were first appearing in English and in French, Pope's *Essay on Man* [11] carries on the poetic tradition of Dryden's serious verse, though aiming to transcend in a more general view the kind of religious and philosophical differences that are carefully marked out and debated in *Religio Laici* and *The Hind and the Panther*. In transcending such debate, in fact, the poem exults with an exuberance almost worthy of Voltaire :

> For Forms of Government let fools contest;
> Whate'er is best administer'd is best :
> For Modes of Faith, let graceless zealots fight;
> He can't be wrong whose life is in the right :
> In Faith and Hope, the world will disagree,
> But all Mankind's concern is Charity :
> All must be false that thwart this One great End;
> And all of God, that bless Mankind or mend.

(iii. 303–10)

But besides being a reasoned ethical and psychological argument [12] on the great traditional theme of constructive renunciation (losing one's life to find it again), the *Essay* is nourished as a poem by equally traditional dramatic symbols of man's nature and fate. His past, for example :

> Pride then was not; nor arts, that Pride to aid;
> Man walk'd with beast, joint tenant of the shade;
> The same his table and the same his bed;
> No murder cloath'd him, and no murder fed.

(iii. 151–54)

His environment :

> Far as Creation's ample range extends,
> The scale of sensual, mental pow'rs ascends :
> Mark how it mounts, to Man's imperial race,
> From the green myriads in the peopled grass....

(i. 207–10)

His perils:

> Vice is a monster of so frightful mien,
> As, to be hated, needs but to be seen;
> Yet seen too oft, familiar with her face,
> We first endure, then pity, then embrace.

> (ii. 217–20)

His fragility:

> As Man, perhaps, the moment of his breath,
> Receives the lurking principle of death;
> The young disease, that must subdue at length,
> Grows with his growth, and strengthens with his
>   strength . . .

> (ii. 132–35)

His future:

> To each unthinking being, Heav'n a friend,
> Gives not the useless knowledge of its end:
> To Man imparts it; but with such a view
> As, while he dreads it, makes him hope it too. . . .

> (iii. 71–74)

Such poetry, however little it advocates specific doctrines, reveals its own roots in the same general response to existence that gave rise to much of the best pre-Enlightenment English poetry: to Milton's accounts, for example, of man's prelapsarian state in Paradise, or of the seven days of Creation, or of Satan's temptation by the allegorical enchantress, Sin, or of death's various terrors, or of possible attitudes towards death. One might compare the last passage quoted with four lines of Waller's that Pope and his age knew well (he had even parodied them in his *Dunciad*):

> The soul's dark cottage, battered and decayed,
> Lets in new light through chinks that time has made.
> Stronger by weakness, wiser men become
> As they draw near to their eternal home.

> ('Of the Last Verses in the Book', 13–16)

A recurrent mysticism—a sense of man's home as somehow elsewhere—balances Pope's vivid sensitivity to immediate sensual experience and helps give the *Essay on Man* its multi-dimensional quality.

THE VANITY OF HUMAN WISHES (1749). The topic of the fourth Epistle of the *Essay on Man*, false and true notions of human happiness—

> There, in the rich, the honour'd, fam'd and great,
> See the false scale of Happiness complete! . . .
> Know then this truth (enough for Man to know)
> 'Virtue alone is Happiness below'—
>
> (iv. 287–88, 309–10)

is taken up again in Samuel Johnson's *Vanity of Human Wishes*,[13] the finest long poem of the man who became as much the dominant literary sage in his own generation as Pope had been before him. As a poem it contrasts with Pope's in that its best effects come in short symbolic biographies rather than in the nature symbolism ('The Ant's republic, and the realm of Bees' [III, 184]) so pervasive in Pope's *Essay*. Johnson loves the dramatic gesture—Charles XII of Sweden at the height of power and hubris:

> 'Think nothing gain'd,' he cries, 'till nought remain,
> On Moscow's walls till Gothic standards fly,
> And all be mine beneath the polar sky'—

followed by the disastrous anticlimax:

> But did not Chance at length her error mend?
> Did no subverted empire mark his end?
> Did rival monarchs give the fatal wound?
> Or hostile millions press him to the ground?
> His fall was destin'd to a barren strand,
> A petty fortress, and a dubious hand:
> He left the name, at which the world grew pale,
> To point a moral, or adorn a tale.
>
> (202–204, 215–22)

A second difference from Pope is that Johnson's values (though basically like Pope's) have been embedded in a specifically non-Christian vehicle, Johnson's imitation of Juvenal's tenth satire. We can trace here a complex continuity from the specific doctrinal engagements of *The Hind and the Panther* and the partisan satire of *A Tale of a Tub*, through the *Essay on Man's* synthesizing metaphysics to the highly generalized 'religion' with which Johnson concludes:

> Where then shall Hope and Fear their objects find?
> Must dull Suspence corrupt the stagnant mind? . . .

Enquirer, cease, petitions yet remain,
Which heav'n may hear, nor deem religion vain.

(343–44, 349–50)

The poem dramatizes one religious act, and one only, prayer:

Still raise for good the supplicating voice,
But leave to heav'n the measure and the choice,
Safe in his pow'r, whose eyes discern afar
The secret ambush of a specious pray'r.

(351–54)

The strength of the poem is in its defence of an unworldly view
by means of a majestic philosophic disgust or disdain:

How wouldst thou shake at Britain's modish tribe,
Dart the quick taunt, and edge the piercing jibe?

(61–62)

From every room descends the painted face,
That hung the bright Palladium of the place, . . .
The form distorted justifies the fall,
And detestation rids th'indignant wall.

(83–4, 89–90)

. . . mark what ills the scholar's life assail;
Toil, envy, want, the patron, and the jail.

(159–60)

Mark'd out by dangerous parts [talents] he meets the
shock,
And fatal Learning leads him to the block [to be
beheaded]:
Around his tomb let Art and Genius weep,
But hear his death, ye blockheads, hear and sleep.

(171–74)

OF MIRACLES. The same generalizing tendency to treat 'religion' rather than a particular set of beliefs or practices marks
David Hume's essay on miracles (Section X of his *Enquiry concerning Human Understanding* [1748])[14] as much as it does
Johnson's *Vanity of Human Wishes*. Hume's antecedents, however, are not really the imaginative, often narrative or dramatic poetry and prose which we have seen leading up to
Johnson (the works of Dryden, Swift, and Pope discussed so
far); Hume's true antecedents are much less these than a different, and increasingly influential, tradition of more purely
abstract writing—tending ideally toward mathematical form—
connected with and accompanying the rise of science from
Galileo and Copernicus in the sixteenth century, through Bacon,

Harvey, and Newton in the seventeenth, down to Hume's own day. In works like Descartes' *Discourse on Method* (1637), Locke's *Essay concerning Human Understanding* (1690), and Berkeley's *Three Dialogues between Hylas and Philonous* (1733), a brilliant if inconclusive debate had been going on about the nature, and even the possibility, of human knowledge—taking 'knowledge' in its hardest sense, as distinct from faith, belief, opinion, or hypothesis. In an age when the first new scientists since Greco-Roman antiquity had shown how much could be created by questioning accepted premises (including the premises of ancient science), it was not surprising that new philosophical debaters should stage a sort of contest in how many commonly received ideas they could manage to doubt or at least to question. Thus Descartes reduced the very evidence for his own existence to the fact that he could think about such a question (*Je pense donc je suis*—*Cogito, ergo sum*); while Berkeley attacked Locke's division of sense experience into primary ('real') and secondary (subjective, illusory) qualities by finding that he could just as easily doubt the independent reality of primary qualities like mass and extension as he could the reality of supposedly secondary qualities like colour and sound. (Berkeley's abolition of 'matter' is really a defence of the complexity of experience against tendencies to reduce 'reality' to the measurable data of physics.) Hume's contribution to all this was his dismantling of the law of cause and effect. Our knowledge that an egg will break if we drop it reduces, in Hume, to the fact that a series of experiences has caused us to get into the habit of associating together the idea of subsequent breakage and the mental image of an egg in descent. Such a tendency to concentrate on the processes by which we receive experience rather than on what we ordinarily think experience consists of has been epitomized in a modern writer's conception of a hypothetical impersonal, nounless language for communicating such a world outlook: in this language 'The moon rose above the river' would come out 'upward behind the onstreaming it mooned'.[15]

The central ploy in Hume's essay on miracles is to attack the notion of miraculousness not by simple emphatic rebuttal as in a comic writer like Chaucer (who simply asserts that the Pardoner's allegedly sacred relics are nothing but 'pigges bones'), but rather by asking the rational question, 'Which, in the light of all my experience, is more probable : that the allegedly miraculous event took place as reported; or, that there is some reason to question the accuracy of the report itself?' Such a reason might be the selfish interest of the reporters, or their known ignorance and credulity, or the general tendency of people to believe some kinds of report even without evidence—

> This is our natural way of thinking, even with regard to the most common and most credible events. For instance, there is no kind of report which arises so easily, and spreads so quickly, especially in country places and provincial towns, as those concerning marriages; insomuch that two young persons of equal condition never see each other twice, but the whole neighbourhood immediately join them together. The pleasure of telling a piece of news so interesting, of propagating it, and of being the first reporters of it, spreads the intelligence; and this is so well known, that no man of sense gives attention to these reports, till he finds them confirmed by some greater evidence.
>
> (pp. 134–35)

The passage illustrates the lucidity and concreteness which Hume's writing shares with Berkeley's, and which helped his essay become a minor classic of mid-century scepticism.

THE DECLINE AND FALL OF THE ROMAN EMPIRE CHAPTERS 15 and 16 (1776).

Although Hume's essay starts by citing an Anglican archbishop's attack on the Roman Catholic doctrine of transubstantiation, its intent is much more general than merely anti-Catholic, and its conclusion was correctly understood to be heavily ironic at the expense of almost *any* form of Christianity:

> So that, upon the whole, we may conclude, that the Christian Religion not only was at first attended with miracles, but even at this day cannot be believed by any reasonable person without one. Mere reason is insufficient to convince us of its veracity: and whoever is moved by *Faith* to assent to it, is conscious of a continued miracle in his own person, which subverts all the principles of his understanding, and gives him a determination to believe what is most contrary to custom and experience.
>
> (p. 150)

Twenty-eight years later (1776), Gibbon extended an attitude and ironic method not unlike Hume's to encompass an account of the Christian church in its earliest centuries. For neither Hume nor Gibbon was such a topic a central concern, Hume being most interested in philosophical psychology and Gibbon in the history of Rome; so that there is a certain irony in the fact that his dealings with religion have contributed so much to making each man as well remembered as he now is. Basically Gibbon's attitude is ambiguous—he was at one time in his youth temporarily converted to Catholicism partly by reading and mentally refuting an attack on miracles written about the same time as Hume's—; and the ambiguity no doubt contributes to the success of Chapters 15 and 16 of his history, which introduce the Christian topic.[16] Gibbon's method is to arrange a continuing drama in which the most outrageous events take place on the stage of history to the accompaniment of thundering ejaculations of mock-surprise delivered by the one-man chorus, Gibbon himself. 'The scanty and suspicious materials of ecclesiastical history,' he sighs, 'seldom enable us to dispel the dark cloud that hangs over the first age of the church' (p. 1); but the curtain nonetheless rises. At times the commentator lifts his hands in horror : 'the condemnation of the wisest and most virtuous of the pagans on account of their ignorance or disbelief in the divine truth seems to offend the reason and humanity of the present age' (p. 28). A moment's reflection, however, induces ironic acquiescence : 'But the primitive Church, whose faith was of a much firmer consistence, delivered over, without hesitation, to eternal torture the far greater part of the human species' (p. 28). ('Primitive' here is made to have a double significance : 'pristine' and 'savage'.) The actors awaken in the chorus a sort of fascinated consternation : '[The clergy were] a celebrated order of men which has furnished the most important, though not always the most edifying, subjects for modern history' (p. 50). On the subject of their otherworldliness the spectator drily reserves his own opinion : 'Cyprian had renounced those temporal honours which it is probable he would never have obtained' (p. 57). But the central (divine) actor always elicits apparent approval : 'Some deities of a more recent and fashionable cast might soon have occupied the deserted temples of Jupiter and Apollo, if . . . the wisdom of Providence had not interposed a genuine revelation fitted to inspire the most rational esteem and conviction . . .' (p. 59). As a historian, however, Gibbon can only shake his head over the source materials surviving to him : 'the obscure and imperfect origin of the western churches of Europe has been so negligently recorded that, if we would relate the time and manner of their foundation, we must supply [=fill in] the silence of antiquity by those legends which avarice or superstition afterwards dictated to the monks in the lazy gloom of their convents' (p. 67). And on Hume's favourite topic of miracles, the choric

426

murmur rises to heights of pretended incomprehension:

> . . . how shall we excuse the supine inattention of the Pagan and philosophic world to those evidences which were presented by the hand of Omnipotence, not to their reason, but to their senses? . . . The lame walked, the blind saw, the sick were healed . . . But the sages of Greece and Rome turned aside from the awful spectacle, and . . . appeared unconscious of any alterations in the moral or physical government of the world.
>
> (p. 74)

Every drama must have its conflict, and in Chapter 16 Gibbon's topic is the persecution of the early church by various Roman governments. Here ambiguity and irony tend to yield to the chorus's evident emotional involvement in the action, as Gibbon defends Rome by a series of implications in her behalf: authentic church memorials are sometimes 'polluted' with 'extravagant and indecent fictions' (p. 103); the Christians were themselves more intolerant than the Romans; Cyprian couldn't have been executed in a more humane manner; indeed, he *wanted* to be executed, for 'the crown of martyrdom must have appeared to him as an object of desire rather than of terror' (p. 110); only a few died, and they made the most of it (being morbid neurotics and masochists); but of course few wanted death and many repudiated their principles to escape it; persecutions were, after all, *good* for the church; some of the bishops were a disgrace to their calling; even in the worst persecution, important people were seldom harmed ('Adauctus [was] . . . the only person of rank and distinction who appears to have suffered death during the whole course of this general persecution' [p. 138]); many accounts of martyrdoms are unhistorical; and from Eusebius we gather that only nine bishops, in all, died. Clearly, a number of these arguments cut both ways, perhaps more than Gibbon himself is always aware; but the force of the final reference to the religious wars of recent times, at the conclusion of Chapter 16, can hardly be denied:

> In the Netherlands more than one hundred thousand of the subjects of Charles the Fifth are said to have suffered by the hand of the executioner . . . If we are obliged to submit our belief to the authority of Grotius, it must be allowed that the number . . . who were executed in a single province and a single reign far exceeded that of the primitive martyrs in the space of three centuries of the Roman empire.
>
> (p. 148)

BOSWELL'S LIFE OF JOHNSON (1791). No Restoration or eighteenth-century work still widely read brings forward the transcendental themes of religion and philosophy with more liveliness or variety than Boswell's great biography.[17] Johnson himself combines two of the largest interests of his age— Greco-Roman studies and theology—and, though not a clergyman, can often serve as a spokesman on divine topics with at least as much skill and conviction as, for example, the Reverend Jonathan Swift. Boswell, free-thinking friend of reprobates (from Johnson's point of view) like Rousseau or John Wilkes, is never at a loss to introduce ideas, or people, that will highlight by contrast the Johnsonian presence. A single brief scene (dated 15 April 1778) will illustrate how sectarian differences, religious principles (like loving one's enemies), and sceptical preference of first-hand experience to abstract ideas may combine to make up the perfectly natural, but well composed and highly suggestive fabric of Boswell's narrative:

Dr. Mayo having asked Johnson's opinion of Soame Jenyns's 'View of the Internal Evidence of the Christian Religion,'— . . . BOSWELL. '*You* should like his book, Mrs. Knowles, as it maintains, as you *friends* do, that courage is not a Christian virtue.' MRS. KNOWLES. 'Yes, indeed, I like him there; but I cannot agree with him, that friendship is not a Christian virtue.' JOHNSON. 'Why, Madam, strictly speaking, he is right. All friendship is preferring the interest of a friend, to the neglect, or, perhaps, against the interests of others; so that an old Greek said, "He that has *friends* has *no* friend." Now Christianity recommends universal benevolence, to consider all men as our brethren, which is contrary to the virtue of friendship, as described by the ancient philosophers. Surely, Madam, your sect must approve of this; for, you call all men *friends*.' MRS. KNOWLES. 'We are commanded to do good to all men, "but especially to them who are of the household of Faith."' JOHNSON. 'Well, Madam, The household of Faith is wide enough.' MRS. KNOWLES. 'But, Doctor, our Saviour had twelve Apostles, yet there was *one* whom he *loved.* John was called "the disciple whom JESUS loved." [John 19:26]' JOHNSON. (with eyes sparkling benignantly) 'Very well, indeed, Madam. You have said very well.' BOSWELL. 'A fine application. Pray, Sir, had you ever thought of it?' JOHNSON. 'I had not, Sir.'

From this pleasing subject, he, I know not how or why,

made a sudden transition to one upon which he was a violent aggressor; for he said, 'I am willing to love all mankind, *except an American:*' and his inflammable corruption bursting into horrid fire, he 'breathed out threatenings and slaughter;' calling them, 'Rascals—Robbers—Pirates;' and exclaiming, he'd 'burn and destroy them.' Miss Seward, looking to him with mild but steady astonishment, said, 'Sir, this is an instance that we are always most violent against those whom we have injured.'—He was irritated still more by this delicate and keen reproach; and roared out another tremendous volley, which one might fancy could be heard across the Atlantick. During this tempest I sat in great uneasiness, lamenting his heat of temper; till, by degrees, I diverted his attention to other topicks.

DR. MAYO. (to Dr. Johnson.) 'Pray, Sir, have you read [Jonathan] Edwards, of New England, on Grace?' JOHNSON. 'No, Sir.' BOSWELL. 'It puzzled me so much as to the freedom of the human will, by stating, with wonderful acute ingenuity, our being actuated by a series of motives which we cannot resist, that the only relief I had was to forget it. . . . The argument for the moral necessity of human actions is always, I observe, fortified by supposing universal prescience to be one of the attributes of the Deity.' JOHNSON. 'You are surer that you are free, than you are of prescience; you are surer that you can lift up your finger or not as you please, than you are of any conclusion from a deduction of reasoning. But let us consider a little the objection from prescience. It is certain I am either to go home to-night or not; that does not prevent my freedom.' BOSWELL. 'That it is certain you are *either* to go home or not, does not prevent your freedom; because the liberty of choice between the two is compatible with that certainty. But if *one* of these events be certain *now*, you have no *future* power of volition. If it be certain you are to go home to-night, you *must* go home.' JOHNSON. 'If I am well acquainted with a man, I can judge with great probability how he will act in any case, without his being restrained by my judging. GOD may have this probability increased to certainty.' BOSWELL. 'When it is increased to *certainty*, freedom ceases, because that cannot be certainly foreknown, which is not certain at the time; but if it be certain at the time, it is a contradiction in terms to maintain that there can afterwards be any *contingency* dependent upon the exercise of will or any thing else.' JOHN-

SON. 'All theory is against the freedom of the will; all experience for it'.

(iii. 288–91)

There could hardly be a better image than Boswell here creates of a society supremely confident about its central values, in some perplexity about their exact application or their detailed exposition, but at peace with itself and embarked on an enterprise of harmonious clarification : a nation in possession of its own historic experience.

1. All quotations from Dryden's *Poems and Fables*, ed. James Kinsley, Oxford, 1962.

2. Actually a traditional view. For a discussion of the poem's backgrounds, see Phillip Harth, *Contexts of Dryden's Thought*, Chicago, 1968.

3. Quotations from Kinsley (see note 1 above).

4. There is a good modern commentary in Earl Miner, *Dryden's Poetry*, Bloomington, Indiana, 1967.

5. All quotations from the Shakespeare Head edition of Defoe's *Novels and Selected Writings*, 14 vols., Oxford, 1927–28, vol. xiv.

6. All quotations from the brilliant modern edition by A. C. Guthkelch and D. Nichol Smith, Oxford, 1920, revised 1958.

7. All quotations from Herbert Davis's edition of Swift's *Prose Works*, Oxford, vol. ii (1939).

8. All quotations from J. M. Robertson's edition, 2 vols., London, 1900.

9. Quotation from *Prose Works*, ed. Herbert Davis, Oxford, vol. xii (1955).

10. All quotations from the translation by Ernest Dilworth, Indianapolis, 1961.

11. All quotations from *The Poems of Alexander Pope*, ed. John Butt, London and New Haven, 1963.

12. An argument whose shapely symmetries have been beautifully traced and clarified by the poem's latest editor, Maynard Mack (Twickenham Edition of Pope, vol. III. i), 1950.

13. All quotations from Johnson's *Poems*, ed. E. L. McAdam, Jr. and G. Milne, New Haven, 1964 (Yale Edition of the Works of Johnson, vol. vi).

14. Quotations from Hume's *Philosophical Works*, 4 vols., Boston, Mass, 1854, vol. iv.

15. Jorge Luis Borges, *Labyrinths*, New York, 1962, p. 8.

16. All quotations from J. B. Bury's edition, 7 vols., 1909–14, vol. ii.

17. Quotation from *Boswell's Life of Johnson*, ed. G. B. Hill, revised L. F. Powell, 6 vols., Oxford, 1934–50.

BIBLIOGRAPHY

Select Bibliographies for Gibbon, Hume and Shaftesbury

Gibbon

The Decline and Fall of the Roman Empire, ed. J. B. Bury, 7 vols., London, 1896–1900, 1909–14, 1926–29 (revised text).

The Autobiographies of Edward Gibbon, ed. J. Murray, London, 1896.

The Letters of Edward Gibbon, ed. J. E. Norton, 3 vols., London, 1956.

The Memoirs and Life of Edward Gibbon, ed. G. Birkbeck Hill, London, 1900.

Bond, H. L., *The Literary Art of Edward Gibbon*, Oxford, 1960.

McCloy, S. T., *Gibbon's Antagonism to Christianity*, Chapel Hill, N.C., 1933.

Hume

The Philosophical Works, including all the Essays, 4 vols., London, 1826, 1836, Boston, 1854.

The History of England from Caesar to 1688, 8 vols., London, 1763 (many subsequent editions).

Broad, C. D., 'Hume's Theory of the Credibility of Miracles', *Proceedings of the Aristotelian Society*, xvii (1916).

Flew, Antony, 'Hume's Check', *Philosophical Quarterly*, ix (1959), 1–18.

—— 'Miracle and History', *The Listener*, lxv (1961), 963–4.

Gaskin, J. A. C., 'David Hume and the Eighteenth-Century Interest in Miracles', *Hermathena*, xcix (1964), 80–92.

Maidment, H. J., ' In Defence of Hume on Miracles', *Philosophy*, xiv (1939), 422–33.

Mossner, E. C., *The Life of David Hume*, Austin, Texas, 1954.

Noyes, Charles E., 'Samuel Johnson : Student of Hume', *Univ. of Mississippi Studies in English*, iii (1962), 91–4. Illustrates the process of implicit dialogue in the late eighteenth century.

Pomeroy, Ralph S., 'Hume on the Testimony for Miracles', *Speech Monographs*, xxix (1962), 1–12.

Stewart, John B., *The Moral and Political Philosophy of David Hume*, London, 1963.

Taylor, A. E., *David Hume and the Miraculous*, London, 1927.

Shaftesbury

Characteristics of Men, Manners, Opinions, Times, Etc., ed. John M. Robertson, 2 vols., 1900.

Aldridge, A. O., 'Shaftesbury, Christianity, and Friendship', *Anglican Theological Review*, xxxii (1950), 121–36.

—— 'Shaftesbury and the Deist Manifesto', *Transactions of the*

American Philosophical Society, new series, xli (1951), pt. 2, 297–385.

Brett, R. L., *The Third Earl of Shaftesbury: A Study in Eighteenth-Century Literary Theory*, London, 1951.

Crane, R. S., 'Suggestions toward a Genealogy of the Man of Feelings', *English Literary History*, i (1934), 205–30.

Moore, C. A., 'Shaftesbury and the Ethical Poets in England 1700–1760', *PMLA*, xxxi (1916), 264–325.

—— 'The Return to Nature in English Poetry of the Eighteenth Century', *Studies in Philology*, xiv (1917), 243–91.

Tuveson, E., 'The Origins of the "Moral Sense" ', *Huntington Library Quarterly*, xi (1948), 205–30.

—— 'The Importance of Shaftesbury', *ELH*, xx (1953), 267–99. (1953), 267–99.

—— 'Shaftesbury and the Age of Sensibility', in *Studies in Criticism and Aesthetics 1660–1800*, ed. H. Anderson and J. S. Shea, Minneapolis, 1967, pp. 73–93.

INDEX

442

A Short History of the Russian Revolution

JOEL CARMICHAEL

Why did Russia, the most backward state in Europe, become the first country to establish a communist regime? What paralysis gripped the Tsarist government and prevented its ruthlessly suppressing the February uprising as it had all such previous insurrections? What part did Marx's dogmatic insistence on the proper sequence of economic evolution—feudalism to capitalism to socialism to communism—play in the counsels of the successful revolutionaries? Joel Carmichael poses and answers all these and many other questions to do with the Russian Revolution. His narrative is swift and succinct. He cuts through the confusion of events to the central dramas of these world-shaking times.

For easy reference, there is an abridged chronology, a glossary and biographical notes on the main personages from Antonov-Ovseyenko to Zinoviev.

All Sphere Books are available at your bookshop or
newsagent: or can be ordered from the following address:

Sphere Books, Cash Sales Department,
P.O. Box 11, Falmouth, Cornwall.

Please send cheque or postal order (no currency), and allow
4p per book to cover the cost of postage and packing
in U.K., 5p per copy overseas.